REFLECTING ON AMERICA

Second Edition

REFLECTING ON AMERICA

Anthropological Views of U.S. Culture

Second Edition

Edited by
Clare L. Boulanger

Routledge
Taylor & Francis Group

NEW YORK AND LONDON

Second edition published 2016
by Routledge
711 Third Avenue, New York, NY 10017

and by Routledge
2 Park Square, Milton Park, Abingdon, Oxon OX14 4RN

Routledge is an imprint of the Taylor & Francis Group, an informa business

© 2016 Taylor & Francis

First edition published 2007 by Pearson.

Library of Congress Cataloging-in-Publication Data
Names: Boulanger, Clare L. | Boulanger, Clare L.
Title: Reflecting on America : anthropological views of U.S. culture / edited by Clare L. Boulanger.
Description: Second edition. | Walnut Creek, California : Left Coast Press, Inc., [2016] | Includes bibliographical references and index.
Identifiers: LCCN 2015040415 | ISBN 9781629583693 (pbk. : alk. paper)
Subjects: LCSH: Anthropology—United States—History. | Anthropology—United States—Philosophy. | Ethnology—United States—Philosophy. | United States—Civilization—1945- | United States—Ethnic relations.
Classification: LCC GN17.3.U6 R44 2016 | DDC 306.0973—dc23
LC record available at http://lccn.loc.gov/2015040415

ISBN: 978-1-138-68434-8 (hbk)
ISBN: 978-1-62958-369-3 (pbk)

Typeset in 10/12 pt, Palatino Linotype by Diligent Typsetter India Private Limited.

Contents

Ritual and Religion

Ideology

1

Introduction: Upon Further Reflection

Clare L. Boulanger

There is a discernible culture, a river, a thread, connecting Thomas Jefferson to Lucille Ball to Malcolm X to Sitting Bull. The panhandler at one corner is related to the pamphleteer at the next, who is related to the bank executive who is related to the Punk wearing a FUCK U T-shirt. The immigrant child sees this at once. But then he is encouraged to forget the vision.

When I was a boy who spoke Spanish, I saw America whole. I realized that there was a culture here because I lived apart from it.

— Richard Rodriguez, *Days of Obligation*

The popular impression of "culture" is that it is a timeless matrix in which its practitioners are embedded. Anthropology has been justly criticized, chiefly by anthropologists themselves, for helping to promulgate this view. Today's anthropologists try to atone by conducting longitudinal studies and employing methods that see well beyond the immediacy of participant observation, but still there is discontent on the part of prominent scholars in the field that has led some to jettison the concept of culture entirely. What is "a culture," they ask, if it is constantly changing, transformed by developments that erect, realign, and dissolve boundaries that are already tenuous? I maintain, however, that the concept remains valuable as a means of grasping and explaining the continuity that emerges from the shifts of time and context. I maintain as well that "culture" is newly helpful in attempts to understand the wealthy and powerful as they pull even further away from an expanding global majority.

The readings in this book on American culture are sorted into the categories one might find in a classic ethnography—"ecology/economy," "family life and leisure," "class and power," "ritual and religion," "ideology"—but of course the complexities of culture are not so easily contained, and readers might well wonder why my chapter on *The Big Bang Theory* isn't included in "ecology/economy," or Micaela di Leonardo's essay on the concept of "home" hasn't been placed in "family life and leisure." Frankly, all of the chapters, whether ostensibly about buttons (Grebinger) or commuting (Descartes, Kottak, and Kelly) or heroin addicts (Bourgois) or Groundhog Day (Myers), could all appear under the heading of "class and power," because the United States continues to dominate the world not only in terms of the amount of resources it commands but also in terms of ideology, especially that hallmark component we call the American Dream. The Dream mesmerizes those within as well as outside the country; it remains possible for a poor American to look at a rich American and think, "That could be me," even as the income gap widens. This is the myth that the young Richard Rodriguez (1992), quoted above, had not yet absorbed; thus he could see an "Americanness" that Americans themselves often deny (see Chapter 20 [Cerroni-Long]).

All the groups discussed in the chapters that follow are shaped by the American Dream. Whether they have lived it (so they think), whether they are chasing it, whether they are deprived of it (and wondering if they are at fault), whether they believe it is threatened, or whether they believe they are challenging it, they are all in the grip of its power.

Reference

Rodriguez, Richard. 1992. *Days of Obligation: An Argument with My Mexican Father*. New York: Penguin Books.

2

AMERICA—THE VIEW FROM ACROSS THE (REFLECTING) POND

Clare L. Boulanger

The majority lives in the perpetual utterance of self-applause; and there are certain truths which the Americans can only learn from strangers or from experience.

—Alexis de Tocqueville, *Democracy in America*

Americans are a commercial people par excellence. But of all the consumer goods we sell around the globe, perhaps the most important is ourselves. Throughout our history, despite brief moments of doubt, we have been supremely proud of our values and way of life. Further, we have distributed these generously worldwide, not only through direct colonization but also through such ideological weapons as the Voice of America and a vast array of entertainment products advertising our global preeminence, our wealth, our piety, our happy families, our passion for justice, and our sense of fun. This ideological barrage is a savvy marketing strategy—purveying our ideals softens the ground for the passage of objects that are all the more salable when they embody Americanism. But the strategy works precisely because it is not calculated. We Americans believe in what we sell, and our confidence increases the desirability of our goods.

This trade is ingeniously organized—with every item sold both our economy and our national ego are bolstered. The American way of life is a high-maintenance project; it asks much of us in terms of practical and psychic work and thus must be constantly renewed in both areas. Fortunately, our ethnocentrism is a powerful reality-treatment system. Once passed through its filters, the poverty and filth we observe in other countries disappear in our own. The beggars we pity elsewhere become, on urban U.S. streets, shiftless bums too drunk and lazy to get a job; the government corruption we decry as endemic around the globe is reduced in the United States to a few "bad apples" bobbing to the surface of the political system from time to time; and while we wring our hands about the world's wars of aggression, we understand our own military actions as just and justified.

Through the prism of ethnocentrism our privileged lives become, simply, natural. We believe (to the extent we are able to think about such things) that our advantages do not stem from the historical and ongoing exercise of national power but from the desire and hard work of individual Americans; hence, anyone in the world who takes up these practices will enjoy a similar level of success. This vision is compelling even to those most insulted and injured by it, both inside and outside the United States. But without benefit of American ethnocentrism, what do outsiders actually see?

Since 2014, I have been teaching at a university in the People's Republic of China. My students are learning English and have already reached a level that is far better than my Mandarin. Once I got the go-ahead to work on this second edition of *Reflecting on America*, I thought of giving my students the opportunity to write its lead-in chapter. No other contribution to the book will hold up such a "distant mirror" (DeVita and Armstrong 1992) to our culture, and, in fact, the other chapters demonstrate to American students that it is possible to adopt an intellectually constructive insider/outsider perspective even as a member of one's own society. Nonetheless, my Chinese students may help American students jump-start their ability to develop, in line with this volume's subtitle, "anthropological views of U.S. culture."

Before I could ask my Chinese students to provide material, I had to clear the project with the organization for which I teach and the university at which I teach. These authorities attached the following conditions: my organization would not be identified, my university would not be identified, my students would not be identified. In fact, I cannot identify which students said what, because I had them write in groups and most of what is quoted below is the product of collaboration. I am sure my students understand the value of preserving their privacy even as they might want their names to appear in an American textbook. But when I read them the passages I would include in the chapter, they likely recognized their own groups' contributions and took a deserved, if secret, pride in their work.

It is perhaps not divulging too much about my university to say that it lies in an inland province that is, for the most part, developing rather than developed. Many of my students come from rural backgrounds. None has visited the United States; in fact, few have traveled to Beijing or Shanghai. However, the students are not ignorant of the world, or even greatly naive. The internet has transformed formerly distant mirrors into the long, infinite tunnel of a mirror facing a mirror. Much of what my students wrote about the United States has the same arch tone American students of the same age might use, and I have tried to preserve this tone in what I quote below. I have also preserved the writing nearly exactly, editing only to eliminate confusing wording. My intention was not to point up my students' difficulties with English but to avoid, to the extent possible, reworking their views in line with what *I* think they must have meant.

In keeping with the classic anthropological quest to find the extraordinary in the ordinary, I asked my students (eighty-five in total) to answer five questions on everyday American life. All of the questions began with "If you were an American, . . ." and continued as follows: "what would you like to eat?"; "what job would you have?"; "what would you do for fun?"; "what would your family life be like?"; and "how would you feel about your country, and why?"

"IF YOU WERE AN AMERICAN, WHAT WOULD YOU LIKE TO EAT?"

Supporters of American meat industries will be happy to know that my Chinese students think of the United States as a land overflowing with animal products, notably beefsteak (mentioned eight times on my three answer sheets), hamburger (also mentioned eight times), and turkey (mentioned seven times), known in China as an important American ritual food. Coffee and various forms of alcohol showed up frequently as favored American drinks. Some sample menus:

> For lunch, I would like to eat steak and red wine. I'll cook some pizza with chicken, tomato sauce, eggs, and butter.

> I would like to eat egg tart with hot dogs. And I would like to eat turkey and American big lobster and drink coca cola. It's very delicious. I would like to eat pasta and all kinds of pie, drink some kind of coffee. And I'd like to eat salmon. It's very famous in America.

> In the morning, I'd like to eat sandwich, hamburger, butter, cake, milk and egg for breakfast. In the afternoon, I'd like to eat beefsteak, pizza, salad, spaghetti, and vegetable for lunch. I usually like to drink wine. In the evening, I'd like to eat turkey, cheese, hot dog, splashed potato, and chocolate for dinner. . . . After supper, I'd like to eat dessert and fruit. I'd like to eat junk food when I'm watching TV.

> In the evening, we'll hold a barbecue party with a lot of beer.

"IF YOU WERE AN AMERICAN, WHAT JOB WOULD YOU HAVE?"

In response to this question, students did not necessarily dream big in American terms. One said, "I would like to be a cleaner," while another mused, "Maybe a supermarket cashier." Yet another student proclaimed, "I am going to be a bartender, which looks like very cool." Several students thought they might be farmers, though the following passage does not really describe a rural life in either China or the United States:

> I want to be a farmer. Driving my secondhand tractor to transport some meats and vegetables to the restaurant and factory in the downtown everyday. After doing this, I drink champagne and watch TV.

A similar mix of the practical and fanciful distinguishes this ambition:

> I want to keep a store which can sale flowers and bread and coffee and I also want to keep a zoo.

Finally, the list below runs the gamut of modest and grand occupations:

> If I were an American, I will be a teacher, or dentist, president, the star of Hollywood, the seller of spicy noodles, and you can have a Chinese restaurant. . . . You can earn a lot of money, CEO of a big company, director of the Fast and Furious Eight, host, reporter, painter, writer, singer, farmer, guide, editor, chief, waiter, airline stewardess, pilot, kindergarten leader, custom[er] service staff, designer, nail artist.

"IF YOU WERE AN AMERICAN, WHAT WOULD YOU DO FOR FUN?"

In a landlocked part of China, it is unsurprising that my students often mentioned the beach as a desirable destination, though they might be surprised to realize that many Americans have no more access to the seaside than they do. Driving, which none of my students can do (in terms of either operating a car or owning one), is also attractive.

> I will take part in some adventurous activities to enrich my spare time.

> I will travel with my friends driving a car.

> I would like to surf. I would like to swim.

> I would like to build a band and participate in all kinds of music festival.

> I will drive a car at the top of speed on the motorway which around mountains. And in summer, I will surf with my friends, and swim in winter with my friends who are adventurers.

> Have my own big house and just sit in front of the window to enjoy it.

> I'd like to have a gun.

"IF YOU WERE AN AMERICAN, WHAT WOULD YOUR FAMILY LIFE BE LIKE?"

Admittedly, my students are at a tender age—they are breaking away from their parents while at the same time feeling pressure from them to return home. It is little wonder, then, that the students are intrigued by the egalitarianism that is often featured in American depictions of family life. References to domestic violence, or the lack thereof, not only idealize American family life in line with TV sitcom portrayals but also indicate that all is not well in the Chinese family despite its preeminent place in social life.

> Children have their own choices and they can make decisions by themselves.

> Every family member is equal to each other.

> Most parents don't quarrel in front of their children.

Most parents don't hit or beat their children.

I want to live with my father and my mother. We have a very big and comfortable house and we have a big car. We can drive it to everywhere we want. Besides, I want to have a big enough kitchen. We can make delicious food in our spare time. All of us just like friends.

If I were an American, I will live in a big beautiful house standed by sea. My husband is a CEO and earns a great deal of money. We will drive Lamborghini to catch the wind. As usual, we can swim in our big private pool and take our private plane to travel around the world.

I and my family will be together forever and we will have endless food.

"If you were an American, how would you feel about your country, and why?"

My students are puzzled when I say "the U.S." The Chinese know us as "America," or *Meiguo* in Mandarin. *Meiguo* is clearly modeled on the sound of "America," but additionally, it means "beautiful country." The rendering of foreign terms in Mandarin is especially artful when sound and meaning come together, as most Chinese, including my students, would agree has happened in this instance.

I would be proud of my country because the infrastructure such as traffic, entertainment, makes people's life convenient and happy.

I think our country is much opener than any other countries. There are many new ideas in people's mind and they always would like to try new things. What's more, we prefer to do challengeous sports. . . . In my opinion, our country is filled with adventurous spirit.

Our leisure activities are followed by other countries, and progresses in movies or TV field attract people all over the world.

Dangerous, because the gun is legal.

I am proud that our president [Obama] is such a handsome man.

The positive tone of much of the above commentary suggests that the United States has succeeded in marketing its ideals even in places like China, which has ideals of its own. In the answer that follows, however, an admiration for America is tempered by a recognition of the country's flaws and deficits.

If I were an American, I feel my country is freedom, we can parade, free speech, but, crime and a lot of teenagers take drugs and excessive drinking. On the other hand, we should agree with homosexuality. At the same time, we hope our country is developed, rich, and democracy, but it is pity that [we] have no long history like China.

However, I'm happy to allow my students to end this piece on a flattering note:

> I will extremely like my country, because in my mind this country is fashionable and fastanstic.

I will personally support "fastanstic" as an English word. We Americans welcome new superlatives.

REFERENCES

DeVita, Philip R., and James D. Armstrong, eds. 1992. *Distant Mirrors: America as a Foreign Culture*. Belmont, CA: Wadsworth/Thomson Learning.

Tocqueville, Alexis de. 1835. *Democracy in America*, vol. 1. Henry Reeve, trans. London: Saunders and Otley.

ECOLOGY/ECONOMY

3

MICKEY, NICKY, AND BARBIE: KINDERCULTURE IN AMERICA

Richard H. Robbins

The idea of culture is central to anthropology, culture being, among other things, the symbols, objects, and meanings that allow people to turn the chaos of shifting impressions that constitute raw experience into a seemingly ordered and coherent universe. But, in some ways, culture has become our enemy.

That may seem a strange thing for an anthropologist to say. The study of culture is, after all, the anthropologist's stock-in-trade; culture is what anthropologists claim makes human beings unique, what distinguishes us from the rest of the animal world. It has permitted the birth of language, reason, and the building of seemingly great civilizations. I believe, however, that in the United States today, a case can be made for the possibility that culture has become our greatest threat.

In traditional, small-scale, and relatively isolated communities, certain persons—the elderly, male and female family heads, shamans, and priests—were assigned the task of maintaining culture and the values that supported the community. But virtually everyone was active in the maintenance of the culture and given the opportunity to introduce innovative variations.

In modern society, however, with its vast global communications technology, culture is no longer communally created and maintained; rather, it is created and maintained by those with the political and economic power to control how the world is represented and the mechanisms through which these representations reach us. This is an awesome power, for it truly is the power to influence, even determine, the meanings we assign to our experiences. Never in the course of human history have so few been empowered to dictate how so many define the purpose of their existence and define the values that they live by.

Reflecting on America, 2nd edition, edited by Clare L. Boulanger, 17–27 © 2016 Taylor & Francis. All rights reserved.

A word commonly used to describe the power to define how society members define their world is *spin*. Politicians, of course, are constantly "spinning" the versions of events or policies that they want people to accept. Public-relations specialists earn their living by spinning, getting people to view their clients in ways favorable to them. And advertisers, of course, use the power of spin to control the meaning that consumers attribute to everything from baby formula to sex enhancement products. "The job of a leader is to define reality and give hope," said Kenneth Chenault, chief executive of American Express, of President George W. Bush after 9/11, "and you are giving us a great deal of hope" (quoted in Walsh 2006). Ron Suskind (2004) wrote in the *New York Times Magazine* of boasts by officials in the Bush administration that they did in fact get to define reality. People like Suskind, one official (likely Karl Rove) told him, live "in what we call the reality-based community," which he identified as people who "believe that solutions emerge from your judicious study of discernible reality." When Suskind responded with a remark about enlightenment principles and understanding the facts, the official interrupted:

> That's not the way the world really works anymore. We're an empire now, and when we act, we create our own reality. And while you're studying that reality . . . we'll act again, creating other new realities, which you can study too, and that's how things will sort out. We're history's actors . . . and you, all of you, will be left to just study what we do.

Americans do not talk much about power. One of the reasons, I suspect, is that power works in such a subtle and hard-to-define manner. Ask Americans how McDonald's, or Disney, or General Motors, or Barack Obama has shaped them or constructed their consciousness, and you will likely draw blank stares. What does it mean to argue that power involves the ability to ascribe meanings to various features of our lives?

Let me illustrate. In the 1960s, Ray Kroc dedicated his organization to ensuring that people associated his company, McDonald's, with the American nation-state. In what up to that time was the most costly advertising campaign ever, he succeeded in making McDonald's into an American icon, a place where the American flag was to fly twenty-four hours a day, a place decorated with a wall plaque depicting an eagle carrying a banner in its beak that proclaimed, "McDonald's: The American Way." Little effort or expense was spared to ensure that anyone thinking of McDonald's would think of it as American. The association is so complete that protesters in Sweden and France have tried to block the opening of McDonald's restaurants because these represent, to them, "creeping Americanism" (see Kincheloe 1997: 252ff.).

McDonald's, of course, is not alone in the attempt to colonize our consciousness. Globally, businesses spend a half trillion dollars a year on advertising—an amount higher than the gross domestic products of 163 countries listed by the World Bank. Disney, for example, spent almost $2 billion in 2014 to define its image and persuade us to purchase its products, while McDonald's remains number one among television advertisers. American corporations employ almost 200,000 public-relations specialists engaged in manipulating news, public opinion, and public policy to serve the interests of paying clients. These public-relations specialists now outnumber actual news reporters by about 40,000—and the gap is growing. A 1990 study found that almost 40 percent of the news content in a typical U.S. newspaper originates from public-relations press releases, story memos, and suggestions, and there is little to indicate that the percentage has declined.

Some observers have certainly warned about how advertising and other forms of corporate persuasion influence our lives: Vance Packard's classic work *The Hidden Persuaders* (1957) did that almost sixty years ago. But I don't think we are yet aware of the extent to which these efforts and the power they represent define our entire culture and consequently influence our behavior.

THE CONSTRUCTION OF CHILDHOOD

What I propose to do in this chapter is to illustrate how corporations control our culture by focusing on one aspect of it—what Shirley Steinberg and Joe Kincheloe (1997) call "kinderculture." One thing that anthropology teaches us is that childhood, much like the rest of our culture, is socially created. That is, childhood, and how it is defined, varies from society to society and from era to era. In the nineteenth century, childhood in America was very different from what it is today. Prior to the twentieth century, the major role of children in the capitalist economy was as workers (Lasch 1977: 14ff.). Few industries did not employ children at some level, and few families did not expect children to contribute economically in one way or another, through either their farm or factory labor. This began to change dramatically in the twentieth century, largely because of the effort by business, with the cooperation of the government, to change children from laborers into consumers. This is not to say that there was no childhood culture. Children's culture in America has always existed in playgrounds and schools, but this culture was produced by children and maintained through child-to-child contact. Today's childhood culture is created by adults and maintained largely by the mass media, especially TV, and schools for the purpose of convincing children to consume (see, e.g., Milner 2006).

The economic stakes in kinderculture are considerable, and so it should come as no surprise that children have become a main target of corporations. As one marketing specialist told the *Wall Street Journal*, "Even two-year-olds are concerned about their brand of clothes, and by the age of six are full-out consumers" (quoted in Durning 1992: 120). Almost 60 million school-age children spend well over $100 billion a year of their families' money as well as their own on sweets, food, drinks, electronic products, toys, games, clothes, and shoes. Children under the age of twelve spend more than $12 billion of their own money and influence over $165 billion in family spending. One study determined that children influence $9 billion worth of car sales. As one car dealer put it, "Sometimes the child literally is our customer. I have watched the child pick out the car" (quoted in Beder 1998).

McDonald's, along with Disney, Mattel, and other corporations such as Saban Entertainment, the producer of what was once the top-rated children's TV show, *Mighty Morphin Power Rangers*, have created a kinderculture that is designed to produce consumers and to separate them from any other institution that might challenge that goal. If you have a problem conceptualizing power, you only need to examine the extent to which kinderculture works to promote childhood hedonism, instill an ethic of pleasure, and separate children from parents, teachers, and other community members who might challenge corporate authority.

This kinderculture represents a cultural pedagogy, an educational curriculum taught largely outside the school on TV and in movies, newspapers, magazines, toys, advertisements, video games, books, sports, and so on. The curriculum of kinderculture has replaced traditional classroom lectures and seatwork with "dolls, 'magic kingdoms,' animated fantasies, interactive videos, virtual realities, kickboxing TV heroes, spine-tingling horror books, and an entire array of entertainment forms produced ostensibly for adults but eagerly consumed by children" (Steinberg and Kincheloe 1997: 4).

Our most important teachers are already no longer in schools, and educational policy is no longer being constructed by elected officials. Instead, our educational curriculum is being crafted by corporate producers in the interests of generating consumption and accumulating profit. Corporate America, as Steinberg and Kincheloe (1997: 11) put it, has revolutionized childhood by creating a "consumption theology" that in effect promises redemption and happiness via the consumptive act.

THE CURRICULUM OF KINDERCULTURE

If anthropologists unfamiliar with American culture were to examine the way that kinderculture represents such things as the family, gender, and ethnicity, they would find some things that even they, aware of the variety of human cultures, might find bizarre. Let us first take a look at the family curriculum in kinderculture.

The Family Curriculum in Kinderculture

While anthropologists have described hundreds of varying family structures, none, with which I am familiar, shares the dominant feature of the family in kinderculture—the irrelevance of parents in general and the absence of mothers in particular. Think for a moment about how the family is depicted in the classic Disney releases *Aladdin*, *Beauty and the Beast*, *The Little Mermaid*, *Pocahontas*, and *The Hunchback of Notre Dame*. None of the major characters has a mother. Ariel has none, Belle has none, neither Aladdin nor Jasmine has one, Pocahontas has none. Quasimodo's mother is killed by his protagonist and substitute father Frodo at the opening of the film, while Esmeralda, the Gypsy dancer, has, I believe, neither father nor mother. Interestingly, this has long been a feature of Disney characters. In fact, the only mothers I can recall in Disney films are the elephant mother in *Dumbo*, the short-lived mother in *Bambi*, and the evil stepmothers in *Snow White* and *Cinderella*.

The Duck family is made up of Donald, his three nephews, his uncle Scrooge, and Grandma Duck, who is Donald's aunt (but not Scrooge's wife), along with all kinds of cousins such as Gus and Moby Duck; even Daisy's family consists only of nieces. Mickey Mouse also has only his nephews Morty and Ferdy, while Goofy has Gilbert and Gyro Gearloose has Newton. The Beagle Boys have only uncles, aunts, and nephews, though their female cousins occasionally appear (see Dorfman and Mattelart 1975). Whether this absence of parenthood is a way to obliterate any suggestion of sexuality, as some have suggested, or whether it is an expression of Disney's own unhappy relations with his parents is difficult to judge. But because the same meanings about parents are present in other classic films—such as the *Home Alone* movies, in which a ten-year-old does quite well when his parents leave him behind, and in such movies as *Halloween* and *Friday the 13th*, in which parents are irrelevant or hostile—it is safe to say that the absent mother is a common theme in kinderculture.

We might speculate that these representations are simply based on the reality of the American family today. But my own suspicion is that, intentionally or unintentionally, the goal is to create in children a sense of their own agency that clearly isolates them from any parental authority and suggests, to borrow a line used by sociologist Robert Bellah and his associates (1996), that "they have given birth to themselves."

The ultimate mythic expression of children as their own creators occurs in the movie *Back to the Future*, in which the hero, played by Michael J. Fox, is shot back into the past, where he faces the task of ensuring that his mother and father fall in love lest he, and his siblings, are never born.

The practical consequence of this family form, or lack of it, is anything but benign, for it suggests to children that they live in a world in which they must act alone, a world in which collective, or at least family, action is nonexistent or futile. The result is to leave the corporation (or the state) as the only benevolent agency capable of exerting collective power, and as the major benevolent force in the lives of children. Don't worry, children—Ronald McDonald, Mickey, and Barbie will always be there to fulfill your needs, as long as you can pay for them. *American society has succeeded in commodifying nurturance.*

Gender: Women as Altruist-Shoppers

While women as mothers are largely absent in kinderculture, women are not absent altogether. On the contrary, they play an important role as "altruist-shoppers," beings characterized first and foremost by their evident mandate to subordinate their interests to those of men and secondarily by their proclivity to buy things. Disney films are good examples of this. Ariel in *The Little Mermaid* trades her beautiful singing voice for a chance to pursue her handsome prince, while Ursula, the evil octopus, assures Ariel that men do not like women who talk anyway, a sentiment with which the prince clearly concurs, since he bestows the kiss of true love on Ariel even though she has never spoken to him.

In *Beauty and the Beast*, Belle first sacrifices herself for her father, then falls in love with the Beast, whom she attempts to civilize by instructing him to eat, control his temper, and dance. In the end she has become another woman whose life is valued for solving a man's problems. *The Lion King* portrays the animal kingdom as clearly ruled by males, and even the evil Scar is served by unresisting lionesses as he assumes control, defeated only by the return of the grown-up Simba. The *Pocahontas* story, of course, was just made for the woman whose major role is to sacrifice herself for a man (see Giroux 1997).

The altruistic theme is further developed with Barbie, who, like Disney's Ariel, Belle, Pocahontas, and Esmeralda, is the ultimate altruist, giving up something for the good of men or mankind. Barbie stories, in case you haven't seen them, revolve around Barbie's willingness to take in everyone and to sacrifice her own interests for theirs.

It is clear, I believe, that the gender curriculum in kinderculture instructs little girls to believe that it is better to give up one's goal than to disappoint anyone else. It is the place of the female in our society to sacrifice for the good of others (see Steinberg 1997: 216ff.). For some, this in itself might be an appropriate goal, but only if boys were also instructed in the same value. However, it is the boys or the men who always achieve the goals they have set for themselves. Aladdin marries the princess and rules the kingdom, the Beast fulfills his goal of achieving his past glory, and Simba becomes king of the jungle.

Of course, sacrificing is not all that girls do. The real power of Barbie is her power to consume. It is unlikely that any female has escaped unscathed from "Barbie buying," leading Shirley Steinberg (1997) to label Barbie "the bitch who has everything." Barbie has clothes galore, of course, and virtually every form of transportation—cars, dune buggies, motorcycles, speedboats, yachts, and horses—and virtually every sort of pet, appliance, and beauty aid. From a marketer's point of view, Barbie defines the cultural inventory of what every young woman should possess.

The Collective Other

Finally, while the family is devalued and women are reduced to altruist-shoppers, adult groups do appear in kinderculture. The problem is that these groups generally take the form of evil "others" who are often racially coded.

In Disney films racial stereotyping is apparent. For example, the opening song in *Aladdin*, "Arabian Nights," originally contained a lyric that identified Arabs as casually violent barbarians. Clearly Howard Ashman, who wrote the lyric, was sufficiently aware of its racism to submit an alternative verse, describing the physical as opposed to the (alleged) social landscape, along with the original he evidently preferred. The less offensive version replaced the original in the video release.

Nonetheless, the characters themselves remain stereotypes. As one representative of an Arab organization put it:

> All of the bad guys have beards and large bulbous noses, sinister eyes and heavy accents, and they're wielding swords constantly. Aladdin doesn't have a big nose; he has a small nose. He doesn't have a beard or turban. He doesn't have an accent. What makes him nice is they've given him this American character.... I have a daughter who says she's ashamed to call herself an Arab, and it's because of things like this. (quoted in Giroux 1997: 61)

Worse yet is the racial stereotyping in *The Lion King*, in which the despicable hyena storm troopers speak with the voices of Whoopi Goldberg and Cheech Marin in racially coded accents that have the nuances of black and Latino youths. These films suggest to viewers that cultural differences that do not bear the imprint of white, middle-class ethnicity are deviant, ignorant, inferior, and a collective threat to be overcome.

Particularly interesting is how Mattel, through Barbie, defines ethnicity. Mattel Toys, the creators of Barbie, sought to contribute to ethnic and racial tolerance with a series of Barbies representing different cultures. There is the Jamaican Barbie, the Polynesian Barbie, the Indian Barbie, the Native American Barbie, and the German Barbie, whose country is known for its "breathtaking beauty and hard-working people," as if south of the equator Barbies don't work.

At first one might applaud Mattel's efforts to increase cultural awareness. From an anthropological perspective, however, the message is quite different. Mattel, like Disney, defines ethnicity as anything other than white. The multicultural Barbies are all defined by their foods, their "dances," and their languages. Because white, middle-class Barbie is the norm from which others are defined, no "regular" Barbie ever talks about her culture's favorite foods (hamburgers, French fries, and milk shakes), the personality of "her" people, or their customs. In the words of one researcher, "Barbie has otherized dolls into dominant and marginal cultures. Barbie's whiteness privileges her to not be questioned; she is the standard by which all others are measured" (Steinberg 1997: 214).

In brief, then, I would suggest that kinderculture portrays a world in which goal-oriented, white, Christian, American men and their altruistic female companions alone face the forces of ethnically coded, evil others. It is as if the only forces remaining to protect them, the only remaining sanctuaries, are Disney World and McDonald's.

THE MASKING OF REALITY

I mentioned earlier that our culture has become our enemy, partially because we have lost any semblance of control over it. It is our enemy in another sense as well: not only does culture portray a particular world for us, but it also has the capability to mask other realities. One of the more ironic things about kinderculture is that it subtly hides from us the real state of childhood in the United States and the world.

In Ronald Reagan's final address from the White House in 1989, he called for Americans to adopt "an informed patriotism," to return to the basics of American history and emphasize what it means to be an American. He suggested to the children in the audience that all great change in America begins at the dinner table and that if their parents had not been teaching them what it is to be an American, the children should "nail 'em on it," adding that that would be the "American thing to do."

Yet only 50 percent of the children President Reagan was talking to lived with two parents, and only 12 percent lived with their two biological parents, let alone sat down to dinner with them. Furthermore, one in five of those children lived in poverty—one in four if they were under the age of five, and seven out of ten if they happened to be African American females.

American children likely had more than patriotism on their minds. Adolescent suicide was not even a category fifty years ago, yet by the 1980s it was second to accidents in accounting for teenage deaths. By 1994, some 400,000 adolescents were attempting suicide each year (Ferguson 1994).

How many Americans are aware that the toys and clothing that they purchase for their children are made in sweatshop conditions, often by children, in countries such as Haiti, Thailand, Indonesia, and Guatemala? One reporter who visited a factory just outside Bangkok, where Barbies and Disney toys are made by 4,500 (mostly female) workers, was greeted by a rally of women and children who carried banners saying, "We are not slave labour!" These workers, earning the equivalent of 60 to 70 U.S. cents an hour, were astonished to hear that two Barbies are sold somewhere in the world every second, that more than a billion pairs of shoes have been made for Barbies (many in Bangkok), and that the Mattel corporation grosses from $3 billion to $4 billion a year.

But perhaps the most powerful contrast can be drawn between American twelve- and thirteen-year-olds playing soccer with balls made in sweatshop conditions by twelve- and thirteen-year-old children in Bangladesh. How are these things kept from us, how are they masked?

This is where Nicky—Saint Nicholas, or Santa Claus—comes in. Every culture has its myths, the stories that purport to explain how things came to be. Santa Claus, and his accompanying ritual of Christmas, is perhaps the ultimate myth of kinderculture, one that idealizes consumption, production, and profit. This is a grossly simplified and idealized model of the American political economy. It depicts a world in which commodities (toys) are manufactured by happy elves working in Santa's workshop and distributed, free of charge, to good boys and girls by a corpulent, grandfatherly male in fur-trimmed clothes. It is perhaps ironic that when political cartoonist Thomas Nast created, in 1862, what has become the contemporary image of Santa Claus, he modeled Santa's costume on the fur-trimmed clothes worn by the fabulously wealthy Astor family (Restad 1995: 149).

Nast also created Santa's workshop, perhaps in nostalgic remembrance of the days before factory production. Writers as early as the 1870s recognized the irony of this idealized version of Christmas and toy production. One magazine editorial in 1873, commenting on a picture of Santa's elves working gaily in their workshop, noted the reality of the situation: poor immigrants working six days a week in factories, not some magical workplace, turning out dolls, boats, tops, and toy soldiers. The writer added that "the cost of these toys is small; and yet there is a profit in them" (quoted in Restad 1995: 149). In *The Modern Christmas in America: A Cultural History of Gift-Giving*, William Waits (1992: 25) suggests that Santa's major role was to "decontaminate" Christmas gifts, removing the stigma of industrial manufacture.

So, What Can We Do about It?

If the above analysis is valid, a question then follows: What can parents, schools, and others do to regain a role in building the cultural reality in which our children live?

Parents

What can we do as parents? Very little, I suggest. As popular movies, such as *Home Alone* and *Halloween*, tell children, parents have become largely irrelevant. When she was five years old, my daughter Rebecca doted on her collection of

Barbie dolls, spent too many hours engrossed in the Disney Channel, and anxiously awaited the arrival of Santa. I did not accept this passively. I was constantly pointing out to her that Disney just wanted her to buy stuff, and that nobody looks like Barbie, and I tried to convince her that "Terrible Sid," the little boy in *Toy Story* who tears the heads off his sister's Barbie dolls and replaces them with the heads of dinosaurs and is depicted as the villain, is the real hero of the movie, but to little effect. She just said dismissively, "Oh, Daddy."

Corporations, largely but not exclusively through TV and movies, have taken over the task of child rearing. They have been allowed to do so partially because of our collective sense that what they do is trivial, that it is only entertainment, and also because of the economic realities and necessity of the multiworker household. With the absence of any meaningful national day-care program, TV and its corporate sponsors have been handed the responsibility for day care in America, much to the relief of many parents grateful for the free time they gain through the largesse of the Disney Channel, *Mighty Morphin Power Rangers*, Barbie, and Barney.

Schools

How about the schools? I suspect that they too are largely irrelevant in American kinderculture. Furthermore, corporations are threatening to take over our schools, as McDonald's, Disney, and Mattel, along with scores of others, have targeted the public schools for child marketing. McDonald's has its "A's for hamburgers" program along with advertising-based learning packets for science, foreign languages, and other subjects; McDonald's and other fast-food firms have attempted to operate school cafeterias; and Disney is establishing a model school while it promotes its "Teacher of the Year" awards. These and other corporations freely distribute promotional materials to be used in classrooms, materials that financially strapped schools are only too happy to accept. Privatization of our schools, if the penchant to "downsize government" continues, will likely occur within the next decade, and along with it the emergence of dominant "education corporations" (Disney and McDonald's will probably be in the forefront) that will parallel the development of megacorporate health management organizations.

Even the so-called charter school movement, groups of concerned people empowered by the federal government to begin their own schools, will likely fall prey to the easy money of corporations only too anxious to begin building consumer loyalty at earlier and earlier ages.

Holding Corporations Responsible for What They Do

We could make more of an effort to hold corporations responsible for what they do. This approach is certainly a possibility, but one for which I hold no great hope. Not that the potential is not there. As consumers, after all, we have, collectively, as much if not more power than the corporations. They depend on us. Yet I think that, as consumers, we are so disciplined by our possessions and convinced of the evils of collective action that any effective national consumer movement is unlikely.

TAKING BACK OUR CULTURE

Anthropologist Ruth Benedict used to tell her students, "You can't beat your culture." Anthropology, she said, by bringing to bear knowledge of other cultures, can help you gain a useful perspective on your own culture, but, to quote another anthropologist, Eleanor Leacock (1993: 14), "it is folly to think one can transcend it."

In his 1991 novel *The Sweet Hereafter*, Russell Banks describes a community plunged into grief by the deaths of many of its children in a school bus accident that leaves few families untouched. The parents hire a lawyer, Mitchell Stephens, to handle their suit for damages. At one point Stephens, who has had problems with his own daughter, muses about the fate of children in America. His soliloquy is worth repeating at length:

> The people of Sam Dent are not unique. We've all lost our children. It's like all the children of America are dead to us. Just look at them, for God's sake—violent on the streets, comatose in the malls, narcotized in front of the TV. In my lifetime something terrible happened that took our children away from us. I don't know if it was the Vietnam war, or the sexual colonization of kids by industry, or drugs, or TV, or divorce, or what the hell it was; I don't know which are causes and which are effects; but the children are gone, that I know. So that trying to protect them is little more than an elaborate exercise in denial. Religious fanatics and superpatriots, they try to protect their kids by turning them into schizophrenics; Episcopalians and High Church Jews gratefully abandon their kids to boarding schools and divorce one another so they can get laid with impunity; the middle class grabs what it can buy and passes it on, like poisoned candy on Halloween; and meanwhile the inner-city blacks and poor whites in the boonies sell their souls with longing for what's killing everyone else's kids and wonder why theirs are on crack.
>
> It's too late; they're gone; we're what's left.
>
> And the best we can do for them, and for ourselves, is rage against what took them. Even if we can't know what it'll be like when the smoke clears, we do know that rage, for better or worse, generates a future. (Banks 1991: 99–100)

QUESTIONS FOR DISCUSSION

Which cartoons and films influenced you most as a child? Did you accumulate the consumer goods associated with these media products? How did these cartoons and films have an impact on your development as a person, as a boy or girl, as an American?

REFERENCES

Banks, Russell. 1991. *The Sweet Hereafter*. New York: Harper Perennial.

Beder, Sharon. 1998. "Marketing to Children." www.uow.edu.au/~sharonb/children.html#fn6 (accessed October 29, 2015).

Bellah, Robert N., Richard Madsen, William M. Sullivan, Ann Swidler, and Steven M. Tipton. 1996. *Habits of the Heart: Individualism and Commitment in American Life*. Berkeley: University of California Press.

Dorfman, Ariel, and Armand Mattelart. 1975. *How to Read Donald Duck: Imperialist Ideology in the Disney Comic*. David Kunzle, trans. New York: International General.

Durning, Alan. 1992. *How Much Is Enough? The Consumer Society and the Future of the Earth*. New York: W. W. Norton.

Ferguson, S. 1994. "The Comfort of Being Sad." *Utne Reader* 64 (July/August): 60–61.

Giroux, Henry A. 1997. "Are Disney Movies Good for Your Kids?" In Shirley R. Steinberg and Joe L. Kincheloe, eds., *Kinderculture: The Corporate Construction of Childhood*. Boulder, CO: Westview Press.

Kincheloe, Joe L. 1997. "McDonald's, Power, and Children: Ronald McDonald (aka Ray Kroc) Does It All for You." In Shirley R. Steinberg and Joe L. Kincheloe, eds., *Kinderculture: The Corporate Construction of Childhood*. Boulder, CO: Westview Press.

Lasch, Christopher. 1977. *Haven in a Heartless World: The Family Besieged*. New York: Basic Books.

Leacock, Eleanor. 1993. "Being an Anthropologist." In Constance Sutton, ed., *From Labrador to Samoa: The Theory and Practice of Eleanor Burke Leacock*. Washington, DC: American Anthropological Association.

Milner, Murray, Jr. 2006. *Freaks, Geeks, and Cool Kids: American Teenagers, Schools, and the Culture of Consumption*. New York: Routledge.

Packard, Vance. 1957. *The Hidden Persuaders*. New York: D. McKay.

Restad, Penne L. 1995. *Christmas in America: A History*. Oxford: Oxford University Press.

Steinberg, Shirley R. 1997. "The Bitch Who Has Everything." In Shirley R. Steinberg and Joe L. Kincheloe, eds., *Kinderculture: The Corporate Construction of Childhood*. Boulder, CO: Westview Press.

Steinberg, Shirley R., and Joe L. Kincheloe. 1997. "Introduction: No More Secrets—Kinderculture, Information Saturation, and the Postmodern Childhood." In Shirley R. Steinberg and Joe L. Kincheloe, eds., *Kinderculture: The Corporate Construction of Childhood*. Boulder, CO: Westview Press.

Suskind, Ron. 2004. "Faith, Certainty and the Presidency of George W. Bush." *New York Times Magazine*, October 17. www.nytimes.com/2004/10/17/magazine/17BUSH.html?ei=5090&en=890a96189e162076&ex=1255665600&adxnnl=1&partner=rssuserland&adxnnlx=1157297345-WE/kdbziLwV7Q0HvQZORMw (accessed March 26, 2007).

Waits, William, 1992. *The Modern Christmas in America: A Cultural History of Gift-Giving*. New York: New York University Press.

Walsh, Kenneth T. 2006. "Leadership." *U.S. News & World Report*. www.usnews.com/usnews/9_11/articles/911bush.htm (accessed March 26, 2007).

4

Consuming Ourselves to Death

Richard Wilk

Defining "the Cause" of Global Climate Change

The ways in which different experts define the causes of global climate change tell a great deal about their training, their worldviews, and the limitations of the partitioned knowledges we have inherited from the nineteenth-century division of the world into physical, natural, and social sciences. Ask atmospheric scientists and they will tell you that the cause is greenhouse gases, cloud cover, and the balance of the carbon cycle. An ocean specialist is likely to talk about thermohaline circulation, currents, glaciers, and sea levels. You get the same myopia from economists, who focus on the industries that spew carbon dioxide and other gases into the atmosphere, and from political scientists, who talk about the failure of regulatory regimes. A tropical ecologist is likely to give you a lecture about deforestation and the burning of Amazonia.

At the other extreme are consumer activists and the "simple living" movement, telling us that climate change is the result of Western society's extravagant lifestyles, which consume too many of the world's resources, and other world areas emulating the West. From this perspective, consumption is "using up" the resources of the world, leaving nothing but a despoiled wasteland for the next generations. While this is an easy way of defining the problem, with a clear moral vision of "good guys" and "bad guys," it is in many ways as myopic and inaccurate as a technical focus on smokestack emissions or rain-forest destruction. It may work as an agitation tactic to wake people up and get them to see the urgency and magnitude of the problem of climate change, and warn them that the solution

From Crate, Susan A. and Mark Nuttall, eds. 2009. *Anthropology and Climate Change*, 265–76. © Left Coast Press, Inc. Republished in *Reflecting on America*, 2nd edition, edited by Clare L. Boulanger, 29–39 (© 2016 Taylor & Francis). All rights reserved.

will affect all of our lives. However, in some important ways, this image of "using things up" misrepresents the problem and can make consumers think that just using less of everything is the answer.

If the world were simply a shopping bag of groceries that humans could either open and eat or store for later, then the idea of "using up" would make sense. Instead, human impacts on the planet are far more varied than simply using up stocks of resources. Most of the nonrenewable resources, like copper, iron, and coal, are still abundant and are in no danger of running out. In fact, cost, not availability, is usually the obstacle to obtaining them. Additionally, the oceans have an almost inexhaustible supply of gold and other valuable minerals, but the cost of recovering them is very high. The irony is that *renewable* resources, like timber and fish, are the ones most in danger of being destroyed by human overexploitation. The most immediate ecological dangers of pollution, extinction, and climate change are due more to waste, poor regulation, and unregulated emissions than to the "using up" of resources.

The vast engines of the economy, especially in rich developed countries, *are* ultimately driven by the relatively luxurious lifestyles of what is called the "consumer economy," a way of life based on moving and transforming huge amounts of materials and energy. Averaged on a per person basis, for example, U.S. citizens use about sixty times as much material each year as citizens of poor countries like Mozambique, and ten times as much as people in middle-income countries like Turkey and Mexico (Redclift 1996). On the other hand, populous countries like China and India, even though they consume far less on a per capita basis, are now rivaling the national consumption and carbon emission levels of rich countries with far smaller populations. Said another way, if 1.3 billion Chinese were to start producing waste and emitting CO_2 at the same level as North Americans, the rate of climate change would increase dramatically. The Chinese, however, see this is an issue of development and justice, and ask why they should stay in poverty in order to compensate for the past greed and wealth of North Americans and Europeans (Paterson and Grubb 1992).[1] Even though rich countries want to focus on the present and the future, the legacy of past injustice and inequality will not go away in debates over sustainability. There is always a moral and political dimension to issues of consumption, and because moral standards vary from place to place, we also have to think about different cultural ideals concerning justice, comfort, needs, and the future. Anthropology is uniquely situated to address just these issues, all of which have historically been part of the discipline's research program.

But defining the cause of climate change as "overconsumption" and prescribing a kind of global belt-tightening tends to put the burden of *systemic* change on individuals. Many of the ways North American consumers live are beyond their individual control. Suburbs are built in a way that requires people to own cars, since there is no public transportation. Businesses are actually the largest consumers of many kinds of goods, such as paper and cardboard, so even if every private citizen were to recycle every single piece of household paper waste, this would still account for less than 10 percent of the paper used in the country. Many consumption decisions are not made by consumers at all, but by governments, regulatory agencies, and businesses. To give just one example, the automobile industry in the United States has not produced and sold large numbers of electric vehicles to a mass public market since 1914. Archaeologist Michael Schiffer (2003) has persuasively argued that the death of the electric car at the time was a cultural event, related to the marketing of electric cars as "feminine," rather than an economic or technical imperative. The industry's antipathy to the electric car has continued into the recent past, when General Motors, forced to produce an electric vehicle by the state of California, eventually killed its program and destroyed the vehicles despite strong public demand (Sartorius and Zundel 2005).[2]

My point is that it is easy to condemn overconsumption in general terms. On a large scale there is no question that many of the environmental problems the world faces are due to the high levels of material and energy that are used, wasted, and disposed of. But the devil is in the details. A simple admonition to "consume less" may be a satisfying moral message, but in different contexts it can carry class, cultural, and religious overtones. Most religions of the world tell us to be charitable, because wealth is corrupting and materialism distracts us from spiritual and ethical matters (Belk 1983; Miller 2005). But on the other hand, poor people are often accused of wasting their money and other resources, consuming improperly or immorally with respect to clothes, drink, or drugs. The moral critique of consumption is a difficult terrain where we have to tread carefully to make sure we are not passing along class or religious prejudices rather than thinking about environmental ethics and issues (Horowitz 1988; Miller 2001; Wilk 2001).

In practice it is very hard to separate "good" consumption from bad. Why should visiting museums to view fine art be inherently better than going to amusement parks? Is a collection of old master paintings less materialistic than a box of comics, or a garage full of motorcycles? Why should a fast-food hamburger be censured, while a plate of fresh foie gras in a gourmet restaurant is praised? Recent studies show that eating centrally prepared, highly processed food is actually more energy efficient than eating the same number of meals cooked at home using fresh ingredients purchased individually (Sonesson, Anteson, et al. 2005; Sonesson, Mattsson, et al. 2005). When it comes to organic, ethical, local, and energy efficient, what yardstick do we use to measure the negative aspects of consumption, and when do we acknowledge the importance of aesthetics and pleasure? Even tracking the total energy cost, or CO_2 emissions, of a single product turns out to be a complex task, full of uncertainties and arbitrary choices. For the problem of climate change, some kinds of consumption are pretty irrelevant—what is most important is how much fossil fuel was burned to produce, move, and dispose of an item, and how much fossil fuel an item (such as a lawn mower) consumes over its lifetime (measurement of these factors is referred to as life-cycle analysis).

So far most of the information provided to the consumer public about these kinds of issues has been oriented toward helping individuals be "smart consumers" who make the right choices. But what do consumers do as public citizens, as politically engaged members of society, and as anthropologists who want to address the major pressing issues that face humanity during our lifetime?

At the general, strategic level, anthropologists can contribute to an understanding of the complex dynamics of consumer culture so that they can play a part in the modeling and prediction that has become so crucial to the public policy battles going on at the national and international levels. In other words, anthropologists can use what they know about society in general to understand consumer culture in a way that is precise and concrete enough that their findings can have an influence on government policy. Anthropologists can also work at the tactical level of applied anthropology, on specific projects aimed at changing specific kinds of consumption. Perhaps anthropologists can, for example, find ways to encourage people to weather-strip their houses or compost their organic trash.

ANTHROPOLOGY AND CLIMATE CHANGE STRATEGY

One way to recast the problem of consumer culture and climate change in anthropological terms is to phrase it this way: What makes human wants and needs grow? How do things that were once distant luxuries—say, hot water—become basic necessities that people expect on demand for civilized life (see Illich 1977)? Air-conditioning in personal automobiles, an expensive and uncommon option just twenty years ago, is now standard, even in cars sold north of the Arctic Circle in Norway! Why do Western consumers expect their standard of living to keep rising?[3]

Anthropology offers the scope and sweep of time, stepping back and offering a bigger picture of how the human species got itself into its present dilemma of rapid growth in greenhouse gas emissions. Archaeology shows that the growth of human wants and needs is not a new thing. The Neolithic period, for example, saw human societies all over the world becoming used to a wide assortment of new goods and possessions, from pottery to personal jewelry. Once people built a way of life around these goods, they seem to have been very reluctant to give them up and go back to being mobile hunters and gatherers. But compared to the pace of change today, the consumer culture of most early civilizations was relatively stable, and new wants and needs grew very slowly. The Nile valley of Egypt and Sudan hosted a civilization that seems to have provided a stable modest life with the same basic domestic consumer culture for millions of people over at least three thousand years, with only short periods of instability. A small urban elite class lived in relative luxury, with bigger houses, servants, and many kinds of exotic arts and crafts, but even their repertoire was, by our standards, remarkably conservative and slow to develop. The daily material culture and rhythm of everyday life did not change substantially until cheap manufactured goods and machines arrived from Europe in the late nineteenth century.

These historical examples contrast sharply with today's furious pace of change in Chinese and Indian consumer societies, and with the constant stream of new goods flowing into supermarkets, electronics stores, clothing stores, and car dealerships in the United States and other rich countries. Marketing and selling, as Kalman Applbaum (2003) persuasively argues, are the dominant ideology, the unquestioned daily work, of Western consumer society. Disposing of no-longer-wanted goods has itself become a major enterprise and environmental problem. North Americans are buying bigger and bigger houses (and renting huge amounts of extra space) just to have room to keep all of their possessions.

Why have human beings become so insatiable? Social science, to date, has provided only fleeting and partial answers to this query. Here anthropology can potentially play an important role. Economic anthropologists have convincingly argued that the modern capitalist economic system, itself an enormous engine of growth requiring constant expansion, is a cultural artifact (Miller 1997;

Yang 2000). Humans are operators and participants whose behavior is not simply determined by advertisers. Because anthropology has a systemic view of human society that commands the full sweep of the human past and does not isolate our evolutionary heritage from our technology, economy, consumption, morality, and religion, it alone has the potential to assemble a comprehensive approach. But since the time of Leslie White's now-outdated evolutionary model of human energy use, anthropologists have not used their magnificent cross-cultural and long-term data on human societies to think synthetically about the problems of growth and consumption.

This is not to say that anthropologists have not recognized consumption's key importance to the problem of climate change. Since the mid-1980s, an interdisciplinary approach to understanding consumer culture has been growing slowly under the rubric "sustainable consumption" (Murphy and Cohen 2001). However, anthropologists have not had a notable presence in discussions about how public policy can respond to the challenge of making consumer culture more sustainable. Willett Kempton, a cognitive anthropologist trained at Berkeley, and I were the only anthropologists who presented papers at the 1995 National Research Council conference on "environmentally significant consumption" (Stern et al. 1997). Since then, sociologists, social psychologists, and ecological economists have taken the lead in thinking about solutions to the problem of high consumption in North America (e.g., Jackson 2006; Princen 2005; Princen, Maniates, and Conca 2002).

The idea of making consumer culture more sustainable through changes in taxation and government policy is much more widely discussed and accepted in Europe than in the United States, and there have been many European congresses and high-level policy groups addressing the issue (Organisation for Economic Co-operation and Development 1997). There have already been some dramatic results—for example, German legislation now requires companies to take responsibility for recovering and recycling the consumer products they sell (see Reisch and Ropke 2005). Yet anthropologists have again been almost invisible in these discussions, their place taken by social scientists whose global perspective does not take cross-cultural differences into account.

At least anthropologists have begun to take consumer culture seriously as a research topic.[4] The number of studies and their breadth is truly impressive (e.g., Miller 1995), though some find the anthropological approach fragmented, overly symbolic, and poorly contextualized within political economy (Carrier and Heyman 1997). Anthropologists have also been lumped together with cultural studies scholars, whose approach to consumer culture is often less to critique it than to celebrate the opportunities it offers for expression, agency, and developing identity.

Nevertheless, for a globally contextualized picture of how consumer culture is becoming established in new territories around the world, or for a detailed understanding of the social and moral meaning of daily grocery shopping in rich countries, anthropologists offer rich and comprehensive case studies and sophisticated theory. So far what anthropologists have not done is to sit down together to compare and synthesize results, or put them into the kind of language or format that could be useful to policy makers. Why not?

Fundamentally, anthropologists are methodological individualists. We are not trained in collaborative research, and we are not socialized to work together. Instead, we compete for publications, jobs, and visibility. Our collaborations tend to be fleeting affairs, at most on a single research project or publication, often confined to a few days of conference discussion or committee meetings. Contemporary anthropology departments rarely offer the time or the resources for faculty members to actually do research together, much less synthesize and discuss their work with an eye toward policy. These are not the kinds of work that the academic reward structure supports.

In contrast, the disciplines that have made effective contributions to policy have developed appropriate institutions that bring numbers of scholars together for extended periods of time in specialized research institutes, think tanks, and policy centers, often with direct foundation support. About the closest thing anthropologists have to such institutions today are the three multidisciplinary Sloan Foundation–supported centers on American working families at Emory University, the University of Michigan, and the University of California, Los Angeles, all of which have done a great deal of innovative research and produce policy-relevant publications.[5] But otherwise there are no Brookings Institutions, World Resources Institutes, or Russell Sage Foundations to support groups of anthropologists in translating research into useful advice and policy, or to act as public voices for the discipline. There have been a few applied anthropology "shops" associated with major anthropology departments over the years, but they have usually been field research oriented and contract supported, with limited policy capabilities.[6] The result is that anthropologists are left to their own devices to try to bring the relevant results of their own research into government and public discourse, a task akin to whispering in a room full of people screaming through bullhorns.

TACTICAL RESPONSES TO THE PROBLEMS OF CONSUMPTION

Global climate change has brought the issue of consumption forward into public and academic attention, but it was the so-called first energy crisis in the early 1970s and the OPEC oil boycott that gave the American public its first taste of what a world with energy scarcity and higher prices would be like. This initiated a first round of scientific research on conservation, energy efficiency, and alternative energy, funded by the U.S. government and American electric utilities. For a time in the early and mid-1980s, several anthropologists became involved in what was a flowering of applied social science in the field of energy consumption.

Willett Kempton was perhaps the most prominent and prolific researcher, and his innovative ethnographic work on home hot-water use, the way people used and understood thermostats, and folk knowledge about energy costs was widely read and cited among energy researchers (Kempton 1986; Kempton, Darley, and Stern 1992; Kempton, Feuermann, and McGarity 1992). He had influence on the eventual shape of the U.S. Department of Energy's Energy Star labeling program. He conducted pathbreaking experimental work in which people were encouraged to lower their electricity use by seeing their neighbors' electricity consumption on their own monthly bills. He also did important research on how Americans think about and understand global climate change, which attracted attention from congressional legislators (Kempton 1997). Steve Rayner is another anthropologist who had a major role in energy research through his leadership position at the

Oak Ridge National Laboratory and then the Pacific Northwest National Laboratory, where he was chief scientist (see Rayner and Malone 1998).

During this time, Harold Wilhite and I conducted an ethnographic study, funded by the University of California Energy Research Group, contrasting people who were and were not investing in home energy-saving improvements. We were the only anthropologists who applied for funding. The funding organization was initially quite skeptical, but once it saw our results, it became quite supportive. We found a receptive audience for our research in the energy community, and our technical publications continue to be cited (Wilhite and Wilk 1987; Wilk and Wilhite 1984, 1985). But even with grant funding, neither of us was able to find a secure university position in anthropology, and we both had to leave California to pursue our work. Wilhite moved to Norway, where he continued to do innovative research on culture and energy consumption (Wilhite 1996; Wilhite and Ling 1995). I left academia for a position as a rural sociologist with the U.S. Agency for International Development.

If anyone knows how to change consumer behavior, it is advertisers and marketers. Consumer research is the applied science of consumption, taught in marketing programs in hundreds of business schools in the United States and elsewhere. During the 1980s business schools became a haven for anthropologists interested in the applied study of consumption. Eric Arnould, John Sherry, Barbara Olsen, and Grant McCracken, among others, effectively introduced cultural anthropology to marketing programs previously dominated by social psychologists, survey researchers, and demographers. They produced a huge volume of new and creative research, textbooks, and collaborations (e.g., Arnould, Price, and Zinkhan 2003; McCracken 1988; Sherry 1995; Sunderland and Denny 2007).

Anthropology has become both an accepted part and a fashionable trend in mainstream consumer research and marketing. Anthropologists have also helped bring a critical perspective on consumer culture into business schools, questioning the effects of consumption on culture, gender, class, individual identity, and the environment in ways previously quite alien in a pro-business environment. This movement matured in 2005 with the "Transformative Consumer Research" initiative and conferences sponsored by the Association for Consumer Research, both of which explicitly seek to turn the tools of marketing toward socially positive ends.[7] In 2006, the University of Auckland founded an "anti-consumption" institute within its business school, a radical initiative unmatched by anything imagined so far by anthropologists or sociologists.

Given the potential for an applied anthropology of consumption, however, the total response of our discipline has been late, random, and feeble. Anthropologists have started to study the environmental movements that have spawned simple living, bioregionalism, farmers' markets, community-supported agriculture, local currencies, and a host of other initiatives. However, anthropology plays catch-up with popular movements for ethical consumption, vegetarianism, and global equity, and against the World Trade Organization, genetically modified organisms, and the industrialization of the food system. These movements are constantly developing and changing in the United States, and many of these groups have also formed effective international networks. Not only have anthropologists been slow to recognize the importance of consumption activism and study it as a significant phenomenon in the world, but they have also lagged in putting anthropology to work as an applied tactical tool in furthering activist goals.

The Teaching Mission

Our students live and breathe consumer culture, and just as fish living in water never really see the water they live in, our students pass through their four years at a university without ever learning anything systematic about the consumer culture that forms the very fabric of their daily lives. In some ways this is a paradox— the most conspicuous aspect of modern life and the part with which students have direct daily experience is largely passed over during their studies. This is a great tragedy, for it misses an important chance to show students how their daily lives engage them with global issues, complex moral choices, and cultural complexity. A liberal arts curriculum is supposed to equip them for intellectual engagement with the world they live in.

This huge gap also presents an enormous opportunity for anthropology to step in as the one discipline that can integrate a topic otherwise fragmented and scattered across the entire university curriculum, from nutrition to economics, history to physics. Teaching about consumption is also a great opportunity to bring ethnography right into the classroom and to get the university connected with its surrounding community through various kinds of service learning and community engagement in active learning.

Among other consumption-related classes, I have taught a freshman course on "global consumer culture" to 120 students several times.[8] I gave the students a variety of assignments that required them to go out into the community to talk to people in supermarkets, shops, restaurants, and food banks, and I also asked them to inventory their own food, bottled water, and clothing consumption. A smaller group engaged in service-learning projects with Bloomington's Center for Sustainable Living.[9] Each time I taught this course, a significant number of the students found thinking about their own consumption to be challenging, transforming, and exciting, and I was always gratified when the experience recruited new anthropology majors, but I was equally happy to see others heading off toward history, psychology, media studies, international studies, and other useful majors.

Teaching this class reminded me that teaching university students is itself one of the most important kinds of applied anthropology. Each public-speaking occasion, every lecture is an opportunity to bring anthropology to bear on problems of consumption and to spread the message that sustainability is not an issue that can wait for the next generation. Students want to see the university itself as a laboratory for a more sustainable way of life. Anthropologist Peggy Barlett is among the pioneers of the "Greening the Campus" movement, first working effectively to get sustainability ingrained into the mission of her own Emory University and then investigating how to extend the message to other institutions around the country (Barlett and Stewart 2009; see also Barlett and Chase 2004). Any anthropology class can take up fair trade coffee, bottled water, or another global or equity issue as an applied project with direct relevance to daily campus life.

Conclusion

"Sustainability is a term like truth or beauty," says Fred Kirschenmann, a senior fellow at the Leopold Center for Sustainable Agriculture at Iowa State University. "We struggle but never get there" (quoted in Brown 2007). We have no choice but to join this struggle, because the world cannot survive any more business as usual. Since we are all consumers, we have power to change our own participation in the system as users, though many of our decisions will be negative ones—for example, we will decide not to eat certain things, not to buy particular products, to travel by train instead of by air. But this is only a small and relatively passive part of our possible role in building a sustainable future, which is going to depend on new kinds of social, cultural, and economic systems. The challenge for the next generation will be to invent those systems and get them deployed in the world while there is still time. Anthropology has tremendous potential to play a productive role in the transformation to a more sustainable economy, but only if we are willing to enter new fields of study, improve our communication skills, and think of ourselves as participants in change rather than just critics.

So far we have mainly exploited our methodological skills as specialists in ethnography and participant observation to gain entry into areas that are already full of active and engaged social scientists from rival disciplines. Now that we have an entry, it is time to use our knowledge of social change and process, our synthesis of biology and culture, our command of global issues, and our holistic understanding of the economy to make a greater contribution and increase our voice. It would help us a great deal in this enterprise if we could find a way to temper methodological individualism and create fresh models of comparison and collaboration, so that we can represent anthropology as more than a quarreling and fractious gaggle of scholars.

Questions for Discussion

Do you think it will ever be possible to convince people to consume less? What can anthropologists do to help convey the importance of reducing consumption?

Notes

1. The present greed and wealth of North Americans and Europeans also figure here. A good portion of China's emissions result from the manufacture of goods intended for export. The United States condemns countries like China for their rising emissions levels while consuming mass quantities of imported goods.
2. This incident was the topic of the 2006 documentary film *Who Killed the Electric Car* (www.whokilledtheelectriccar.com).
3. Surprisingly few philosophers and theorists have written extensively about this question, which Adam Smith considered fundamental to economics but later economists dropped.
4. Eric Arnould and I remember submitting a paper on growing consumer culture in developing countries to *American Anthropologist* in 1982, only to have it rejected on the grounds that "consumption was not an anthropological topic."
5. These are the Center for Myth and Ritual in American Life (MARIAL) at Emory University (college.emory.edu), the Center for the Ethnography of Everyday Life (CEEL) at the University of Michigan (www.psc.isr.umich.edu), and the Center on Everyday Lives of Families (CELF) at UCLA (www.celf.ucla.edu).
6. One of the longest-lived is the Bureau of Applied Research in Anthropology at the University of Arizona, which has concentrated on border-studies issues, and there have been similar institutions at Harvard and SUNY Binghamton focused on international development.
7. See the Association for Consumer Research website at www.acrwebsite.org.

8. The syllabus from the last time I taught the course can be found at www.indiana. edu/~wanthro/e104_05.htm.
9. See the center's website at www.simplycsl.org.

REFERENCES

Applbaum, Kalman. 2003. *The Marketing Era: From Professional Practice to Global Provisioning.* London: Routledge.

Arnould, Eric, Linda Price, and George Zinkhan. 2003. *Consumers.* 2nd ed. Columbus, OH: McGraw-Hill.

Barlett, Peggy F., and Geoffrey Chase. 2004. *Sustainability on Campus: Stories and Strategies for Change.* Cambridge: MIT Press.

Barlett, Peggy F., and Benjamin Stewart. 2009. "Shifting the University: Faculty Engagement and Curriculum Change." In Susan A. Crate and Mark Nuttall, eds., *Anthropology and Climate Change: From Encounters to Action,* 356–69. Walnut Creek, CA: Left Coast Press, Inc.

Belk, Russell. 1983. "Worldly Possessions: Issues and Criticisms." *Advances in Consumer Research* 10: 514–19.

Brown, Corie. 2007. "Hot Topic: Our Fragile Food System." *Los Angeles Times,* May 23. articles. latimes.com/2007/may/23/food/fo-monterey23 (accessed October 22, 2015).

Carrier, James, and Josiah Heyman. 1997. "Consumption and Political Economy." *Journal of the Royal Anthropological Institute* 3 (2): 355–73.

Horowitz, Daniel. 1988. *The Morality of Spending.* Baltimore: Johns Hopkins University Press.

Illich, Ivan. 1977. *Toward a History of Needs.* New York: Pantheon.

Jackson, Tim, ed. 2006. *The Earthscan Reader in Sustainable Consumption.* London: Earthscan.

Kempton, Willett. 1986. "Two Theories of Home Heat Control." *Cognitive Science* 10: 75–90.

———. 1997. "How the Public Views Climate Change." *Environment* 39 (9): 12–21.

Kempton, Willett, John M. Darley, and Paul C. Stern. 1992. "Psychology and Energy Conservation." *American Psychologist* 47 (10): 1213–23.

Kempton, Willett, Daniel Feuermann, and Arthur McGarity. 1992. "'I Always Turn It on Super': User Decisions about When and How to Operate Room Air Conditioners." *Energy and Buildings* 18: 177–91.

McCracken, Grant. 1988. *Culture and Consumption: New Approaches to the Symbolic Character of Consumer Goods and Activities.* Bloomington: Indiana University Press.

Miller, Daniel. 1995. "Consumption and Commodities." *Annual Review of Anthropology* 24: 141–61.

———. 1997. *Capitalism: An Ethnographic Approach.* Oxford: Berg.

———. 2001. "The Poverty of Morality." *Journal of Consumer Culture* 1 (2): 225–43.

Miller, Vincent J. 2005. *Consuming Religion: Christian Faith and Practice in a Consumer Culture.* London: Continuum International.

Murphy, Joseph, and Maurie J. Cohen. 2001. *Exploring Sustainable Consumption: Environmental Policy and the Social Sciences.* London: Pergamon.

Organisation for Economic Co-operation and Development. 1997. *Sustainable Consumption and Production.* Paris: OECD.

Paterson, Matthew, and Michael Grubb. 1992. "The International Politics of Climate Change." *International Affairs* 68 (2): 293–310.

Princen, Thomas. 2005. *The Logic of Sufficiency.* Cambridge: MIT Press.

Princen, Thomas, Michael Maniates, and Ken Conca, eds. 2002. *Confronting Consumption.* Cambridge: MIT Press.

Rayner, Steve, and Elizabeth L. Malone, eds. 1998. *Human Choice and Climate Change.* Columbus, OH: Battelle Press.

Redclift, Michael. 1996. *Wasted: Counting the Costs of Global Consumption.* London: Earthscan.

Reisch, Lucia A., and Inge Ropke, eds. 2005. *The Ecological Economics of Consumption.* London: Edward Elgar.

Sartorius, Christian, and Stefan Zundel. 2005. *Time Strategies, Innovation, and Environmental Policy.* London: Edward Elgar.

Schiffer, Michael, with Tamara C. Butts and Kimberly K. Grimm. 2003. *Taking Charge: The Electric Automobile in America*. 2nd ed. Washington, DC: Smithsonian Books.

Sherry, John F., Jr., ed. 1995. *Contemporary Marketing and Consumer Behavior: An Anthropological Sourcebook*. Thousand Oaks, CA: Sage.

Sonesson, Ulf, Frida Anteson, Jennifer Davis, and Per-Olow Sjödé. 2005. "Home Transport and Wastage: Environmentally Relevant Household Activities in the Life Cycle of Food." *Ambio* 34 (4–5): 371–75.

Sonesson, Ulf, Berit Mattsson, Thomas Nybrant, and Thomas Ohlsson. 2005. "Industrial Processing versus Home Cooking: An Environmental Comparison between Three Ways to Prepare a Meal." *Ambio* 34 (4–5): 414–21.

Stern, Paul C., Thomas Dietz, Vernon W. Ruttan, Robert H. Socolow, James L. Sweeney, et al., eds. 1997. *Environmentally Significant Consumption: Research Directions*. Washington, DC: National Academy Press.

Sunderland, Patricia L., and Rita M. Denny. 2007. *Doing Anthropology in Consumer Research*. Walnut Creek, CA: Left Coast Press, Inc.

Wilhite, Harold. 1996. *The Dynamics of Changing Japanese Energy Consumption Patterns and Their Implications for Sustainable Consumption*. Summer Study, Human Dimensions of Energy Consumption. Washington, DC: American Council for an Energy Efficient Economy.

Wilhite, Harold, and Rich Ling. 1995. "Measured Energy Savings from a More Informative Energy Bill." *Energy and Buildings* 22: 145–55.

Wilhite, Harold, and Richard Wilk. 1987. "A Method for Self-Recording Household Energy Use Behavior." *Energy and Buildings* 10: 73–79.

Wilk, Richard. 2001. "Consuming Morality." *Journal of Consumer Culture* 1 (2): 245–60.

Wilk, Richard, and Harold Wilhite. 1984. "Household Energy Decision Making in Santa Cruz County, California." In Bonnie Morrison and Willett Kempton, eds., *Families and Energy: Coping with Uncertainty*, 449–59. East Lansing: Michigan State University College of Human Ecology.

———. 1985. "Why Don't People Weatherstrip Their Homes? An Ethnographic Solution." *Energy* 10 (5): 621–31.

Yang, Mayfair. 2000. "Putting Global Capitalism in Its Place: Economic Hybridity, Bataille, and Ritual Expenditure." *Current Anthropology* 41: 477–509.

5

THE BUTTON: NOT A SIMPLE NOTION

Paul Grebinger

The button is no mere appurtenance of costume. In the discussion that follows I treat it as a material reflection of change in American culture.[1] It becomes a lens through which we can develop insight into the dimensions of American life that otherwise might elude us. Although the manufacture of buttons is embedded in cultural contexts that are, strictly speaking, technical and economic, simple infrastructural determinism as set forth in cultural materialist research strategy does not provide a satisfactory explanation for the transformations in button technology discussed here. Even an apparently "simple notion" such as the button exhibits attributes of function *and* of style. It embodies cultural meaning that is not only technological and economic but social and political as well.

In order to explain transformations in button technology we must explore the processes of change in American culture that reach back into the nineteenth century. The locus of change described here was Rochester, New York, a national center of both menswear manufacture and button production since the second half of the nineteenth century. The change was revolutionary in that the fundamental technology of button manufacture was transformed from mechanical to chemical, and was so profound that there could be no return to the previous system.

Cultural materialism (Harris 1999, 2001), with modifications suggested by Magnarella (1993) under the rubric human materialism, is my framework for analysis. As Harris

Author's Note: Dodworth Rowe (deceased), button designer for Rochester Button Company, provided invaluable assistance in preparing the research for the exhibit at the Rochester Museum and Science Center and in making it possible to preserve the business papers of the company. In addition, many thanks to my colleague in sociology, Vincent Serravallo, for his thoughtful and detailed comments on an earlier draft of this chapter.

(2001: xv) notes, cultural materialism "is based on the simple premise that human social life is a response to the practical problems of earthly existence." Therefore, infrastructure will take precedence in human adaptive responses to the environment. In attempting to understand change in any human cultural system, an anthropologist should first look to perturbations in the technological and economic subsystems of culture. In cultural materialist analysis, infrastructure has causal priority. There are feedback links with structure (dimensions of social and political organization) and with superstructure (dimensions of political and/or religious ideology). Investigation of these links follows from careful identification of patterns of production and reproduction.

Proponents of a cultural materialist research strategy have tended to select subjects for analysis that lie at the very boundary of human interaction with the environment. For example, there is Eric Ross's (1980: 183–86) "beef with Sahlins." Marshall Sahlins has argued that human foodways are based on the logic of object versus human subject; hence, we do not commoditize what we tend to categorize as kin, for example, the family pet. By contrast, Ross's materialist explanation is based on the cost/benefit analysis of cattle over dogs as a protein source; the herbivore is a much more efficient converter of energy into proteins than the carnivore. In another context, Harris and Ross (1987) analyze modes of reproduction among preindustrial and developing societies. Cultural mediation of birth and death rates in response to cost/benefit analyses of child rearing, given available food supplies, is a human adaptive response to environmental change.

However, when one's research happens to focus on cultural behaviors that are not so firmly embedded in infrastructure, as are foodways and population, the cultural materialist strategy presents problems. Further, Brian Ferguson (1995: 30–33) has argued that cultural materialism is weak when it confronts short-term historical change. And indeed, for Harris and Ross (1987: 2–3), "causal relationships [in synchronic or slice-in-time analysis] dissolve into an incoherent corpus of middle-range eclectic correlations linking infrastructural, structural, and superstructural components in infinite arrays." They seem to prefer working through broad evolutionary time frames while consigning the analysis of everyday minutiae to historians. Ferguson (1995: 31), however, sees "no reason to abandon the quest for causal regularity in normal historical process." To deny the value of synchronic studies is to throw out the baby with the bathwater. Feedback relationships among infrastructure, structure, and superstructure can be understood as a function of the special nature of the cultural thing and context of events under investigation.

Paul Magnarella (1993: 1–19) and Maria Palov (1993) offer a useful alternative model. Magnarella recognizes the dynamic relationships among infrastructure, structure, and superstructure. However, he divides infrastructure into components: material (technology), human (demography, psychology, biology), and social (leadership and power). These are in feedback relationships among themselves as well as with social structure (kin, economic, and political organization) and superstructure (ideology). In other words, Magnarella embraces complex relationships in the form of general systems analysis. These are asymmetrical, in the sense that change in infrastructure has causal priority with impacts on social structure and superstructure. Further, they are open to change from the natural and sociocultural environment. Finally, Magnarella makes a plausible case for human teleology in these systems. People in power will maximize outcomes for themselves, even when the well-being of others or long-term adjustment to the natural environment is jeopardized.

I attempt to cast the results of research on the button in a form consistent with the nature of the material under study and the cultural contexts in which it is embedded. A descriptive account of the technologies that changed provides insight into the material infrastructure of button manufacture in early twentieth-century Rochester, New York. This is followed by an analysis of change within the general guidelines of human materialism as described above.

TECHNOLOGY OF BUTTON MAKING: MATERIAL INFRASTRUCTURE

Before 1935, buttons manufactured in Rochester were handcrafted from veg-etable ivory, the fruit or nut of the tagua palm (*Phytelephas macrocarpa*). The tagua nut is several times larger than, but similar in shape to, the Brazil nut. When mature it exhibits the color and texture of tusk ivory, hence its generic name, vegetable ivory. The process of manufacture was subtractive. Material was removed from the original matrix in a carefully ordered sequence of steps that were readily adapted to a factory system for mass production. The process included drying to loosen the nut from a flintlike shell casing; tumbling in a barrel or "shucker" with metal weights to crack the shell casing; "scabbing" upon hand inspection to remove minute bits of shell; sizing or sorting accord-ing to size; sawing to cut individual nuts into slabs the thickness of a button, using circular saws that ran at a speed of six thousand revolutions per minute; further drying to remove every bit of residual moisture; immersion in steam-ing hot water in preparation for turning at a lathe to produce the basic button shape; drilling of the holes; dyeing, either in a bath or by spraying to achieve a mottled effect; final polishing and finishing; and carding, in which buttons were sewn onto cards for demonstration or sale (Albes 1913). A different opera-tive performed each major step. The machinery employed was simple: circular saws, polishing wheels, lathes, and drills adapted to the scale of the product. Each slice of the tagua nut was manipulated a hundred times before it was finally carded or boxed. As a result, the labor investment in producing a vegetable ivory button was high—as much as 80.5 percent in some types (Simon 1949: 15). This was a labor-intensive process.

Between 1930 and 1935 changes in the local industry were instituted that would shift manufacturing to capital-intensive processes. The entire technologi-cal transformation dates from 1931 to the end of World War II. During this period techniques for mass-producing buttons from plastic materials manipulated by automatic machines replaced the hand labor and craftsmanship employed in pro-ducing buttons from vegetable ivory. Of three major or national manufacturers of vegetable ivory buttons operating in Rochester during World War I, only one was thriving following World War II. It became the leader of the national plastic button industry.

Among plastics of that time, "beetle" (an early compound of urea), phenolics like Bakelite, and casein were satisfactory substitutes that could be fashioned into machine-made buttons at considerably less cost than vegetable ivory. The synthetic materials from which plastic buttons were produced in the 1930s were actually several times more costly than the unprocessed tagua nuts, but the reduced labor costs offset this disadvantage.[2] Casein was in fact the plastic that figured in the early drama of change in the Rochester industry.

Casein is produced from the protein of skim milk, which, when treated with formaldehyde, produces a thermosetting plastic. One hundred pounds of new skim milk produces approximately three pounds of casein powder. An especially fine grade of casein is necessary in the manufacture of buttons. At the time this grade was available only from abroad, primarily Germany, and consequently was expensive ("Casein and Plastic Buttons" n.d.). Neil O. Broderson, president of Rochester Button Company and the innovator responsible for most of the technological change described in this chapter, determined that he would have to create his own supply of button-grade casein. He established a processing plant near one of the largest creameries in the state of Wisconsin. At that location, ten thousand gallons of skim milk per day could be converted into casein through the application of rennet (Clune 1936).

Production of buttons involved extruding chemically treated casein from machines that compacted and forced the material through nozzles from which it emerged in the form of rods. The rods were then machined to uniform or standard sizes and then turned on automatic screw machines that produced buttons at the rate of two hundred per minute. Or, in some cases, in separate operations the rods were cut into round disks and then faced and backed on automatic lathes. A subsequent formaldehyde bath strengthened the buttons and imparted a varnish-like sheen that in cheaper varieties substituted for polishing and other types of surface treatment. Since dyestuffs in the form of baths do not penetrate the surfaces of casein buttons, coloring agents were added to the casein at the time that it was extruded in rod form ("Casein and Plastic Buttons" n.d.).

The reduction in the number of steps involved in the manufacturing process and the ease with which casein plastic could be adapted to automatic machine processing made it an attractive candidate for mass production of buttons. Casein's chief limitation was its tendency, although it was thermosetting, to absorb water, swell, soften, and break in a hot-water wash, and to discolor and become pliable when subjected to moderately elevated temperatures such as those produced by a clothes iron (Masson 1959: 14–15). Other more durable plastics such as urea-formaldehyde, melamine-formaldehyde, nylon, and polyesters would eventually replace casein in button manufacture.

AN INDUSTRY TRANSFORMED: HUMAN MATERIALIST ANALYSIS

In the summer of 1930, with signs of business slowdown everywhere, Neil Broderson had some doubt about the future of the button business. He took more than a passing interest in a letter dated July 22, 1930, from George Baekeland of the Bakelite Corporation offering to put him in touch with a friend who might be interested in buying Rochester Button Company:

> I do not want to meddle in your affairs, but I did get the impression that you want to get out of your present business. Otherwise I should not be bothering you.[3]

Broderson responded the following day, July 23, 1930, with his typical candor:

> Your assumption that I am not particularly fond of the button business is correct.
> However, I realize that which one has is the best until something better is found. The
> button business is most interesting, the principal criticism is the fact that the entire
> industry is such a small one that a bright future could not be hoped for, unless we can
> develop something aside from buttons.

At that moment, in his early thirties, Broderson was about to embark on a remarkable career as an innovator in plastics technologies and button making.

An intuitive engineer with no formal training in chemistry, Broderson had a network of friends in the nascent plastics industry upon whose advice he could rely. Between 1931 and 1935 he developed and installed a successful casein button manufacturing department in his plant in Rochester. This innovation, like many others in biological and cultural evolution, follows Romer's rule, which states, in effect, "The initial survival value of a favorable innovation is conservative, in that it renders possible the maintenance of a traditional way of life in the face of changed circumstances" (Hockett and Ascher 1964: 137). Plastic substitutes had already begun to replace vegetable ivory in the manufacture of largely functional buttons such as those used to attach suspenders to men's pants and fly buttons. There was a lucrative market in such mundane items. Plastic in general was not yet of a quality that would provide satisfactory substitutes for more stylistically crucial or visible buttons.

Broderson was at the cusp of change in the following evaluation of a plastic button offered for his consideration by the Aladdinite Company on September 11, 1930. His letter reveals both conservative business intuition and creative impulse:

> We are not very optimistic over the possibilities of buttons made from substitutes,
> especially during these times when ivory nuts cost so little. Even in the large sizes
> we can import slabs for as little as 20 cents per pound. [Nevertheless] in regard to
> substitutes we are constantly on the alert, watching for anything ... which might
> become serious competition for ivory buttons, and *consequently are very willing to be
> shown.* (emphasis added)

He was familiar with plastic substitutes. He read *Plastics* magazine. He was searching for and experimenting with plastic materials that would be cost-effective, buttons that would meet his company's high standards, that could become "an index of hidden values" (a company marketing slogan following its transition to plastics in the mid-1930s). Even as late as October 14, 1934, under pressure from his salesmen to rush to plastic alternatives, Broderson counseled:

> The longer we can preserve our ivory button business while building up our sub-
> stitutes, the better it will be for us. It will be difficult to gain the same advantageous
> position in substitutes that we enjoy in ivory and it cannot be done in six months or
> one year's time.

Technological change as it plays out in the lives of real people is often not dramatic. Broderson developed a conservative but successful strategy that led him to further success in plastic button technologies. Following World War II he chaired the button division of the Society of the Plastics Industry. He saved his company from the extinction that overtook a rival vegetable ivory button maker in Rochester, the Art in Buttons Company. Broderson's business papers, however, offer no analysis of the economic, social, and political forces to which he and the industry were responding. Here, then, is a role for the anthropologist who wishes to write culture history.

The economic perturbations of the Great Depression were only a catalyst that precipitated technological change in the button industry. Population growth was the mechanism driving the transformations described in this chapter. Vegetable ivory button manufacture grew up as a subsidiary of the ready-to-wear clothing industry, which was directly linked to the population boom that began in North America in the late nineteenth century. Between 1881 and 1924 more than 21 million immigrants entered the United States, most of them of peasant origin from eastern and southern Europe (U.S. Bureau of the Census 1975). Immigration, not natural increase, provided a market for cheap clothing. Poor immigrants required mass-produced garments of uniform and undistinguished character. Once people were suited in such attire, ethnic distinctions based on dress were obliterated. This was the "democracy of clothing" described by the historian Daniel Boorstin (1973: 91–100).

Vegetable ivory as a raw material was ideally suited for buttons on such clothing. It was collected from palm trees growing under natural conditions in Ecuador, Colombia, and Panama. The raw nuts were harvested by Indian *taguaros*, cheap and exploited labor (Albes 1913: 198). Before the properties of tagua as vegetable ivory were discovered, the nuts were used as ships' ballast (Simon 1949: 13). In short, the cost of the raw material was low. Further, clothing designed to suit everybody did not require buttons in a dazzling array of forms and colors. Consequently, the subtractive technology for transforming the nut into a button was adequate for the need. Finally, with the exception of sawing, turning, and dyeing, relatively unskilled labor was sufficient for the steps in the process of producing a vegetable ivory button. The immigrant consumer of these symbols of mass democracy became the cheap labor that produced them. The industry expanded along with the immigrant population and flourished in the early twentieth century. By the 1920s, thirty to forty factories were producing vegetable ivory buttons in the United States (Simon 1949: 16).

The decline of the industry to which Neil Broderson was responding through technological innovation in the early 1930s had already set in just after World War I. The factors involved can be traced to feedback from the structural and superstructural subsystems. First, the immigrant boom was brought to an abrupt halt as national sentiment against the flood led to quota laws in 1921, 1924, and 1929 (Schaeffer 1984: 120–22). The falloff in immigration from 1924 to 1925 was dramatic. In 1924, 364,399 immigrants from Europe were admitted to the United States; in 1925, the number was only 148,366 (U.S. Bureau of the Census 1975). The quota laws reflected the concern of organized labor that immigrants would lower wage standards. More important was general antipathy toward Europe following the war and jingoistic fears that southern and eastern European immigrants were not assimilating culturally. Further, a eugenics movement with considerable influence in both academia and government played on fears that biologically inferior immigrants would weaken the American gene pool. President Calvin Coolidge signed the 1924 quota law with this admonition: "America must be kept American. Biological laws show that Nordics deteriorate when mixed with other races" (quoted in Harris 1999: 68). In the button industry sales volume is critical, and the impact of these changes was immediate.

Second, styles in women's fashion changed dramatically in the 1920s. The flapper attired herself in dresses with a draped and pinned look. Fashions of the previous decade were festooned with buttons from shoulder to hemline. Among Rochester manufacturers, Art in Buttons produced for both the men's and women's apparel industries and was hardest hit by this downturn in demand. The president of the company, Henry T. Noyes, was an uncooperative member of the community of vegetable ivory button makers. His schemes to undercut and undersell competitors led to business conflict with Broderson that became quite heated, and personal. In a letter of February 28, 1930, Broderson accused Noyes of selling a button imitating one produced by Rochester Button Company for the knitwear trade:

> I am surprised that you have seen fit to resort to such business practices, which in my judgment are not only unethical and unfair, but also a violation of our property rights and if so, illegal.

Noyes retorted the next day, March 1:

> "Those who live in glass houses should not throw stones." Those who copy buttons with the deliberate and malicious purpose of "cutting prices" and pulling down the market are in no place to criticize anyone.

There followed a litany of Rochester Button Company malfeasance. Broderson's letter in reply on March 11, 1930, gave no ground:

> If you have been laboring under the impression that Rochester Button Company has committed such offenses, we can begin to see the motive which prompts you to "tear down and trade down" the industry as you have been doing of late.

Under these circumstances Broderson's efforts later that year to create a vegetable ivory button manufacturers association ultimately came to naught. Here then are additional factors in the cost/benefit analysis that led ultimately to a strategy of technological innovation.

Third, serviceable slide fasteners were first introduced as closures for money belts in 1917. In that year the Hookless Fastener Company sold 24,000 fasteners. In 1923 B. F. Goodrich began producing galoshes with slide fasteners and originated the name "zipper." By 1934 the Hookless Fastener Company sold more than 60 million slide fasteners (Weiner 1983: 132–33). During the 1930s and 1940s the slide fastener would become a substitute for fly buttons and a frequent alternative to buttons on outerwear. Although it is clear from his business papers that Broderson was not concerned about inroads from the slide fastener in 1930–31, by the late 1930s this competing technology was reinforcing his earlier decisions to intensify in the direction of further plastics technologies. He quickly moved to compounds of urea and by the late 1940s, with assistance from professionally trained chemists in his employ, developed a nacreous polyester button that literally drove natural pearl buttons out of the men's shirt market.

From 1924 through the early 1930s, button makers were under assault from forces they did not fully understand. Politically influenced population shifts, changes in fashion, and then the economic downturn of the Great Depression put them under stress. They responded through a process of intensification based on cost/benefit analysis. It is important to note that technological innovation was the last strategy they employed.

Initially, competition among leading producers was resolved through merger. In 1926 two Rochester vegetable ivory button manufacturers, Rochester Button Company and Shantz Button Corporation, merged with a third, the Superior Ivory Button Company of Newark, New Jersey. By the early 1930s the Shantz and Superior companies had been closed, with all manufacturing operations concentrated in the single Rochester Button Company plant at 300 State Street. Broderson was the son of the owner of Superior Ivory Button Company and had become manager of the Newark plant after the 1926 merger. He assumed leadership of the new company in 1928.

Following the stock market crash of 1929, competition intensified between the reorganized Rochester Button Company, under Broderson's leadership, and Art in Buttons, under Noyes. Price-fixing, as yet another strategy for survival, ended when one of the industry leaders excused himself from a meeting where new wholesale prices had been set to pass the information on to a confederate waiting in the men's room. The confederate, of course, contacted customers with offers to fill orders at below the new market price. The evidence in this case points to Henry Noyes.[4]

By the early 1930s, even as he was exploring new plastics technologies, Broderson instituted standard business strategies for hard times, cutting salaries at all levels (executive, sales, and factory), reducing inventories, and, finally, initiating financial reorganization. When board member Maynard S. Bird, who was also a bondholder, suggested liquidation, Broderson's response in a letter of July 12, 1932, was blunt:

> I do not see a possibility of liquidating this business at today's market. Factory buildings are white elephants which cannot be given away—button machinery lacks a market as there are no prospective buyers for same with any capital. Surely the bondholders' best move is to do whatever may be necessary to insure their investment for the future.

In the face of this adversity Broderson engineered the technological transformation from labor-intensive vegetable ivory to capital-intensive plastics technologies as outlined above.

NOT A SIMPLE NOTION

This research project began more than thirty years ago when I received an invitation from the Rochester Museum and Science Center to conduct background research for and create an exhibit on button making in Rochester (funded by the New York State Council on the Arts). Although all buttons manufactured by Rochester Button Company in the 1980s were made from plastic materials, there were still individuals working for the company and retirees living in the city who had worked as vegetable ivory button makers. Through interviews and historical research I was able to establish the outlines of button manufacture presented in this chapter. The technology and the button makers who developed and transformed the industry were the focus of the exhibit. Describing the change from labor-intensive to capital-intensive was a first step in explaining the transformation. As a historically oriented anthropologist, I have been uncomfortable with the limitations of the cultural materialist research strategy as noted earlier. Brian Ferguson's critique and Paul Magnarella's revision in the form of human materialism have provided incentive and a model for thinking anew about these data.

The approach described by Magnarella (1993) has been recast in terms of general systems by Maria Palov (1993: 144), who notes, "A basic tenet of the systems approach is that the whole is greater than the sum of its parts." The whole that I have attempted to define provides insight into changes in American culture in the early twentieth century. At no time between 1925 and 1945 did Neil Broderson, or others with whom he was in contact, make an analysis of change such as I have attempted here. (Broderson's letters through his fifty years as president are available among the papers of the Rochester Button Company.) Further, the model has allowed me to explore the roles of individual actors, such as Neil Broderson and Henry Noyes, as well as the role of a class of people, immigrants, in conjunction with structural components (see Palov 1993: 148). In this way I have been able to preserve the textures of normal historical analysis and achieve materialist insights about transformation in technical and economic systems.

According to *Webster's Third International Dictionary*, a notion is a small article such as a button; it is also an ingenious device. Although low on the horizon of visibility, the button as material culture is affixed to garments worn by human actors engaged in social and cultural life. These actors, here the immigrants of early twentieth-century America, were themselves subject to economic, political, and ideological forces of the time. Button men such as Neil Broderson responded to declining markets through strategies available to them, a process of intensification based on cost/benefit analysis. Their response to perturbations in ideology, society, and economy in America produced a revolution in button making. Throughout this process the button was never just a simple notion.

EXERCISE

Examine the life of the modern button, or a similar "simple notion." Where did the raw material come from? What technology was employed to transform the raw material into the item you see today, and how did it come to be a part of your life? In seeking answers to such questions you expand your view of American culture and its reach beyond the borders of society.

NOTES

1. I returned to this project on summer retreat in the Adirondacks, Osgood Pond, near Paul Smiths, New York. On the eastern shore of the pond is White Pine Camp, Calvin Coolidge's summer White House in 1926. Local guides reported that "silent Cal" fished but did not discuss politics—or much else, for that matter. His comment on the quota law of 1924 (referred to in this chapter) was testament to his political views. This story of change turns on his views and his act of signing that law. I doubt that Coolidge gave much thought to

the implications as he paddled the pond's waters. It has been left to me, ninety years later, to reflect upon them.

2. This information comes from the archives of the Rochester Button Company: Rochester Button Company Papers, Rochester Museum and Science Center.

3. All letters quoted in this chapter are archived in the Rochester Button Company Papers, Rochester Museum and Science Center.

4. Nelson Zimmer, president of Shantz Associates, interview by author, 1983.

REFERENCES

Albes, Edward. 1913. "Tagua-Vegetable Ivory." *Bulletin of the Pan American Union* 37 (2): 192–208.

Boorstin, Daniel J. 1973. *The Americans: The Democratic Experience*. New York: Random House.

"Casein and Plastic Buttons." n.d. Rochester Button Company Papers, Rochester Museum and Science Center.

Clune, Henry. 1936. "Who's Got the Button?" Rochester Button Company Papers, Rochester Museum and Science Center.

Ferguson, R. Brian. 1995. "Infrastructural Determinism." In Martin F. Murphy and Maxine L. Margolis, eds., *Science, Materialism, and the Study of Culture*, 21–38. Gainesville: University Press of Florida.

Harris, Marvin. 1999. *Theories of Culture in Postmodern Times*. London: AltaMira Press.

———. 2001. *Cultural Materialism: The Struggle for a Science of Culture*. Updated ed. New York: AltaMira Press.

Harris, Marvin, and Eric B. Ross. 1987. *Death, Sex, and Fertility: Population in Preindustrial and Developing Societies*. New York: Columbia University Press.

Hockett, Charles F., and Robert Ascher. 1964. "The Human Revolution." *Current Anthropology* 5 (3): 135–47.

Magnarella, Paul J. 1993. *Human Materialism: A Model of Sociocultural Systems and a Strategy for Analysis*. Gainesville: University Press of Florida.

Masson, Don, comp. 1959. *Plastics: The Story of an Industry*. 8th rev. ed. New York: Society of the Plastics Industry.

Palov, Maria Z. 1993. "Appendix: A Systems Analysis of Human Materialism." In Paul J. Magnarella, *Human Materialism: A Model of Sociocultural Systems and a Strategy for Analysis*, 144–52. Gainesville: University Press of Florida.

Ross, Eric B. 1980. "Patterns of Diet and Forces of Production: An Economic and Ecological History of the Ascendancy of Beef in the United States Diet." In Eric B. Ross, ed., *Beyond the Myths of Culture: Essays in Cultural Materialism*, 181–225. New York: Academic Press.

Schaeffer, Richard T. 1984. *Racial and Ethnic Groups*. 2nd ed. Boston: Little, Brown.

Simon, Arthur James. 1949. "The Distribution of Buttons." MBA thesis, Wharton School, University of Pennsylvania.

U.S. Bureau of the Census. 1975. *Historical Statistics of the United States: Colonial Times to 1970*. Washington, DC: Government Printing Office.

Weiner, Lewis. 1983. "The Slide Fastener." *Scientific American* 248 (6): 132–44.

6

SAFETY AND HEALTH IN THE "SAFER AND HEALTHIER" AGRICULTURE

Brandi Janssen

While at a statewide agricultural meeting in Iowa, I had a conversation with a new community-supported agriculture (CSA) producer. He had recently left another career to take over his family's land and start a direct-market farm. Only in his second year, he was optimistic about increasing his customer base and adding more shareholders who would pay in advance for weekly boxes of produce from his farm. I told him about my work directing a center for agricultural safety and health and the center's desire to work more with new direct-market farmers. He was puzzled. "What could hurt you on a vegetable farm?" he asked. "Isn't it the big guys who are more at risk?" His comment underscored a point I had been considering for some time: because we tend to assume that food from a small, organic vegetable farm is healthier and safer than conventionally produced food, we also assume that the farm is safer than a large commodity farm.

In fact, those "big guys" who farm a few thousand acres of corn and soybeans in Iowa actually tend to have safer equipment, and the physical labor on their farms is less demanding. The rollover protective structure of an enclosed combine or tractor cab helps keep its operator safe. Many new tractors even have GPS, so that, if necessary, an operator can be located quickly on the farm. Modern farming equipment has all the safety bells and whistles, and these go a long way toward preventing serious injuries or fatalities so long as operators don't reach into moving parts.

In contrast, the CSA producer I spoke with uses a small antique tractor on his farm. Not only does it not have a rollover protective structure, but also its front tires, called tricycle wheels, are placed very close together. This arrangement is highly unstable and can easily cause the tractor to roll over, crushing the driver. Additionally, an old tractor does not have a bypass starter shield, which means that the operator can start the tractor while standing on the ground in front of the back tires. If the tractor is in gear, it could lurch forward, driving over the person or trapping him or her under the back tires. Basically, my conversation partner's tractor is one of the most dangerous pieces of equipment one could have on a farm; it has none of the recommended safety features. I would worry about this farmer much more than I would worry about someone on his shiny new combine during fall harvest.

The "big guys" in Iowa also benefit from a well-established economic support system that alleviates many of the financial risks, and therefore much of the stress, of farming. Commodity producers have access to federal price supports through the farm bill, and numerous crop insurance programs are in place to cushion the impact of crop failures resulting from natural disasters such as floods, hail, and drought. Commodity producers have to do very little to market their products. Their corn and soybeans go directly to an established grain cooperative, and hogs produced in one of Iowa's many confinement buildings have designated corporate buyers from the moment they are born. Farmers on small CSA farms do not have access to any of these support systems. Instead, they are responsible for marketing their own products and finding their own customers. If their crops fail as the result of a weather event, they are unlikely to have adequate insurance.

We like to think of American farms as wholesome, safe places. Less than 2 percent of the U.S. population lives on farms, so for most of us, agriculture exists only in our imaginations and in the products we find in grocery stores (U.S. Department of Agriculture [USDA] 2014). It is easy to conjure images from our childhoods based on *Charlotte's Web*, complete with friendly livestock and visits to the county fair. In reality, agriculture is one of the nation's most dangerous occupations, accounting for hundreds of deaths and thousands of injuries each year. According to the National Institute for Occupational Safety and Health (2014), 167 workers are injured on farms every day, and nearly 400 farmers and farmworkers die from agricultural injuries each year. This results in a fatality rate of 20.2 deaths per 100,000 workers. In comparison, there are only 3.2 fatalities per 100,000 workers across all industries. In Iowa, about 30 percent of all occupational fatalities are related to agriculture, more than any other industry in the state. Injury numbers are likely underreported, because there are few mechanisms to track farm-related injuries accurately. Some of this difficulty is related to the fact that farmers live where they work. It is challenging to distinguish between a truly "work-related" injury and an injury that may happen on a farm but is not necessarily related to productive activity.

Chief among farm hazards is the tractor, with rollovers and runovers causing the most injuries and deaths. Tractors manufactured after 1985 come equipped with rollover protective structures as well as other safety features, such as shields or guards over moving parts. However, many tractors still in use were manufactured before 1985. Altercations with bulls, cows with newborn calves, and horses are the next most frequent cause of farm casualties; farm animals can be unpredictable and are especially protective of their young. In Iowa and throughout the Midwest, where grain is stored in large bins, there is risk of becoming trapped in the grain and suffocating. Agricultural workers sometimes enter these bins to check the condition of the grain or to fix the equipment that moves grain out of the bin; in so doing they may shift the grain so that it falls and buries them. Also common in rural areas are burn-related injuries from handling anhydrous ammonia and from burning trash, brush, and grass.

In short, there are a lot of ways to be injured or killed on a farm. This reality has driven an entire field of public health dedicated to reducing farm-related accidents. However, most of the focus remains on farmers who produce vast quantities of commodities, such as corn, soybeans, cotton, and wheat, or who manage feedlots or animal confinements (often abbreviated CAFO, for "confined animal feeding operation"). Agricultural safety and health professionals have been less likely to address issues on small farms that produce fruits, vegetables, meat, or dairy products for local markets (Donham and Larabee 2009).

The schism between alternative and conventional production runs deep; it is not limited only to health and safety outreach. The news media, popular authors, and researchers have all directed an increasing amount of attention to the problems with conventional agricultural production and the presumed benefits in alternative farming, especially organic practices and local food. The popular dialogue has become particularly combative. In 2010, the president of the American Farm Bureau Federation, Bob Stallman (2010: 4), criticized a "handful of self-appointed food elitists . . . trying to divide us. . . . They define good farmers and bad farmers, solely on some arbitrary divide based on size or methods of production." Stallman was referring largely to films like *Food, Inc.* (Kenner 2008) and authors such as Michael Pollan (2006) and Eric Schlosser (2001), who have condemned the dominant agricultural system for its vertically integrated structure and reliance on chemicals and fossil fuels.

Social science researchers have also helped to widen the gap between conventional and alternative production. In his early work, anthropologist Walter Goldschmidt (1978) was highly critical of large-scale agricultural production. His research in California showed that larger average farm sizes in a community were associated with more social problems and poorer economic outcomes. In contrast, smaller farms were associated with empowered and democratic rural communities. Likewise, sociologist Thomas Lyson (2004), in his examinations of the relationships between smaller-scale agriculture and community engagement, coined the phrase "civic agriculture" to refer to the embeddedness of economic transactions in social life and communities related to alternative agriculture. He suggested that the direct-market relationships inherent in local food are an important mechanism to increase agricultural literacy in a community and enhance social relationships between and among farmers and consumers.

The agricultural landscape in Iowa features both conventional and alternative production. Iowa produces more corn, soybeans, hogs, and laying hens than any other state in the nation. The massive corn yields support a large ethanol industry; about 25 percent of the country's ethanol is produced in Iowa. The 2012 agricultural census indicates that Iowa is second in the nation in total value of agricultural sales at $30.8 billion (USDA 2014). The technological "machine" (Dudley 2000) is ever present in Iowa agriculture as farms continue to consolidate and mechanize with more precise, computerized technology. Despite the dominance of conventional agriculture, options for direct-market agriculture and alternative strategies such as organic farming are growing. Iowa has more than 200 farmers' markets; the state is ranked fourth nationwide in the number of farmers' markets overall and second in the number of markets per capita (Otto 2010). In 2015 at least 85 farms in Iowa offered a CSA option (Lyons and Trout 2015). More than 200 small meat lockers facilitate the direct marketing of beef and pork, a few creameries are in operation, and some farmers pasteurize dairy products on their farms to sell fluid milk, yogurt, or cheese locally. Iowa ranks fifth in the nation in organic acreage with 467 certified organic farms (USDA 2012).

According to anthropologist Mark Grey (2000), the conventional and alternative production styles described above constitute Iowa's two "food streams." One consists of continuously consolidating, vertically integrated corporations that control production from seed, or egg, to finished products. The other stream is made up of loosely organized small-scale operations that range from backyard chicken growers who occasionally sell a few fresh eggs to larger-scale organic grain producers.

Rhetorically, alternative agriculture has stayed steadfastly within its own stream banks, squarely placed as oppositional to conventional production. Local food, in particular, has very effectively been declared the ultimate form of resistance to corporate control of our centralized food system (Hendrickson and Heffernan 2002; Hinrichs 2000; McIlvaine-Newsad, Merrett, and McLaughlin 2004). But in reality, conventional and alternative farms have many things in common. Not only do alternative farmers in Iowa often take advantage of their neighbors' large-scale equipment, but some also blend conventional and alternative practices on the same farms. They also spend just as much time thinking about yields and economic efficiencies as do conventional farmers (Janssen 2013). When it comes to farm safety, direct-market farms have just as many dangerous pieces of equipment and numbers of ornery livestock as conventional farms. Add to that the physical labor typical in diversified vegetable production, and there may in fact be more potential for injury on a direct-market farm. The lack of economic and social support systems can be stressful for local food farmers, despite the popular romanticized notion that small-scale farming provides an easy lifestyle. Public health professionals are obligated to ask the same questions of alternative farms that they do of conventional farms concerning occupational safety and mental health.

Anthropology provides some tools for investigating these issues. As holistic and comparative thinkers, anthropologists can examine the ways that alternative producers resemble conventional farmers and how they are set apart from the conventional system. Ethnographic methods, with their emphasis on understanding how people actually behave in everyday situations, encourage us to move beyond conventional wisdom about agriculture. Rather than assuming that alternative farming is healthier or safer for farmers, both physically and mentally, anthropology provides tools that enable us to understand the reality of farmers' lives. In what follows, I provide some examples related to equipment, labor, and mental health that should be of concern to public health professionals engaged in agricultural safety and health outreach.

EQUIPMENT

The equipment on small farms is just as likely to cause injury as that on large farms. In some cases, in seeking out affordable equipment, new farmers acquire older machinery that may pose significant safety hazards. Compared with newer equipment, older equipment tends to be less stable (in the case of front tricycle tractor wheels, for example) and louder (contributing to hearing loss) and may producer higher fuel emissions. Rather than going to dealers, farmers may purchase equipment from neighbors or through online listings, making it less likely that they will receive adequate advice about safety features or be provided owner's manuals. Beginning farmers, in particular, may not know to look for equipment with protective features such as roll bars or bypass starter shields.

In addition, it is often challenging for small farmers to find implements that are appropriately scaled for their farms. When looking for a potato harvester, for example, a farmer may find that the choices are limited to a large harvester designed for potato farms of many hundreds of acres or a pitchfork. Farmers who cultivate a few acres for which mechanization would be beneficial are often unable to find the equipment they need. One solution to this problem is for farmers to make their own. One grower, "Neal Jackson" (all names introduced in quotation marks are pseudonyms), who focuses on greenhouse-grown products but also produces sweet potatoes, cabbage, and asparagus for wholesale grocery accounts, built his own planting apparatus for sweet potatoes to avoid the cost of purchasing a planter. I spent a memorable early summer afternoon perched on this particular implement with Neal planting tiny sweet potato plants, called slips. Constructed out of two-by-four lumber, the "planter" resembled a box-like sled that Neal chained to the back of his tractor. Two large barrels, balanced precariously on the front-end loader of the tractor, provided water for the slips as they were planted. One person drove the tractor and held a watering hose connected to the barrels. The farm owner and I perched on the sled to plant the slips. I sat toward the front of the sled and used a trowel to dig holes for the slips. Though the tractor moved slowly, it was challenging to space the holes appropriately, between twelve and fifteen inches apart. The grower sat toward the rear of the sled and dropped slips into the holes and covered them. After the tractor turned to plant the second row, the driver could water the first row of newly planted slips as we went by.

This process required three of us to multitask in close proximity to a large piece of running equipment. Neal and I sat on a beam only four inches wide while we leaned over to dig the holes and drop and cover the tiny plants. The tractor driver had to be attentive to our shouted communications to slow down or speed up so that we could space the slips correctly. The driver was tasked not only with maintaining a steady speed and straight line but also with watering the plants in each previous row as he passed by them. The tractor's loader had to be held fairly high so that the barrels would not slide off, but the barrels were large enough to obstruct the driver's vision.

Fortunately, we all finished our work that afternoon without incident. However, the presence of multiple people around a tractor, all of whom are distracted by various tasks, is a significant hazard. It would have been possible for either the grower or me to slip off the sled or become entangled in the chain attachment. Further, running a tractor with the loader elevated can make it less stable and more inclined to tip. Even on flat ground, carrying a load too high can cause a tractor to roll over if it turns too sharply, for example, between rows.

Some local food producers are quite attentive to the dangers involved when fieldworkers are combined with tractors, a common occurrence on farms engaged in diversified vegetable production. Total mechanization may not be possible on such farms. "David Evans" is a producer from central Iowa who manages a 250-member CSA farm in addition to selling at several farmers' markets and grocery stores. Like Neal, he has had custom implements made for his farm, most notably a potato harvester that fits his small tractor. He has also invested in a waterwheel planter that improves his efficiency when transplanting items like strawberries and potatoes. This implement is designed with two dedicated seats and footrests. The "waterwheel" circulates and simultaneously punches holes in the ground for the plant starts while water trickles down from an attached tank. The driver is able to focus on maintaining a smooth pace and holding a straight line; however, other workers are still needed in and around the moving tractor.

Two people sit on the planter, and David usually has one or two workers trailing behind to ensure that each hole in the soil has a plant and it is covered properly. He pointed out, "We found that the tractor time is the most valuable time and so we now go faster . . . so the person on the wheel just throws the plant down and people trailing will actually plant it into the mud spot." This process has led him to develop a specific communication procedure for when the tractor stops and starts or the planter needs to be raised or lowered. For example, if the workers need the tractor to stop, they shout, "Stop!" The driver must return the command "Stop!" before actually stopping the tractor. Likewise, the command "Go!" must be initiated from behind, and the driver always responds by shouting "Go!" back to the crew. David told me, "Even if you're looking, we still yell it."

One way that local food is different from conventional production in Iowa is the extensive need for labor. The corn and soybeans in Iowa do not require a great deal of human capital to be productive. While there are more labor needs in livestock production, such as in hog barns and laying facilities, finding a labor source is not usually a significant concern for conventional producers. Not so with diversified vegetable production. For a CSA operation to support a household, shareholders must number in the hundreds. To grow, harvest, package, and deliver those shares requires a labor source beyond the farmer's family (in most cases). As a result, farmers sometimes rely on volunteer groups, school groups, or farm interns. Heavy physical labor, the repetitive motions required for weeding and harvesting, and sun and heat exposure all have health implications.

In addition, some tasks on small farms simply require a high level of strength, especially in the absence of large equipment. "Faye Jefferson," a vegetable farmer who has sold at farmers' markets and runs a small CSA farm, reported that there are some tasks she cannot do on her own small acreage. For example, "the stakes that we put in for tomatoes, I can't physically do it, even on a ladder. We've got this thing that drives T-posts into the ground but I can't do it." Faye's husband, who is otherwise not involved in her farming business, helps with some of these heavy chores. According to many of the farmers I spoke with, the physical labor involved in direct-market or organic farming is a barrier for both new and established farmers. Renee Johnson-Berry compared the work involved with an organic farm to conventional farming: "Nobody wants to work, because most people don't farm organically or have a relatively closed system—it's just harder work . . . [and] people don't want to work that hard . . . [or] make that kind of commitment."

While it is not unusual to hear about farming as "hard work," the popular discourse around local food often portrays vegetable farming as a peaceful, leisurely pastime. At a national conference on organic farming, a keynote speaker declared, "I think of all the people who hate their jobs—if you feel detached from life sitting in a cubicle, it's because you are!" He suggested that those who were tired of "cubicle culture" should become farmers and reenergize the food system.

He recounted the impact that young food entrepreneurs have had in his home state of Vermont and lovingly described the rural landscape. His speech conjured more *Charlotte's Web* fantasy than farm reality.

STRESS AND MENTAL HEALTH

As a result of such portrayals, the lure of farming is strong and the myth of the idyllic, slow-paced, pastoral life is a major selling point for farming, especially vegetable farming. Much like starry-eyed newlyweds, new farmers are often unaware of (or choose to ignore) the very high rates of burnout, bankruptcy, and failure. For example, a simple count of existing CSAs paints an initially hopeful picture of direct-market agriculture. In Iowa, there were fifty CSA farms in 2006; by 2015, there were eighty-five. However, of those listed in 2006, fewer than twenty were still in existence in 2015 (Lyons and Trout 2015). This suggests a high rate of turnover or failure. Some of the farms no longer listed are still operating but have changed their primary marketing strategies from CSA to something else.

There is ample evidence that, compared with the general public, people involved in farming may experience higher rates of mental health problems (Fraser et al. 2005). Especially in the decades since the farm crisis of the 1980s, a significant amount of research and outreach activity has been undertaken in the Midwest to address the pressures of farm life. In Iowa, for example, the Iowa Concern Hotline has been fielding thousands of calls per year since 1985. The hotline offers farmers support related to financial concerns as well as help dealing with anxiety, crisis and disaster management, and legal issues. While the economic challenges associated with commodity farming are well known, much less attention has been paid to the stresses and burdens typical in small-scale farming. As one young farmer noted, "Vegetable farming has become trendy and romanticized; it can never live up to the expectations of pastoral bliss that many non-farming local food eaters assume of it" (quoted in Kolbe 2015: 6).

The CSA distribution model—customers pay in advance for weekly shares of a farm's output—has been promoted as a good strategy for new farmers (Galt et al. 2011; Janssen 2010). However, one grower told me, "CSA is not for the faint of heart. You're essentially taking a loan from your customers, and they're paying you in advance for your product. That adds a lot of stress." He spoke at length about the pressure he felt to provide his shareholders their groceries each week. Record rainfall in 2010 caused him to seriously consider canceling the season. The "potatoes and squash drowned, and the carrots rotted because of the rain." He relied on short-season crops that year, especially spinach and kale. But, he noted, "some people liked all the greens . . . others didn't. If you didn't like greens you might not come back." He wondered, "Are we bad at this?"

Another grower who did cancel his forty-share CSA in mid-June because of the repeated flooding in 2010 spoke about the guilt he and his wife felt. He said telling his shareholders that the season would be canceled was "the hardest thing I've ever done." The promise to customers that they will receive a weekly bounty of food is an enormous burden. Farmers feel a great sense of failure if they are unable to fulfill their obligation.

The CSA farmers I spoke with often remarked on the stress they experience if they cannot fill a share box adequately. Some keep their CSAs intentionally small to avoid overextending themselves. One grower stated early one season: "I had fifteen shares last year, nineteen this year. I turned down twenty or thirty people. We did our first deliveries last week: asparagus, eggs, bread, and onions. It felt stressful; I didn't know what was going into the box." Another pushed back the start of her season by two weeks, which "alleviates a lot of stress in the early spring when there usually isn't much to pick from. It's hard to fill out a basket." Sometimes she would add baked goods, but with more than fifty shares, that was too much to manage regularly.

Other farmers suggested to me that selling at farmers' markets provides better opportunities, especially for new growers. One vegetable and poultry producer noted that farmers' markets are still a "lot of work," but they provide a "good low-risk place to learn those lessons." He reported his own experience of selling only six dollars' worth of produce during his first farmers' market, and that only was because two other vendors "felt sorry for us." He went on: "A farmers' market is a clean slate every year, in some cases every week, so if you have a bad year, you can come back the next with very little repercussions. A CSA can't recover that quickly."

Farmers' markets have seen enormous growth in numbers in recent years, with the USDA now estimating that there are more than eight thousand markets nationwide. Even with the increase in the number of markets, producers feel added competition as more new farmers enter the direct-market realm. In some cases, established farmers may not be accepting of newer farmers moving into a market. Faye Jefferson explained how, as a very small farmer who is exclusively organic, she was presumed to be less serious about her business than the other vendors at a new market:

> There was an old guy, he's passed now ... he was a big vendor and he called me a fly-by-nighter. And he wasn't being mean or anything.... I'd usually show up about the same time he did and he was always the one that raised the shutters on the roundhouse and I'd try to help him and he says, "Who are you? Oh yeah, you're one of the fly-by-nighters." And he said, "I'll be surprised if you stick it out more than one season."

She noted that he did eventually realize that she was a serious grower, and she slowly gained legitimacy among the vendors; however, she never felt fully part of the community. Ultimately, the difficult market environment caused Faye to transition to a full-time CSA and stop selling at farmers' markets altogether. "I just got up one morning in the winter between the last time I did the market and thought you know I just really don't want to do this again. Because it's just such hard work, getting up that early. It's difficult."

Small-scale vegetable producers also lack the economic security of price supports, federal crop insurance, and other farm bill protections that are common in commodity production. Crop loss insurance options are among the biggest challenges in that they are limited and, in some cases, completely unavailable to produce growers. A conventional farmer has not only the safety net of the farm program but also access to crop loss insurance in case of a natural disaster. For corn and soybeans this is a pretty straightforward process. The agricultural data in Iowa are very good—we know how much corn will come out of any given acre in any county nearly down to the kernel. We also know what the corn will sell for on the commodity markets. In case of a drought, flood, hailstorm, or tornado, the Farm Services Agency, which manages federal crop insurance, can pretty accurately reimburse the farmer for the lost income.

This program is not available to produce growers. In Iowa there are no "benchmarks" for fruit and vegetable production. Corn farmers can be reimbursed for lost crops because there are precise yield and price calculations, but such calculations do not exist for vegetable and fruit production. Melon grower "Roger Daniels" pointed out that the risk of growing produce is very high. By midsummer he has already invested nearly $25,000 in the watermelons and cantaloupes that will be sold to grocery stores and schools around the state. There is only one crop loss program available to him: if he loses more than 60 percent of his crop, he will be reimbursed the cost of half the remaining 40 percent. As Roger noted, this is "completely inadequate." If he loses more than 25 percent of his crop, he will not break even for the year.

In sum, local food farmers experience both social and economic pressures that big growers do not. CSA producers have taken money in advance from their customers, and the pressure they are under to fill share boxes each week during the season is significant. Farmers' market vendors must navigate sometimes unfriendly relationships with fellow vendors, and the early mornings they put in and the time spent at the markets may not even pay off. Local food farmers are not eligible for most of the federal economic programs that keep commodity production afloat, even in the face of natural disaster. Combined, these pressures are at times a surprise to new farmers who were attracted by the "trendy and romanticized" version of farming.

CONCLUSION

The local food movement has strategically and intentionally set itself apart from conventional production. Instead of anonymous commodities, local food farmers provide handpicked products. The farmers can tell the stories of their farms and food directly to their customers. They argue that their food is safer, healthier, and more sustainable. As a result, we have largely presumed that their farms are also healthier and safer than conventional farms. The popular notion of communing with nature while engaging in the wholesome activity of growing vegetables hides the realities of physical labor, the dangers of equipment, and the tenuous economic and emotional space that most food farmers occupy.

Researchers and public health practitioners who work in agricultural safety and health are often challenged by the diversity of local food farms. These small farms, often combining orchards, vegetable growing, and livestock enterprises in unique ways, are not as comparable to each other as row crop or confinement livestock operations. In particular, occupational safety professionals—who have largely learned their trade in industrial settings where the equipment, machinery, work tasks, and labor needs are all highly specialized—may struggle to apply their knowledge to small farms.

Herein lies the benefit of ethnographic investigation as a way to better understand complex systems. Alternative farming is not radically different from conventional farming, but it does have some characteristics, such as the labor requirements, that set it apart. As a result, we should ask the same health and safety questions of alternative farms that we do of conventional farms, while taking into account those characteristics that may actually add to the dangers on alternative farms. This requires that we let go of assumptions that might cause us to overlook hazards or stress in alternative farming because of the presumed health or safety of the food such farming produces. Ethnography provides us with the tools to examine the real-life experiences of farmers. The next step is to apply ethnographic work to develop culturally competent initiatives that will lead to improving the health and safety of all agricultural producers.

QUESTIONS FOR DISCUSSION

What associations do Americans make when they hear the word *farm*? How accurate are these associations? What role do they play in a sense of "being American"?

REFERENCES

Donham, Kelley J., and Beth Larabee. 2009. "The Changing Face of Agricultural Health and Safety: Alternative Agriculture." *Journal of Agromedicine* 14 (1): 70–75.

Dudley, Kathryn Marie. 2000. *Debt and Dispossession: Farm Loss in America's Heartland*. Chicago: University of Chicago Press.

Fraser, C. E., K. B. Smith, F. Judd, J. S. Humphreys, L. J. Fragar, and A. Henderson. 2005. "Farming and Mental Health Problems and Mental Illness." *International Journal of Social Psychiatry* 51 (4): 340–49.

Galt, Ryan E., Jessica Beckett, Colleen C. Hiner, and Libby O'Sullivan. 2011. "Community Supported Agriculture (CSA) in and around California's Central Valley: Farm and Farmer Characteristics, Farm-Member Relationships, Economic Viability, Information Sources, and Emerging Issues." University of California, Davis.

Goldschmidt, Walter. 1978. "Large-Scale Farming and the Rural Social Structure." *Rural Sociology* 43 (3): 362–66.

Grey, Mark A. 2000. "The Industrial Food Stream and Its Alternatives in the United States: An Introduction." *Human Organization* 59 (2): 143–50.

Hendrickson, Mary K., and William D. Heffernan. 2002. "Opening Spaces through Relocalization: Locating Potential Resistance in the Weaknesses of the Global Food System." *Sociologica Ruralis* 42 (4): 347–69.

Hinrichs, C. Clare. 2000. "Embeddedness and Local Food Systems: Notes on Two Types of Direct Agricultural Market." *Journal of Rural Studies* 16: 295–303.

Janssen, Brandi. 2010. "Local Food, Local Engagement: Community-Supported Agriculture in Eastern Iowa." *Culture & Agriculture* 32 (1): 4–16.

———. 2013. "Herd Management: Labor Strategies in Local Food Production." *Anthropology of Work Review* 34 (2): 68–79.

Kenner, Robert, dir. 2008. *Food, Inc.* Los Angeles: Magnolia Home Entertainment.

Kolbe, Liz. 2015. "Small-Scale Fruit and Vegetable Farms: Financially Viable?" *Practical Farmer* (newsletter of Practical Farmers of Iowa) 31 (2): 6–7.

Lyons, Savanna M., and Stefanie Trout. 2015. *2015 Statewide List of CSA Farms and Organizers Serving Iowa*. Extension and Outreach Publications, Book 10. Ames: Leopold Center for Sustainable Agriculture, Iowa State University.

Lyson, Thomas A. 2004. *Civic Agriculture: Reconnecting Farm, Food, and Community*. Medford, MA: Tufts University Press.

McIlvaine-Newsad, Heather, Christopher D. Merrett, and Patrick McLaughlin. 2004. "Direct from Farm to Table: Community Supported Agriculture in Western Illinois." *Culture & Agriculture* 26 (1–2): 149–63.

National Institute for Occupational Safety and Health. 2014. "Workplace Safety and Health Topics: Agricultural Safety." www.cdc.gov/niosh/topics/aginjury (accessed October 22, 2015).

Otto, Daniel. 2010. "Consumers, Vendors, and the Economic Importance of Iowa Farmers' Markets: An Economic Impact Survey Analysis." Iowa Department of Agriculture and Land Stewardship.

Pollan, Michael. 2006. *The Omnivore's Dilemma: A Natural History of Four Meals.* New York: Penguin Press.

Schlosser, Eric. 2001. *Fast Food Nation: The Dark Side of the All-American Meal.* Boston: Houghton Mifflin.

Stallman, Bob. 2010. "Producing Results." Address to the 92nd American Farm Bureau Federation Annual Meeting, Atlanta, GA.

U.S. Department of Agriculture. 2012. *2011 Certified Organic Production Survey.* Washington, DC: National Agricultural Statistics Service, USDA.

———. 2014. *2012 Census of Agriculture.* Washington, DC: National Agricultural Statistics Service, USDA.

Family Life and Leisure

7

CHAUFFEURING AND COMMUTING: A STORY OF WORK, FAMILY, CLASS, AND COMMUNITY

Lara Descartes, Conrad P. Kottak, and Autumn Kelly

In this chapter we describe how three major domains of contemporary life—work, family, and community—are linked by crisscrossing minivans and SUVs as parents drive back and forth commuting to work and chauffeuring children to school and activities. We examine these daily driving patterns to reveal how intertwining threads of class, gender, and place frame work and family decisions.

Our analysis originates in a study we conducted in Dexter, a small southeastern Michigan town. As we listened to our informants' narratives, we were struck by how the characteristics of the town itself had drawn many families to move there, how that relocation was connected to class-based ideologies of parenting and childhood, and how, once families were there, possibilities for work and family life were shaped and constrained in ways that centered on transportation.

To illustrate, we begin with a day in the life of Gail Fogarty (a pseudonym, as are all informant names cited in the chapter). Gail was a young mother whose three children ranged in age from three to ten. All of the children were involved in extracurricular activities. Gail and her husband, Kevin, both had college degrees, and both were employed, Kevin full-time and Gail part-time. Gail reported that she was glad that she didn't have to work more hours at her job, because if she did there wouldn't be enough time for all of her children's sports. She also said that her working part-time as opposed to not working at all benefited her family, because her income was needed to cover the children's soccer expenses. Gail and Kevin both believed it was important for their children to participate in sports, not only for the health benefits but also because they felt that sports helped develop personal qualities they valued, such as self-confidence and capacity for teamwork.

Reprinted with permission, from Descartes, Lara, Conrad P. Kottak, and Autumn Kelly. 2007. *Community, Work, and Family* 10 (2): 161–78. © Taylor & Francis Ltd. Republished in *Reflecting on America*, 2nd edition, edited by Clare L. Boulanger, 65–80 (© 2016 Taylor & Francis). All rights reserved.

Lara Descartes (lead author) spent a day with Gail in the fall of 2001. At around 11:00 A.M. Gail left her home in the township of Dexter and drove about fifteen miles east to Ann Arbor, the nearest small city. There she dropped off her minivan at a repair shop, where Lara was waiting to pick her up. Gail and Lara drove back to Dexter to spend a few hours volunteering at the school of Gail's youngest son, Jacob. At 2:00 P.M., Gail and Lara left the school and returned to Ann Arbor to retrieve the minivan. For the remainder of the day, Lara rode along as Gail drove the minivan. They stopped at a nearby dry cleaner's shop to pick up clothing, then at another store to get a small gift for one of Gail's relatives. Next, they drove approximately six miles to the relative's house in east Ann Arbor. On the way they got lunch at a fast-food restaurant, using the drive-thru. From her relative's house, Gail telephoned Kevin to confer about picking up their daughter from the babysitter's. The next trip was from Ann Arbor back to Dexter to pick up Gail's eldest son, Ben, from school. This entailed waiting in the minivan in a long line of vehicles in the school driveway. Once Ben was in the minivan, they went to Gail's youngest son's school and repeated the process. They then drove to a township west of Ann Arbor to retrieve some tires left at a shop there. They next got on the highway to go about eight miles to northeast Ann Arbor to get Gail's daughter from the babysitter's. After settling her daughter in the minivan, Gail and Ben changed into their soccer gear in the back of the vehicle. Ben had a soccer game later that day, and Gail planned to play soccer later that night.

By the time all of this had been accomplished, it was after 5:00 P.M. On the way to Ben's soccer practice in Ann Arbor, they stopped at a fast-food drive-thru to get meals for Gail's family. They arrived at the practice field by 5:40. After the initial practice, Ben's game began at 6:30. In the meantime, Kevin got off from work and joined the family at the field, where he ate the fast-food meal. Jacob had a school open house back in Dexter at 7:00 P.M. Kevin was scheduled to attend this event while Gail stayed at the soccer field, but he became engrossed in the game and skipped the open house. At 7:30 P.M., with the soccer game still in progress, Lara needed to leave. The day was far from over for Gail, however. She planned to drive the children from Ann Arbor back to Dexter after the soccer game and put them all to bed. She then intended to return to Ann Arbor to play her own game, which had a start time of 10:00 P.M. After that ended, she told Lara, she would be stopping on her way home to pick up work-related material for the next day.

In addition to the length and complexity of this schedule, the amount of driving Gail did stands out. She performed one task, such as dropping off the minivan for repairs, then spent thirty minutes driving to another town to do another chore, then crossed town again for the next appointment. During the day detailed above she drove well over one hundred miles performing chores and transporting children.

Gail's tale may sound familiar. Many children in the contemporary United States are involved in a number of extracurricular activities, and most mothers end up driving a great deal while going about their daily tasks. But Gail's story, representative of those of a number of other women at our research site, was what initially led us to examine the overlapping effects of structure and culture in framing and constraining these middle-class parents' work and family choices. We came to recognize the links between the specific community in which our informants chose to locate their families and contemporary middle-class ideologies of child rearing, gender, and parenting.

To interpret the phenomena we observed, we found a life-course perspective, specifically as articulated by Moen and Sweet (2004), to be constructive. This approach examines the individual in the context of time, considered at different but interconnected levels: historical time, or "the significance of the times in which one lives"; social time, "the socially constructed and institutionalized entry and exit portals into and out of various roles and relationships at various ages and stages, and for particular subgroups of the population"; and biographical time, or individual experience and background (Moen and Sweet 2004: 211). Moen and Sweet add:

> Permeating these interlocking temporal constellations are other key life course themes: *agency* (the degree to which individuals shape their own life course and the strategic choices they make within existing constraints), *relationships* (the fact that individuals are embedded in communities of close and distal ties that affect their choice sets, their information, their beliefs, their values), *meaning* (how individuals and groups define their own identities and values, as well as various objective circumstances, and come to hold certain temporal expectations), and *context* (the multi-layered demographic, economic, technological, community, organizational, and situational ecologies in which biographies unfold). (211–12)

To this we add the concept of practice, which Ortner (1989: 12) defines as "action considered in relation to structure.... [It] emerges from structure, it reproduces structure, and it has the capacity to transform structure." Practice theories acknowledge "that individuals within a society or culture have diverse motives and intentions and different degrees of power and influence. Such contrasts may be associated with gender, age, ethnicity, class, and other social variables" (Kottak 2006: A8). Practices are thus the everyday doings of individuals who occupy unequal social locations based on their specific identities. Those locations shape their practices, and those practices in turn help reinforce structure, although they may lead to structural change as time brings shifting circumstances, ideas, and/or cultural contexts.

Our ethnographic research provides an on-the-ground snapshot of these diverse forces as they shaped our informants' decisions about where and how best to live a family life, raise children, and divide up the paid and unpaid labor needed to accomplish those tasks. Neither inevitable nor natural, these practices were bound in interrelated ways to their specific chronological moment. Cultural and structural factors influence the range of choices that individuals see as possible and desirable, while further choices are in turn constrained by resultant actions.

RESEARCH SITE

Dexter was originally a small farming community, but it underwent rapid expansion due in part to its pleasant small-town atmosphere and the fine reputation of its public schools. It also is within fairly easy driving distance of the universities, colleges, and hospitals of the Ann Arbor area and within commuting distance of larger industry and government centers such as Detroit, Dearborn, Flint, Jackson, and Lansing. A number of parents we spoke with explicitly cited these factors when discussing why they lived in Dexter.

Older farmhouses were spread throughout the township, interspersed with new subdivisions of high-end homes built on converted farmland. The farther from the village center, the larger a subdivision's lots and houses tended to be. The drive from the outer limits of the township to the town center could take half

Table 7.1 Gender and paid labor status

Sex by work status in 1999, usual hours worked per week in 1999	Village	Township
Male (number)	879	1,964
Usually worked 35 or more hrs/week (%)	75.77	75.71
Usually worked 15 to 34 hrs/week (%)	10.92	6.87
Usually worked 1 to 14 hrs/week (%)	1.25	2.39
Did not work in prior year (%)	12.06	15.02
Female (number)	975	1,946
Usually worked 35 or more hrs/week (%)	52.41	47.23
Usually worked 15 to 34 hrs/week (%)	21.23	136.27
Usually worked 1 to 14 hrs/week (%)	3.90	5.50
Did not work in prior year (%)	22.46	26.62

Source: U.S. Census Bureau (2000d).

an hour or more, and could involve long stretches of dirt roads. All of the schools and most of the township's services were located in the central village.

Between 1990 and 2000 the Dexter village and township populations increased, with the number of village residents rising from 1,497 to 2,338 and the township growing from 4,407 to 5,248 (U.S. Census Bureau 1990a, 1990b, 2000b, 2000c). The racial/ethnic composition, however, remained overwhelmingly (98 percent) non-Hispanic white (U.S. Census Bureau 1990b, 2000c). Family households made up 63 percent of the village and 80 percent of the township. Of those, the majority were married-couple families: 47 percent in the village and 72 percent in the township (U.S. Census Bureau 2000b, 2000c). The township was where most new housing was in the form of large, expensive, single-family homes, unlikely to be afford-able for most single parents. Most children in the village and the larger township lived with two parents. Again, this pattern was more marked in the township (96 percent) than in the village (61 percent) (U.S. Census Bureau 2000a).

Roughly 65 percent of the two-parent families in Dexter were dual income (U.S. Census Bureau 2000a). If only one parent worked, it was most likely to be the father. Table 7.1, however, provides more insight into the definition of "dual income." Women working for pay were far more likely than men to work part-time: looking at both the village and the township, about 76 percent of the men who worked did so full-time, in contrast to approximately 50 percent of the women (U.S. Census Bureau 2000d). This was low compared to the national average of 71 percent of employed women working full-time (U.S. Census Bureau 2000e).

METHODS

We spent two years conducting fieldwork in Dexter. To contact parents of young children, we worked through a public school system. Five first-grade classrooms and five second-grade classrooms, out of a total of approximately twenty, were chosen by the school principal based on her judgment of which teachers would be most willing to help. The total number of students in the ten classrooms was approximately 250, and an explanatory letter and request for interviews was sent home with each. Half of the letters specifically asked that a mother participate and half asked for a father. We conducted in-depth inter-views with thirty-six parents, eight of whom were men, using a guide that

Table 7.2   Employment statuses of research participants and their spouses[a]

	Employed full-time	Employed part-time	Out of paid labor force	Spouse employed full-time	Spouse employed part-time	Spouse out of paid labor force
Interviews						
8 men	7	1	0	2	3	2
28 women	6	15	7	28	0	0
Focus groups						
14 men	11	1[b]	2[c]	5	1	8[d]
32 women	16	4[e]	12	31	1[b]	0
Ethnographic observation						
12 women	1	6	5	12	0	0

[a]Or ex-spouses.
[b]Due to retirement.
[c]One due to disability.
[d]Four due to retirement, disability, or student status.
[e]One due to retirement.

had been prepared and tested through preliminary interviews with other local parents. The goal of the interviews was to gain comparable data on parents' personal histories along with information on the work and family ideologies that influenced family decisions.

Of the eight male interview participants, nearly all worked full-time, and few had wives who worked full-time. Of the twenty-eight female interview participants, most were employed part-time, and all of their husbands worked full-time. Many of the employed women did at least some of their work from home. Nearly all of the men, however, worked in conventional office settings. Table 7.2 provides a more detailed description of the employment statuses of the research participants and their spouses.

We conducted focus groups as another means of exploring our topics. These group interviews allowed us to listen to informants as they developed and exchanged ideas in collective discussions. There were forty-six participants, fourteen men and thirty-two women.

Two focus groups were held with the men. The majority worked full-time and had wives who worked part-time or stayed home full-time. We segregated the six women's focus groups by the employment statuses of the thirty-two women. Twenty worked for pay and twelve stayed home full-time, and the majority were married to men who worked full-time. There was a higher incidence of remarriage and cohabitation among the women in the working mothers' focus groups than in the stay-home mothers' groups (see Han and Moen 1999).

In addition to the individual interviews and focus groups, we conducted ethnographic observation with twelve research participants. Only women signed up for this phase of the research, but in the interactions that we had with families, their children frequently were present and sometimes their husbands. Six of the mothers worked part-time and five stayed home full-time. The only single mother worked full-time, and all the fathers worked full-time. We spent time with the families in a variety of situations: preparing and eating dinner, doing housework, watching videos, working for pay, driving children to and from sports practices, attending holiday parties at school, and so on. The intent was to experience firsthand what parents faced in their daily lives as they cared for their families and earned a living, to see the contexts in which their actions took place, and, through conversation, to learn about the meanings of these actions.

All but three of the research participants in this project were non-Hispanic white and nearly all were middle-class. We use the term *middle-class* broadly, to indicate that one or both parents had a college education, worked at a white-collar position, and/or owned their own home. Nearly all the research participants possessed all three of these criteria. All the couples were heterosexual couples. All but five of the research participants were married at the time of the interview, and of those five, two were cohabiting with their partners. Most of the couples had two children. The participants in this study were representative of the town's demographic profile.

Class, Child Rearing, and Community

Many of the men involved in our project were doctors, lawyers, scientists, and engineers. Most of their wives tended to have less professional training, but many had degrees in such fields as nursing, dental hygiene, education, and social work. These parents thus had an expectation of middle-class lifestyles for their children, and this guided their child-rearing practices. The work of other researchers helps provide insight into middle-class parenting and values transmission. In a classic 1960s study, Kohn (1969; cited in Gilbert and Kahl 1993) reported that middle-class parents emphasized values that oriented their children toward professional success: self-direction, management of internal states, and initiative. In more recent work, Hays (1996: 159) similarly observed that middle-class mothers stressed "self-discipline and independent decision-making skills" and believed that having their children participate in diverse activities provided them with "appropriate cultural capital" for their future class positions (see also Warner 2005). These perceived connections between extracurriculars and the development of skills that lead to later success have made extracurriculars seem a necessary part of a normal middle-class childhood. Lareau (2003) describes the many benefits such activities provide these children in their subsequent employment in the white-collar world, such as self-confidence in interactions with authority. And indeed, there are demonstrated links between extracurricular activities and success. Fletcher, Elder, and Mekos (2000), for example, show that adolescent involvement in extracurriculars corresponds to better high school performance and increased likelihood of attending college.

Children's participation in such activities and enrichment programs is complicated, however, by the transportation distances involved in life in Dexter. Extensive driving time was necessary to convey children to the many activities of middle-class childhood. The activities in which our informants' children were involved included T-ball, Little League, soccer, hockey, dance, horseback riding, drama workshop, language class, religious studies, basketball camp, specialized medical care, tutoring, and music therapy. Many of these activities took place outside the community proper. The relatively recent expansion of the town meant that there was not yet a population density sufficient to support more localized provision of specialized services and activities. Thus, parents may have had to get one child to music therapy at a site in Ann Arbor at the same time that another child was scheduled for private soccer coaching in a town twenty miles away.

Even if services were available in Dexter, the selection was limited, and parents sometimes needed or chose to go elsewhere. For example, some parents drove their children an extra thirty minutes one way to see a preferred allergy specialist or attend a particular day-care center.

Daily child transportation was further complicated by the fact that many of these parents did not wish their children to ride the school buses on routes that could last for thirty to sixty minutes each way. Quite a few of the parents felt that such long rides and the earlier rising times they entailed were burdens on their children. Kinney, Dunn, and Hofferth (2000: 16) noted the same pattern among their own southeastern Michigan middle-class informants: "Surprisingly, we found a substantial number of parents who drove their children to school, even though their children could take the school bus, walk, or ride their bikes." Even parents who were willing to have their children ride the buses may have had to pick up their children directly from school themselves if the children had scheduled events elsewhere that were timed close to the end of the school day. One mother, for example, complained that she had no choice but to pick up her son directly from his school because thirty minutes after school was let out he had soccer practice in a town that was a twenty-minute drive away. According to the informant, this particular activity was actually scheduled by the school system, yet no school-based transportation was provided.

In Dexter, however, picking up children after school could involve up to a twenty-minute wait by the parent, because the process was strictly controlled and the lines were very long. One mother kept newspapers in her minivan to have something to read while she waited for her children. Because schools in the town were divided by grade level, quite a few parents had children at different schools and therefore waited in more than one school pickup line in an afternoon. In addition, because the population of the community had burgeoned in recent years, the buses and hence the schools ran on staggered shifts. The older children went to and returned from school an hour ahead of the younger children. Thus, any parent with more than one child in the school system could face a very complex daily schedule.

The end result of these community-specific factors of school schedules and country roads, in combination with middle-class ideologies of childhood, was that quite a few stay-home mothers and mothers employed part-time, like Gail, discussed their choices to stay home or work only during school hours in terms of accommodating their preferences regarding their children's lifestyles and resultant transportation needs. The majority of the mothers we interviewed who worked part-time or stayed home full-time stated that they had no desire to return to full-time paid employment as their children got older. Most expressed a wish to work for pay only during school hours, if at all. The most frequently heard explanation for this was that the women expected their maturing children's activity schedules to become even more hectic, and thus to demand more of their mothers' time.

Providing child transportation themselves was a part of good mothering for quite a few of the women with whom we spoke. Some were part of organized or informal carpool arrangements, but most were not. Getting one's own children to and from school could hold great significance as a symbol of maternal care, as shown in the case of Polly Jordan, a mother who was employed full-time. Polly reported that she would leave work early specifically to provide rides to one or more of her three preteen children, even though her husband was at home during the day and could do it: "I'm fortunate that I get to pretty much make a schedule and I get to get off to pick up the kids . . . that's important to me. Even though [my husband's] home now, he's at the house . . . it just is important to me." This well illustrates the concept of "maternal visibility" discussed by Garey (1999), in which women's performance of specific activities demonstrates to themselves and others their status as involved, caring mothers.

The mores that lead parents to settle in communities such as Dexter thus made it difficult for women to engage in full-time paid labor, even if working was part of their value systems. For many of the parents in our sample, however, full-time work for mothers of young or school-aged children was emphatically not part of their ideal. As Hays (1996) notes, there exists a hegemonic ideology of mothering, reinforced by child-care manuals and the wider culture, that is very time-intensive. To be a mother is presented as an all-consuming activity, concomitant with the idea that children's well-being is more important than mothers' convenience.

Arendell (1999) similarly argues that the ideology of the "good mother" is that she stays home and is economically dependent on her husband. Her family comes first. All the women we interviewed consistently agreed with this latter point. However, there was some divergence in how they thought family needs were best served, and that variation was related to individual background. For example, June Deschamps, a mother of two, was the daughter of a stay-home mother. Living on one income caused financial difficulty for the family, to which June attributed her own desire to work full-time: "That's probably what it stemmed from, was seeing how unhappy my parents were because they weren't able to do certain things for us." In contrast, Zoe Gibbens, a mother who worked part-time, related that she had always envisioned devoting herself to her family rather than a career, in part because of her own family background: "I mean work is fine, but my dad's a physician, and he was never home. And I'm like 'I'm not doing that.'" Some of the women's lives were shaped more by circumstances than by intent. Kelly Putney, for example, was a stay-home mother who planned to work part-time after she had children but then was unexpectedly laid off. Of this she said, "Actually that was great, it was a big relief!" Despite such individual differences among the women, however, none questioned the primary tenets of hegemonic motherhood: that to be a mother is to sacrifice for children. As one mother who gave up her job to stay home put it, "It really drains me sometimes being at home with kids all day. But I think it's just going to be such a short time and then I'll have my time back to myself again. It's a sacrifice for the kids."

Arendell's (1999) contention that the "good mother" is socially institutionalized was supported by our observations of the Dexter school system. Not only did parents deal with the staggered bus schedules and the transportation gaps between the end of the school day and late-afternoon activities, but they also were encouraged to do quite a bit of volunteering at the school during the day. Especially in the younger grades, parents were recruited to help at parties, go on field trips, assist with school events, and spend time assisting the teacher. Some of our informants had acted as "room mothers," people assigned to organize other parents for such activities by phoning them at home. One room mother, who stayed home full-time, grumbled to us about employed mothers, who she said did not return her phone calls or seem interested in helping out. However, many mothers with whom we spoke, both those who were employed and those who stayed home full-time, talked about spending time in their children's classrooms and how much they enjoyed it (for a discussion of classroom volunteering as another domain of maternal visibility, see Garey 1999).

We viewed this ethos of intensive parental classroom volunteering as an example of the escalation of expectations for the involvement of parents, particularly mothers, in their children's lives outside the home. Few fathers participated in daytime classroom activities, and if any did, it was remarked upon by mothers. Arendell (1999) notes that the normative activities of middle-class children's lives create more work quite specifically for women. Women, but not men, often cut back on their work hours to accommodate children's schedules (Arendell 2000; see also Kinney et al. 2000). Dunn, Kinney, and Hofferth (2001: 12) noted similar findings in a study they conducted with middle-class families in Michigan:

> For many parents—and particularly for mothers—the late-afternoon and early-evening time on most weekdays was spent driving children to their after-school activities and/or attending these activities; preparing, serving, and eating the evening meal; and overseeing children's homework and daily chores. Mothers who did not work outside the home or who worked part-time had more time available for these duties than mothers who worked full-time, but it was also not uncommon among Parkside families for mothers (and a few fathers) who worked full-time to adjust their work schedules to fit the school and after-school schedules of their children.

Kinney et al. (2000) also observed that parents became involved in their children's activities in order to exert some control over their children's peer groups. The women we interviewed who volunteered in the classroom echoed these concerns, saying how they liked to be able to get to know their children's teachers and classmates. Ortner (1991) makes a similar point, saying that middle-class parents in particular express a great deal of concern about their children's friends, worrying that if their adolescents mix with the "wrong crowd"—often a coded term for children of the working class—their offspring may deviate from the life path their parents want for them.

It turned out that our community of study was one where parents were able to exert a great deal of control over their children and their environment, in part because of the children's need for transportation, but also because Dexter was quite homogeneous along almost any axis of identity, including marital status. Single parents as a rule could not afford to buy much of the new housing in Dexter. The census data cited above confirm that most families there were headed by married couples, something a number of our informants mentioned with approval. As stated, the area's population was almost entirely white. There was little poverty, the schools were modern and well equipped, and there were large lots and large houses spread throughout the township in similar-appearing subdivisions. Though houses were cheaper in Dexter than in some of the more suburban middle-class communities nearby, the prices were still quite substantial, with large homes in the new subdivisions listed at up to $500,000 in 2000. Thus, residents of the subdivisions were solidly middle-class, and their children were raised in de facto middle-class peer groups. Our informants talked about feeling safe in Dexter, perceiving it to be a wholesome community. In discussing this phenomenon, which to differing extents is playing out in suburbs nationwide, Duany, Plater-Zyberk, and Speck (2000) aptly label it a "balkanization" along class lines.

The type of location parents sought to avoid in moving to Dexter is illustrated by the words of Jack Tanner, a father of three. He commented that his wife had been working full-time because "two-income families now are pretty much what you have to have if you don't want to live in the bowels of Detroit." Jack and his wife, Susan, both professionals, and their children lived in a large house they designed themselves on the outskirts of Dexter. Susan now worked part-time, enabled by telecommuting technology to work regularly from home. This had given her the flexibility to accommodate her children's schedules, which she appreciated. It also gave her time free of her husband and older children to clean house and run errands. Susan tried to finish her paid work early in the day in order to do this. On a morning Lara spent with Susan, for example, Susan had been up since 5:00 A.M. working in her home office, which had a play area set aside for her infant daughter. By midmorning, Susan completed her paid work, turned to housework, then drove into Dexter to purchase a gift for a birthday party to which one of her children had been invited. Later that afternoon Susan was going on a Scouting trip with another of her children.

Although part-time employment and telecommuting gave Susan flexibility and allowed her to avoid driving to work, most of the parents in our sample did not have this option. Living in Dexter could impose lengthy commutes on parents, which in turn could have profound impacts on their personal, family, and career options. To illustrate, we relate the story of one evening Lara spent with Brad Kingston. Brad was a married father of three children, all of whom were under the age of eight. When Lara asked Brad for an interview time, he was only able to schedule for the late evening of a weekday. When Lara arrived at the Kingstons' home, Brad looked physically exhausted. His voice confirmed this impression, as did his wandering replies to the interview questions. As Brad discussed his day, the reasons for his weariness became clear. On weekdays he got up at 6:30 A.M., drove an hour to get to his job, worked for nine hours, and then commuted home. He was away from home for eleven or more hours each day. Many of Brad's evenings and weekends were taken up with his children's activities, which included violin and piano lessons, soccer, and swim class. On the evening he was interviewed, Brad had gone to work, come home, and then attended his daughter's choral recital before meeting with Lara; thus, he had had a fourteen-hour day even before beginning the interview.

When discussing why he lived in Dexter, more than an hour away from his job, Brad cited his wife Connie's extended family and her well-paying part-time job as the determining factors keeping them in the area. Connie's relatives, however, did not live in Dexter, nor did Connie work in Dexter. Connie's commute to her job was far shorter than Brad's, but it was still about a half hour one way, as was the children's commute to school by bus. The daily travel times for all the Kingston family members had to do with Brad and Connie's choice to buy their home in Dexter. The Kingstons lived in a very large, well-appointed new house on a neatly landscaped corner lot that bordered the woods. The home was located in a high-end subdivision fairly removed from the central village. When discussing why Connie was employed when both would prefer she stay home, Brad referred to the mortgage payment on their house.

Dexter's low population density and small-town character came at a cost: there were very few local professional jobs. Parents with sufficient income to purchase Dexter's high-end homes tended to have postsecondary degrees and to occupy white-collar positions. However, local jobs were generally service oriented, aside from those available in town administration and at the school. Main Street in Dexter had some of the primary employment venues in the area: a diner, a pub, a drug-store, a hardware store, a gasoline station, a grocery store, a greeting card store, a barbershop, and a gift store. Elsewhere in Dexter there were other stores and a few small manufacturing and agricultural enterprises. Scattered legal, tax, and medical businesses tended to have only small numbers of white-collar employees.

Essentially, then, Dexter had a burgeoning middle-class population but a com-parative lack of middle-class occupations. In some ways it was a bedroom com-munity to the region's more populated urban areas, but this was a bedroom in the back of the house and up an extra flight of stairs. The ramifications of this set of circumstances for work and family life in Dexter differed for parents according to gender. First, in order to maintain their high-level incomes, most middle-class residents had to commute to their jobs. The shortest possible driving time to a more densely populated area where professional jobs were concentrated was twenty minutes, but we heard of far longer commutes: the longest was two and a half hours one way. Second, because American ideologies of parenting still center on female caregiving and male breadwinning, the member of the couple most often undertaking an extensive commute was the husband. The men took this on to provide their families with the homes and lifestyles they and their wives desired (for a discussion of men's commuting as an expression of their commitment to their families, see Townsend 2002). Hence some men were absent from the home for extended periods of time, and when they were home they were tired. Regular participation in family life could become difficult even for a highly motivated father.

Additionally, when men are involved in long commutes but women are not, women, regardless of their individual commitments to intensive mothering ide-ologies, end up performing the bulk of child transportation, child care, and home care simply because their husbands are not there (for examples of how gendered inequalities are expressed and replicated through discourse around what is "practical" in dividing up the tasks of paid labor and family care, see DeVault 1991; Walzer 1998). Several women we interviewed spoke of feeling like single mothers due to their husbands' job situations. The men in turn could become almost tangential to family life. A few mothers we spoke with said that their husbands' extensive time away from home did not in fact affect their own or their children's schedules very much. The men were such a small part of daily home life already that the mothers arranged activities without taking the possible presence of the fathers into consideration.

Bridget Arnold was one such mother. She stayed home full-time. Her husband worked from 8:00 A.M. to 4:30 P.M., but because of his commute, he was gone from 6:15 A.M. to 7:00 P.M. Bridget did all the inside housework and all the care and transportation associated with their child, even if her husband was home. Their son was simply used to coming to her for his needs since Bridget was always there and her husband was not. Bridget laughingly called the division of labor in her marriage "Old World." Of her relationship with her husband, she said:

> Sometimes I think it's like we just happen to cohabitate . . . because I've got like what me and my son are doing, [my husband's] got his job, [which] is the majority of his day. We see each other in the evening, he's tired, he eats and goes downstairs and

wants to watch TV. I'm still taking care of the kid, watching TV upstairs, sometimes we don't even talk.

Just as men's family lives could be affected by the choice to live in Dexter, so could women's careers. If one partner undertook a long commute, somebody must be home to take care of daily life, and in our sample almost universally that person was the wife. As noted, most women with whom we spoke were committed either to staying home full-time or to working at a job close to home so that they were available to care for their children and transport them to all their activities. It could be difficult, however, for women to find any nearby jobs that were commensurate with their educational levels. This situation was further complicated by the fact that many women wanted part-time hours so that they could be home when their children got out of school. Professionally oriented part-time work was hard to find, but work that was professional, part-time, *and* in or around Dexter was rare indeed. A number of the stay-home mothers with whom we spoke were off their original career tracks entirely. Some who hoped to return to work planned on applying to be paraprofessionals (formerly called teacher's aides). These were some of the few local part-time jobs that were not service oriented, but the pay was still negligible, the requisite skills were frequently mismatched to the individual woman's training, and opportunities for advancement were fairly limited.

Our research shows why middle-class parents want to live in communities like Dexter, which they see as providing the best environment for their children's development and education. Once settled in such communities, however, men can spend a great deal of time commuting between their workplaces and their homes, while women spend a great deal of time transporting their children. In Dexter, the ethos of middle-class life that led parents to encourage their children's participation in a variety of activities, combined with the limitations of such offerings in this small semirural town, imposed a great burden of transportation on parents. Even when publicly funded transportation was available, as was the case with the school bus system, reliance on it was discouraged by ideologies that stressed the desirability of individual parental care for children, as well as the perception that a middle-class child should not be expected to wake up early to ride the bus when a parent could be made available to transport the child to school. In most cases this parent was the mother, due to her classic position as the primary caretaker of young children and her lesser earning potential. Given these constraints on the lives of middle-class women, they might never enter or rejoin the workforce at the level for which they were educationally prepared. In middle-class professions there are negative consequences, in terms of income and advancement, to straying from the traditional full-time career path (Epstein et al. 1999; Schneer and Reitman 1997). Prior research, such as that conducted by Shelton (1990) and Stier and Lewin-Epstein (2000), suggests that it is only women holding full-time jobs who make measurable gains toward gender equity in the home, according to measures such as male participation in housework.

We close by returning to the life-course and practice theories discussed at the beginning of this chapter, which link the many themes that emerged in our work. Briefly, life-course theory presents the concepts of historical, social, and biographical time as interrelated and postulates that other factors simultaneously affect individuals' life courses, including agency, meaning, context, and—our addition—practice. The idea of historical time helps illuminate the broader context of why middle-class families are locating in places like Dexter. The post–World War II expansion of the middle class, growth of the suburbs, and concomitant white exodus from urban areas set the stage. As the rings of suburbs surrounding the nation's cities aged and became more accessible to low-income and minority residents, white flight continued into newer housing stock available in outer-ring suburbs (Leigh and Lee 2005). The rapid expansion of Dexter typified the next step in this trend and exemplified a national pattern of the development of what Marx (1991) calls "ruburbia," the push of suburban development into primarily agricultural areas.

After World War II, ideologies of child rearing and parenting changed. A growing middle class had more discretionary income to spend on children (Arendell 2000). An increasingly child-focused ethos gained greater cultural presence at the same time that women's roles as family nurturers and men's roles as family breadwinners were reinforced by government and media (Hays 1996). As the late twentieth-century economy shifted from manufacturing to information and services, middle-class parents became "increasingly sensitive to the need to raise children prepared to succeed in the high-tech world" (Kottak and Kozaitis 2003: 277), which led to an even greater focus on childhood preparation for adult success. The emergence of this postindustrial economy, however, led to reduced job security and falling real earnings. This, coupled with the women's movement, corresponded to the rise of the dual-earner household as it became more normative, and more necessary, in terms of maintaining a middle-class lifestyle, for women to work outside the home.

Thus, family life changed in historical time, but social time preserved traditional family and career paths. For our middle-class white research population, socially legitimated families were still built by the marriages of men and women in their twenties and thirties who then had children, thus forming self-sufficient, nuclear units. There was little government support for either subsidized child care or extended parental leave (for a discussion of how the loss of government programs to support families has hurt the middle class, see Warner 2005). These are the same years institutionally structured as "career building"; most middle-class professions are based on the assumption that one trains for, enters, and then continues, uninterrupted, at full-time status in one's field.

These chronological norms clashed with the contexts of the school day and year, both mismatched to most professional employment schedules. They also were in conflict with the meanings that middle-class men and women assign to parenting and child rearing. Although the couples participating in our research divided up paid labor and child care differently based on their backgrounds and circumstances ("biographical time"), all held in common an intensive mothering ideology and expectations for active child involvement in a variety of extracurriculars.

How individuals responded to these sets of circumstances in the context of their time, location, and cultural values can be understood in part through the concept of practice. The middle-class families with whom we worked had the agency to create a family environment of their own choosing—one of homogeneity, prosperity, and security. Parents were able to procure spacious upscale homes in white, middle-class developments by moving to a semirural area well removed from major urban centers. Driving emerged as a particularly salient practice that allowed these diverse and sometimes conflicting threads of community, work, and family to coexist. Parents were able to supply the money to finance those homes by driving long distances to well-paid professional-level jobs. They further were able to provide their children with the upbringing they desired, in terms of both parental monitoring and enrichment, by personally driving the children to school and to an array of extracurricular activities.

This practice of driving also seems destined to replicate the structural factors leading to it in the first place. With so many parents choosing to handle transportation themselves, changes in community funding of public transportation or how the schools structure their transportation schedules seem unlikely to happen. Dividing up driving labor in ways that seem "practical"—that is to say, along gendered lines—with men commuting long distances to their higher-paying jobs and women staying closer to home to chauffeur children, results in the reproduction of unequal social and familial gender relationships. Additionally, through all their driving, these middle-class families were able to keep homes in homogeneous, prosperous, and secluded semirural communities, thus maintaining geographically based class separation and inequities.

However, recall that practice also can alter structure as times and contexts change. In Dexter, as more and more middle-class professionals take on the commuting and chauffeuring entailed by life there, the population density may increase to the point where more services and professional jobs are locally available, decreasing some of the need for driving (a development that in turn will likely create its own middle-class exodus into even more remote areas). Or perhaps more companies will start to offer telecommuting options to suit employees' preferences for living far from urban centers, shortening men's commutes and enabling more women to work at part-time yet professional positions. If such changes were to take place, they may have the potential to lead to greater male participation in family life and greater female participation in wage-earning labor.

Questions for Discussion

Does the kind of childhood described in this chapter sound like your childhood? What was the same and what was different about your childhood? Why?

References

Arendell, Teresa. 1999. "Hegemonic Motherhood: Deviancy Discourses and Employed Mothers' Accounts of Out-of-School Time Issues." Working Paper No. 9, Center for Working Families, University of California, Berkeley.

——. 2000. "'Soccer Moms' and the New Care Work." Working Paper No. 16, Center for Working Families, University of California, Berkeley.

DeVault, Marjorie L. 1991. *Feeding the Family: The Social Organization of Caring as Gendered Work.* Chicago: University of Chicago Press.

Duany, Andres, Elizabeth Plater-Zyberk, and Jeff Speck. 2000. *Suburban Nation: The Rise of Sprawl and the Decline of the American Dream.* New York: North Point Press.

Dunn, Janet S., David A. Kinney, and Sandra L. Hofferth. 2001. "Parental Ideologies and Children's After-School Activities." Working Paper 021-01, Center for the Ethnography of Everyday Life, University of Michigan, Ann Arbor.

Epstein, Cynthia Fuchs, Carroll Seron, Bonnie Oglensky, and Robert Sauté. 1999. *The Part-Time Paradox: Time Norms, Professional Life, Family and Gender*. New York: Routledge.

Fletcher, Anne C., Glen H. Elder Jr., and Debra Mekos. 2000. "Parental Influences on Adolescent Involvement in Community Activities." *Journal of Research on Adolescence* 10 (1): 29–48.

Garey, Anita Ilta. 1999. *Weaving Work and Motherhood*. Philadelphia: Temple University Press.

Gilbert, Dennis, and Joseph A. Kahl. 1993. *The American Class Structure: A New Synthesis*. 4th ed. Belmont, CA: Wadsworth.

Han, Shin-Kap, and Phyllis Moen. 1999. "Work and Family over Time: A Life Course Approach." *Annals of the American Academy of Political and Social Science* 562 (March): 98–110.

Hays, Sharon. 1996. *The Cultural Contradictions of Motherhood*. New Haven, CT: Yale University Press.

Kinney, David A., Janet S. Dunn, and Sandra L. Hofferth. 2000. "Family Strategies for Managing the Time Crunch." Working Paper 011-00, Center for the Ethnography of Everyday Life, University of Michigan, Ann Arbor.

Kohn, Melvin L. 1969. *Class and Conformity: A Study in Values*. Homewood, IL: Dorsey Press.

Kottak, Conrad P. 2006. *Anthropology: The Exploration of Human Diversity*. 11th ed. Boston: McGraw-Hill.

Kottak, Conrad P., and Kathryn A. Kozaitis. 2003. *On Being Different: Diversity and Multiculturalism in the North American Mainstream*. 2nd ed. Boston: McGraw-Hill.

Lareau, Annette. 2003. *Unequal Childhoods: Class, Race, and Family Life*. Berkeley: University of California Press.

Leigh, Nancey Green, and Sugie Lee. 2005. "Philadelphia's Space in Between: Inner-Ring Suburb Evolution." *Opolis: An International Journal of Suburban and Metropolitan Studies* 1 (1): 13–32.

Marx, Leo. 1991. "The American Ideology of Space." In Stuart Wrede and William Howard Adams, eds., *Denatured Visions: Landscape and Culture in the Twentieth Century*, 62–78. New York: Museum of Modern Art.

Moen, Phyllis, and Stephen Sweet. 2004. "From 'Work-Family' to 'Flexible Careers': A Life Course Reframing." *Community, Work & Family* 7 (2): 209–26.

Ortner, Sherry B. 1989. *High Religion: A Cultural and Political History of Sherpa Buddhism*. Princeton, NJ: Princeton University Press.

———. 1991. "Resistance and Class Reproduction among Middle Class Youth." Paper presented at the annual meeting of the American Anthropological Association, Chicago, November.

Schneer, Joy A., and Frieda Reitman. 1997. "The Interrupted Managerial Career Path: A Longitudinal Study of MBAs." *Journal of Vocational Behavior* 51 (3): 411–34.

Shelton, Beth Anne. 1990. "The Distribution of Household Tasks: Does Wife's Employment Status Make a Difference?" *Journal of Family Issues* 11 (2): 115–35.

Stier, Haya, and Noah Lewin-Epstein. 2000. "Women's Part-Time Employment and Gender Inequality in the Family." *Journal of Family Issues* 21 (3): 390–410.

Townsend, Nicholas W. 2002. *The Package Deal: Marriage, Work, and Fatherhood in Men's Lives*. Philadelphia: Temple University Press.

U.S. Census Bureau. 1990a. "General Population and Housing Characteristics: Dexter Township, Michigan." American FactFinder. factfinder.census.gov/servlet/QTTable?_bm=y&-context=qt&-qr_name=DEC_1990_STF1_DP1&-ds_name=DEC_1990_STF1_&-CONTEXT=qt&-tree_id=100&-keyword=dexter%20township,%20MI&-all_geo_types=N&-redoLog=true&-geo_id=06000US26161025&-search_results=16000US260695&-format=&-_lang=en (accessed February 20, 2006).

———. 1990b. "General Population and Housing Characteristics: Dexter Village, Michigan." American FactFinder. factfinder.census.gov/servlet/QTTable?_bm=y&-context=qt&-qr_name=DEC_1990_STF1_DP1&-ds_name=DEC_1990_STF1_&-CONTEXT=qt&-tree_id=100&-all_geo_types=N&-redoLog=true&-geo_id=label&-geo_id=16000US260695&-search_results=16000US260695&-format=&-_lang=en (accessed February 20, 2006).

———. 2000a. "Family Type by Employment Status: Dexter Township and Village, Michigan." American FactFinder. factfinder.census.gov/servlet/DTTable?_bm=y&-state=dt&-context=dt&-ds_name=DEC_2000_SF3_U&-CONTEXT=dt&-mt_name=DEC_2000_SF3_U_P044&-tree_id=403&-keyword=dexter%20township&-redoLog=false&-all_geo_types=N&-geo_id=06000US2616122180&-geo_id=16000US2622160&-search_results=04000US26&-format=&-_lang=en (accessed February 20, 2006).

————. 2000b. "Profile of General Demographic Characteristics: Dexter Township, Michigan." American FactFinder. factfinder.census.gov/servlet/QTTable?_bm=y&-context=qt&-qr_name=DEC_2000_SF1_U_DP1&-ds_name=DEC_2000_SF1_U&-CONTEXT=qt&-tree_id=100&-redoLog=false&-all_geo_types=N&-geo_id=06000US2616122180&-search_results=16000US260695&-_sse=on&-format=&-_lang=en (accessed February 20, 2006).

————. 2000c. "Profile of General Demographic Characteristics: Dexter Village, Michigan." American FactFinder. factfinder.census.gov/servlet/QTTable?_bm=y&-context=qt&-qr_name=DEC_2000_SF1_U_DP1&-ds_name=DEC_2000_SF1_U&-CONTEXT=qt&-tree_id=100&-redoLog=false&-all_geo_types=N&-geo_id=16000US2622160&-search_results=16000US260695&-_sse=on&-format=&-_lang=en (accessed February 20, 2006).

————. 2000d. "Sex by Work Status in 1999 by Usual Hours Worked per Week in 1999 by Weeks Worked in 1999 for the Population 16 Years and Over: Dexter Township and Village, Michigan." American FactFinder. factfinder.census.gov/servlet/DTTable?_bm=y&-state=dt&-context=dt&-ds_name=DEC_2000_SF3_U&-mt_name=DEC_2000_SF3_U_P047&-CONTEXT=dt&-tree_id=403&-keyword=dexter%20township&-all_geo_types=N&-geo_id=06000US2616122180&-geo_id=16000US2622160&-search_results=04000US26&-format=&-_lang=en (accessed February 20, 2006).

————. 2000e. "Sex by Work Status in 1999 by Usual Hours Worked per Week in 1999 by Weeks Worked in 1999 for the Population 16 Years and Over: United States." American FactFinder. factfinder.census.gov/servlet/DTTable?_bm=y&-geo_id=D&-ds_name=D&-_lang=en&-mt_name=DEC_2000_SFAIAN_PCT082 (accessed February 20, 2006).

Walzer, Susan. 1998. *Thinking about the Baby: Gender and Transitions into Parenthood.* Philadelphia: Temple University Press.

Warner, Judith. 2005. *Perfect Madness: Motherhood in the Age of Anxiety.* New York: Riverhead Books.

8

Military Families: The Long Journey Home

Sarah Hautzinger and Jean Scandlyn

America's post-9/11 wars, the first protracted conflicts fought with an all-volunteer force, have occasioned unprecedented multiple deployments for U.S. military service members, with some seeing tours of up to five years long in Afghanistan or Iraq. In response to rising levels of psychological injuries and particularly of suicide among soldiers, the U.S. Army invested $125 million in the Comprehensive Soldier Fitness (CSF) program in 2009. According to the CSF website, the program was designed to "help prevent potential problems due to stress by shifting the focus from intervention to prevention, from illness to wellness." Comprehensive fitness is based on five "pillars" of strength: physical, emotional, social, family, and spiritual. As a consequence, the army relegates its historical focus on physical strength to but one facet of overall fitness. Although the army's evaluation of the CSF program in 2011 showed improvement in scores on resilience and psychological health (Lester et al. 2011), critics argued that by focusing on individual soldiers' resilience or strength, the program's approach deflected attention from other sources of distress and suffering: the horrors of war and the added demands of repeated deployments (see, e.g., Eidelson 2011).

Army Families

Perhaps the most important aspect of CSF is its identification of the family as a base for soldier fitness. In part, this reflects a historical shift in the composition of today's army, in which a higher proportion of junior enlisted military personnel are married and have children. Further, in this group there is an extension of the role of spouses and families

From Hautzinger, Sarah, and Jean Scandlyn. 2014. *Beyond Post-Traumatic Stress: Homefront Struggles with the Wars on Terror*, 117–42. © Left Coast Press, Inc. Republished in *Reflecting on America*, 2nd edition, edited by Clare L. Boulanger, 81–95 (© 2016 Taylor & Francis). All rights reserved.

as sources of stability and unremunerated support and care, and an increasingly explicit acknowledgment of the demands that multiple deployments place on family life.

Over time, the army has significantly changed its policies toward marriage and the family, particularly for junior enlisted men and women. From World War II until the army became an all-volunteer force (AVF) in 1973, marriage was the purview of officers. Older officers (at that time almost exclusively heterosexual males) were expected to marry, and their wives' role was to support their spouses' careers through managing the couples' social lives (Goldman 1976). Military policies discouraged marriage among enlisted personnel, requiring that they get approval from their commanding officers to marry.

With the institution of the AVF, military leaders had to compete with civilian employers to attract and retain personnel, and a significant aspect of appealing to potential recruits was supporting a lifestyle that included marriage and family life (Janofsky 1989; Karney and Crown 2007). Thus, one of the biggest changes since the AVF was initiated has been in the number of junior enlisted personnel who are married. In 1953, 38 percent of all active-duty service members were married (Segal 1986: 24). By 2005, 54.6 percent of all military personnel were married, including 51.6 percent of enlisted members (Hogan and Seifert 2010: 425). Today's enlisted personnel in the junior grades (E1–E4) are more likely to be married than their civilian peers ages eighteen to twenty-four. The relative economic stability offered by the military—full-time work for a specified, contracted period of time with benefits—makes marriage possible for many young people, in particular men who are not college-bound, at younger ages than in the civilian workforce. Because the military links housing and medical benefits to marriage, active-duty military personnel are more likely to marry their partners than are civilians (Lemmon, Whyman, and Teachman 2009). This is not only a matter of financial incentives. As a Family Readiness Group (FRG) specialist told us, the military officially recognizes blood relations and legally married spouses, but not partners who live together. Cohabiting partners, even in relationships of many years, cannot receive official notification of their partners' injury or death.

Several factors contribute to the army's large proportion of young families with young children. The bulk of the active-duty army (85 percent) consists of enlisted personnel who are generally twenty-nine years old or younger. Their spouses are also young: in 2004, just over half (53 percent) of army spouses were thirty years old or younger. Just under half (47 percent) of army personnel have children, with an average of two children per parent. The children are young, too: in 2005, half of army children were seven years old or younger. Since the start of the AVF, the American family has also changed, and these changes are reflected in the variety among soldiers' families. In 2007, 7 percent of soldiers were single parents (Booth, Segal, and Bell 2007: 20), and with the repeal of "Don't ask, don't tell" in 2012, the army began to at least acknowledge gay and lesbian couples and include them in family and counseling services, even if federal law at the time prohibited their being legally recognized as married and eligible for spousal benefits. Many soldiers are members of blended families, and it is important to remember that single soldiers have families, too.

All of this means that family members outnumber service members and that significant numbers of civilians are thus directly affected by multiple deployments and the absence of family members for military duty for periods of days to years at a time. Here it is important to consider the army as a social institution. Sociologist Mady Segal (1986) proposes that the army is less a total institution (Goffman 1961) than a "greedy institution." A greedy institution does not control every aspect of its members' lives, but it does ask much of them in terms of loyalty, time, commitment, and energy. Although many civilian occupations make considerable demands on workers and their families, Segal argues, the way these demands combine in military work creates a "unique constellation" of requirements. This pattern includes risk of injury or death, geographic mobility, separations, residence in foreign countries, and normative constraints. By "normative constraints," Segal means that the behavior of spouses and children reflects on their military family members. This kind of social control is most apparent when families live in military housing, where how they maintain their yards and houses is subject to inspection. Additionally, spouses, especially officers' spouses, may feel pressured to participate in military social networks.

The combination of demands on military families and aspects of military culture that separate it from civilian culture—such as the use of acronyms, ritualized behaviors signaling rank and authority, and the emphasis on hierarchy—means that spouses and children undergo rites of passage into their roles as members of military families. As the National Military Family Association states on its website: "Some people have compared military culture to a foreign country without a guidebook." The need to learn military culture was brought home to Zena Bailey, who, although she had been married to a soldier for many years, had not been "military minded" until her husband's first deployment to Iraq in 2003. With him overseas, she realized she needed to know more. She enrolled in the army's family team-building classes "to learn about the military, from the simplest Level One class of learning how to read his LES, which is his pay stub, to learning military acronyms and rank—the basics—to leadership, how to be an FRG leader."

Initiation into military life may also coincide with initiation into marriage, as many couples are recently wed and may have had little time to establish their own patterns of intimacy, communication, and roles prior to deployment. Tracey Hall is an elementary school teacher married to a senior noncommissioned officer (NCO). "Just last week we celebrated our fourth anniversary, and we have been together for twenty months of that. So not even two years." The challenges of establishing a new relationship with a spouse who is absent for long periods are compounded for spouses who are also immigrants and who may not speak English.

Greedy institutions like the military must compete with other institutions, such as hobbies, clubs, service organizations, and religion, for their members' time and energy. The institution in most direct competition for most military personnel is the family.

While competition and conflict between the demands of family and those of work also exist in civilian life, they can be even greater for military families in time of war, and in particular in the post-9/11 wars, in which the military has depended on ground troops on two fronts for more than a decade. Almost every brigade has served multiple deployments, some as long as fifteen months, with extensive mobilization of army national guard and army reserve troops, with a significant increase in the regularity, number, and length of family separations (Booth et al. 2007; Faber et al. 2008; Karney and Crown 2007).

To retain personnel and increase soldier readiness for deployments, the army has devoted considerable resources to supporting families. Health care benefits, signing bonuses, increased pay during deployments, child care, support for disabled children, housing benefits for married couples and couples with children, and a number of programs to assist soldiers and families in preparing for and managing deployments and reintegration may all contribute to military couples staying married despite the separations and challenges. A study by the RAND Corporation that explored the effects of multiple deployments on military marriages found that increased length of deployments actually reduced the risk that a marriage would dissolve; this effect was strongest for young couples who married after 2002. The authors conclude that structural factors outside the marriage, such as those listed here, may outweigh the emotional and other stresses of multiple deployments in terms of whether or not a couple stays together (Karney and Crown 2007). When learning to adjust to deployments coincides with the development of patterns of responsibility, problem-solving skills, intimacy, and communication in a new marriage, the two may reinforce each other. In other words, these newly married couples learn to be military couples. Couples who married in 2002 or later knew that their soldiers would be deployed. They expected that deployment would be difficult but had norms and support to aid them in adjusting to this new situation. Through the army's extensive programs on marriage and family life, preparing for deployments, the work of the FRGs during deployments, and the preparation for reintegration, these young couples, if they chose to participate, had access to a wealth of free resources and support.

While families have always been affected when soldiers go to war, the space–time compression of contemporary life has brought the living room to the battlefield and the battlefield into the living room. Each deployment incorporates a cycle that moves soldiers and their families through different patterns of routines, communication, and interaction. The "deployment cycle" consists of three phases: notification and preparation, separation, and reunion (Karney and Crown 2007: xix). So there are big transitions and little transitions, epic transitions and those that happen every day.

FRGs serve as the primary contexts through which the U.S. Army involves families in deployment and reintegration challenges. Across the years of the post-9/11 wars, army units have grown increasingly dependent on spousal labor for sustaining the tempo of repeated deployments. Yet until 2000, when FRGs were "brought under the chain of command" and made a "Green Suit responsibility" (U.S. Army War College 2009: 38–39), they were nominally civilian, women-controlled, and autonomous spaces. FRGs were made explicitly "command sponsored" to emphasize family readiness as a necessary counterpart to soldier readiness and to impose such structural changes as the mandatory incorporation of junior enlisted wives, previously largely excluded when earlier wives' clubs and coffee groups were run by officers' wives. A 2009 FRG guide titled *The Battlebook IV* stresses that the FRG is "not a democratic group but has to *feel* like one!" (U.S. Army War College 2009: 33).

Thus, the 9/11 wars brought sharply rising expectations and pressures for a counterpart all-volunteer force, but unlike the 86.5 percent of male and 13.5 percent of female soldiers whose work is paid, those who provide the FRGs' spousal volunteer labor remain overwhelmingly female and unpaid. Even with growing numbers of "MANspouses" (as one blogger pointedly calls himself), a 2010 FRG study still concludes, "Expectations for Army husbands differ from those for their female counterparts in that there are simply no expectations of the male spouses" (Gassmann 2010: 87).

In speech and formal publications, the tenacious use of "Army Wives" as a category proudly claims competencies and accomplishments for women. One wife shared her reaction to the prospect of integrating men: "No, this isn't your playground. Go play somewhere else." She speaks for numerous women who resist the complete de-gendering of FRG wife-work into spouse-work because for them, the turf represents hard-won accomplishments. Social reproduction on the home front is work for which wives want credit and some portion of control. As unpaid support work becomes increasingly official and public, the persistence of feminine gender markers is remarkable amid new complexities like the lifting of the bans on women in combat and on openly gay and lesbian soldiers. In communities surrounding Fort Carson, we found domestic, largely women's work increasingly of a piece with the public, home-front labor required for deployment readiness.

IN DEPLOYMENT MODE

It's so much harder when they come home than when they leave. It's so much harder.

—Theresa Thayer

In *The Odyssey*, Odysseus's wife, Penelope, must endure what may be the longest deployment in history. Her husband wages war in Troy for ten years only to take another ten years returning to Ithaca and the embrace of his wife and now adult son. Although Odysseus's journey is the focus of the epic, we do learn of the many challenges Penelope faces during his absence. How do today's army spouses manage the transitions surrounding multiple deployments for their families? Perhaps not surprisingly, several of the spouses who agreed to interviews or that we met in a variety of community settings were coping well, even thriving, and were eager to share their experiences with us. While they acknowledged that deployments are stressful and may have long-term consequences for themselves, their marriages, and their families, they manage, viewing the challenges as a source of growth and strength. Looking at how these families cope well reveals how many different factors must come together positively to make a "successful" adjustment.

Faber et al. (2008: 223), in a study of families in the reserves, use the concept of "ambiguous absence" to describe families' experience during deployments: "Ambiguous absence occurs when a person is perceived by his or her family members as physically absent but psychologically present." Family members may be preoccupied with the absent member's safety or feel uncertain about what kinds of information they should share or what role they should take in the family. The stories that follow show how several spouses managed this ambiguity.

As we walk out of the Canyon Café after talking with JJ Thomas, a military spouse, her words echo in our minds: "We're just fine here—everything's great!" She finishes her statement with thumbs up and a smiling, tilted pose to her head, as if she's taking a snapshot of herself. And indeed, we think later, when she's Skyping with her husband, Derek, in Afghanistan, she would be watching herself have those conversations on a smaller, inset window next to his image. "I'm safe, nobody's shooting at me. I'm not sitting out there in 130-degree weather with no air-conditioning, you know, sand and those big crab things that look like spiders." For JJ, the deployment is not about her, but about her husband. Taking care of things at home, finding fun things for the kids to do, and setting goals for herself is how she supports him in his work. "He would call every so often, and he'd say, 'Great! I hear the kids are fine.' You know, I don't want him worrying about that. Because it's not about me."

Despite her strong self-assurance, JJ acknowledges that handling deployments wasn't always easy. "The first deployment to Iraq was hard. The kids were little, two and five. We had just moved back here. I really didn't know a whole lot of people at first, and it was scary because it was right after 9/11 . . . everybody was just afraid." But his second deployment to Iraq was the most dangerous: "That was when he was in the middle of all kinds of things."

> It was fresh; it was new. But you know, I just had my pity party for a few days and just said, "Ok, I got to move on. I've got these kids. We gotta do this and that." So I got them involved in music and in gymnastics and I keep them really busy. And that's just what I do.

She notes that anybody's first deployment is going to be difficult. "But you've just got to 'Buckle up, buttercup' and move on. You have to be independent, you have to be resourceful, you have to have goals. You have to want to progress and move on and well, be able to handle it."

For Theresa Thayer, the key to handling deployments is to maintain a stable home routine, especially for her two young children. Theresa met her husband when they were both enrolled at the Defense Language Institute in Monterey. They started their family right away. While Theresa admires women with children who remain on active duty, she says, "I know a lot of moms who are active duty, and yay on them, but I saw what it was like when my next-door neighbor had to turn over her six-year-old and deploy." So Theresa left the military and takes care of her children and household full-time. She keeps track of such details as when the car's registration will expire and when the children need checkups, and she insists that her soldier-husband respects this. "Because they're gone for so long, you have to pick up the pieces. You put together a very specific life as to how and when things get done." Like JJ, Theresa attributes her ability to cope to her independence. "I think we were very lucky because we were raised by a family of fiercely independent women. My grandmother raised five children in the military and my grandpa was never around. There's pictures of her flying back from Paris with my two uncles on leashes. It's chaos."

Husbands and wives also develop ways of protecting each other from distressing news or events. Several of the wives labeled this "compartmentalization." Theresa Thayer says that she and her husband are lucky because "neither one of us are people who need large amounts of emoting." When he is deployed and they need to emote, they "have other people that we go and talk to so we don't blur those lines." They have "some very clear lines" about what kinds of information they share. "If it's not important, he doesn't need to know. When my one-year-old broke her leg, I told him that. At the end of the lice adventure [head lice in school], I told him that." But she doesn't tell him about things he cannot fix.

Both JJ and Theresa emphasize the importance of maintaining daily routines. JJ plans fun things for her kids around the holidays that give them something to look forward to. "We have good times for Christmas and New Year's and birthdays, make a big deal of that, but we don't go," she adds, imitating a sobbing voice, "'Ohh, Daddy's not home.' Let's plan some fun things. . . . We got Halloween coming up, we got Thanksgiving coming up. We have Christmas—what are we going to do?"

Despite parents' best efforts, deployment can be a time of marked stress for the children. Young children with deployed parents see pediatricians more frequently for mental and behavioral health issues than do those whose parents are not deployed (Chartrand et al. 2008; Gorman, Eide, and Hisle-Gorman 2010). Older children and girls of all ages have more problems with school, family, and peer relationships (Chandra et al. 2009), and younger children and boys are at higher risk for depressive and behavioral symptoms (Cozza, Chun, and Polo 2005).

Mary Estrada, a mental health consultant with the Community Partnership for Child Development in Colorado Springs, reports that she has observed behavior in preschool-age children with deployed parents that is "very, very explosive and aggressive." Estrada says that children of deployed parents show decreased scores on measures of resilience, and some have been kicked out of preschools for aggressive behavior. A Head Start teacher spoke at a public event about preschoolers' aggression that she thought was depression based; she even worried that her young charges might become suicidal. Noreen Landis-Tyson, who heads the Community Partnership, says that children experience very high levels of stress related to continued cycles of deployment (Lane 2009).

Laurie Wilson is the principal of Milton High School, an alternative high school for at-risk students. About half of her students come from military families. "How do I handle the kiddos who are drawing machine guns and war . . . tell them, 'You can't do that' when that's their life, reality, that's what Dad is doing? That's what is in their house. Camo . . . it's just their culture." She attributes this to military culture rather than to problems with aggression and anger. "I do struggle with that. Because the majority of it comes from a military kiddo, drawing that type of thing. And, just, boys in general. . . . How do you teach them how to handle that appropriately, instead of just . . . cutting it all out?"

Wilson says that adolescents learning new roles in the family when a family member deploys experience high levels of stress. "Whether they're stepping in as Dad or whether they're stepping in as Mom . . . having to get a job, or having to become babysitters to the brothers and sisters. Or they're taking on extra responsibilities at home. And that cuts into their school time, whether it's attending school or doing their [home]work." Students often miss school to spend time with parents who are about to deploy or who are home on midtour leave, or to prepare for their homecoming. Stress often manifests in bad behavior. "Kiddos will snap more often. They'll get in trouble more often. Not serious trouble, necessarily, but you can just tell that that stress level is higher." Wilson says that although some students will use a parent's deployment as an excuse for absences or bad behavior, for the most part they are honest in reporting when a deployment affects their schoolwork. "Definitely, you could tie anxiety to deployments. I think a lot of depression . . . too, and lack of motivation. Just not caring, not doing their schoolwork, not doing their homework." She adds that at times this can be severe. "We've had a couple kiddos in the hospital for really severe depression. Not just with the thoughts, but also plans. There's a big range, but big time is the lack of motivation."

Over the past few years the schools at Fort Carson have increased resources for mental health. One of the post's elementary schools has a counseling office near the front entrance so that parents can drop by when picking up their children and have informal, unscheduled conversations with a mental health professional. Wilson says the marriage and family life counselors (MFLCs, or "Em-Flacs") have been a wonderful source of support for many of her school's families, although the relationships they can form are limited by the temporary nature of their assignments. The school's family advocate, part of the Army Community Service program, is working to decrease the stigma that some families associate with getting help. "Instead of her calling up just when there is something bad going on, she goes and visits every home proactively, so that they already have a relationship with her."

Kathy Edwards, the children's program manager at a Colorado Springs agency that provides services to victims of sexual abuse and assault, reports high levels of child abuse during deployments. "Children can't emotionally regulate, so they're having significant behavior problems, they're having significant academic problems in school, they're having problems with their relationships with peers—they're fighting because they have this overwhelming fear." If the mother is overwhelmed herself, she is not able to "create the safety, stability, security they need." Families often look to the returning spouse to establish stability, but if soldiers are having difficulty regulating their own emotions after returning from deployment, they end up escalating the children's distress and acting out, a setting for child abuse. As JJ so astutely recognized, how well children do during deployments is "strongly determined" by the quality of their relationships with their parents and how well the nondeployed parent is coping. Deployments of nine months or longer, and more frequent deployments, place female spouses at greater risk for depression, anxiety, and sleep disorders (Mansfield et al. 2010; Sherman and Bowling 2011).

As JJ puts it: "You cry, you know, when you have to. And you try not to worry about it because my whole philosophy is you've got little kids, don't be cryin' every single minute of the day and freakin' them out, you know. It's all about how mommy handles it, and how the kids are going to handle it."

REINTEGRATION

If deployment puts soldiers and families in the middle of the labyrinth, then redeployment (return and reintegration) represents their journey out, back to a life in the civilian world of extended family and community. How do they negotiate this journey, and what programs and services are there to assist them?

As the time of the soldier's homecoming nears, anxiety rises with anticipation (Allen et al. 2011). This is the time of greatest risk, and one that the army is increasingly taking seriously. While family members and counselors describe the initial days and weeks following return as the "honeymoon" period, in which family members enjoy seeing each other again and are eager to make the transition smooth and easy, the period thirty to sixty days following return is often fraught with conflict and unease. During deployment, spouses and children have established routines and roles that have a certain efficiency of energy that resists change. Faber et al. (2008) characterize this as the time of "ambiguous presence," when the soldier is perceived as physically present but psychologically absent. As with ambiguous absence, family members also experience ambiguity about their roles, how to communicate, and how to fit the formerly absent member into the routines established while he or she was away.

Karen Levine, an army wife who provides training in parent nurturing at Fort Carson, explains: "We were very well-functioning without him ... became very self-sufficient. Do you want to really welcome that person and embrace them in? ... You know they are going to be leaving again for another nine to twelve months. I think that's hard."

Theresa Thayer's husband is in special forces, which means that in addition to deployments, one of which lasted almost eighteen months, he is often gone for several weeks to a month at a time for training classes. "In February, he was gone for two weeks, came home for three weeks, left for a month, came home for thirty-six hours, and left for another month." So when he came home and wanted to take her and the children out to lunch, she said, "I understand you want to go out to lunch, but nap time starts at 12:30 and there's nothing that I can say or do to change that at this point. We have to be at this house and in this bed at 12:30." She acknowledges his need to reconnect ("I know how much you missed everybody"), though she adds, "but you can't come back and change everything in an afternoon."

Theresa says that her insistence on maintaining the routines that she establishes when her husband is gone when he returns has been a source of frustration for him and conflict between them. "Especially parenting kids. We disagree about that all the time. When he comes back after a year and a half he's like, 'I just want to be involved.' I'm like, 'That's cool. How about we do it this way?' He's like, 'Well, I don't feel included.'" For JJ, midtour breaks, when husbands return for a few days, are the hardest. "Especially that two-week R&R [rest and relaxation] thing in the middle which eventually they're going to get rid of as soon as they go to nine-month deployments, it's going to go away. That is a big problem." Not only does it place major logistics demands on the army, which must manage getting personnel to and from Iraq or Afghanistan, but it also creates problems at home. JJ explains:

> And then all the problems that happen when the soldier comes home in that two weeks. You have a lot of domestic violence issues ... and a lot of marital problems because they come home and nobody knows how to interact with each other.... So a lot of us don't even want them coming back for that two weeks because it's just not enough time to adjust, for them to fit into the family.

One of the biggest difficulties that spouses related was the compression of these phases, particularly in the early years of the wars. In principal, dwell time—the time between deployments—is supposed to be a time for soldiers and families to readjust to being together and recover from the stresses of separation and the intensity of military missions (Doyle and Peterson 2005). But in the early phases of the post-9/11 wars, as the army faced rising insurgency in Iraq, the tempo of deployments increased along with the intensity of conflict. Frequently the reunion phase from one deployment was interrupted by the preparation for the next, so that although soldiers were in the United States, they were still absent for considerable periods of time. Soldiers spoke of "feeling deployment stress, including predeployment arguments," with one sergeant adding, "It's easier to leave if you are arguing." By 2007, the army shortened time at home still further, with some troops spending less than a year at Fort Carson between tours in Iraq. "We're getting mad over here and, yes, it's destroying morale," one soldier wrote from Iraq in an e-mail to the Colorado Springs newspaper the *Gazette* (quoted in Roeder 2013). As Susan Wilson, who teaches classes on traumatic brain injury (TBI) at Fort Carson, told us, this deployment tempo often means that families are never able to make the transition. "And it's a long time to be in a war where you are supposed to have downtime between.... So they're always in that mind-set," stuck long term, as it were, betwixt and between.

But after a deployment, family members must readjust to one another and make that transition. For Theresa, the experiences her husband has during deployments mean that he returns a different person. "I've gotten a new husband three different times. So much change ..." They renegotiate their marriage, and who will do what, each time. She attributes some of this to changing phases in the family, and some to the different experiences they've had while separated. And here the mechanisms that couples develop to handle deployments, such as compartmentalization, may make the process of reestablishing intimacy more difficult:

> If you're interrogating and working in the community trying to find people you have to learn how to completely compartmentalize everything, you can't have emotions. Coming home, you have to turn that off, and sometimes it takes a while. Sometimes it's hard to remember his kids are his kids and you're allowed to have emotion.

Wives who have become more independent while their husbands have been deployed may not be willing to give up the control they have worked hard to achieve, and this can be a source of conflict as husbands return and try to find roles for themselves in the family. Adolescents often worry that their returning parents will not recognize or acknowledge how much they have changed and matured or the new responsibilities they have assumed while the parents were deployed (Chartrand et al. 2008; Huebner and Mancini 2005; Richardson et al. 2011). Theresa adds that financial matters can be another source of stress as families must adjust to losing the $150 to $225 of monthly "combat pay."

While many families negotiate this transition without too many bumps in the road, for others it brings serious and long-lasting problems. Doreen Brennan married John, an NCO in the infantry, and moved to Fort Carson a month prior to her husband's first deployment to Iraq. While preparing to deploy he spent little time with her, preferring to spend time with men from his unit. Though disappointed, she understood this as anxiety over the upcoming deployment. "The last ... month before they leave their behavior might be a little more irrational just because their clock is ticking and they get nervous and scared." In contrast, his deployment was a time of greater intimacy because they communicated more. "When he was gone he would call me almost every day.... I liked that and our relationship actually grew a lot when he was gone because we had to communicate. John always had a problem with communication."

But after John had been home a month, Doreen noticed changes. "He was a different person every day. He didn't want to go out anymore; he wanted to stay at home.... His spending habits went through the roof." She said that he bought a car without telling her, saying that he deserved it. "He had really bad mood swings, and he would throw stuff and kick things, which he never used to do. For instance, the little things, little tiny things would set him off, like Cheerios in the sink." Their physical intimacy was affected as well. "Weird sounds in his ears reminded him of flesh and blood and body I guess. If I got close to his ears he would freak out." He no longer wanted her to touch him. "He never wanted me to do any form of massage, scratch, tickle.... The only thing he wanted was for me to just sit there with my arms around his waist, which was very weird." She stopped looking him in the eye, because he would look down at her and point, treating her like one of his privates. When she reminded him, "I am not one of your soldiers. I am your wife. Do not talk to me like that," he would apologize. "He would say, 'Oh, I'm really sorry.' But it is almost like he didn't know he was doing it." Doreen wanted to help him, to hear about his experiences in Iraq, but while he would show pictures from his deployment to his grandparents, he wouldn't share them with her. He began drinking heavily, got a DUI, and abandoned her at a downtown bar at two o'clock in the morning. "He just got drunk and went home and left me there."

John got treatment for post-traumatic stress disorder (PTSD) and TBI at Fort Carson and from a civilian therapist off-post. But nothing seemed to help. Doreen acknowledges that some of John's behaviors presented before he joined the army, but "Iraq really, really heightened his negative aspects, made him so bad." Raised as a devout Baptist, John is tortured by the memory of shooting an Iraqi civilian who would not stop at a checkpoint. "He is tortured. Every single day he lives through the torture, and I think a part of him wants to try and be normal, but he can't." Feeling increasingly isolated and abandoned, and without her family to help keep John's behavior toward her in control, Doreen filed for divorce and moved to be near her family.

Sarah Jones, a counselor at an agency that assists victims of domestic violence, noticed a distinctive pattern in domestic violence following deployments. "I was able to pull queries from this access database and find that the numbers were doubling" for domestic violence cases "in the units that had returned from Operation Iraqi Freedom, ninety days out. So in other words, when they returned, rates were pretty average, maybe even a little lower for the first thirty [days], normal at sixty, and doubled at ninety." She explains that symptoms of combat-related PTSD and depression may not appear immediately following return from a combat zone. "It takes two or three months before the depression sets in."

She adds that many of these cases are different from those she and her colleagues usually see. "We see people who are arrested for domestic violence that we wouldn't consider a crime of power and control. So there are instances, for example, when a soldier has a flashback in the middle of the night and strangles his wife." But she cautions that in many of these cases, combat-related stress and the means soldiers use to self-medicate—alcohol and drug abuse—amplify relationship dynamics that existed prior to deployment (Bell et al. 2004). "The general excuse was it's PTSD. Then I talk to the wife and find out, he had done this before deployment, he had done this before he was in the army, but now it's being excused as PTSD." While PTSD can escalate domestic violence, the two are separate issues that both demand treatment. "So you have to treat both of them. But you don't ignore one and treat the other and think that one is causal of the other; it's just not effective. We're not doing our service members any good by pretending that there aren't two issues when they're doing both."

Not only does PTSD contribute to domestic violence, but it is also associated with significant psychological distress in spouses, often referred to as secondary traumatic stress or secondary traumatic stress disorder (STS/STSD) (Renshaw et al. 2011). Children of veterans with PTSD may exhibit many of the same symptoms as their affected parents as a way to identify and connect with them, act as rescuers by assuming some of the parents' responsibilities, or withdraw emotionally (Price 2009). Many soldiers and veterans who experience PTSD and depression self-medicate with alcohol or drugs (Brady, Back, and Coffey 2004). The combination of combat-related mental health issues, alcohol and drug use, and violence often lands soldiers in jail, with felonies, debt, and other consequences that can contribute to long-term economic and social problems.

The army has responded to the potential dangers of reintegration with post-deployment sessions, known at Fort Carson as Reintegration University. The program is mandatory for all returning soldiers and includes classes for couples, singles, and couples getting divorced, as well as classes on drug and alcohol issues, financial matters, sexual assault, domestic violence, and child abuse. Spouses are invited and encouraged, but not required, to attend. The army has combined this approach with increased screening for PTSD, TBI, and depression at multiple points after deployment in the hope of detecting issues earlier and getting soldiers into treatment.

We attended an FRG pre-reintegration training session for spouses on the topics of domestic violence and communication with children, led by a counselor from Army Community Service. He talked about patterns in relationships that are healthy and those likely to lead to conflict and domestic violence during reintegration. The training was intended to help spouses recognize these patterns, so that they would be able to understand the dynamics of the situation and be more likely to find alternative ways to resolve or diffuse conflict before it could escalate to violence.

APPROACHING THE LIMITS OF HUMAN FLEXIBILITY

Although humans can adapt to a wide range of social settings and communicate across differences in language and culture, in settings as radically different as war and civilian peace we may be bumping up against serious limitations to our flexibility. JJ, Theresa, and many other wives of deployed soldiers are functioning well, by and large. Theirs are the success stories, and they might be quick to point out that despite the "problem wives" who "can't handle deployments," most spouses do handle them. Many even thrive, developing skills and a newfound independence and strength. Karen Davis is an army wife married to a senior NCO for many years. We asked her what advice she might give to her daughter. "Just be prepared for some tough times, mentally and physical, 'cause it's going to be exhausting. But the rewards . . . You'll know how strong you are, that you can do it."

Kay Ogden, who leads training sessions on reintegration through Army Community Service, says that "there are a lot more families that are strong and figuring it out than aren't. But I think it impacts everybody." Nor does reintegration necessarily get easier over time, with more deployments. Zora Bates, who has found a fulfilling career serving military families, nonetheless confesses, "The military families are just fractured. They are truly fractured. I personally, with three deployments, I didn't think we would make it. It's a challenge. . . . It's across the board; with multiple back-to-back deployments it has broken the family."

Although deployments may strengthen good marriages, they may hasten the dissolution of troubled ones. Even in the time of relative peace prior to the post-9/11 wars, military personnel had higher rates of divorce than civilians (Lundquist 2007). Active-duty infantry soldiers we interviewed spoke repeatedly about marriages falling apart. For Don Haskins, it's a matter of families being able to sustain themselves while soldiers fully readjust:

> And I think they give up too fast, because they might think the help's [therapy] not working or whatever. It takes time. It takes a long time. I hear the shrink say it takes six months to a year and by that time you're deploying again. So by the time you're just getting over it, you're starting another one. You got to really have a patient family.

Kelsoe Fitzgerald is single and wishes that his parents had access to programs to prepare them for the changes they see in him following his deployments. "Every time I come home they expect me to be like I was before I even left for the army. I keep telling them, 'Hey, I'm not that person anymore. I'm different.'"

Then there are the soldiers who never fully come home. Beryl Makris was leaving the next day for a family trip to the Caribbean with her injured veteran husband and daughter. "This trip is about making family memories for our [fourteen-year-old] daughter," she said. "Especially memories with her dad." She took a breath and went on, her voice steady: "He's been declared terminal. He's deteriorated to the point where there's no hope of recovery. They're giving him a year, maybe." She shared details of their arrangements, adding, "We're not going to be able to go to Australia like we'd always planned; his health and our finances make it impossible. So three days in the U.S. Virgin Islands will have to do."

After Beryl's husband, Charles, returned from Iraq in 2006 with a debilitating TBI following exposure to multiple bomb and weapon blasts, his functioning steadily worsened. When we next saw her a few months later, his behavior was "out of control," and to protect herself and daughter, Beryl had committed him to institutional care.

Charles will never recover from multiple head injuries to exit the labyrinth and be home. Beryl and her daughter will recover, but their journey has already been arduous, filled with unanticipated twists and turns, and they will likely face more detours in the coming years. Thousands more will live out their lives with chronic pain, illness, and disabilities resulting from their war experiences. Others will choose to end their distress with suicide. For such soldiers and those closest to them, neither comprehensive fitness nor compartmentalization may suffice to help them weather the back-and-forth of war and home without devastating, permanent costs.

EXERCISE

Hold a class roundtable on life in the military and in military families, using this chapter as a guide for discussion. If no one in the class has had military experience or experience in/with a military family, invite guests who have.

REFERENCES

Allen, Elizabeth S., Galena K. Rhoades, Scott M. Stanley, and Howard J. Markman. 2011. "On the Home Front: Stress for Recently Deployed Army Couples." *Family Process* 50: 235–47.

Bell, Nicole S., Thomas Harford, James E. McCarroll, and Laura Senier. 2004. "Drinking and Spouse Abuse among U.S. Army Soldiers." *Alcoholism: Clinical and Experimental Research* 28 (12): 1890–97.

Booth, Bradford, Mady Wechsler Segal, and D. Bruce Bell. 2007. *What We Know about Army Families: 2007 Update*. Washington, DC: Caliber and U.S. Army.

Brady, Kathleen T., Sudie E. Back, and Scott F. Coffey. 2004. "Substance Abuse and Posttraumatic Stress Disorder." *Current Directions in Psychological Science* 13 (5): 206–9.

Chandra, Anita, Sandraluz Lara-Cinisomo, Lisa H. Jaycox, Terri Tanielian, Rachel M. Burns, Teague Ruder, and Bing Han. 2009. "Children on the Homefront: The Experience of Children from Military Families." *Pediatrics* 125: 16–25.

Chartrand, Molinda M., Deborah A. Frank, Laura F. White, and Timothy R. Shope. 2008. "Effect of Parents' Wartime Deployment on the Behavior of Young Children in Military Families." *Archives of Pediatrics & Adolescent Medicine* 162 (11): 1009–14.

Cozza, Stephen J., Ryo S. Chun, and James A. Polo. 2005. "Military Families and Children during Operation Iraqi Freedom." *Psychiatric Quarterly* 76 (4): 371–78.

Doyle, Michael E., and Kris A. Peterson. 2005. "Re-entry and Reintegration: Returning Home after Combat." *Psychiatric Quarterly* 76 (4): 361–70.

Eidelson, Roy. 2011. "The Dark Side of 'Comprehensive Soldier Fitness.'" *Psychology Today*, March 25. www.psychologytoday.com/blog/dangerous-ideas/201103/the-dark-side-of-comprehensive-soldier-fitness (accessed August 30, 2012).

Faber, Anthony J., Elaine Willerton, Shelley R. Clymer, Shelley M. MacDermid, and Howard M. Weiss. 2008. "Ambiguous Absence, Ambiguous Presence: A Qualitative Study of Military Reserve Families in Wartime." *Journal of Family Psychology* 22 (2): 222–30.

Gassmann, Jaime Nicole Noble. 2010. "Patrolling the Homefront: The Emotional Labor of Army Wives Volunteering in Family Readiness Groups." PhD dissertation, Department of American Studies, University of Kansas, Lawrence.

Goffman, Erving. 1961. *Asylums: Essays on the Social Situation of Mental Patients and Other Inmates*. New York: Anchor Books.

Goldman, Nancy L. 1976. "Trends in Family Patterns of U.S. Military Personnel during the 20th Century." In Nancy L. Goldman and David R. Segal, eds., *The Social Psychology of Military Service*, 119–34. Beverly Hills, CA: Sage.

Gorman, Gregory H., Matilda Eide, and Elizabeth Hisle-Gorman. 2010. "Wartime Military Deployment and Increased Pediatric Mental and Behavioral Health Complaints." *Pediatrics* 126 (6): 1058–66.

Hogan, Paul F., and Rita Furst Seifert. 2010. "Marriage and the Military: Evidence That Those Who Serve Marry Earlier and Divorce Earlier." *Armed Forces & Society* 36 (3): 420–38.

Huebner, Angela J., and Jay A. Mancini. 2005. "Adjustments among Adolescents in Military Families When a Parent Is Deployed." In *Final Report to the Military Family Research Institute and Department of Defense: Quality of Life Office*. Falls Church: Department of Human Development, Virginia Tech.

Janofsky, Barbara J. 1989. "The Dual-Career Couple: Challenges and Satisfactions." In Gary L. Bowen and Dennis K. Orthner, eds., *The Organization Family: Work and Family Linkages in the U.S. Military*, 97–115. New York: Praeger.

Karney, Benjamin R., and John S. Crown. 2007. *Families under Stress: An Assessment of Data, Theory, and Research on Marriage and Divorce in the Military*. Santa Monica, CA: RAND Corporation.

Lane, Anthony. 2009. "Little Kids, Big Problems." *Colorado Springs Independent*, February 12. www.csindy.com/coloradosprings/little-kids-big-problems/Content?oid=1327878 (accessed August 30, 2013).

Lemmon, Megan, Mira Whyman, and Jay Teachman. 2009. "Active-Duty Military Service in the United States: Cohabiting Unions and the Transition to Marriage." *Demographic Research* 20 (10): 195–208.

Lester, Paul B., P. D. Harms, Mitchel N. Herian, and Dina V. Krasikova. 2011. "The Comprehensive Soldier Fitness Program Evaluation, Report #3: Longitudinal Analysis of the Impact of Master Resilience Training on Self-Reported Resilience and Psychological Health Data." www.ppc.sas.upenn.edu/csftechreport3mrt.pdf (accessed August 30, 2013).

Lundquist, Jennifer Hickes. 2007. "A Comparison of Civilian and Enlisted Divorce Rates during the Early All Volunteer Force Era." *Journal of Political and Military Sociology* 35 (2): 199–217.

Mansfield, Alyssa J., Jay S. Kaufman, Stephen W. Marshall, Bradley N. Gaynes, Joseph P. Morrissey, and Charles C. Engel. 2010. "Deployment and the Use of Mental Health Services among U.S. Army Wives." *New England Journal of Medicine* 362 (2): 101–9.

Price, Jennifer L. 2009. "When a Child's Parent Has PTSD." National Center for PTSD, U.S. Department of Veteran Affairs. www.ptsd.va.gov/professional/treatment/children/pro_child_parent_ptsd.asp (accessed August 30, 2013).

Renshaw, Keith D., Galena K. Rhoades, Elizabeth S. Allen, and Rebecca K. Blais. 2011. "Distress in Spouses of Service Members with Symptoms of Combat-Related PTSD: Secondary Traumatic Stress or General Psychological Distress?" *Journal of Family Psychology* 25 (4): 461–69.

Richardson, Amy, Anita Chandra, Laurie T. Martin, Claude Messan Setodji, Bryan W. Hallmark, Nancy F. Campbell, Stacy Ann Hawkins, and Patrick Grady. 2011. *Effects of Soldiers' Deployment on Children's Academic Performance and Behavioral Health.* Santa Monica, CA: RAND Corporation.

Roeder, Tom. 2013. "Iraq: Ten Years Later." *Gazette,* March 15. gazette.com/article/152318 (accessed August 30, 2013).

Segal, Mady Wechsler. 1986. "The Military and the Family as Greedy Institutions." *Armed Forces & Society* 13 (1): 9–38.

Sherman, Michelle, and Ursula Bowling. 2011. "Challenges and Opportunities for Intervening with Couples in the Aftermath of the Global War on Terrorism." *Journal of Contemporary Psychotherapy* 41 (4): 209–17.

U.S. Army War College. 2009. *The Battlebook IV: A Guide for Spouses in Leadership Roles.* Carlisle Barracks, PA: U.S. Army War College. www.carlisle.army.mil/usawc/mfp/battlebook/default.cfm (accessed August 30, 2013).

9

EVERY TIME WE TYPE GOODBYE: HEARTBREAK AMERICAN-STYLE

Ilana Gershon

In the fall of 2008, Lynn sat in my office at Indiana University and told me a story about how a long-term relationship of hers began to unravel. I had been searching for volunteers for a study on how people were using new media to end romantic relationships, and Lynn, like all the others, had agreed to be interviewed in a face-to-face conversation. She told me about the consequences of sharing passwords. "I was abroad last semester, and he snooped onto my e-mail account and claimed that he was deleting an e-mail that he had sent me, but he had seen an e-mail that I had received from another mutual friend of ours, and he decided to take it upon himself to read it and, um, then he told my two best friends here at school that he had read this e-mail and they of course came and told me. And then I confronted him on it. And then he said, 'Yeah, I did look at it.' And I was like, okay, you shouldn't have. It is one thing to know my password, but it is another thing to be looking through my e-mail."

There are parts of Lynn's story that I have grown to think of as part of how American undergraduates tell breakup stories. The story was a string of conversations, in which each medium that people used to communicate was marked. Lynn, the wronged party, has to figure out what was happening in the first place, and then she has to decide to confront her boyfriend. But when she ascribes motivation to him, as she does in the following quote, she attributes a level of innocence to his practice. He violates her expectations that her communication will be private, but does so by accident:

ILANA: How did he get to see this e-mail?

LYNN: Right, well, she wrote back to me and wrote a response to this e-mail. This is when he logged on to my e-mail account, claimed he was deleting an e-mail he sent me,

Reprinted with permission, from Gershon, Ilana. 2013. *Anthropology Now* 5 (1): 93–101. © Taylor & Francis Ltd. Republished in *Reflecting on America*, 2nd edition, edited by Clare L. Boulanger, 97–104 (© 2016 Taylor & Francis).

saw that my best friend, who is also a good friend of his, but through me, saw that my best friend had written me an e-mail, assumed it was about Little 500 [an annual bicycle race at Indiana University] activities, because it was during when Little 500 was going on here, so he decided to read this e-mail.

There is quite a bit to analyze in this story, including Lynn's belief that sharing passwords is not the same as granting her boyfriend unconditional access to all her conversations with others through Facebook and e-mail (at different points in their relationship, they shared with each other their passwords to both accounts). In my book *The Breakup 2.0* (2010), I discuss how sharing passwords can be a marker of intimacy as people respond to the ways communicative technologies are shifting what counts as public or private conversation. Here I'm interested in how this story is similar to the other breakup stories that U.S. undergraduates told me and, in particular, why I have begun thinking of the elements I mentioned as culturally specific ways that people are using and thinking about new media when they break up.

Media, both old and new, are part and parcel of how the people I interviewed are performing the complicated daily tasks of living among other people. They are, as Mark Deuze (2012) puts it, living in media, not with media. These breakup narratives become glimpses into specifically American ways that people understand their own and others' uses of media.

THE "HOW" OF A BREAKUP

I was inspired to interview people about their mediated breakups because of an improvised class exercise I regularly use to reveal common cultural assumptions. I teach an introductory linguistic anthropology course every year. On the second day of class, I ask students to write down individually all the rules for a first date. The students don't know each other that well, and yet the U.S. undergraduates invariably come up with remarkably similar answers. This allows me to point out that the American students in the class, so far always the vast majority, have shared tacit expectations about this ritual. After five or six years of teaching this course, I looked down at my notes and couldn't bring myself to ask the question yet again. I had heard the answer "the guy pays" one too many times. On the spot, I decided to ask them to write down, on their own and without talking to anyone else, what they thought constituted a bad breakup. I was expecting stories about infidelity; DVDs that were never returned; or loud, dramatic arguments. I did not expect what actually happened—everyone answered "breaking up by e-mail" or "breaking up by text." The consensus was that a bad breakup was a mediated breakup. I became curious why the medium used was so important, but it wasn't until after I had collected many breakup stories that I realized my students had told me something quite revealing that would come up time and time again when I interviewed their peers—American undergraduates focus on the "how" when describing their breakups, not the "why" or the "who."

After this classroom moment, I decided to research mediated breakups further. I conducted seventy-two interviews at Indiana University during 2007 and 2008 with anyone who would volunteer to be interviewed. I primarily interviewed undergraduates, although six people I interviewed had advanced degrees and were over twenty-five years old. I spoke to fifty-four women and eighteen men about how they used new media when dissolving romantic relationships and friendships. These people were self-selected. They volunteered to be interviewed in response to requests I made by word of mouth and in large lecture classes. I also found people to interview by sending e-mail to campus-based student organizations and, via departmental lists, to students in popular majors. All but two of the people I interviewed were raised in the United States. The majority of students I interviewed were upper-working-class to middle-class and white. I interviewed six Asian American students, seven African American students, and one Latino student. Indiana University is a sizable midwestern state university with about 30,000 students enrolled on the Bloomington campus from 2007 to 2009. In academic year 2008–9, 1,749 of these 30,000 students were minorities (7.2 percent). At a state university, there is a difference in tuition (and thus potentially class background) between in-state and out-of-state students. This was reflected in my interview sample—the out-of-state students were from more middle-class backgrounds than some of my in-state interviewees. During academic years 2007–8 and 2008–9, 56 percent of the university's students had in-state residency (Indiana University 2007–8, 2008–9).

When U.S. undergraduates told me their breakup stories, these were well-rehearsed stories about all the different media they were using to end a relationship, not only stories about one conversation that they might label "The Breakup Conversation." They had told the tales to friends and family and had gotten feedback that was sometimes interwoven into the stories as well. For example, Halle explained to me what her mother thought in the middle of a story about an ex-boyfriend who ended the relationship in a series of text messages:

> I called my mom, and told her about it.
>
> She said, "This is all a big joke, this isn't serious."
>
> I told her, "No, this really happened."
>
> She goes, "What a schmuck!"

I want to point out two aspects of this snippet of a breakup story. First, Halle, like the others I interviewed, mentioned the medium used for every conversation (she called her mother on the phone). Second, her narrative chronicled the array of conversations she had with her lover/ex-lover and with others in the course of the relationship's dissolution. In short, these stories were primarily collections of conversations in which the medium used for the conversation mattered enough to be almost always mentioned.

People would invariably mark when a different medium was used, explaining when communication shifted from voicemail to texting to Facebook and then to phone. At first, when I noticed that they were doing this, I thought that they were simply being generous interviewees. After all, we were conducting an interview because I had asked people to tell me about how they were using new media in their breakups. As I looked at more and more examples of widely circulated breakup accounts on websites as well as in books, television shows, and movies, I realized that marking the medium is a standard element of how many other Americans tell breakup stories. This is just one of the ways that people in the

United States call attention to the "how" of a breakup when they tell their stories about the disintegration of a romantic relationship.

A story about a breakup does not have to be a story about how the breakup happened. This is a cultural choice. I think one can analyze this as a narrative pattern that American undergraduates use, in part because I have read other ethnographers' research on divorce in Britain and Japan, where the divorce narratives have a substantively different focus.

When Bob Simpson did his anthropological research in England in the late 1980s and early 1990s, the people he interviewed did not tend to talk about the ways the relationships ended. Instead, their stories tended to be justifications— why the person might still be a good person despite being willing to end a relationship. Character was the focus, not method. Simpson (1998) notes how often the people he interviewed were concerned with justifying their decisions, with continuing to be seen as decent human beings in the eyes of their families and communities and in their own self-assessment. Admittedly, he was interviewing people who were at a different stage of life from those I have been interviewing—these were people who had children and entangled families they were rearranging. But I believe that there is still something culturally specific about his interviewees' focus on personal character. Even accounts of U.S. divorces from research done only a few years earlier than Simpson's interviews, such as Diane Vaughan's *Uncoupling* (1986), often stress the "how" instead of the "who." This seems to indicate that people in Britain and the United States might use different narrative structures to explain the same phenomena.

Japanese couples, by contrast, often discuss their efforts to figure out the right mix of dependence and independence when going through breakups or divorces, as Allison Alexy found in her anthropological research. Until relatively recently, a good marriage in Japan was characterized, as Alexy (2011: 900) puts it, as "un- or under-stated affection, highly gendered familial roles, separate hobbies and social spheres, and a relationship as partners rather than friends." While this kind of marriage is increasingly becoming less appealing to Japanese couples—not all that surprisingly, many people in Japan do not want their parents' marriages—relationships that privilege intertwined dependence are still highly valued. Partners want some independence, but not too much. Japanese stories about breakups and divorces thus often revolve around people's struggles to find the right kind of dependence, the one that is most comfortable and emotionally satisfying for them. Women explained to Alexy that their husbands or boyfriends had grown too dependent and kept demanding services and care from the women instead of working toward companionate relationships. But too much independence in a relationship was also a problem. One of Alexy's Japanese interviewees, after describing her divorce and relating that she chose to find her true self and to be more independent, asked Alexy if she knew any available men. The woman had divorced her abusive husband a decade before. This request surprised Alexy.

> She [the interviewee] had been alone for long enough, [now she] was looking for someone with whom to share a partnership. Using a metaphor of a bicycle built for two riders, and invoking classic images from ideals of companionate love, she described wanting a man with whom she could share daily struggles and "pedal together." She didn't mind if this hypothetical man leaned on her because she planned

to lean on him, and that is what love is about. For these women, dependence is a key ingredient of romantic love. (913)

Japanese divorce narratives are often all about finding a middle ground between acceptable and unacceptable dependence.

The American undergraduates I interviewed were not discussing their breakups in terms of the right balance of dependence, or even the kinds of people who might break up. The interviewee who came closest to describing herself as a particular type of person was a woman who decided not to show anyone else the breakup text message her ex had sent her. She explained that she didn't want to be known as "the girl who was dumped by text message." Even this example shows that U.S. undergraduates use the "how" of the breakup as the narrative frame to explore what the end of a relationship might mean for them.

They also focus on the "how" in the context of other cultural assumptions about the ways conflicts begin and then unfold. Jane Collier outlines some of these cultural assumptions in her 1989 article "Whodunits and Whydunits," in which she compares Zinacanteco (indigenous Mexican) narratives of conflict with narratives from the United States. Collier collected conflict narratives from her undergraduates at Stanford, who were asked to write conflict journals for a term. Collier found that most of the narratives revolved around perceived victims, their emotions and their interpretations, not around perceived wrongdoers and their motivations. That is to say, the information about the wrongdoer tended to be relatively brief, and the reasons given for this misbehavior tended to focus on two kinds of explanations—the person acted either out of ignorance or out of selfishness. Collier (1989: 140) writes: "Because the American students equated selfishness with thoughtlessness, they did not posit deliberate malice on the part of those who harmed them. Wrongdoers were merely thoughtless. They had not put themselves in others' shoes to think about how they would feel if they were the recipients of their own acts." It is easy to imagine Americans telling long, complicated stories about long-standing familial antagonisms generating embittered individuals who spend years planning revenge—television shows like *Dallas* and *The Sopranos* are filled with such plotlines. But this element did not appear in the conflict stories of Collier's American undergraduates.

Because the offenders in these undergraduate narratives were being selfish or didn't know better, they were not seen as the ones provoking open attempts to address the conflicts. The victims were the ones who instigated the conflicts, in a sense, by revealing that what the other persons did affected them. Collier found that most of the students' conflict narratives were devoted to explaining the victims' carefully reasoned decisions either to make it clear that wrongdoing had happened or, perhaps more frequently, to avoid conflict entirely. The victims tended to avoid conflict to protect valued relationships or because they decided they cared too little about the relationships to go to the trouble of making the conflicts visible.

When a confrontation happened, it tended to take the form of the victim informing the offender indirectly or directly that his or her actions had inspired negative feelings. No third parties were asked to mediate the conflict or help the two reach a resolution. If the injured party did decide to confront the offender, he or she might do so indirectly—for example, by announcing at a house meeting that "some people are leaving dirty dishes in the sink." Or a victim might initiate a direct confrontation, explaining to the wrongdoer what he or she had done that was hurtful and how it had made the victim feel. The confrontations rarely involved trying to establish the facts of what had happened or allocating blame. Instead, they quickly became about creating "shared understandings about goals for the future" (Collier 1989: 152–53).

The events in the breakups of my interviewees didn't always fit neatly into the types of conflicts that Collier describes. In her article, Collier doesn't mention romantic breakups. Instead, she relates stories of conflicts involving a mother who asks her son in front of his roommates if he remembers to change his underwear and a male professor who makes sexist jokes all the time. In both instances, the narrators thought the authority figures were being thoughtless—they would not have acted as they did if they had realized what impact their actions would have on their audience. Wrongdoers were represented as unaware that they had created conflict. In contrast, when you are breaking up with someone, you tend to think of this as a moment of conflict. Who exactly is the aggrieved one can be up for grabs, and in some sense, this is precisely what focusing on the "how" of the breakup can draw attention to. So I am suggesting that when breakup stories focus on the "how" of the breakup, this narrative structure brings the dilemmas that a breakup might raise more closely in line with the other cultural script for addressing conflict outlined by Collier.

The American undergraduate conflict narratives Collier describes and the breakup narratives I collected have in common a particular technique for addressing the audience. In both sets of stories, the storyteller is expecting the listener to validate the storyteller's tacit understanding of how responsibility should be allocated and how what took place should be defined (see also O'Barr and Conley 1997). As Collier (1989: 154) explains: "Student narrators assumed the role of detective. They gave careful accounts of the clues they uncovered, providing a reader/listener with the evidence he/she would need to assess responsibility and allocate blame." When undergraduates told me their breakup stories, the medium was crucial evidence that I, as audience, was expected to interpret as a sign that these were indeed bad breakups. However, in the stories that I collected, assessing blame was only part of the point of the narrative. Breakup conversations turned out to be quite confusing in practice—people might think that they have had breakup conversations but still find themselves in the same relationships the next week or the next month. Framing the breakup as a detective story led the storyteller and listener(s) to agree on whether a breakup had taken place and how bad it was in terms of the method used.

Calling attention to the ways that their breakups took place allows people to talk about the other familiar motivations that U.S. undergraduates seem to like to attribute to others in moments of conflict. One of the most common descriptions I have heard applied to breaking up using a medium, any medium, is how cowardly it is. And in this instance, cowardice is a form of selfishness, seeing one's own comfort and emotional security as more important than anyone else's. When a story focuses on how someone used texting or Skype to end a relationship, the storyteller is often reframing the ending of the relationship into a conflict with a clearer victim. The fact that someone wants to end a relationship does not make the dumped individual into a victim. It is the way the breakup is done that makes someone into the aggrieved party. My interviewees, just like Collier's American students, spent a considerable amount of time talking about their rationales, how they understood what was happening, and why they responded in the ways that they did.

CONCLUSION

One day I was showing a short video clip in an undergraduate class when I noticed Rebecca starting to get teary-eyed. Dave Chappelle can inspire some strong reactions, but he never seems to drive people to tears, so I asked her discreetly what was going on. Rebecca told me that her boyfriend had just broken up with her by text. I advised her to go home and recover, which she did. A year or two later, when I started doing this research, I contacted her to find out what had actually happened that day. She explained that they had been dating for four and a half years, but the relationship had become rocky. They would break up, get back together, and then break up again. It had become a cycle until he texted her to say that it was no longer working out (a message she received while walking to my class) and then refused to talk to her through any other medium. He would interact with her only by text. As she told me the story, she kept stressing that she wanted to talk to him by phone about what was happening. He refused, claiming she wouldn't be able to change his mind. This too offended her greatly. As she pointed out, she simply wanted to talk on the phone in order to have what she considered a proper ending to the relationship. She did not want to change his mind. She said that whenever she told the story to her friends, she focused on how her ex-boyfriend had ended the relationship—by texting her and refusing to speak to her using any other medium *but* text for months afterward.

As in most of the narratives I collected, the "how" of the breakup was the central focus of Rebecca's story. And this "how" stood in for another question that haunted Rebecca as well—namely, why her ex-boyfriend decided to break off the relationship. Rebecca and others did not focus on the "why" or the "who" of their breakups, although these elements would of course come up in the narratives as secondary themes. By focusing on the "how," Rebecca was able to avoid these often unanswerable questions. She was also able to structure the story of the breakup so that it resembled some other typically American ways to discuss conflict. She, like others, was able to present herself as aggrieved because of someone else's selfishness, cowardice, or thoughtlessness. Focusing on the messy "why" of a breakup might not lead to such a clear-cut division between victim and aggressor and risks raising the distressing possibility that the person who broke off the relationship had a very good reason to do so. It might spark a different set of judgments about the persons involved in the relationship, giving the lie to the clichéd American breakup line, "It's not you, it's me." Rebecca managed to deflect those questions by emphasizing how poorly her ex-boyfriend behaved in the manner he chose to end the relationship. She could also recruit the support of her friends and family in presenting herself as aggrieved in the process of the breakup because the method was so inappropriate.

What I also found striking about Rebecca's account and other similar stories was the way in which the medium helped clarify that a breakup had in fact happened. Both undergraduates and older adults told me about breakups that "didn't take," relationships filled with cycles of fighting, ending, and then getting back together. This pattern could turn the end of a relationship into something of a mystery, and the stories told became detective stories of a sort. In telling a breakup story, a person was piecing together a series of ambiguous and unclear conversations to create an overarching narrative that revealed a breakup had happened. And for Americans, often the medium becomes a key piece of this narrative.

QUESTIONS FOR DISCUSSION

Is it appropriate to break up with someone by text or on social media? Why or why not?

REFERENCES

Alexy, Allison. 2011. "Intimate Dependence and Its Risks in Neoliberal Japan." *Anthropology Quarterly* 84 (4): 897–920.

Collier, Jane. 1989. "Whodunits and Whydunits: Contrasts between American and Zapotec Stories of Conflict." In Victoria Bricker and Gary Gossen, eds., *Ethnographic Encounters in Southern Mesoamerica: Essays in Honor of Evon Zartman Vogt, Jr.,* 142–58. Albany: Institute of Mesoamerican Studies, State University of New York.

Deuze, Mark. 2012. *Media Life.* London: Polity Press.

Gershon, Ilana. 2010. *The Breakup 2.0: Disconnecting over New Media.* Ithaca, NY: Cornell University Press.

Indiana University. 2007–8. *Indiana University Factbook.* Bloomington: Indiana University Reporting and Research.

———. 2008–9. *Indiana University Factbook.* Bloomington: Indiana University Reporting and Research.

O'Barr, William, and John Conley. 1997. *Just Words: Law, Language, and Power.* Chicago: University of Chicago Press.

Simpson, Bob. 1998. *Changing Families: An Ethnographic Approach to Divorce and Separation.* Oxford: Berg.

Vaughan, Diane. 1986. *Uncoupling: Turning Points in Intimate Relationships.* New York: Oxford University Press.

10

Striptease, Leisure, and Labor in the Midwestern United States

Beth Hartman

> Everybody, including my people, my family, thought I was making a whole lot of money.... [I earned] a hundred and a quarter [per week]. Three shows a night. Six or seven nights. You got yourself there. No one paid your fare from one town to the other. You paid your own hotel ... and all your food and everything.... When I think about it now, I wonder how I [managed], because a hundred and a quarter was never a lot of money ... [and] because of my color, I couldn't get a job just anywhere.
>
> —interview with Toni Elling

I first met Toni Elling at Diversitease, a three-day neo-burlesque festival held at the Minneapolis Ritz Theater in February 2014. Performers from around the country came into town to participate in the festivities, which included shows every evening and workshops during the day. In addition to nationally known headliners like Sydni Deveraux and the World Famous *BOB*, both from New York, the festival's producers invited Toni to serve as the guest of honor, a feature performer, and a lecturer, covering her lodging and travel expenses to and from Detroit as well as paying her an honorarium for her time and expertise.[1]

In the 7:00 P.M. Friday-evening showcase, the eighty-five-year-old former striptease artist took to the stage amid thunderous applause, parading and posing to Duke Ellington's "Satin Doll" while two stagehands helped her keep her balance (Toni later told me she had been experiencing difficulties with her vision and hips, making stage appearances an increasingly precarious endeavor).[2] The following afternoon, she gave a public lecture in which she recounted her days as a burlesque performer and discussed the challenges, and often overt racism, she faced as an African American woman working in the strip-show business. Since her real name is Rosita, her agent had encouraged her to market herself as "Spanish" so that she would get better-paying gigs—something she refused to do, although she suffered for the decision financially. She described how surprised and confused she was when white performers at a club in Portland, Oregon, asked to see her "tail," and she was treated with suspicion by white male venue owners who questioned her work ethic and capabilities. Toni felt she had to put more creative energy into her acts than white performers, many of whom could get by with doing "straight strips" and utilizing fewer gimmicks. As a result, she did themed acts, ranging from an African-inspired number to an Orientalist act in which she lip-synched to a Japanese song while dressed as a geisha. Finally, although she performed internationally (including in Japan) and toured throughout the United States from 1960 to 1974, Toni was denied access to some of the most high-profile and lucrative burlesque venues, and she was never allowed to perform in Las Vegas, one of the top cities for showgirl-style striptease entertainment through the 1960s.

In 2006, Toni was officially welcomed into the Burlesque Hall of Fame (BHOF), an organization based in the very city that shut her out forty years earlier.[3] While she was thrilled to receive recognition by BHOF for her accomplishments, Toni also acknowledges the irony of it, and she has expressed concern that some performers today do not accurately depict the past:

> Take what you can get. That's what I had to do. That's what blacks had to do. Don't you let any one of them tell you any different. Some of them like to change history. They don't want to admit that they worked under such conditions. I'm telling you like it is. (interview, August 4, 2014)

Toni has, indeed, been "telling it like it is" to the generation of dancers who constitute the burlesque revival—a cultural movement that took root in New York, Los Angeles, and London in the 1990s. Often involving the nostalgic reconceptualization of early to mid-twentieth-century striptease performances—evident through dancers' musical, sartorial, staging, and/or choreographic choices (Ferreday 2008: 48–50)—neo-burlesque has spread across the United States, with most major metropolitan areas now offering striptease as "middlebrow" entertainment for middle-class people (Levine 1990). Unlike previous iterations of burlesque and the contemporary "gentlemen's club" industry, neo-burlesque is predominantly run by women, with female producers and producer-performers organizing and performing in shows, festivals, workshops, and classes.[4]

Over the course of four years (2011–15) of observing performances, participating in classes and shows, and conducting formal and informal interviews (primarily in Minneapolis–St. Paul and Chicago but also in Detroit, Seattle, Las Vegas, and New York), I have become increasingly aware that this new wave of performers is deeply passionate about burlesque, interested in striptease history, and attentive to issues of inequality within what is now a performance community.[5] Perhaps less apparent to some participants, however, is how the very notion of community makes something like burlesque viable in today's saturated "culture market" (Gopinath 2013).[6] And although scholars have described various facets of the "new burlesque" (Baldwin 2004; Buszek 2006; Ferreday 2008; Nally 2009; Willson 2008), an investigation of what—and, more important, who—makes it tick has yet to be undertaken.

In what follows, I consider some of the ways in which burlesque has reemerged as a popular form of live entertainment and has also changed significantly since its "Golden Age" (the 1920s to the 1950s), focusing on two groups within the larger burlesque community: the "Living Legends" and students/hobbyists. No longer primarily a job for working-class women, today's burlesque constitutes a hobby for most participants; it is a full-time occupation for only a select, skilled, entrepreneurial few. I will argue that this new leisure-labor compact is central to the formation, maintenance, and unevenness of the community itself.

COMING OUT OF RETIREMENT: THE LIVING LEGENDS OF BURLESQUE

After hearing Toni Elling's stories, one might wonder why she ever opted to do burlesque, why she stuck with it for nearly fifteen years, and why she would return to it again so late in life. In fact, from the 1920s through the 1960s, "striptease"—live entertainment that involved female dancers gradually removing their clothing in front of mostly male audiences—was a potentially lucrative profession for young, working-class American women, including working-class women of color, providing them with more remunerative employment than low-level clerical and other service-sector jobs (Shteir 2004: 4–6). At $125 a week in 1960, for example, Toni would have made approximately $5,000 a year (based on forty weeks of work), which, when adjusted for inflation, would be approximately $40,000 a year today (U.S. Bureau of Labor Statistics 2015). According to the U.S. Bureau of the Census (1961), American women's annual income averaged $1,200 in 1961, and full-time female workers' yearly income averaged only $3,200.

In addition to the relatively good pay, many of the former performers with whom I spoke, Toni among them, were quick to point out that they had enjoyed aspects of their work, despite the fact that they may have wanted to do something else or struggled to make a living at various points in their careers (see also Zemeckis 2013). Some were given the opportunity to travel across the United States and internationally, meet famous people like Frank Sinatra and John F. Kennedy, and perform in front of packed houses and adoring fans.[7] The work enabled some to support their families and purchase homes, cars, and luxury items. And a select few also managed to land roles in film and television.[8]

Nonetheless, for most performers, life onstage and on the road was not easy, and the everyday and structural racism faced by performers of color made the strip-show business even more difficult for women like Toni. And over time, post–World War II legal changes, the advent of adult movie houses, the flourishing of men's magazines like *Playboy*, and topless go-go dancing all contributed to a gradual shift in the industry—from the "slow reveal" accompanied by live music in large burlesque theaters to pole and lap dances occurring in nightclubs to the sounds of "canned music" (Shteir 2004: 5). Although burlesque did not "die," as some scholars have claimed (Allen 1991: 257–58; Shteir 2004: 5), it did change shape, with smaller venues that featured shorter acts, more dancers, more nudity, and prerecorded music becoming increasingly common.[9]

"Exotic dance" emerged in the United States in the late 1950s and continues to this day. Like their burlesque precursors, exotic dancers appear in various states of undress (depending on the venue and legal restrictions) in front of predominantly male audiences. But with less of a theatrical "fourth wall" now in place between audience members and performers, emotional and affective labor involving close bodily and verbal interaction (Hochschild 1983; Irvine 1990) has become more prevalent in the "intimate economy" (Wilson 2004) of gentlemen's clubs. In addition to performing on stages and/or selling lap or table dances to individual customers, exotic dancers may make physical contact and/or provide services like talk, fantasy, and companionship (Frank 2007: 502).

The women who performed burlesque in the 1950s and 1960s not only witnessed considerable shifts in the industry; they also had to decide whether to remain a part of it, either adjusting their acts to fit the new nightclub format and embracing the performance practices of exotic dance or opting to retire. Some women, like Shannon Doah, continued performing into the 1980s and 1990s and consider exotic dance and burlesque to be one and the same (as Shannon put it, "We're all related"). Others, like Holiday O'Hara, draw a clear line between what they see as legitimate and illegitimate kinds of stripping (field notes, June 8, 2014). Regardless of whether and where they draw a line, dancers of this era nonetheless share a similar history and trajectory: burlesque was their job.

Today, with the support of organizations like BHOF and the members of the neo-burlesque community, former stripteasers can reflect on and share their past experiences—the good, the bad, and everything in between—without fear of stigmatization, a luxury many of them did not have when they were performing. Dubbed "Living Legends" by BHOF, these women are now considered role models worthy of respect, praise, and, importantly, financial support. Given the lack of social safety nets, benefits, and job security available to them during their prime working years, a number of the Legends now struggle to cover their daily living expenses. Thus, community members take up collections to help their elders make ends meet, host charity shows to fund their trips to the annual BHOF Weekender in Las Vegas, and invite them to teach courses, give lectures, and, if they are still able, perform as headlining acts in shows and festivals across the United States. In other words, the Legends have been included within what historian David Hollinger (1993) refers to as the "circle of the we."

As former professionals themselves, the Legends can perhaps relate to current performers for whom neo-burlesque is a career; as Penny Star, Sr., an eighty-one-year-old Legend, remarked, burlesque was definitely "not a hobby" for her and her contemporaries (field notes, June 8, 2014). But the way that professional performers make their money today is considerably different from that experienced by their predecessors, as is their customer base. Nowadays, hobbyists are key to the success of full-time neo-burlesquers. Thus, creating appropriate and appealing environments in which hobbyists can learn the art of the tease is of the utmost importance to those seeking to support themselves solely through burlesque.

Taking It Off for Fun (and Money): Students and Professional Ecdysiasts[10]

Over the past decade, performers like Michelle L'amour, Indigo Blue, and Jo Weldon have managed to establish themselves as professional burlesque dancers, adapting to market changes and successfully increasing their currency as artists in urban nightlife scenes across the country. Indeed, with the neoliberal expansion of the service sector continuing to draw increasing numbers of women into the "symbolic economy" (Zukin 1995) and the gentrification of certain neighborhoods beckoning both businesses and the middle class back into cities, burlesque seems to be in an ideal position to fill niche markets, providing entertainment for audiences while operating in tandem with existing service-oriented businesses like bars, theaters, and nightclubs, thus allowing for the diversification of many establishments' cultural offerings with minimal financial commitment.[11]

While burlesque is a potential boon for small business owners looking for a supplementary, inexpensive, and popular form of entertainment, professional burlesque dancers must deal with the uncertainties and inconsistencies of freelance work in an industry where flexibility and independent contracting are taken for granted. Some dancers, like Michelle, Indigo, and Jo, have therefore opted to augment the services they offer by teaching, opening up dance studios and schools of burlesque in response to the desires of female audience members who are eager to learn how to take it all off—or, perhaps, pretend to take it all off.

My First Burlesque Class

In January 2011, I signed up to take an introductory four-week course, "Basic Burlesque," at Studio L'amour, one of the few dance studios in the United States dedicated entirely to teaching students the art of the tease. Michelle L'amour and her husband, Franky Vivid, opened the studio in 2008 in Chicago's West Loop, an area that recently has been subject to gentrification.[12] Over the next two years, as I walked along Randolph Street from the Green Line El stop to attend burlesque classes, signs of a still-changing neighborhood were evident: brick buildings occupied by wholesalers distributing fresh produce, dry food goods, meat and poultry, and paper products butted up against warehouses recently converted into condominiums. Neighborhood bars and diners were slowly being replaced by expensive restaurants, trendy cafés, wine bars, and gastropubs—bars with high-class food—and I frequently would pass young urban professionals getting drinks or dinner after work, walking their dogs, handing off car keys to valets, or jogging.

The first time I went to Studio L'amour, I literally walked right by it. Nestled between two storefronts with only a small, subtle banner hanging over the door, the entrance to the studio was somewhat discreet and safeguarded. In order to gain entry into the third-floor space, one had to punch in a code on a keypad and be buzzed in. And while the code itself was posted near the entryway, the system allowed for a certain level of security, with individuals gaining access to the space only when an instructor was present.

After someone buzzed me in, I climbed the three flights of stairs, checked in, and sat down on one of the ornate couches in the lounge area, taking in the vintage decor. Particularly striking was a long red velvet curtain separating the lounge from the studio, which permitted me to hear, but not see, the class currently in session. Although I knew from the studio website that we would not be taking our clothes off during these classes, I wondered what sorts of activities we would do and learn. What does a striptease class look, sound, and feel like? And what inspires individuals to take such a class in the first place?

Soon, more women began to come in, and they, too, sat down in the lounge to await the beginning of our class. Some shared stories about why they were there.

The woman sitting next to me had seen Michelle L'amour perform and thought it would be fun to take a class. Another woman said she knew one of the other instructors. Two friends had come together—they had wanted to do something like this for a while. No one seemed to know what to expect, and the nervous energy was palpable.

At 6:15 p.m., our teacher, an energetic white woman in her late twenties, gestured for us "girls" to come into the studio. Leaving behind the lounge area and with our high heels in tow, eleven of us—one African American, one Middle Eastern American, and nine Euro-American women appearing to be between the ages of twenty-five and forty—filed into the dance studio, a moderate-size exposed-brick space with hardwood floors and mirrors on one wall. After introducing herself, our teacher described what we would be learning: "In classic burlesque, what we're doing is exaggerating our femininity." Perhaps sensing some uncertainty, she then quickly reassured us that "there are no wrong moves, only 'better' moves." After selecting a big band jazz track on her iPod, she proceeded to lead us through a series of semi-aerobic dance moves—"bumps," "grinds," and "shimmies." Watching myself in the mirror and feeling rather self-conscious and clumsy, I tried my best to mimic our fearless and smiling leader, who shouted words of encouragement as we all took our first burlesque steps (field notes, January 5, 2011).

An Invitingly Sexy Home

Thirty-five-year-old Michelle L'amour has proven herself to be a prominent and respected producer, performer, and instructor within the burlesque community, with her husband, Franky Vivid, comanaging and coproducing alongside her. Voted Miss Exotic World in 2005 and a semifinalist on the prime-time television show *America's Got Talent* in 2006, Michelle teaches weekly classes and regular workshops, produces monthly shows in the Chicago area, travels as a headlining performer throughout the United States and internationally, oversees her "Naked Girls Reading" franchise, directs the award-winning Chicago Starlets, and much more.

In terms of developing her niche in the market, Michelle specifically targets women, and she tries to emphasize the nonperformance benefits of burlesque classes, such as confidence building, feeling desirable and sexy, and the possibility of making new female friends. On the Studio L'amour website, the studio is described as "an invitingly sexy home for her students . . . a place where sensuality is explored through dance, confidence and social experiences." This social space stands as a "welcoming oasis for women of all ages, shapes and professions," and Michelle and the Studio L'amour instructors are "bridging the gap for thousands of women who want to know how to feel and be sexy" (Studio L'amour n.d.). Thus, providing a welcoming, inviting space for women is one of Michelle's explicit goals, and the studio's location, limited access, and interior design all contribute to a sense of sociospatial semiexclusivity and safety.

For many women, an introductory course like the one I took marks the beginning and end of their kinesthetic dabbling with burlesque. Offering a small taste of the movements, music, and overall aesthetic of neo-burlesque, beginner courses, one-time workshops, and lessons at bachelorette parties allow women to experience some aspects of striptease under the guidance of burlesque performers in fun, low-pressure, often all-female environments. Ranging in price from $15 to $30 per class to substantially more for private parties (starting at $300 per hour at Studio L'amour), burlesque classes tend to cater to a middle-class clientele with some disposable income. Generally held after the workday is over and/or on weekends, these classes also fit the schedules of those who work 9-to-5 jobs, making it more difficult for working-class women with unorthodox work schedules to participate.

Women who decide they want to continue to learn more about this dance form and who have the financial means to do so may choose to enlist the services of someone like Michelle L'amour to help guide them through further explorations. At Studio L'amour, students can immerse themselves in the learning process, with purposely contained and structured performance possibilities available only to the most advanced students who have been taking classes at the studio for months or even years. In this way, women may feel that they can comfortably experiment with their own sexual self-expression in semiprivate dance classes without the immediate pressure of performing for an audience—a pressure that professional burlesque and exotic dancers must deal with on a regular basis.

The L'amour Method—"There are no wrong moves, only better moves"

Michelle's background in dance contributes to her success in burlesque, and years of training and teaching separate her from her students, many of whom have little to no previous dance experience.[13] By her own description a shy kid raised in a conservative Christian household in small-town Illinois, Michelle did not start taking dance classes until she was fifteen, which, she noted, is too late for a young woman who hopes to achieve a professional career as a modern or ballet dancer. So instead of pursuing a purportedly unattainable professional career, Michelle began teaching dance to seven- to seventeen-year-olds—ballet, modern, lyrical, and hip-hop—when she was just out of high school and attending community college. When she moved to Champaign-Urbana to work on an undergraduate degree in finance (which she finished, although she ended up hating the field), she continued to teach and dance. And once she relocated to Chicago in the early 2000s, teaching in Champaign-Urbana provided her with a meager income while she looked for opportunities in the city. Finally, as her burlesque career began to take shape in the early years of the revival—which she says was a natural fit in terms of her own movement style and sense of sensuality and sexuality—she was forced to stop teaching dance to children, as some of her students' parents found out about her involvement with burlesque and were uncomfortable with it. Additionally, burlesque instruction had become an economically viable career possibility, as female audience members and women with backgrounds in the performing arts started to experience burlesque in Chicago for the first time. Michelle began offering workshops at a lingerie shop, followed by regular classes at a belly dancing studio and, finally, at Studio L'amour.

Now that she runs her own studio, Michelle says she has more freedom to invest her time fully in burlesque, and she seeks out ways to make burlesque accessible to individuals with varying backgrounds, ability levels, and performance desires. She has also developed the L'amour Method, a personal brand and pedagogical approach that she hopes will someday be thought of as akin to the Graham Method of modern dance. The L'amour Method presents students with "the basics," builds on that skill set as the students advance to higher levels

over time, and helps them perfect a certain bodily repertoire through the purpose-
ful selection of a core set of movements, or what Bill Lepczyk (1981: 7) refers to
as the "baseline of the movement style." Once a student has mastered (or at least
adequately managed) that baseline, Michelle makes decisions about what movements, attitudes, and gestures to "layer" on top and how to communicate corrections according to the student's skill level and interests.

Ideally, and primarily because she believes in burlesque as an art requiring
training, Michelle wants students to immerse themselves in the dance form for
long periods, becoming part of the Studio L'amour community. Of course, this
expectation provides Michelle with necessary income and expands her client base,
but it also nurtures students' initial excitement for burlesque and helps them hone
their craft should some sort of performance be the end goal. But absorbing particular "techniques of the body" (Mauss [1935] 1973) over time is only one facet
of the L'amour Method. Instructor feedback, sartorial constraints, music choices,
and the aerobicization of "sexy" movements all structure students' experiences at
Studio L'amour, providing them with a specific framework within which to learn
this dance form as well as encouraging continued involvement in this and the
larger burlesque community.

Feedback

Michelle and the other instructors at Studio L'amour bring students into the
burlesque world rather gently, wanting to ensure that they feel comfortable during
their first experiences with striptease.[14] In terms of feedback, all of the instructors
with whom I took classes tailored their remarks to students based on the courses in
which they were enrolled: "Basic Skills," "Beginner/Intermediate Choreography,"
"Intermediate/Advanced Choreography," and "Advanced Performance."[15]
Michelle indicated to me she would never give notes to individual students in
the "Basics Skills" class, opting instead to offer general, sweeping comments to
the whole group. In contrast, in the invitation-only performance class, in which
a select group of students meets once a week (if not more) for a period of six
months, Michelle frequently gives pointed and direct corrections to individual
dancers—which, she noted, sometimes surprises students who have reached that
level. Prior to this class, students are rarely singled out, but since the performance
class culminates in a public recital, Michelle sees the feedback as necessary in
order to help soon-to-be performers prepare adequately for this next step. So
while students at the basic level are told there are "no wrong moves, only better
moves," as they continue to advance to higher levels the feedback changes, with
the instructors offering constructive criticism to individuals who have made
longer-term commitments of time, effort, and money.

Sartorial Separation

In addition to strategic and level-appropriate feedback, Michelle provides another
layer of security for middle-class hobbyists through sartorial restrictions. Since
only one of Michelle's classes—the performance class—requires seminudity, most
women never fully strip, as they place items of clothing to be removed on top of

workout clothes. This added layer of clothing distinguishes students from performers in a very visible, tangible way, with their fully clothed bodies positioned in opposition to the more risqué stages of undress that are part and parcel of contemporary and past burlesque performances and exotic dance.

Even at the performance class level, learning to strip happens very slowly and over a long period of time. When I was in the performance class (January–June 2012), more than four months elapsed before we had to remove any of our clothing in front of our classmates. This perhaps alleviated the concerns of some of my classmates, a number of whom initially expressed reservations about being seminude onstage. At our first class meeting, several of the more experienced student performers assured us that come July 1 (the date of our first public performance), nudity would be the furthest thing from our minds, and that we would get very comfortable with it in the studio first, making it less scary onstage. Michelle added that she would make sure we felt fully prepared for our first true "reveal." Much of that preparation, she noted, had already taken place, because all of us had been enrolled in classes for an extended period of time and had learned how to align our burlesque moves with appropriate burlesque music.

Music and Aerobicization

Many of the classes I attended at Studio L'amour featured prerecorded mid-twentieth-century big band jazz during warm-ups and choreographed routines. According to Michelle, a dancer must be sure to match musical style to movement style. Because jazz is the music Michelle believes best expresses sexuality, the marriage between jazz and burlesque makes artistic sense, thus the abundance of jazz used in her classes and performances; the weekly "Speak Easy" held at the now-closed Everleigh Social Club that featured a live jazz combo and improvisatory burlesque; and the addition of specialty classes like the eight-week "Music Theory and Burlesque" workshop that teaches dancers basic musical terminology through the use of jazz standards.

The use of big band jazz also can serve to distance embodied movements and associated behaviors from the present day, allowing students to move their pelvises, hips, and breasts in mildly suggestive ways to music that is decidedly not what one would hear at a modern gentlemen's club. Additionally, the music itself has within it certain "affordances" (Butler 2014: 71–72; see also Gibson [1979] 2014), or suggestions, as to how one might move at any given moment. As ethnomusicologist Tia DeNora (2000: 93) explains, music can become "a medium of describing 'how'—how to move, how to think, how to include, how to begin, how to end, how to mingle." Using her fieldwork conducted in an aerobics studio in the 1980s in Britain, DeNora shows that music is able to become a "medium of describing 'how'" because of the involvement and direction of instructors. Similarly, as Michelle and the other instructors at Studio L'amour teach students a standardized movement repertoire, with the development of a particular aesthetic being the goal, students are also learning what kinds of movements "match up" with big band jazz and which ones do not.

Like the individuals in DeNora's study, instructors at Studio L'amour seem to use music to ground participants' experiences in more familiar, up-to-date territory: an aerobics studio. A compilation CD mixed by Franky, called "Franky Vivid and

Hisorchestra," combines jazz standards with prominent, consistent dance beats. Often used in classes at Studio L'amour, Franky's mixes appear to help students more easily locate the pulse of the music during the warm-up period, a fifteen- to twenty-minute segment of most classes that, in addition to providing some low-impact aerobic activity, serves to solidify technique prior to the introduction of new choreography.

For example, in the basic class I attended, the instructor utilized this CD to help students follow the repeated series of aerobicized bumps, grinds, pin-up poses, and shimmies. And just as in an aerobics class, our instructor frequently yelled out directions to us while demonstrating the moves we would be doing next. Meanwhile, the sounds of big band jazz mixed with a dance beat kept us more or less unified as we repeated "sexy" pelvic thrusts and circles over and over again. The familiar feelings of an aerobics studio—a prominent steady pulse, mirrors on one wall, continuous verbal and nonverbal guidance by an instructor, the sporting of workout clothes, and the unison repetition of movements by a group of women—all seemed to position striptease as a form of fitness, with sexualized elements somewhat toned down. When considered in the context of Studio L'amour's other class offerings, which range from choreography and specialty classes (including floor work, fan dance technique, and improving one's "bumps"), to the more explicitly workout-focused "PilaTEASE" and "Tease & Tone" (which is also available for purchase as a DVD), one can see how Michelle draws on contemporary notions of what it means to be fit, feminine, and sexy, fashioning striptease as a healthy aerobic and performance practice suitable for women with varying burlesque interests and ability levels.

Conclusion

This chapter has admittedly not addressed all the ways individuals engage with burlesque today. Between the professional and hobby/student levels, for instance, are amateurs and semiprofessionals who may not be able to make a living from burlesque but would not consider themselves hobbyists. Many of these performers spend countless hours assembling their costumes and props, editing music, creating and practicing choreography, and perfecting their hair and makeup styles. They may never get paid enough in burlesque to quit their day jobs or even offset their expenses, but for them, striptease is still a serious business—if only a career imaginary. Some performers may look to someone like Michelle L'amour and envision a possible future for themselves, but the reality is that very few performers can do burlesque full-time. Most who can have to do more than perform in order to stay afloat financially.

This is precisely why the predominantly female hobbyists—those who enjoy going to shows, taking classes and workshops, and perhaps performing on occasion—are financially and socially indispensable to the burlesque community and, in many ways, make its existence possible. Unlike exotic dance, which caters to heterosexual cis-men (though some nonheterosexual cis-men, cis-women, and transgender individuals also frequent gentlemen's clubs), burlesque needs to attract both women and men. Shows produced by women, featuring female (semi) professional and amateur performers and drawing mixed-gender audiences, and classes that allow women to "try on" striptease for their own entertainment and pleasure make burlesque viable in today's culture market. Without its female consumer base, striptease likely would be relegated to the past.

Attempts by members of the burlesque community to extend financial support to "Living Legends" like Toni, both in the form of donations and by offering them work, also would fall short were it not for hobbyist participation. Professional and semiprofessional producers/performers are, of course, instrumental in terms of organizing and producing shows and fund-raisers, lining up Legends as headliners, ensuring that the women are compensated, and generally making sure that Legends continue to be included within the burlesque "circle of the we." But the continued support of the Legends would be untenable without hobbyists populating audiences, classes, and workshops; volunteering to help out at charity events; making monetary and other donations; and often performing for little to no compensation. The burlesque community, therefore, relies heavily on the involvement of women who are not necessarily attempting to earn a living at striptease, rendering clothing removal a hobby perhaps unlike any other today.

QUESTIONS FOR DISCUSSION

What are some of the differences between burlesque of the early to mid-twentieth century and neo-burlesque? What might these differences tell us about shifting notions of gender, sexuality, labor, and culture/entertainment in the United States?

NOTES

1. A fellow former performer advised Toni to "not go out of [her] house for less than $500" (interview, August 3, 2014), so although I do not know the precise amount she was paid, it was likely at least $500. Sydni Deveraux purportedly was paid $800—a fee that falls within the expected range for a major headliner (about $400–$2,000).

2. According to Toni, Duke Ellington wrote "Satin Doll" for her, and her stage name is also based on his. One of her frequently used taglines was "the Duke's Delight."

3. The Burlesque Hall of Fame owes its existence to Jennie Lee, a founding member of the Exotic Dancers League. That union, incorporated in the summer of 1955, fought for better pay and clean, safe dressing rooms and against the unfair arrests of performers. Today, according to the BHOF website (www.burlesquehall.com), the Burlesque Hall of Fame is "the world's premier organization dedicated to preserving the living legacy of burlesque as an artform and cultural phenomenon."

4. Although I am focusing on cis-women (*cis* refers to people whose gender identification is in line with the sex they were assigned at birth) in this chapter, in large part because of the unprecedented number who are consuming stripping, more cis-men and transgender individuals have begun to get involved in burlesque. As a result, a number of burlesque studios and schools, such as Vaudezilla in Chicago, are now offering explicitly queer-, trans-, and gender-inclusive classes.

5. Performers of color have started to voice their concerns regarding the burlesque community's white image and lack of performance opportunities for brown and black women and men. See *21st Century Burlesque* magazine's recent series of articles on "race and burlesque" (www.21stcenturyburlesque.com). Producers have also begun to create their own shows featuring performers of color exclusively, such as Foxy Tann's "Afrodisiac" (Minneapolis) and Jeez Loueez's "Jeezy's Juke Joint" (Chicago).

6. Music theorist Sumanth Gopinath (2013: 101) uses the term "culture market" to describe the commodification of art and entertainment in what he perceives to be an increasingly dense array of consumer choices, in terms of both live performance and the competing — and increasingly more mobile—realms of television, film, and the internet. Although cultural offerings differ from one geographic location to the next and are unevenly distributed (for example, some urban areas in the United States are perhaps better equipped than many rural areas to support a wide variety of live music, dance, and theatrical productions), individuals in various locations can now more easily access culture products that were once available only in person, resulting in increased competition among cultural producers. Thus, because consumers have so many choices, burlesque's growing popularity within the urban nightlife economy—and the fact that it now seems to count as "culture," unlike exotic dance and pornography—is something that warrants further research and informs my discussion below.

7. Toni met Frank Sinatra and many other musicians (interview, August 3, 2014). Tempest Storm is infamous for having had affairs with John F. Kennedy and Elvis Presley, among others (Ortiz 2011: 5; Zemeckis 2013: 208).

8. Gypsy Rose Lee and Ann Corio both made appearances in film, though neither had much success crossing over from burlesque to a career as an actress (Shteir 2004: 189–90, 218; Zemeckis 2013: 28, 162).

9. As Jo Weldon (2010: 5, 9), a former gentlemen's club feature dancer and current burlesque performer and teacher, notes, dancers in some U.S. gentlemen's clubs continued to create and perform burlesque-style acts throughout the 1970s and 1980s and into the early 1990s.

10. In 1940, H. L. Mencken created the word *ecdysiast* at the behest of burlesque dancer Georgia Sothern, who had asked Mencken to come up with a new, purportedly more elegant-sounding word for "stripteaser" (Shteir 2004: 216). The term, which is based on the scientific word for molting (*ecdysis*), was not universally embraced, however. As Gypsy Rose Lee put it, "We don't wear feathers and molt them off.... What does he know about stripping?" (quoted in Shteir 2004: 216).

11. As sociologist Sharon Zukin (1995: 2) explains, a city's "symbolic economy," that is, "its visible ability to produce both symbols and space," is driven, in part, by the consumption of food, music, theater, dance, and other cultural offerings. Neo-burlesque thus contributes to the symbolic economy of many U.S. urban areas, and its proliferation shows that culture has, indeed, become "more and more the business of cities" (Zukin 1995: 2).

12. Perhaps reflective of increasing rents and further gentrification of the area, Michelle and Franky opted to close their West Loop studio location in March 2015, reopening further north, in the Lakeview neighborhood.

13. Much of the information provided in this section comes from an interview I conducted with Michelle at Studio L'amour in 2012.

14. I have purposely refrained from using the instructors' stage names in this section for privacy reasons. Michelle is a prominent public figure, but her staff members have other jobs in addition to their work teaching classes at the studio.

15. Michelle recently changed the names of these classes, and it appears she has made some minor adjustments in scheduling, class duration, content, and requirements as well. However, the overall progression seems to be more or less intact. See the Studio L'amour website (studiolamour.com) for details.

References

Allen, Robert C. 1991. *Horrible Prettiness: Burlesque and American Culture*. Chapel Hill: University of North Carolina Press.

Baldwin, Michelle. 2004. *Burlesque and the New Bump-n-Grind*. Golden, CO: Speck Press.

Buszek, Maria Elena. 2006. *Pin-up Grrrls: Feminism, Sexuality, Popular Culture*. Durham, NC: Duke University Press.

Butler, Mark J. 2014. *Playing with Something That Runs: Technology, Improvisation, and Composition in DJ and Laptop Performance*. Oxford: Oxford University Press.

DeNora, Tia. 2000. *Music in Everyday Life*. Cambridge: Cambridge University Press.

Ferreday, Debra. 2008. "Showing the Girl: The New Burlesque." *Feminist Theory* 9 (1): 47–65.

Frank, Katherine. 2007. "Thinking Critically about Strip Club Research." *Sexualities* 10 (4): 501–17.

Gibson, James J. (1979) 2014. *The Ecological Approach to Visual Perception*. New York: Psychology Press.

Gopinath, Sumanth. 2013. *The Ringtone Dialectic: Economy and Cultural Form*. Cambridge: MIT Press.

Hochschild, Arlie Russell. 1983. *The Managed Heart: Commercialization of Human Feeling*. Berkeley: University of California Press.

Hollinger, David A. 1993. "How Wide the Circle of the 'We'? American Intellectuals and the Problem of the Ethnos since World War II." *American Historical Review* 98 (2): 317–37.

Irvine, Judith T. 1990. "Registering Affect: Heteroglossia in the Linguistic Expression of Emotion." In Catherine Lutz and Lila Abu-Lughod, eds., *Language and the Politics of Emotion*, 126–61. Cambridge: Cambridge University Press.

Lepczyk, Bill. 1981. "A Contrastive Study of Movement Style in Dance through the Laban Perspective." PhD dissertation, Teachers College, Columbia University.

Levine, Lawrence. 1990. *Highbrow/Lowbrow: The Emergence of Cultural Hierarchy in America*. Cambridge, MA: Harvard University Press.

Mauss, Marcel. (1935) 1973. "Techniques of the Body." *Economy and Society* 2 (1): 70–88.

Nally, Claire. 2009. "Grrrly Hurly Burly: Neo-burlesque and the Performance of Gender." *Textual Practice* 23 (4): 621–43.

Ortiz, Johnny. 2011. *My Life among the Icons: A Fascinating Memoir of a Raconteur Whose Life Intersects with the Giants of Sports and the Glamour of Hollywood*. Bloomington, IN: AuthorHouse.

Shteir, Rachel. 2004. *Striptease: The Untold History of the Girlie Show*. Oxford: Oxford University Press.

Studio L'amour. n.d. "About Studio L'amour." http://studiolamour.com/chicago_burlesque_school_about (accessed November 3, 2015).

U.S. Bureau of the Census. 1961. "Consumer Income." *Current Population Reports*, Series P-60, no. 35, January. www2.census.gov/prod2/popscan/p60-035.pdf (accessed November 3, 2015).

U.S. Bureau of Labor Statistics. 2015. "CPI Inflation Calculator." www.bls.gov/data/inflation_calculator.htm (accessed November 3, 2015).

Weldon, Jo. 2010. *The Burlesque Handbook*. New York: HarperCollins.

Willson, Jacki. 2008. *The Happy Stripper: Pleasure and Politics of the New Burlesque*. New York: I. B. Tauris.

Wilson, Ara. 2004. *The Intimate Economies of Bangkok: Tomboys, Tycoons, and Avon Ladies in the Global City*. Berkeley: University of California Press.

Zemeckis, Leslie. 2013. *Behind the Burly Q: The Story of Burlesque in America*. New York: Skyhorse.

Zukin, Sharon. 1995. *The Cultures of Cities*. Malden, MA: Blackwell.

CLASS AND POWER

11

Talk of "Broken Borders" and Stone Walls: Anti-immigrant Discourse and Legislation from California to South Carolina

Ann Kingsolver

Anti-immigration or anti-immigrant legislation has been making its way through state-houses across the United States over the past two decades. This is the latest round of legislation blaming recent immigrants (often from a specific nation or set of nations) for economic hardship or criminal activity in the United States, problems portrayed as manageable so long as undocumented ("illegal") immigrants are removed or prevented from entering the country. The research question taken up here is this: What larger discursive projects (e.g., racializing or economic projects) do specific acts of anti-immigrant legislation fit into, and how might state legislation—most recently proposed in southeastern states—be understood as part of a national political project?

In this chapter, I demonstrate some ways to situate local anti-immigration legislation within that larger national context using the concepts and methods of anthropology. I argue that anthropological perspectives can contribute to both academic and activist analyses of the most recent anti-immigrant legislation (focused especially on immigrants from Latin American nations, often glossed as "Mexico" in public discourse) and that such analyses are particularly needed in southeastern U.S. states like South Carolina, which has a rapidly growing new immigrant population from Latin America and other regions of the world. In these states, both the infrastructure of nongovernmental organizations concerned with immigrant rights and a changing government infrastructure for immigration enforcement (the U.S. Immigration and Customs Enforcement, or ICE, system devolving such enforcement to local authorities) may lack the linguistic and cultural resources emphasized as vital by anthropologists.

Reprinted with permission, from Kingsolver, Ann. 2010. *Southern Anthropologist* 35 (1): 21–40. © Southern Anthropological Society. Republished in *Reflecting on America*, 2nd edition, edited by Clare L. Boulanger, 121–134 (© 2016 Taylor & Francis). All rights reserved.

This chapter emerges from a long-term ethnographic research project on how individuals (often without access to legal documents) make sense of policies related to globalization, like the North American Free Trade Agreement, and anticipate the effects of those policies on their everyday lives. In this larger project, I use political economic and interpretive theoretical lenses to focus on the cultural logics (e.g., the logic of neoliberal capitalism) that both inform and are constructed through individual explanations and actions. As Fleck ([1935] 1979) and Douglas (1986) have noted, it is extremely challenging to think outside our own "thought styles"—the cultural logics into which we have been socialized. Weber's ([1905] 1977) pathbreaking project on interpreting the logic of capitalism and how it relates to other logics (religious ones, in his work) has inspired quite a few anthropologists, like me, to see how applying both political economic and interpretive theoretical perspectives illuminates the cultural context of economic and political decisions.

This project also falls within the anthropology of law, or political anthropology. Carol Greenhouse (2006: 189) has pointed out that today, "anthropologists are working on legal doctrine, and lawyers are working on cultural practice." Discourse analysis, or the tracking of collective strands of explanation and action, is a method commonly used in legal anthropology. As Greenhouse explains, "A theory of discourse helps to account for how states are rendered social through language and the interplay of subjective experience among ordinary people in their everyday lives, as well as how states figure in history through collective identities created in those very processes" (200). In looking specifically at how anti-immigration legislation fits into a larger cultural landscape of contested assertions of rights, identity, and power, I join Nicholas De Genova, among others, in utilizing ethnography to investigate the broader cultural logics involved. About such work, De Genova (2002: 423) states, "It thus becomes possible for the ethnographic study of undocumented migrations to produce migrant 'illegality' as the kind of ethnographic object that can serve the ends of a distinctly anthropological critique of nation-states and their immigration policies, as well as of the broader politics of nationalism, nativism, and citizenship."

From 1993 to 1996, when I was doing ethnographic interviewing and discourse analysis on what people (in many occupations, identifying themselves in many ways) in the United States and Mexico thought of the North American Free Trade Agreement (Kingsolver 2001), I found that racialized and national identities were often conflated in narratives about threats to economic nationalism and job security. As I researched those narratives more and studied speeches and political advertising and cartoons related to California's Proposition 187 (an anti-immigrant bill proposed in 1994, the year NAFTA was being debated and voted on), I learned that metaphors related to the U.S.–Mexico border—a stone wall, a leaky membrane, the Berlin Wall—became vehicles for what was being said both overtly and between the lines about citizenship and economic entitlement.

In 1996, I moved from California to South Carolina and continued to study anti-immigration legislation, which helped me to see state and local anti-immigration laws within a national and transnational context. It is the larger pattern of anti-immigration legislation and the selective marking and unmarking of individuals and groups as "citizens" or "illegal immigrants" (whatever their actual status might be) that interests me here. Pablo Vila's (2000) research on the use of metaphors and the variety of narratives in constructing "border" identities demonstrates how anthropological techniques can figure productively in this type of research. The work I have done for this chapter is much more limited to discourse analysis, but, as I have noted, it is part of a larger ethnographic project. National movements fund local anti-immigration campaigns at strategic moments, I have observed, promoting this wave of state laws across the country.

In May 2010, the day before I submitted an earlier version of this chapter for initial publication as a journal article, I received a mass e-mail from Jim DeMint, then U.S. senator from South Carolina, asking me to "tell Congress to build the fence!" He referred to the Secure Fence Act passed five years earlier, in which "we promised to build 700 miles of double layer fencing on our border with Mexico. . . . Less than 35 miles of fencing have been completed!" The message continued: "Americans have demanded a real fence to combat the very real problems of illegal immigration that have led to human trafficking, drug trafficking, kidnapping and violence on our border." This quest to build an actual fence (or wall) at the border gives concrete form to a metaphor that has figured in anti-immigration talk for years. Hence "wall talk" is a useful place to start my analysis.

In 2007, South Carolina's Senator Lindsey Graham proposed an amendment to the Homeland Security Department appropriations bill, requesting "emergency" funding to secure the U.S.–Mexico border. Through his support for this amendment, the Republican senator could begin distancing himself from the title commentator Rush Limbaugh had given him—"Lindsey Grahamnesty"— and the related conservative dissent over the immigration reform bill he had not been able to get passed earlier in the year. The emphasis in national discussions of immigration shifted from the Z visa and the legal and cultural meanings of "amnesty" to the language of national security, national emergency, and the threat of terrorism that has characterized both American political discourse and some of the most egregious hate crimes and sanctioned discrimination in the United States since September 11, 2001.

After the Senate passed his amendment, Senator Graham said, "Securing our border is a national emergency because it's a national-security problem not to be able to control who comes into your country" (quoted in Rosen 2007b). Such discourse is *selective*: the *southern* border of the United States is represented as more of a security threat than the northern border, despite arrests defined as terrorist related being more frequent on the Canadian border. "The vote was overwhelming," Senator Graham stated, "because everybody agrees that the broken borders we have today are not in our national security interests" (quoted in Rosen 2007c). Lou Dobbs of CNN also used the term "broken borders" in describing immigrants from Mexico as an "army of invaders" (Fairness & Accuracy in Reporting 2006). This choice of the word *broken* suggests a disturbing current rupture in what was once a hermetically sealed boundary—an image that does not reflect experience but it has tremendous rhetorical power. *Broken* also conveys a need for repair, and the assumption that it would be natural to spend money on such a repair, in the same way as those in Holland might vote to repair a breach in a dike.

Graham's legislative efforts on immigration succeeded only after the senator was told by his colleagues to focus on the need to secure the southern border.

Representative Duncan Hunter, a Republican from California, said that there ought to be "a very strong sense of urgency in this country to simply carry out the law, the mandate, for 854 miles of fence that we passed. . . . They've only built 13 miles of the fence so far" (quoted in Babington 2007).

This obsession with enclosure is not unique to the United States. "Wall talk" often arises when a nation's economic or political sovereignty appears diminished. Recent European discourse has also turned toward border fortification ("Fortress Europe") to counter the immigration threat posed by selectively blamed groups. In addition, new social means of constraining mobility have been proposed. Ong (2007: 15) cites discussions in Europe concerning the granting of different kinds of graduated citizenship, or postnational citizenship, with different levels of rights, to different immigrant groups within the European Union. Fox (2005) calls such stratification of rights and claims "multi-layered citizenship." As Ong (1999) has pointed out, citizenship is not fixed but flexible. We need to understand how changes in rules about who "belongs" reflect other forms of power.

In the United States, there is a long tradition of privileging whiteness in relation to rights, and there is little criticism of this by those who benefit from it. But such discrimination is obvious to those who experience it daily, both within and outside the nation. When California's Proposition 187—the ballot initiative that would have made it illegal to provide health care or educational services to undocumented immigrants—was being debated before the vote, political cartoonists in Mexico were not hesitant about bringing the link between anti-immigrant legislation and white supremacist political projects (and funding) into the public eye; several cartoons equated Governor Pete Wilson's advocacy of Proposition 187 with Hitler's role in the Holocaust. While hyperbole is the stock-in-trade of political cartoonists, I argue that it was more possible to talk publicly about white supremacy and U.S. immigration legislation as overlapping political projects in Mexican civic space than it was in the United States. For example, after the 2007 immigration reform bill was voted down, Senator DeMint stated: "We've gotten thousands of calls, and I haven't gotten one call that could have been interpreted in any way as anti-immigration. . . . I have not sensed any racism or any fear of diversity or the things that have been leveled against some of us" (quoted in Rosen 2007a).

Researchers such as Jean Stefancic (1997) and William Tucker (2003) have discussed the relationship between white supremacist funding and well-financed campaigns for anti-immigrant legislation across the United States. In California, for example, in the run-up to the Proposition 187 vote, the Federation for American Immigration Reform (FAIR), probably with Pioneer Fund backing (Stefancic 1997), targeted the "white" vote in California with the "Save Our State" campaign (although by no means did the vote break down along the lines of stated identities). That rhetoric aligned citizenship with whiteness and placed the responsibility for the state's economic downturn on the undocumented workers (assumed to be nonwhite) whose labor actually made a key contribution to California's status as the eighth-largest trading body in the world at that time. FAIR also "bankrolled Proposition 200" in Arizona (Judis 2006).

The links between dollars going to specifically white supremacist causes and the anti-immigrant publicity are hard to trace. Disguised as populist groundswells, such targeted campaigns often appear and disappear in ways that seem a bit mysterious to those not funding them, but I would join others in arguing that these campaigns are coordinated nationally. For example, in the spring of 2000, as John McCain, George W. Bush, and other Republican contenders for the presidential nomination moved into South Carolina and worked the state before the primary vote, Project USA anti-immigration signage went up around the state—there was even a billboard right over one of Columbia's two mosques that said "90 percent of U.S. population growth in the 21st century will result from current immigration; stop it, Congress." Anti-immigration television advertisements were broadcast frequently. The ads stopped as soon as the vote was over.

FAIR's website (www.fairus.org) gives the impression that the organization focuses strictly on information—it has data available for anti-immigration researchers and tracks legislation such as S.1842, the "Protecting American Lives Act," proposed in the U.S. Congress in 2015. However, as indicated by the "Save Our State" campaign in California, FAIR has been activist as well. It was reported to be involved in the formation of Sachem Quality of Life (SQL), a group brought together in Farmingville, New York (on Long Island), to support a local anti-immigrant legislative initiative. James Claffey (2006: 75) describes SQL's attempts "to speak for" the entire community in protesting the presence of undocumented workers:

> Composed of thirty to forty working-class, native-born residents, this group began a media blitz demanding that public officials at the local and federal levels act immediately. They also spoke to immigration officials (the INS) and began a generalized campaign to rid the town of the undocumented.

Claffey goes on to note that FAIR sent in a national organizer, and violence against undocumented workers began to escalate. While SQL members did not claim any responsibility for hate crimes, as their anti-immigrant rhetoric and harassment increased, two Mexicans looking for construction work were brutally beaten in an abandoned building by two young local men.

> Picked up a few days later, one of the perpetrators was found to have Nazi and white-supremacy tattoos. As became clear during the trial, they were "out to get some Mexicans," clearly a hate crime. They are currently serving twenty-five years for attempted murder. (Claffey 2006: 78)

Then, Claffey reports, "five white teenagers, residents of Farmingville, firebombed the house of a Mexican family of four in town" (79). Additional research, of the kind Kathleen Blee (2002) has done on local and national Ku Klux Klan activity, is necessary to bring accountability to white supremacist organizations—perpetrators of hate speech—for such hate crimes.[1]

As more and more new immigrants from Latin America arrive in U.S. regions that have no strong histories of Latino settlement, national anti-immigrant and hate groups see growth opportunities. In South Carolina, the proposal of national immigration legislation in 2007 was quickly mirrored by local anti-immigration organizations orchestrated through national groups. The state president of the national Minuteman Civil Defense Corps spoke to the 150 members of the new Horry County chapter about the "invasion" of "illegal immigrants": "We've got to get rid of them, one way or another" ("150 Turn Out to Fight" 2007). Once again, more studies are needed to identify the links between this kind of violent speech and all the levels of violence Bourgois (2001: 6–7) has described: political, structural, symbolic, and everyday.

One form of symbolic violence is the selective use of the term *immigrant* in dominant discourses in the South over time. Labor has been global in this region since before the United States was a nation, but, unlike free Europeans with capital, enslaved Africans were never described as immigrants. The marking of groups as immigrants or not, desirable or not, has been ongoing in powerful public venues in South Carolina. A recent iteration was the bill that State Senator Glenn McConnell introduced in the 2009–10 session of the South Carolina State Senate: S 306 would prevent undocumented workers (called illegal aliens) from receiving workers' compensation for job-related injuries if their employers were aware of the workers' undocumented status before they were injured. This dovetailed with the structural violence of ICE devolving its functions to local law enforcement officials across the South. These officials now carry federal authority and have restructured the poultry workforce in South Carolina through immigration raids.

The 2008 and 2009 raids rendered visible labor relations and marginalized workers who had not often been represented in mainstream media, and that exacerbated anti-immigrant feeling. As Benson (2008: 596) points out, "Power and perception overlap." Once South Carolina's undocumented poultry workers were stigmatized in the news, fears of broader anti-immigrant and anti-Latino discrimination arose (Ordonez 2008), and many recent Latino immigrants lost jobs in the poultry plants in Greenville and Columbia, replaced mostly by prison workers (another form of structural violence that is not always visible in public discourse, although on almost any day, prison uniforms worn by grounds crews can be seen on the South Carolina statehouse lawn). De Genova (2002: 439) has clearly described the relationship between the need to maintain a low-wage labor force that includes workers with varying degrees of citizenship and control of that labor force through fear of deportation:

> Migrant "illegality" is lived through a palpable sense of deportability, which is to say, the possibility of deportation, the possibility of being removed from the space of the nation-state.... Thus, the legal production of "illegality" as a distinctly spatialized and typically racialized social condition for undocumented migrants provides an apparatus for sustaining their vulnerability and tractability as workers.

The racialization that is part of this process is discussed in the next section.

SELECTIVE RACIALIZATION AND THE POLITICS OF BLAME

A "moral" aspect of the neoliberal capitalist project is the displacement of responsibility for economic and social difficulties onto a strategically stigmatized group, as in the politics of blame (see Farmer 1992) that propelled the passage of California's Proposition 187 in 1994. I have discussed this moralizing process elsewhere as *strategic alterity*, or "shifting between different assertions of devalued group identity in order to valorize free-trading citizens of the market and to mask the labor of those making that free market participation possible" (Kingsolver 2007: 87). The text of Proposition 187 (later ruled unconstitutional) did in fact blame undocumented immigrants for economic hardship during Governor Pete Wilson's administration. The ballot version of Proposition 187 began with these words:

> The People of California find and declare as follows:
>   That they have suffered and are suffering economic hardship caused by the presence of illegal aliens in this state.
>   That they have suffered and are suffering personal injury and damage caused by the criminal conduct of illegal aliens in this state.
>   That they have a right to the protection of their government from any person or persons entering this country unlawfully.

Note also that the proposition blamed undocumented migrants for a rise in criminal activity—it is all too easy to move from the "illegality" of "illegal aliens" to broad brushstrokes painting all Latinos as criminal, as Michael Finewood (2005: 57) found when he analyzed representations of Latino immigrants in South Carolina. It was thus no accident that Proposition 187 packed its first few lines with words like *illegal, unlawful,* and *criminal.*

Which Californians needed protection from whom? The rhetorical sleight of hand here between citizenship, "whiteness," and the threat posed by (a selectively marked group of) immigrants was a powerful one. Proposition 187 was promoted—in speeches and media advertisements—through language that smoothed over the complexity of identity and immigration by equating the term *immigrant* with the term *Mexican,* which was problematically racialized, gendered, and nationalized (see Kingsolver 2001; Vila 2000) against a threatened white California self (Zavella 1997). This rhetoric clearly did not match the diversity of California residents, but it was used to rationalize discrimination.

Racializing stories are attempts to normalize the equation of whiteness with entitlement in political and economic life. As Charles W. Mills (1997: 32–33) has said, "The whole point of establishing a moral hierarchy and juridically partitioning the polity according to race is to secure and legitimate the privileging of those individuals designated as white/persons and the exploitation of those individuals designated as nonwhite/subpersons." I think that market citizenship (Kingsolver 2001) is distinct from national citizenship, and I see the former as being used to argue for or against groups' rights within nation-states regardless of legal status. This is what Aihwa Ong (2007) calls "graduated citizenship." Whether we talk about this as othering, alterity, xenophobia, or racial formation (Omi and Winant 1994), the collapsing of multiple ethnic, transnational, class, and gender identities into a transgressive male "Mexican" single-handedly responsible for California's economic hardship and high crime rate was prominent in the discussions of Proposition 187. Undocumented immigrant groups currently racialized as "white" were never spoken of in the same way; similarly, as Joseph Nevins (2002) has pointed out, it is "Mexican workers," rather than their employers, who are most often represented as having broken the law.

The stereotype of a male migrant worker coming to steal jobs, or lure them, with a "giant sucking sound" (Perot 1993), over the U.S.–Mexico border, has long been used as a nationalist ax to divide workers and actively *un*mark the result of neoliberal capitalist policies—an increase in unemployment and economic inequity. Gendering, racializing, and otherwise stereotyping the "Mexican" was facilitated by the availability of vilifying images in Hollywood representations of a Mexican "other" as a storytelling foil over most of the twentieth century (Flores 1995). In his analysis of representations of new immigrants on U.S. magazine covers, Leo Chavez (2001: 21) found that alarmist imagery always rose in moments of economic downturn. In 2015, anti-immigrant and wall-building discourse became more prominent than ever in the rhetoric of some U.S. presidential candidates, most notably Donald Trump.

POLICING THE MARGINS: CITIZEN SURVEILLANCE AND MARKET CITIZENSHIP

How can a population be mobilized to police the margins of who is allowed to be a free-trading market citizen and who is strategically altered to be a silenced noncitizen of that market despite laboring to support it? Lee Baker (1998: 24) has detailed how the Louisiana statute affirmed by the U.S. Supreme Court in the *Plessy v. Ferguson* decision required train conductors to assign and enforce constructions of passengers' race or be fined and possibly imprisoned. In the early twentieth-century Atlanta described by Du Bois (1903), a law forbidding those racialized as black and white from having conversations with one another would have to have been enforced not only through police surveillance but also through citizen participation in the kind of racial profiling that has its descendants in the Neighborhood Watch and crime-tipoff programs of the twenty-first century. Legally sanctioned racialized segregation in the United States *required* citizen surveillance—the "vigilance" at the heart of the word *vigilante*. I argue that the political legacy of California's Proposition 187 is the resurgence of citizen surveillance, with those racialized as white policing the borders of whiteness both figuratively and literally. Smith (2006) has pointed out the pitfalls of leaving it up to the individual to identify those who represent a threat to the nation. Racial profiling is more about disciplining the public and reinforcing the role of government in our lives (see Foucault 1977) than about personal or national security.

Even though Pete Wilson, reelected governor of California on the same ballot on which Proposition 187 appeared, stated in a preelection debate that he knew the initiative could never become an enforceable law, the role Proposition 187 played in affirming an explicitly and implicitly white supremacist discourse in California was powerful, as were the associated expressions of violence, ranging from renters being turned out of their housing to beatings and killings of those perceived as undocumented immigrants. The stereotypes promoted through the support and passage of Proposition 187 were not merely annoying or misleading; they were very, very dangerous. Hate crimes against Latinos increased sharply after passage of the proposition (Finnigan 1995). The Coalition for Humane Immigrant Rights of Los Angeles documented this increase in hate crimes, as well as acts of discrimination, aimed at people who "looked Latino"; noncitizenship was presumed.

Many of the experiences of discrimination were specifically racialized. A Latina mother (with U.S. citizenship) and her children, for example, were told by their apartment complex manager that they could not use the pool after 6:00 P.M. because in the evenings it was "for whites only" (Finnigan 1995). Another Latina (again a U.S. citizen) was turned away from a hospital while she was hemorrhaging; she was told that the hospital no longer treated Hispanics. As a result, she lost her baby (Martinez 1995). The Coalition for Humane Immigrant Rights of Los Angeles reported even more violent examples of empowered hatred against visually targeted Latinos in California. These acts, especially when carried out or sanctioned by police officers, seemed to support a white supremacist notion of who constituted the public of, or who had a right to citizenship in, California and the United States.

Renato Rosaldo (1999: 257) states that "Proposition 187 was arguably in large measure an expression of white supremacy." Tomás Almaguer (1994) has written about the white supremacist paradigm underlying the Lights on the Border program, which urged U.S. citizens (symbolically "white") to park their vehicles in lines facing the Mexican side of the U.S.–Mexico border and use their high beams to discourage border crossing by those symbolically seen as the nonwhite couriers of all California ills. Members of the Minuteman Civil Defense Corps also took border policing into their own hands, reflecting the broader privatization logic of neoliberal capitalism. In 2014 and 2015, similar vigilante activity by the Oath Keepers in Ferguson, Missouri, illustrated that assertions of private/civic defense by individuals who are visibly armed and patrolling public space are not options equally available to those identifying as white, African American, and Latino in a nation-state in which cultural citizenship is elided with white privilege.

Governor Pete Wilson urged the national passage of a corollary to Proposition 187 (Ono and Sloop 2002: 62), and similar bills were considered first in Texas, Florida, and Arizona (Ono and Sloop 2002: 4)—states also tending toward English-only initiatives. More local and state ballot initiatives followed in Hazleton, Pennsylvania, and Riverside, New Jersey; then came the passage of Arizona's State Senate Bill 1070, the Support Our Law Enforcement and Safe Neighborhoods Act. Provisions of that act include enforcing trespassing charges against "illegal aliens" who are "present on any public or private land in this state" (Section 3, Title 13, Chapter 15) and providing "for any lawful contact made by a law enforcement official or agency of this state or a county, city, town or other political subdivision of this state where reasonable suspicion exists that the person is an alien who is unlawfully present in the United States, a reasonable attempt shall be made, when practicable, to determine the immigration status of the person" (Section 2, Title 11, Chapter 8). Governor Jan Brewer made a statement on April 23, 2010, upon signing the bill into law, saying that the law was necessary for Arizona to address a crisis "the federal government has refused to fix . . . the crisis caused by illegal immigration and Arizona's porous border." She stated that the bill would protect "all of us, every Arizona citizen and everyone here in our state lawfully. . . . We cannot delay while the destruction happening south of our . . . international border creeps its way north."

Although Governor Brewer avowed, in that same speech, "I will not tolerate racial discrimination or racial profiling in Arizona," the passage of the bill had several immediate results that illustrated the political and cultural logics connecting the actual wording and implementation of legislation to larger debates and public anxieties. The act was modified by later legislation, and parts of it were ruled incompatible with the U.S. Constitution, but passage of the act inspired further anti-immigration legislation across the country. Archibold (2010) reported in the *New York Times* that in 2009, "there were a record number of laws enacted (222) and resolutions (131) in 48 states [related to immigration policy], according to the National Conference of State Legislatures." Discourse analysis of these legal texts, accompanied by an anthropological exploration of the contexts that produced them, throws a different light on the contention that increased surveillance of all persons in the United States is justified to protect "lawful citizens" from the criminality of "illegal immigrants" and other racialized subjects.

Not since the McCarthy era has the United States seen so much state-sponsored citizen surveillance (see Lind and Otenyo 2006). Although the rhetoric for the current increase in surveillance harks back most directly to the events of September 11, 2001 (see Haggerty and Gazso 2005), there is clear continuity from the anti-immigrant discourse and practice supporting the passage of California's Proposition 187 to more recent anti-immigrant legislation to today's antiterrorist policies. Similarities include the conflation of constructions of race and nation in the targeting of individuals for state-sanctioned reductions of rights and the retreat from an inclusive national identity to one that equates full citizenship with "whiteness." With respect to the perceived threats from both immigration and terrorism, "security" is discursively associated with this symbolic whiteness, and blame and danger are associated with nonwhiteness.

Nativist appeals to anti-immigration legislation have waxed and waned with the economic and political tides in the United States. In the 1870s, for example, the country was experiencing a severe economic depression (Zinn 1995: 240). One response was to blame Asian immigrants for job shortages, and the Chinese Exclusion Act was passed in 1882 (Frank 1999: 74). After that act became law, the United States increased patrols along both the U.S.–Canada and U.S.–Mexico borders and pressured those neighboring North American nations to adopt the same immigration policies (Lee 2002). More than a century later, in 1996, the U.S. Congress passed the Illegal Immigration Reform and Immigrant Responsibility Act, kicking off another round of talks with representatives of the Canadian and Mexican governments on coordinating immigration controls. In 2002, racial profiling in U.S. immigration practices was the target of very public protests in Canada.

How is "freedom from terrorism" being used to selectively invoke and ignore global citizens' rights under international agreements? How is current U.S. immigration policy, as enforced by paid officials and by individuals acting out a sense of "citizen watch" entitlement, privileging whiteness and stigmatizing nonwhiteness to the point of stripping away citizenship rights? Alejandro Portes (2003: 51) argues:

> While coping with the terrorist threat is an urgent concern, it should not derail us from the long-term priorities of the nation, or be used to justify chauvinism. An unfortunate consequence of this sense of national urgency is that the words "immigration" and "terrorism" are often joined in the same sentence, as if one necessarily led to the other.

Joanne Mariner (2003) discusses the increasingly discriminatory national regulation of citizenship status despite nations' being signatories to the 1969 International Convention on the Elimination of All Forms of Racial Discrimination. Teresa Hayter (2000: 165) argues that "immigration controls are inherently racist." Brian Keith Axel (2002) writes about the representation of diasporas as a "national interruption," going along with the fantasy of homeland—as in the Homeland Security Act—and suggests that we view citizenship as a commodity. I would argue that market citizenship, like cultural citizenship, is a way to think about degrees of inclusion in the national public apart from legal status, and that it is tied to moral and racializing arguments about whose free-marketeering status is meritorious and who is meant to serve the free-marketeering citizens as labor. If the fear is that noncitizens will commits acts of terror, why are noncitizens encouraged to serve in the U.S. military as a route to citizenship? Like the wall, arguments about threats to security are largely symbolic and used to promote citizen surveillance of a shrinking default national citizenship. Legal status does not always matter at such moments, as Japanese Americans in California learned during their World War II internment.

Concluding Strategies

Anthropology is well equipped as a discipline, theoretically and methodologically, to situate anti-immigrant legislation in particular moments and places within broader contexts and cultural logics. In this chapter, for example, I have shown how California's Proposition 187 and subsequent anti-immigration legislation—often not intended by proponents to be lasting laws, given obvious unconstitutionality—have served as focal points for a collection of fears about economic decline across the United States and a perception of diminishing political control by those racialized as white, often conflated with "U.S. citizens" in public discourse and anti-immigration political advertisements. Activist anthropologists whose scholarship is informed by social justice concerns may well ask what can be done about these dominant and arbitrarily racializing representations of new immigrants as threatening to personal, economic, and national security.

A number of useful suggestions have already been made. Otto Santa Ana (2002) suggests that we engage in a campaign of countermetaphor—for example, countering representations of immigrants as violating the national body with representations of immigrants as the lifeblood of the nation, necessary to its economic and cultural vitality. He proposes that rather than allowing disease metaphors to be used for new immigrants, we apply them instead to racism, publicly calling it a cancer in the United States. Racializing discourse itself also introduces the possibility of transnational organizing against racialized discrimination. As Silverstein (2005: 377) argues, it is our responsibility as scholars "to explore the cultural conditions of not just disjuncture and difference, but also of conjuncture and convergence." Expanding on this, it is possible to see convergence not only between neoliberal and neoconservative agendas, and white supremacist and anti-immigrant agendas, but also between social science research and social justice work. The hate crimes spurred by anti-immigrant discourse need to be understood not only in local contexts but also in national, transnational, historical, political, economic, and cultural contexts, and anthropological analyses contribute usefully to such a project.

Exercise

Look into immigration-related initiatives that have been introduced in the United States over the years. How has "immigrant" been defined? Can any of the initiatives be said to be "anti-immigrant"? Justify your view.

NOTE

1. In related research, I followed events leading to the lowering of the Confederate battle flag, a symbol of power for white supremacists, from above the South Carolina statehouse to the front lawn in 2000 (Kingsolver 2006). After the 2015 assassinations in Charleston by a white supremacist, the flag was removed from the grounds entirely, but hate speech and violence continue across the United States. In 2014, the Southern Poverty Law Center mapped 784 active hate groups across the nation (see www.splcenter.org/hate-map).

REFERENCES

Almaguer, Tomás. 1994. *Racial Fault Lines: The Historical Origins of White Supremacy in California.* Berkeley: University of California Press.

Archibold, Randal C. 2010. "Arizona Enacts Stringent Law on Immigration." *New York Times,* April 23. www/nytimes.com/2010/04/24/us/politics/24immig.html (accessed May 12, 2010).

Axel, Brian Keith. 2002. "National Interruption: Diaspora Theory and Multiculturalism in the U.K." *Cultural Dynamics* 14 (3): 235–56.

Babington, Charles. 2007. "Can Immigration Reform Be Salvaged? Farmers and Others Try to Get Remnants of Failed Legislation Passed." *The State* (Columbia, SC), June 30, A12.

Baker, Lee D. 1998. *From Savage to Negro: Anthropology and the Construction of Race, 1896–1954.* Berkeley: University of California Press.

Benson, Peter. 2008. "El Campo: Faciality and Structural Violence in Farm Labor Camps." *Cultural Anthropology* 23 (4): 589–629.

Blee, Kathleen M. 2002. *Inside Organized Racism: Women in the Hate Movement.* Berkeley: University of California Press.

Bourgois, Philippe. 2001. "The Power of Violence in War and Peace: Post–Cold War Lessons from El Salvador." *Ethnography* 2 (1): 5–37.

Brewer, Jan. 2010. Address upon signing Arizona Senate Bill 1070 (transcription by Michael E. Eidenmuller). April 23. American Rhetoric Online Speech Bank. www.americanrhetoric.com/speeches/janbrewersenatebill1070speech.htm (accessed October 26, 2015).

Chavez, Leo R. 2001. *Covering Immigration: Popular Images and the Politics of the Nation.* Berkeley: University of California Press.

Claffey, James E. 2006. "Anti-immigrant Violence in Suburbia." *Social Text* 24 (3 88): 73–80.

De Genova, Nicholas P. 2002. "Migrant 'Illegality' and Deportability in Everyday Life." *Annual Review of Anthropology* 31: 419–47.

Douglas, Mary. 1986. *How Institutions Think.* Syracuse, NY: Syracuse University Press.

Du Bois, W. E. B. 1903. *The Souls of Black Folk.* Chicago: A. C. McClurg.

Fairness & Accuracy in Reporting. 2006. "CNN's Immigration Problem: Is Dobbs the Exception—or the Rule?" April 24. www.fair.org/index.php?page=2867 (accessed September 2, 2007).

Farmer, Paul. 1992. *AIDS and Accusation: Haiti and the Geography of Blame.* Berkeley: University of California Press.

Finewood, Michael. 2005. "'They're Taking Our Jobs': Representations of Latino Immigrants in the Carolinas." MA thesis, University of South Carolina.

Finnigan, David. 1995. "Hate Crimes Up since Proposition 187, Group Says." *National Catholic Reporter,* December 29, 6.

Fleck, Ludwik. (1935) 1979. *The Genesis and Development of a Scientific fact.* Chicago: University of Chicago Press.

Flores, Richard. 1995. "Alamo Images and the Birth of 'Otherness.'" Paper presented at the annual meeting of the American Anthropological Association, Washington, DC, November.

Foucault, Michel. 1977. *Discipline and Punish: The Birth of the Prison.* New York: Vintage Books.

Fox, Jonathan. 2005. "Unpacking 'Transnational Citizenship.'" *Annual Review of Political Science* 8: 171–201.

Frank, Dana. 1999. *Buy American: The Untold Story of Economic Nationalism*. Boston: Beacon Press.

Greenhouse, Carol. 2006. "Fieldwork on Law." *Annual Review of Law and Social Science* 2: 187–210.

Haggerty, Kevin D., and Amber Gazso. 2005. "Seeing beyond the Ruins: Surveillance as a Response to Terrorist Threats." *Canadian Journal of Sociology* 30 (2): 169–87.

Hayter, Teresa. 2000. *Open Borders: The Case against Immigration Controls*. London: Pluto Press.

Judis, John B. 2006. "Border War." *New Republic*, January 16, 15–19.

Kingsolver, Ann E. 2001. *NAFTA Stories: Fears and Hopes in Mexico and the United States*. Boulder, CO: Lynne Rienner.

———. 2006. "Strategic Alterity and Silence in the Promotion of California's Proposition 187 and of the Confederate Battle Flag in South Carolina." In Maria-Luisa Achino-Loeb, ed., *Silence: The Currency of Power*, 73–91. New York: Berghahn Books.

———. 2007. "Farmers and Farmworkers: Two Centuries of Strategic Alterity in Kentucky's Tobacco Fields." *Critique of Anthropology* 27 (1): 87–102.

Lee, Erika. 2002. "Enforcing the Borders: Chinese Exclusion along the U.S. Borders with Canada and Mexico, 1882–1924." *Journal of American History* 89 (1): 54–86.

Lind, Nancy S., and Eric E. Otenyo. 2006. "Administrative Agencies in a Technological Era: Are Eavesdropping and Wiretapping Now Acceptable without Probable Cause?" *International Journal of Public Administration* 29: 1397–1409.

Mariner, Joanne. 2003. "Racism, Citizenship, and National Identity." *Development* 46 (3): 64–70.

Martinez, Demetria. 1995. "Hatred Rumbles along New Fault Line Called Proposition 187." *National Catholic Reporter*, February 10, 18.

Mills, Charles W. 1997. *The Racial Contract*. Ithaca, NY: Cornell University Press.

Nevins, Joseph. 2002. *Operation Gatekeeper: The Rise of the "Illegal Alien" and the Making of the U.S.-Mexico Boundary*. New York: Routledge.

Omi, Michael, and Howard Winant. 1994. *Racial Formation in the United States from the 1960s to the 1990s*. 2nd ed. New York: Routledge.

"150 Turn Out to Fight Illegal Immigration." 2007. *Sun News* (Myrtle Beach, SC), reprinted in *The State* (Columbia, SC), November 11, B11.

Ong, Aihwa. 1999. *Flexible Citizenship: The Cultural Logics of Transnationality*. Durham, NC: Duke University Press.

———. 2007. *Neoliberalism as Exception: Mutations in Citizenship and Sovereignty*. Durham, NC: Duke University Press.

Ono, Kent A., and John M. Sloop. 2002. *Shifting Borders: Rhetoric, Immigration, and California's Proposition 187*. Philadelphia: Temple University Press.

Ordonez, Franco. 2008. "Immigration Arrests Spark Fear among S.C. Poultry Workers." *The Herald*, September 5. www.heraldonline.com/109/v-print/story/795178.html (accessed January 11, 2010).

Perot, Ross, with Pat Choate. 1993. *Save Your Job, Save Our Country: Why NAFTA Must Be Stopped—Now!* New York: Hyperion.

Portes, Alejandro. 2003. Ethnicities: Children of Migrants in America. *Development* 46 (3): 42–52.

Rosaldo, Renato. 1999. "Cultural Citizenship, Inequality, and Multiculturalism." In Rodolfo D. Torres, Louis F. Mirón, and Jonathan Xavier Inda, eds., *Race, Identity, and Citizenship: A Reader*, 253–61. Malden: Blackwell.

Rosen, James. 2007a. "DeMint Applauds Defeat of Bill—Immigration Measure Supported by Bush, Graham Dies in Senate." *The State* (Columbia, SC), June 29, A1.

———. 2007b. "Senate Backs Plan to Beef Up Border." *The State* (Columbia, SC), October 4, A6.

———. 2007c. "U.S. Senate Approves Graham Border Measure—Amendment Would Provide Money for Fencing, Agents, Detention Centers." *The State* (Columbia, SC), July 27, A4.

Santa Ana, Otto. 2002. *Brown Tide Rising: Metaphors of Latinos in Contemporary American Public Discourse*. Austin: University of Texas Press.

Silverstein, Paul A. 2005. "Immigrant Racialization and the New Savage Slot: Race, Migration, and Immigration in the New Europe." *Annual Review of Anthropology* 34: 363–84.

Smith, Mark M. 2006. "Looking Blindly for Terrorists." *The State* (Columbia, SC), August 2, A9.

Stefancic, Jean. 1997. "Funding the Nativist Agenda." In Juan F. Perea, ed., *Immigrants Out! The New Nativism and the Anti-immigrant Impulse in the United States*, 119–35. New York: New York University Press.

Tucker, William H. 2003. "A Closer Look at the Pioneer Fund: Response to Rushton." *Albany Law Review* 66 (4): 1145–60.

Vila, Pablo. 2000. *Crossing Borders, Reinforcing Borders: Social Categories, Metaphors, and Narrative Identities on the U.S.-Mexico Frontier.* Austin: University of Texas Press.

Weber, Max. (1905) 1977. *The Protestant Ethic and the Spirit of Capitalism.* New York: Prentice Hall.

Zavella, Patricia. 1997. "The Tables Are Turned: Immigration, Poverty, and Social Conflict in California Communities." In Juan F. Perea, ed., *Immigrants Out! The New Nativism and the Anti-immigrant Impulse in the United States,* 136–61. New York: New York University Press.

Zinn, Howard. 1995. *A People's History of the United States 1492–Present.* Rev. ed. New York: HarperCollins.

12

GENDER, RACE, AND CLASS IN AMERICA: HOME IN NEW HAVEN

Micaela di Leonardo

Over the past four decades, our understanding of gender, race, and class processes and politics has matured in an extraordinary way. But the same period has also witnessed, coincident with the demise of the Soviet sphere and China's "capitalist turn," the rise of a new, intensified form of global capitalism: neoliberalism.

Neoliberalism is both an ideology and a practice. Neoliberal ideology asserts that only through governmental retreat from social program spending, the associated widespread privatization of public resources, and the abolition of regulations on business and trade can we experience economic growth and widespread prosperity. And indeed, since the 1970s, governments around the world, whether through choice or under duress from the International Monetary Fund or World Bank, have enacted precisely these "economic reforms" (di Leonardo 2008). We have seen extraordinary global economic growth—but growth for whom? The results have been disastrous: rapidly increasing populations of the very poor and very wealthy and the thinning out of middle classes worldwide.

But while neoliberal ideology lionizes small governments that do not interfere in business affairs, in practice, neoliberal governments have repeatedly bailed out "too big to fail" corporations in economic downturns such as the 2008 recession and have also regularly subsidized corporate functioning—for example, through infrastructure giveaways and tax abatements. Neoliberal ideology has gained enormous purchase worldwide through both its celebration of individualized consumption and its novel joining of neoclassical economic theory with an identity-politics reading of civil liberties. Thus politicians, North and South, can claim to stand for the rights of women, racial and religious minorities, and

Reprinted with permission, from Nugent, David, and Joan Vincent, eds. 2008. *Companion to an Anthropology of Politics*, 135–151. © Wiley Blackwell. Republished in *Reflecting on America*, 2nd edition, edited by Clare L. Boulanger, 135–150 (© 2016 Taylor & Francis). All rights reserved.

even LGBTQ populations while ignoring the growing immiseration that disproportionately affects most of those populations (di Leonardo 2008; Harvey 2005;
Went 2000).

As these decades-long shifts have taken place, feminist scholarship has shifted
as well in the ways in which it construes the gender/politics arena. The first, pathbreaking work both established female political sentience and agency worldwide
and asserted that the unpolitical, "private" domestic domain of Parsonian theoriz-
ing and general scholarly neglect was, on the contrary, as much a hotbed of power
politics as the public arena. In anthropologist Sylvia Yanagisako's (1979) formulation, we needed to provide thicker descriptions of domestic domains worldwide,
acknowledging their political centrality.

The "sentience and agency" impulse also led to the rediscovery of female political actors, as in American historian Gerda Lerner's (1998) work on the antebellum
white Grimke sisters of South Carolina, who moved to Philadelphia to work for
abolition and then joined the fight for suffrage in the face of their Quaker brethren's
discrimination against them as women. Outside the West, scholars devoted new
attention to, for example, the early twentieth-century Egyptian women's movement activist Huda Sharawi and her contemporaries throughout the Middle East,
Africa, Asia, and Latin America (Jayawardena 1986).

The "rethinking public and private" impulse inspired an entire domestic
domain literature and a rewriting of earlier Marxist work on "the woman question." Theorists reconceptualized "reproduction" to include all the labor of bringing
the next adult generation into existence and attempted to account for the varying
reproductive roles of women—and even of men—in multiple social locations, particularly those inflected by race and class. Using both historical and contemporary
materials, looking at what were then labeled the First and Third Worlds, feminist
scholars considered the political implications of women's varying intersections
with this larger vision of economy.

A significant element of this retheorizing, along with the renascent Marxism
of the period, was social constructionism. Second-wave feminists coined the
opposition between sex, or biological differences, and gender, or all differences
between human males and females based on enculturation. Social construction
has been extraordinarily productive both theoretically and pragmatically and
is, if possible, even more important now, given the rebirth of sociobiology and
its takeover of U.S. popular culture. Acknowledging the mutability of human
categorizations, which we could also derive from Marx's analysis of class under
capitalism, sets the stage for progressive intellectual and political projects dealing with class, race, gender, and sexual orientation in the context of today's
global neoliberalism.

Yet constructionism poses a political problem in two ways. First, a wide
variety of political actors around the world have found essentialist arguments
congenial in their attempts to effect change. Whether these actors are pan-
Mayan activists, LGBTQ rights workers, feminist environmentalists, or Native
American or Australian Aboriginal land-claims disputants, the notion of the
eternal, unchanging subject whose traditions have the imprimatur of history can
be extremely compelling, especially if, as in the cases of Native Americans and
Australians, states themselves assert that only such subjects can bear rights. And
of course, as Eric Hobsbawm and Terence Ranger note in their seminal anthology

The Invention of Tradition (1983), states and elites are among the key historical inventors of traditions.

Second, the 1980s rise of poststructuralism and postmodernism also tended to create a false antinomy between culture and economy—even, in some scholars' work, to declare political economy itself simply another fictional representation and thus not worthy of study. And this set of claims became part of the vitiation of progressive politics in the West from the Reagan era forward. Joan Wallach Scott's widely hailed piece "Gender: A Useful Category of Historical Analysis" (1988), for example, adjures historians to study gender as historical discourse, entirely eliding any concern for actual male and female historical subjects and the shifting political economies in which they lived and live.

These new postmodern antinomies have tended to fuse with earlier scholarly tendencies to locate specific kinds of stratification-based politics in particular social spaces: class, of course, in workplaces, gender in households, and race or ethnicity and immigrant statuses in neighborhoods. (The "hybrid" identities celebrated in postmodern writings seem to be located, appropriately, in no particular social space.) Some second-wave scholars have helped to disrupt these spatial givens through considering, for example, the gender politics in proletarian workplaces, in neighborhood or village organizing, and in feminist and antifeminist organizations in a wide variety of locations around the globe. In addition, research on sexuality and reproduction from the 1980s forward has opened up our understandings of the myriad ways in which mutually imbricated constructions of gender, sexuality, and race are part of all nationalist, colonialist, capitalist, and anticapitalist projects.

More recent work has achieved further complexity and breadth. Susan Gal and Gail Kligman's *The Politics of Gender after Socialism* (2000), for example, engages simultaneously with shifting labor and reproductive processes, the complex gendering of official discourses, and the varying popular framings of "proper" gender in the former Soviet sphere. Roger Lancaster's *The Trouble with Nature* (2003) considers the renaissance of antiempirical and misogynist sociobiology in contemporary American popular culture. Gina Pérez's *The Near Northwest Side Story* (2004) simultaneously narrates postwar circular labor migration between Puerto Rico and Chicago, the specifically raced and gendered economic and familial effects, and the heavily freighted and shifting places of *la isla* and the mainland in her female subjects' fertile imaginaries. And Jane Collins's *Threads* (2003) analyzes material shifts in the global garment industry and the changing gendered discourses of work and community among firm managers, female workers, and union activists in the United States and Mexico.

In what follows, I offer my own efforts to illuminate shifting gender, class, and race politics in one Northern location—the United States—through the prism of what Marx labeled the "historical and moral element" that we must always consider in gauging class formation and capitalist development: the gendered construction, across class and race, of the workings of the "proper home." Like the scholars mentioned above, I engage gender within the full historical political economic contexts of its shifts over time. Thus we can and should consider "the political" both in terms of our older understandings of politics and political organizations and in terms of the newer sense of cultural politics—but without succumbing to the wan idealism of postmodernism without political economy.

Home in New Haven, Connecticut

Let me begin with some urban ethnographic snapshots. First, from the summer of 2000, the tag end of the Clinton years: I am in New Haven, Connecticut, in The Hill, one of the three named ghettos of the town, about four blocks from my former home. My black male companion and I park outside a nondescript brick building with a single neon sign, Cavallaro's. We approach the building and open the door onto a dark barroom. Black faces at the full bar turn toward me, then back to their conversations. Rhythm and blues pumps from the jukebox at the back of the room. My companion and I find spaces at the bar and order drinks. But the bartender is an elderly white woman, in a dress and matching pearl necklace and earrings, who seems to be having trouble understanding "Stolichnaya." On a hunch, I address her formally, "Signora, e` Italiana, lei?"

Italian benedictions rain down on me as the signora, overjoyed to find a *paesana*, calls loudly for her husband and son to come meet me. The drinks are free, the great beauties of our mother country, my appearance, and my competence *nella lingua bella* extolled. The husband tells me at length about his recent trip back to the Abruzzi, checking every paragraph or so, "Ha capito, signorina?" Bar life goes on around us as the excitement fades. A hard-bitten woman in a baseball cap, in response to TV news of an international Catholic gathering, shouts, "I want to go the fuck to Rome." The recent gospel convocation comes up, to much criticism of the arrangements: "This is Gospel Fest, you don't rope off shit. It's supposed to be free." Then the signora takes off her apron, totters around from behind the bar, bids me a flowery Italian adieu, and announces to the room, "Io vado adesso." Every bar-stool habitué turns toward her to call in chorus, "Goodnight, Mom." Baseball cap says minatorily to Giuseppe, the son, now behind the bar, "She's been on her feet all night!" On a later evening, I wander in and suddenly realize there are only (almost all black) women customers and a female DJ. The place is hopping, and it is clearly Lesbian Night. I engage the patrons in conversation, and a young black firefighter throws her arms around Giuseppe, declaring, "Joe and I went to school together, didn't we, Joe? I been comin here thirteen years!"

Then: moving back to 1989—deep in the Reagan–Bush Senior recession—and I am still living in, not just visiting, New Haven. I have developed a friendly relationship with the black couple who recently moved in next door in my largely white working-class neighborhood a couple of miles from the Yale University campus, and I go over one evening to interview them. Patti Hendry had said upon meeting me, "I'm not knockin my kind you know, but I never lived with a lot of black people around." I walk into an apartment much like mine in that it is a floor-through flat that was created from a 1920s vintage multifamily house. But Patti's apartment, definitely unlike mine, is a miracle of white, cream, oatmeal, and glass surfaces—and she has a toddler son. She accepts my compliments as only her due and fusses over providing refreshments.

Much happened during that interview, but here I want to note two key points. The first is that Patti repeatedly noticed tiny imperfections in her domestic environment—her little son leaving a handprint on the glass tabletop, a napkin falling to the impeccable white rug—and sharply directed her husband to remedy them. The second is that he and Patti, engaging with my life-history questions, got caught up in a fierce disagreement with one another over whether or not poor black people were to blame for their poverty. Patti was furious about crime and drugs in the neighborhood and said, "And then you have to fault the parents," while her husband focused on the economy: "I'm just saying, there's some kids that don't know no way out . . . people doing what they have to do to survive. . . . I'm saying there's no jobs out there right now."

In the summer of 2000, having kept in touch, I catch up with Patti again. She has moved off my old block, due west, into a neighborhood that had been all white in the 1980s. She is still renting, but now an entire house. This environment is even more impressive than her old apartment, and at the end of our interview, Patti gives me a tour of both floors of the house, pausing to explain how she sponge-painted the bathroom and stenciled a bedroom wall, showing off the vintage furniture and crystal and linens she has collected by haunting yard sales. While all this is going on, her two children wander in and are sharply told what they are allowed to eat in the kitchen and that they cannot go out to the front yard to play. Some little children playing outside come up to the screen door, trying to find out who I am. Patti teases them but complains to me later that they are poorly trained. "You know, you don't talk to adults that way."

Through the years I have known her, Patti has repeatedly laid out for me her sense of the city and its suburban surround, which areas are "nice" and which are "drug city," where she is willing to go and where not. She explicitly warns me against the block where Cavallaro's is located and also tells me that she won't walk on the small business block a few streets away from her home, where I regularly attend a storefront black working-class aerobics center in an excess of ethnographic zeal.

In the same more recent period, I also visit with two white families living in Patti's new neighborhood. Both are professional-class heterosexual couples with children, both heavily involved in the renaissance of a local Orthodox Jewish congregation, both with progressive politics. And their home environments are similar as well. Just like Patti and her family in the 1980s, both families rent flats in 1920s multifamily houses. But unlike Patti's home, their apartments are dingy with old paint and crowded with mismatched, beat-up furniture; children's toys and clothes are flung all over, and no effort at decoration is apparent. In each home, the children wander freely and engage the guest, taking over the conversation with their parents' happy approval. And in both homes, the women talk about New Haven in expansive terms. One boasts to me of her broad knowledge, despite her recent residence in the city, of different black and Latino neighborhoods as a result of exploring them in search of the best thrift shops, driving her beat-up station wagon with the kids in the back.

Finally, there is the New Haven native, Frances Jones, a progressive black lawyer in her late fifties with a Black Panther past, who befriended me in the aerobics class (I was wearing a T-shirt with a local civil rights message). For this woman, a wide-ranging familiarity with all areas of the city, specific long-term relationships with black neighborhood shopkeepers, and consumption of local minority journalism are all points of personal pride. She lives with her husband, a retired blue-collar worker, and elderly mother in a nice two-story Victorian house furnished in high style, with Orientalist touches, in a neighborhood known since the 1980s as the residential center of the city's black middle class—just a few blocks from my old block, in the opposite direction from Cavallaro's. Her sense of the city, as I have noted, is expansive, and she tends to frame local crime issues in terms of improving communication and saving poor children's lives rather than in terms of avoidance of certain areas or increased home or neighborhood security. One night she takes me to the Black Elks Lodge, located in the ghetto right next to her neighborhood, to listen to live jazz, and afterward we drive around the area so she can show me, with great pride, newly constructed town houses where falling-down public housing had been. "Where would we go?" she asks me rhetorically, talking about the city and its problems, and announces, "New Haven is home."

Home is an extraordinarily resonant term in American life—a point highlighted by former President George W. Bush's post–September 11 creation of the bureaucratic behemoth of the Department of Homeland Security. My own engagement with the gender, class, and race politics of home arose through the accident of setting up my own residence. In 1986, while teaching at Yale University, I rented an apartment in a working-class neighborhood in New Haven and thereby backed into doing fieldwork in the poor, deindustrialized, and richly engaging city. The "home" theme of this piece is abstracted from the array of issues in my study as a whole, which is a historical ethnography of race, class, gender, and representation in the city from the optic of a shifting working-class neighborhood.

The late French sociologist Pierre Bourdieu (1977, 1984) wrote compellingly about homes and habitus among both village Algerians and the French working and middle classes—about how the very physical organization of housing space enacts a population's apprehensions of social order, and about the ways in which class habitus is reflected in home organization and decor. Historians and social scientists have also contributed greatly to our understanding of shifting local apprehensions of domesticity in the contexts of global colonial, capitalist, and postcolonial transitions. But as we will see, these insights have not really been adequately translated to the contemporary American scene. God is in the details, and we need to engage with details of home in American history. The people with whom I worked in New Haven, like all of us, have inherited this array of representations, and they made and make selective use of them in explaining their lives to themselves and others. So we should be clear at the outset about what they are. For that reason, rather than entering immediately into the lives and apprehensions of Patti Hendry and her sister New Haveners, I will go the long way around, through a historical and political economic review of "home" in the United States.

"Home" underscored the nineteenth-century sense of American differences from Europe—in the (Henry) Jamesian sense that "we" somehow had nice homes without the decadent baggage of the European class system. This idea explains the deep strength of the notion of the American family farm and lies behind Manifest Destiny mythology—that Americans could and should domesticate what we define as uninhabited wilderness. And, of course, as in all of Europe and indeed its colonies, in the United States notions of home became deeply gendered as female over the course of the long nineteenth century with the rise of an ideology of separate spheres. Many scholars have articulated the development of the paired notions of the outer, urban, business world as both dirty and corrupting and inherently male and the inner, tranquil, psychological, spiritual, "noneconomic" domestic realm as entirely female. So we have inherited a tendency to think about home as a female realm somehow outside the world of economy and labor.

In the post–World War II environment of rapid economic expansion, home took on added symbolic baggage. Widespread suburbanization, widely available household technologies like improved vacuum cleaners and automatic washing machines, and postwar anti–working woman ideology (American women stayed in the labor force in this era but were newly invisible after their wartime apotheosis as Rosie the Riveter) combined in an image of the safe suburban home presided over by the contented housewife aided by labor-saving devices. This construction became official in the notorious Cold War "kitchen debates," in which President Richard Nixon boasted to Soviet leader Nikita Khrushchev about the splendor of American women's household lives.

Betty Friedan's *The Feminine Mystique*, first published in 1963, predated the actual second wave of the feminist movement, but it helped put the ball—the critique of the "housewife in splendor" model—in play. Feminists of the 1970s exploded the notion of the "economy-less" domestic realm, succeeded in shifting popular consciousness to an apprehension of housework and child care as real labor, and brought women's labor force participation, which was in any event already rising rapidly, into sharp visibility. "Home" began to be represented as a site of gender struggle as well as a haven from a heartless world.

This early second-wave period, however, was also the era of the civil rights and black power movements, anti–Vietnam War mobilizations, early gay rights organizing, and the general youth revolution symbolized by the silly but notorious trinity of "sex, drugs, and rock 'n' roll." Popular American notions of home shifted to include—at least for some—unmarried couples, gay couples, and hippie, communal, or movement households. And as a result of civil rights organizing, Americans came to understand the United States as a nation of segregated housing. They varied enormously, however, in their understanding of what should be done about that state of affairs.

Most discussion of housing segregation focused on urban neighborhoods, and here yet another element of the era enters, one I in fact cut my scholarly teeth on back in the 1970s. The very term *white ethnicity*—meaning European Americans from backgrounds more diverse than WASP (white Anglo-Saxon Protestant)—hails from the 1970s, from what came to be called the "white ethnic renaissance," which had a short flurry of media attention and then was crowded off the public stage by other concerns. White ethnics are important for our discussion, though, both because New Haven historically was a largely white ethnic and black city—the growing Latino population is of more recent vintage—and because the nationwide construction of "white ethnics" in that era was both heavily gendered and tied into shifting notions of proper and improper homes.

"White ethnics" discovered themselves and were discovered by others in early 1970s American cities in the context of complex cultural and political economic shifts: continuing economic expansion, the ongoing war in Vietnam, and the social movements, identified above, that arose from these two key political economic realities. These multiple movements for reform and liberation challenged federal, state, and institutional structures—such as those of colleges and universities—and individuals who perceived themselves to be threatened by particular demands for social change. The Nixon administration (1969–74), in particular, sought to exploit and enhance these social divisions through the use of the polarizing discourse of the "silent majority"—as opposed to the protesting antiadministration "minority." Between administration rhetoric and media response, an image of this stipulated entity grew: members of the silent majority were white—implicitly white ethnic—blue-collar workers, largely male. They were held to be "patriotic" and to live in "traditional" families—ones in which males ruled, women did not work outside the home for pay, and parents controlled their children.

This media image, of course, did not reflect an aggregate social reality. This was the era, after all, in which married working-class women were entering the labor force at record rates, and in which their additions to family income maintained working-class living standards in the face of declining real incomes. And sexual adventurism and drug use in the late 1960s and early 1970s were the property of working-class no less than middle-class youth. Nevertheless, as a media construct, as a symbol of the hemorrhaging of Democratic voters to the Republican Party, the conservative white ethnic blue-collar worker—Archie Bunker from the popular television show *All in the Family*—gained salience in this period. This salience was much enhanced by the shifting populations and power relations in American cities.

In the 1960s, poor black Americans became newly visible and newly defined as a social problem in northern cities. The two great waves of black migration from the South during World Wars I and II had resulted in cohorts of permanent northern black urban residents. These men and women had moved to the North (often through employer recruitment) both to take advantage of lucrative war jobs and to flee Jim Crow and the effects of the mechanization of southern agriculture. They had then often been laid off, and many had become part of a permanent reserve army of labor (available to be employed during periods of high business demand). Urban renewal projects in the 1950s and 1960s—an employment boondoggle for white ethnic blue-collar workers—destroyed countless urban black and Latino neighborhoods, replaced them with office blocks and sports complexes, and shifted and concentrated the poor minority populations in areas dominated by inhospitable, poorly built, and badly maintained government housing projects. Approximately 90 percent of the housing destroyed by urban renewal was never replaced, and two-thirds of those displaced were black or Puerto Rican. The Federal Housing Authority deliberately fostered segregated white housing and refused loans to blacks until the passage of the Fair Housing Act in 1968. Big-city governments refused to shift budgetary resources to basic services for these impoverished areas.

Neighborhood deterioration, increased crime, and urban uprisings—combined with intensive political organizing—stimulated the establishment of highly visible federal Great Society programs. At the same time, a small cohort of socially mobile blacks, emboldened by the civil rights movement, attempted to buy homes in formerly white urban and suburban neighborhoods. The resulting "white flight" greatly enriched the real estate speculators who fanned its flames and exacerbated inner-city white racism. Black (and Latino) struggles for higher-quality public education, neighborhood services, and civil service and union jobs led to increased friction between white, often white ethnic, and minority citizens in northern urban environments. The first scattered fringe of desuburbanizing better-off whites entered into this polarized and often dangerous environment, benefiting, of course, from its resulting low real estate values.

Thus the white ethnic community construct arose from an extraordinarily complex historical ground, and this complexity was reflected in its multiple expressions and political uses. Notions of the strength and richness of white ethnic cultures and their repression by WASPs mimicked black cultural nationalist (and white scholars') celebrations of black culture's endurance despite white domination. Both popular journalistic accounts and grassroots white ethnic discourse focused on the strength and unity of white ethnic families as opposed to black families—whose popular image had been shaped in the early 1960s as a "tangle of pathology" by the Moynihan Report. In my own first study, many Italian Americans' racist expressions against blacks focused on inferior black family behavior as both explaining and justifying widespread black poverty. The argument was that, as the undeserving poor, blacks were not entitled to the largesse of Great Society programs and the approval of elite sponsors, which should instead flow to "deserving" white ethnics.

This relative entitlement frame is attached, as I have argued elsewhere, to a "report card mentality" in which shifting American class divisions are seen as caused by proper and improper ethnic or racial family and economic behavior rather than by the differential incorporation of immigrant and resident populations in American capitalism's evolving class structure (di Leonardo 1984). Scholarship, journalism, and grassroots expressions celebrated white ethnics for their family loyalties and neighborhood ties. In fact, advertising in this period began to exploit "cute" white ethnic imagery (the pizza-baking grandmother, the extended family at the laden dinner table) in order to invest frozen and canned foods with the cachet of the gemeinschaft—of community in the deepest sense, of knowing how to live in and reproduce proper homes.

This gemeinschaft was delineated as an urban phenomenon existing alongside and in opposition to urban black populations. In fact, there was the distinct flavor of a "three bears" analogy in much 1970s and 1980s rhetoric on white ethnicity. While WASPs were "too cold" (bloodless, modern, and unencumbered) and blacks were "too hot" (wild, primitive, and overburdened), white ethnics were "just right." They could and did claim to represent the golden historical mean between the overwhelming ancientness and primitiveness of gemeinschaft and the exhausted modernity of gesellschaft. For a hot minute in the 1970s, American white ethnics commandeered Baby Bear's chair (nonblack Latinos, Asians, and other minorities were written out of the story altogether).

Central to the new construction of white ethnic community was the Madonna-like (in the older sense) image of the white ethnic woman. Early 1970s popular writers extolled her devotion to home and family, and many of the more conservative Italian Americans in my late 1970s study echoed this fusion of ethnic chauvinism and antifeminism. Part of the appeal of this construction was the notion that white ethnic mothers, unlike "selfish" WASP and "lazy" black mothers, could control their children and thus were exempt from blame for then-current youth protests. But in fact, white ethnic women were no less subject to the pressures and opportunities of the shifting American political economy of the 1970s, and many more of the Italian American women with whom I worked actively altered or rejected the popular image of the self-sacrificing, kitchen-bound ethnic mother.

In an era of rising feminist activism, the sudden celebration of a group of women socially labeled as backward, stolid, and possessive wives and mothers functioned very clearly as antifeminist rhetoric—particularly against women's participation in the workforce. As well, in focusing on women's "duties" to husband and children, it worked against prevalent civil rights imagery of heroic black women in the movement whose duties lay in the public sphere. Many feminist scholars celebrated the strength and endurance of "traditional" ethnic women and used, for example, narratives of past union and strike activities or consumer protests to suggest a vision of innately progressive, rebellious ethnic womanhood. This attempt, however, was overwhelmed by dominant conservative media images, images that live on in, say, Olive Garden commercials, while their original political usage has withered.

White ethnic community is no longer a hot topic for academic papers and popular cultural accounts. Festivals and meetings of ethnic historical associations and social groups do not receive the public attention they once did. During the Reagan era (1981–88), we saw instead a return in public culture to the *Great Gatsby* romance—the notion that the really proper American homes were those of wealthy WASPs. *Good Housekeeping* began its "New Traditionalist" advertising campaign, which featured obviously affluent, nonworking, blond women and their well-groomed children on the spacious grounds of their suburban or country estates: "She knows what she values—home and family." Wealthy whites took back Baby Bear's chair with a vengeance, and a new romantic halo was constructed over the image—embodied by First Lady Nancy Reagan—of the elegant, dignified, adorned, and (publicly at least) devoted wife and mother, the curator of the proper WASP bourgeois home and children. Through the presidencies of George H. W. Bush, Bill Clinton, and George W. Bush, these images waxed and waned and ultimately retreated to the backstage of American life, but, together with notions of white ethnic community, they remain "on hold" for activation in particular social settings for particular ends. The stage itself was soon populated by a new construct involving race, class, gender, and notions of home—that of the "minority underclass." Let me lay out its evolution.

The mid-1970s energy crisis, so profitable for the big oil companies, was the first of a series of shocks to the American economy that helped to usher in the new public ideology that we had entered an "era of limits." During Jimmy Carter's administration (1977–80), rapidly escalating inflation, particularly in the rising real estate market, set the stage for the dismantling of Great Society programs, newly seen as "too expensive." Welfare cutbacks under Carter became a wholesale shrinkage of the federal social welfare budget under Ronald Reagan, and then the abandonment of Aid to Families with Dependent Children altogether under Clinton. The concomitant recession drove unemployment figures into double digits. The numbers of individuals and families made homeless by unemployment, real estate speculation, and the federal abandonment of low-cost housing programs grew rapidly.

With the economic recovery of the middle and late 1980s, unemployment shrank to early 1970s levels then rose again with the Bush recession, fell with the Clinton economic renaissance, rose again in the post-9/11 recession, fell during the housing-bubble boom, skyrocketed in the 2008 recession, then fell under President Obama's stimulus program and with economic recovery. However, unemployment always shrinks less for minority Americans, giving rise to the African American aphorism, "When America catches a cold, blacks get pneumonia." Of those successfully reemployed, many worked part-time or at jobs with lower status and pay than their previous positions. As a result of these shifts and regressive tax legislation, from the 1970s onward the numbers of both the very poor and the very rich have risen. The United States now has the highest levels of poverty and the smallest middle class, proportionately, in the industrialized world. Despite much local and national organizing, popular political discourse shifted significantly rightward. Civil rights, women's, gay, and labor groups were newly labeled "special interests." (Only in the 2000s did we begin to see a progressive shift in public opinion concerning LGBTQ rights.) But most crucially, public discourse about the poor, particularly poor blacks and Latinos, turned once again, nearly hegemonically, to automatic deprecation and "blame the victim" rhetoric. Such groups were once again thought to constitute an "underclass" that had deviated from the American mainstream.

The new underclass ideology functioned specifically, as had the older "culture of poverty" formulation, to turn attention away from the political economic production of poverty and toward the "pathological" behavior of the poor, whose characteristics were presumed (in the hard version) to cause or merely (in the soft version) to reproduce poverty. For African American sociologist William Julius Wilson, for example, whose 1987 work *The Truly Disadvantaged* rationalized underclass ideology for scholars and policy makers, advanced capitalism is assumed, and assumed to be benign. Writing in Reagan's second term, Wilson used passive-voice political economy: blacks "get concentrated" in inner cities, jobs just happen to leave. He scorned "racism" as an explanation for any social change, interpreting it narrowly as nasty dyadic encounters in which individual whites do dirt to individual blacks. To put it bluntly, Wilson effectively said, "It's nobody's fault, but poor blacks got screwed and now they're acting ugly." Wilson and other underclass ideologues adduced rising numbers of unmarried mothers, uninvolved biological fathers, welfare abuse, poverty, drugs, and crime to prove the existence of a new pathology in the black and brown poor.

Countering elements of underclass mythology, scholars have noted that black adolescent childbearing rates began falling *in the 1960s*. It was not birthrates but marriage rates that had altered. Further, most poor Americans are white; African Americans were never the majority recipients of welfare, and 40 percent of welfare mothers worked for pay as well. Despite media portrayals, most welfare recipients had few, not many, children—the average was two—and most cycled off the dole whenever they could line up jobs, child care, and health insurance. (Further, it was welfare for the often financially stable elderly—Social Security— not for poor mothers—Aid to Families with Dependent Children—that took up the bulk of the federal social welfare budget.) Black and white pregnant women consume substances (legal and illegal) that may be injurious to their fetuses at the same rates, but doctors report black women to law enforcement authorities for such activity ten times more often. The exception to the rule is cigarette smoking, which of course is legal. A government study indicates that black mothers smoke much less than do white mothers.

Federal government studies indicate that black adolescents consume illegal drugs at lower rates than do their white peers. Studies also show that blacks now graduate from high school at close to the same rates as whites, but that "returns to education" (job remuneration and status), at all educational levels, are significantly lower for both male racial minorities and all women than for white men. Employers openly admit to interviewers that they discriminate against minorities in hiring, and federal studies indicate that minorities with the same resources and credit records as whites are denied home mortgages at twice the rate. Minorities are more frequently harassed, injured, and killed by police, arrested for crimes when whites are not, convicted more frequently, and given heavier prison sentences. Finally, on the family values front, federal data indicate that the higher a man's income, the *less likely* he is to make his court-ordered child-support payments. In sum, underclass ideology, which faded as the Clinton administration eviscerated welfare and the go-go economy of the 1990s took off, both entirely misrepresents empirical reality and is waiting backstage, much like white ethnic community ideology, should the need arise to redemonize the minority poor.

New Haven's historical political economic shifts fit all these national urban patterns only too well. New Haven is a medium-size deindustrialized southern New England city with all the impedimenta of abandoned factories, recurrent municipal financial crises, and white flight so familiar from the situations of other deindustrialized towns and cities. The majority of the population is now black and Latino, though during most of the twentieth century New Haven had a white ethnic majority, with Italians, Irish, Slavs, and Jews of all nationalities predominating.

In the 1980s, in part because of the depredations of urban renewal that I have described for the country as a whole but, more important, in tune with the starvation of American cities by successive Reagan and Bush administration policies, New Haven was repeatedly featured in its own local media, and in the national media, particularly in the *New York Times* and a widely read *New Yorker* series, as an emblem of urban dirt, disorder, and danger writ small, a site of desperate black and brown youth caught up in crack wars. In turn, this image led to a nicely digestible, seemingly empirical rationale for the blame-the-victim pieties of the underclass ideology hegemonic in that era. In *Exotics at Home* (1998), I describe this process from the optic of my working-class neighborhood under the onslaught of large-scale immiseration, a neighborhood that shifted from nearly all white to nearly all black over the five years of my residence.

Spatially speaking, New Haven has an eighteenth-century village green that now defines downtown, with Yale buildings, federal and municipal offices, an urban renewal–era mall and other shopping areas, and a medical complex radiating out in different directions from its orienting grid. What we might call the Yale Zone—and Yale is now, after decades of deindustrialization, the city's largest employer—encompasses some neighborhoods north of campus that had been mixed WASP and white ethnic and now are heavily occupied by faculty and graduate students, and some much shabbier areas east of campus, mixed business and residential, where poorer or more cosmopolitan-minded graduate students live. An Italian literature professor told me she rented in this latter area, which she called the Left Bank, when she was a graduate student, preferring its racial mix and proximity to black areas to the much whiter complexion of the northern neighborhoods. Since the 1980s, Yale has pushed back the Left Bank, and the ghetto it abuts, by buying up and rehabilitating property, even buying and closing off a public street. This expansion of a cordon sanitaire, pushing poor people and their activities away, is not unique to Yale; rather, it is now a common practice on the part of universities and hospitals in the United States, really a part of larger urban growth politics and gentrifying processes.

Due west of the Left Bank, the neighborhood where I lived stretches several miles, with two of the three named city ghettos on its north and south flanks. In terms of what the technocrats call housing stock, New Haven is unlike many large cities in that it has fewer apartment houses and more large multifamily homes that, in poorer areas, have been cut up into individual apartments. My block was made up of such houses, actually in the process of final cutting up and renting out during my five years' residence. Farther east, across a large park, was a somewhat more affluent series of neighborhoods that were, in the 1980s, very white. But during the economically expansionist 1990s, unnoticed by New Haveners, the park boundary was erased as both areas became racially integrated. Most astonishing, from the 1990s into the 2000s, the east–west arterial road, once lined by heavily Jewish-owned small businesses, became dominated by black ones, including innumerable hair and nail salons, various soul food and Caribbean diners, a small music store, and the storefront aerobics center I have mentioned. This shift went unnoticed even by city politicians. In 2002, for example, there was a political fuss over the sale of a small business in the Dixwell area—which is overwhelmingly black—to an Asian couple. A local black alderman, in justifying his protest, astoundingly asked in a public forum whether "Jewish shopkeepers on Whalley Avenue" would welcome black businesses in their neighborhood.

In following urban lives from the mid-1980s to the present, I was highly aware of overarching political economic shifts and associated local demographic, economic, and political changes. During the go-go Clinton 1990s, for example, unemployment fell precipitously, the crack wars abated, and the prostitutes who walked the neighborhood nightly at the end of the 1980s either moved indoors or turned to other means of livelihood. But the New Haveners with whom I worked were simply living out their daily lives and often did not follow these shifts. Thus not only earlier ethnic and racial residential and business patterns but also particular images of urban poverty, crime, and danger that were inscribed in New Haveners' minds in the 1980s remained part of their urban imaginary into the new millennium, despite the evidence of their own daily experiences.

Now we are ready to consider the disjunctive elements of "home" in contemporary American public culture, a disconnection that living in working-class New Haven forced to my attention. That is, since the 1970s, we have seen the development of two major public arenas in which "home" is discussed, which we might label the gentry arena and the underclass arena. On the one hand, with the rising cost of real estate, the glorification of the notion of well-off WASP homes (think Ralph Lauren advertisements and Martha Stewart), and the reestablishment of shelter magazines and online rehab and decor sites, "home," meaning beautifully appointed living spaces for better-off whites, is a major national industry. As American newspapers' "women's pages"—in part under feminist pressure—have been transmogrified into style and living sections, we read more and more each year about sponge-painted walls, great rooms, lofts, ethnic/country/European kitchens, and the installation of vintage or vintage-like bookcases, hardware, and fixtures. Well-off white couples—and sometimes gay couples or single women—pose happily in their "after" living spaces all over mass and middlebrow media.

On the other hand, newspaper front pages periodically run frightening stories, complete with stark black-and-white photos, of ghetto apartments discovered to be overrun with drugs, crime, rats, and roaches, and thus from which social services have just yanked children. Front page versus style section, crime and neglect stories versus fluffy gentrifying ones, narratives of the failure of poor black mothers versus the obsessions and triumphs of well-off white ones: this is the new race- and class-divided representation of home in the United States. Occasionally, particularly in black and Latino media, we see black and Latino actors, music stars, or athletes in their carefully appointed homes—and, of course, President Barack and First Lady Michelle Obama in the White House. But the very rarity of these representations underscores the underclass norm. And the extraordinary misrepresentation of these representations really comes home to us, as it were, when we reflect that the vast bulk of the black American population is neither impoverished nor well-off but solidly working-class. In that sense, Patti Hendry and her family *are* black America.

It is now clear that I developed this analysis of shifts in race, gender, and representation because my New Haven fieldwork virtually rubbed my nose in it. I could not help but be struck by the extraordinarily clean and well-appointed living spaces into which I was welcomed by my black and Puerto Rican neighbors, so utterly at odds with what I was reading in the *New York Times* and the *New Haven Register*. And I was thoroughly amused to go into well-off white homes that could only be described as Martha Stewart's worst nightmare. We can now also see how Patti Hendry's seemingly antiblack statements and class concerns are defensive, an attempt to define herself and her family outside the dominant underclass characterizations, outside the racial report card, while, sadly, their empirical falsehoods seem commonsensical to her, as they do to most Americans since the 1980s. Frances Jones, on the other hand, has both long-term political and religious reasons for explicitly resisting underclass ideology. And, of course, she is aware of her class status, not to mention her appropriately older-model Mercedes, and does not fear being identified with the black poor she defines herself as being in solidarity with and attempting to help.

African American women have inherited not only all the ideological baggage I have just laid out but also the racist white tendency to define them as inherently dirty and degraded, a tendency also extended to other racial minorities and, in the past, to white ethnics. One of the autobiographical sources of my analysis is my strong memory of my Italian American aunts' obsession with cleanliness and gentility. Their 1950s doilies and Patti Hendry's 1990s sponge-painted walls have the same roots in American women's and racial or ethnic history. And my professional-class white New Haven friends literally could "afford," if they wished, to have disheveled homes and unruly children. There is, of course, tremendous variety in the ways in which American women of all racial or ethnic identities and across classes put together interiors, but no one was going to think these Jewish families' households resembled TV video footage of abuse and neglect cases, nor did those wives and mothers worry, as their grandmothers may have done, and my grandmother did, that WASPs would think them dirty, ungenteel sluts.

What can we say, then, about the larger issues of gender, class, and race, and varying home and urban imaginaries on the contemporary American scene? First, individuals in cities extend their notions of "home" outward into other venues, as we saw from the behavior and statements of the patrons at the wonderful bar, Cavallaro's. But sites of urban pleasure and danger are not at all unambiguous, not widely agreed upon, as we also saw. Cavallaro's is a home away from home for large numbers of working-class New Haven black women, straight and gay—literally a site where family is recognized—but for Patti Hendry it is just a building on a dangerous, dirty street. And again, the stretch of the block with the aerobics center strikes her as low-class, but that is not the opinion of the black lawyer who enjoyed the sweat sessions and the lively company there with me. As well as pure issues of habitus, we have here questions of wildly differing notions of gentility. This latter point is underlined by other ethnographic vignettes: hilarious episodes of working-class black women at other bars skillfully swearing like proverbial fishwives and in the next breath extolling their hardwood floors and crystal ornaments at home. It is buttressed as well by the life-history narratives of the elderly black woman, now dead, who lived across the street from me. She deflected attention from her cramped, overstuffed apartment and tended to stress instead her friendships with long-dead white neighbors, her New England ancestry, and her grown son's executive position in the banking industry.

A further important point here is that neither Patti Hendry's home nor the homes of the aerobics center patrons, my elderly neighbor, or the retirement-age librarian with whom I visit—the fulcrum of black womanhood in the United States, statistically speaking—are in any way represented in our contemporary public sphere. Nor, it is important to add, is the easy interracial mingling and open acceptance of homosexuality in the glorious working-class bar part of our public culture, where only since 2014 have we begun to see brave outlier advertising representing interracial and gay couples.

All of these points illustrate the complexities of American civil society in the era of neoliberal capitalism. We can see New Haveners struggling to maintain public spaces and to forge community within the interstices of the capitalist market. We see their struggle to invest "home" with meanings no longer expressible in the public sphere and the particularly privatized class anxieties articulated by African American working-class women in the highly marketized and misrepresentative atmosphere of the neoliberal present.

How New Haveners variously conceive of home, then, is along the lines of eighteenth-century English poet William Blake's world in a grain of sand—it reflects wider national and international historical and contemporary realities. And the class, race, and gender inflections of those realities are both occluded by and parallel to the current international crisis over homelands here and in Central Asia, the Middle East, and beyond. Virginia Woolf is well known for having asserted that her country was the whole world. Our homes, and our understandings of them, in ways that American public culture does and does not allow us to see, are fundamentally political. They both index and manifest gender, class, race, power, and the world of nations.

EXERCISE

Discuss the various ways "home" is and has been political as both a place and a concept in the United States.

NOTE

For American historical and New Haven material and citations, see di Leonardo (1998); on the history of feminist thought, see both di Leonardo (1998) and Lancaster and di Leonardo (1997).

REFERENCES

Bourdieu, Pierre. 1977. *Outline of a Theory of Practice*. Richard Nice, trans. Cambridge: Cambridge University Press.

———. 1984. *Distinction: A Social Critique of the Judgment of Taste*. Richard Nice, trans. Cambridge, MA: Harvard University Press.

Collins, Jane. 2003. *Threads: Gender, Labor, and Power in the Global Apparel Industry*. Chicago: University of Chicago Press.

di Leonardo, Micaela. 1984. *The Varieties of Ethnic Experience: Kinship, Class, and Gender among California Italian-Americans*. Ithaca, NY: Cornell University Press.

———. 1998. *Exotics at Home: Anthropologies, Others, American Modernity*. Chicago: University of Chicago Press.

———. 2008. "Introduction: New Global and American Landscapes of Inequality." In Jane Collins, Micaela di Leonardo, and Brett Williams, eds., *New Landscapes of Inequality: Neoliberalism and the Erosion of Democracy in America*, 3–19. Santa Fe, NM: School for Advanced Research Press.

Friedan, Betty. 1963. *The Feminine Mystique*. New York: W. W. Norton.

Gal, Susan, and Gail Kligman. 2000. *The Politics of Gender after Socialism: A Comparative-Historical Essay*. Princeton, NJ: Princeton University Press.

Harvey, David. 2005. *A Brief History of Neoliberalism*. New York: Oxford University Press.

Hobsbawm, Eric, and Terence Ranger, eds. 1983. *The Invention of Tradition*. Cambridge: Cambridge University Press.

Jayawardena, Kumari. 1986. *Feminism and Nationalism in the Third World*. London: Zed Books.

Lancaster, Roger. 2003. *The Trouble with Nature: Sex and Science in Popular Culture*. Berkeley: University of California Press.

Lancaster, Roger, and Micaela di Leonardo, eds. 1997. *The Gender/Sexuality Reader: Culture, History, Political Economy*. New York: Routledge.

Lerner, Gerda. 1998. *The Grimke Sisters from South Carolina: Pioneers for Women's Rights and Abolition*. New York: Oxford University Press.

Pérez, Gina M. 2004. *The Near Northwest Side Story: Migration, Displacement, and Puerto Rican Families*. Berkeley: University of California Press.

Scott, Joan Wallach. 1988. *Gender and the Politics of History*. New York: Columbia University Press.

Went, Robert. 2000. *Globalization: Neoliberal Challenge, Radical Responses*. London: Pluto Press.

Wilson, William Julius. 1987. *The Truly Disadvantaged: The Inner City, the Underclass, and Public Policy*. Chicago: University of Chicago Press.

Yanagisako, Sylvia. 1979. "Family and Household: The Analysis of Domestic Groups." *Annual Review of Anthropology* 8: 161–205.

13

WELCOME TO AN EAST HARLEM SHOOTING GALLERY

Philippe Bourgois

We passed through a gaping hole smashed out of the rear brick wall of the only abandoned tenement still standing in the middle of an East Harlem rubble field. My friend did not even pause to allow his eyes to adjust to the late-night darkness, and I had to scramble behind him through the entrails of the burned building pretending everything was perfectly normal. We paused by a large slab of plywood that blocked yet another fractured brick wall, and he knocked: "It's me, Mikey—white Mikey ... with a friend. He's white too, but don't worry; he's cool." Shivering wet from the drizzle of a New York City December night, we waited to be invited into the shooting gallery. Fidgeting anxiously, I stepped out of the way of a persistent trail of drops that somehow were making their way through five floors of charred rafters directly onto my baseball cap. I noticed that my mouth tasted of metal and wondered if perhaps I was overstepping my limits as an anthropologist. I also thought of the warning the Puerto Rican crack dealers, operating out of the video arcade next to the tenement building where I lived with my family, had given me when I told them I wanted to visit a shooting gallery: "Stay away from dopefiends. Especially *morenos*. They're bad, all of them. And you're a *blanquito*! Don't be stupid!" But when Mikey invited me to come along with him on his way to buy heroin, I could not resist the opportunity.

Before I knew it, I was ducking sideways through yet another overhanging slab of broken bricks into what had apparently once been a ground-floor apartment. Blinking in what seemed like bright candlelight, I felt a vague warmth from a sputtering fire to my right. Striving to compose myself, I smiled eagerly at Doc, the manager of the shooting gallery,

Reprinted with permission, from Bourgois, Philippe. 1998. *Theory, Culture & Society* 15 (2): 37–66. © SAGE. Republished in *Reflecting on America*, 2nd edition, edited by Clare L. Boulanger, 151–164 (© 2016 Taylor & Francis).

who was introducing himself with a loud, "Welcome to my place." To my surprise he graciously shooed me into one of the four dilapidated chairs ringing a grimy table cluttered with drug debris.

Mikey was not needing or paying attention to any awkward introductions. He no longer needed to prove or justify his identity to anyone, as he was instantly recognizable to everyone as a heroin addict. Intent on his upcoming shot of relief—and possibly of ecstatic pleasure if the quality was as good as everyone waiting on line in the park had claimed—Mikey hardly nodded hello before eagerly dumping the entire contents of both of his ten-dollar packets of heroin into a charred spoon that he picked out of the detritus in the middle of the table. He did, however, turn down Doc's offer to "rent" him the "house needle," as that would have cost him an extra two dollars. I vaguely heard him mumble something to Doc about his "buddy" having "change" for the "house fee."

Not yet fully aware that he was hustling me for his share of the two-dollar admission fee, I somewhat overeagerly pulled out two crumpled dollar bills I had purposely left easily accessible in my outside coat pocket. To my consternation, Doc suddenly tensed up. Mikey, meanwhile, skidded his chair to the far end of the table and ducked his head even closer to his spoon of heroin. My primary concern was to prevent any ambiguity arising from my not being a drug injector—or even a drug user—and nervously I began explaining, in what I feared was a hopelessly lame tone of voice, that I would not be shooting up as I was just drinking tonight and simply wanted to "hang with my buddy Mikey" in order to "learn about the street." In my bubbling confusion, I even heard myself stammering something about being a cultural anthropologist and a college professor who was thinking of writing a book about "life on the street." Persuaded that Doc was now going to be completely convinced that I was an undercover police officer, I struggled to understand why he was ignoring my semicoherent and highly dubious—even though perfectly true—explanation and was instead tapping his finger with irritation on top of the two dollar bills I had placed on the table. I stared at him blankly, prolonging the silence until he finally snarled, "Someone owes me two dollars more, whether you be shooting or not." Mikey was now hissing directly in my ear, "Come on, Phil, can't you cover for me? Just this one time? I don't got no change, brother."

With a flood of relief, I finally realized that all the tension in the room was being caused by Mikey's attempt to make me pay his house fee. Assailing Mikey with what I hoped was an appropriately aggressive flood of curses over his stinginess, I quickly handed Doc the additional two dollars. I now finally understood why Mikey had insisted on my getting one-dollar bills in change at the Yemeni grocery store, where I had bought a quart of malt liquor.

Doc immediately pocketed my money, and his face broke out into a wide, friendly smile. To my surprise, he began to concentrate on making me feel comfortable. In retrospect, I realized that Doc's decision to befriend me followed the straightforward logic of the street economy. Having publicly proved myself to be ineffective at guarding my money and a little too friendly, gentle, and full of smiles, I represented an ideal victim. It was well worth investing the time and energy to build a long-term street hustle relationship with me. Furthermore, Doc was probably a bit bored and looked forward to the curiosity of "conversating" with a white boy who claimed to be—of all outlandish things—a college professor.

It had been difficult to buy heroin tonight because the city's Tactical Narcotics Team was out in force, and two "white boys" stand out like sore thumbs on East Harlem streets, especially after midnight. An emaciated "steerer" advertising that Knockout—a well-established local brand—was "open, workin', and pumpin', man!" had waved us toward the three-man Knockout team (composed of a "pitcher," who actually makes the hand-to-hand sale, and his two helper-bodyguards/touters) selling in the middle of the block. As we walked toward them, however, a hail of whistles pierced the air. I thought perhaps the lookouts at the end of the block had changed their minds and decided we were undercovers rather than heroin addicts, but the whistles switched to calm shouts in street code announcing the arrival of a police car. Despite all being second-generation, New York–born youths, the lookouts rolled their r's with the rural Puerto Rican *jibaro* accents of their immigrant parents and grandparents: "carhrho feo [ugly car], bajando, bajando [coming down] carhrho feo!"

We found ourselves squarely in view of the squad car; it was too late to turn back. The police were bearing down directly on us, flashing their lights but not using the siren. They slowed to a crawl as they passed us, and my pulse began to race. I anticipated we would be thrown roughly against a wall and searched from head to foot—this had happened to me several times when the police caught me out on the street after dark in East Harlem. Behind us we heard more whistles and shouts of *bajando* as customers at the far corner were being turned back so that they would not have to make the dangerously conspicuous trek in front of the raiding officers. I wished we had arrived two minutes later.

Ironically, many of my closest calls with violence during the almost five years I lived and worked among drug addicts and dealers in East Harlem were with law enforcement (Bourgois 2003b). From the perspective of the police, I was an obnoxious provocation violating New York City's unwritten apartheid laws: the only reason for a "white boy" to be in the inner city, especially at night, is to buy drugs. My presence on the street made some officers incredibly angry. They cursed at me, berated me, and shoved me against the wall, no matter how polite and cooperative I tried to be. On this particular night, however, the police left us alone. Perhaps the freezing drizzle dissuaded them from leaving their dry, warm squad car.

Around the corner a woman called out softly from behind a defaced pillar of an abandoned school building: "SunShine at 114th in the park." We did not dare pause lest this self-appointed steerer also demand payment. In fact, both of us pretended not to hear the gentle voice or to notice the huddled, emaciated form. She was what they call a "toss-up" (Bourgois and Dunlap 1993), a woman who sold sex for crack. Toss-ups are the most vulnerable of all street-level prostitutes. In a midwinter drizzle, after midnight, this toss-up seemed especially pathetic.

Arriving at the park entrance six blocks away, we were both relieved to see three orderly single-file lines of heroin addicts buying from three separate teams, all selling the SunShine brand. We were greeted by the angry, barked orders of a steerer, instructing us to proceed to the back of the nearest line along the chain-link fence at the far end of the playground. He also warned us that this was strictly "a place of business," and since Mikey and I were together, only one of us needed to wait in line. Mikey stepped aside and walked a safe distance away into the shadows of some nearby trees, thereby manipulating me to pay for his two packets of heroin. He knew I did not want to call attention to us (the only two white faces in the crowd) by arguing with him and refusing to stand in line.

But nobody seemed to notice our whiteness. Presumably everyone assumed that only full-blown dopefiends could possibly tolerate being so cold and wet on such a miserable late night. I was further reassured when I was immediately included in the line's anxious discussion of the quality of the heroin being sold: "Have you tried it?" "Is it good? Does it work?"

Coincidentally, at this very moment, a legal street hawker, attracted to our huddle of exceptional buying power, walked up with six foldable umbrellas: "Only two dollahs; two dollahs. For the little lady at home. Take a look. These is seventeen dollahs in the store." The lookouts and steerers immediately converged on him in a rage, perhaps suspecting the camouflaged activities of a well-organized stickup crew: "If you ain't buyin', get goin'." Someone in line was trying to buy an umbrella, but the hawker was forced to run away without completing the sale because one of the lookouts had reached conspicuously into the groin area of his baggy jeans as if to draw a firearm. I chuckled at this all-American manifestation of determined, high-risk, cutthroat entrepreneurship in the inner city. Despite what politicians, social workers, or social scientists might claim, U.S. inner cities have emerged as the latest frontier where the descendants of immigrants and other marginalized citizens of color scramble violently for a piece of the proverbial American pie. The multibillion-dollar drug economy is, sadly, an irrefutable testament to how alive and vital capitalism remains among the thousands of people who are dismissed by policy makers as the passive, demoralized "underclass" (see critique by Gans 1996). Rain, snow, or shine, in inner cities across the United States, fistfuls of money and drugs flow among tens of thousands of skinny, sick men and women desperately seeking material sustenance and emotional meaning (see Bourgois and Schonberg 2009).

The pitcher ran out of heroin with only three customers ahead of me in the line, prompting a chorus of groans and curses. To our relief, however, we were not ordered to leave; the pitcher merely trotted fifty yards back into the darkness of the playground, huddled with a newly arrived "runner," then trotted back with a fresh supply of product, announcing, "This is it! This is the last bundle. After this there's no more. Get what you need now!" Those at the end of the line groaned anxiously and someone at the very end begged, "Leave some for me! All's I need is two." Moments later, the pitcher was asking me, "How many?" and I was pushing two ten-dollar bills through the chain-link fence. Without even looking up from his wad of tiny rectangular glassine packets, he handed me two crisp packets of heroin. Each packet was carefully stamped in pink ink, with the SunShine logo covered by a strip of tape to prevent unauthorized opening by addicted employees. I returned to Mikey, and we proceeded to the ruined tenement where Doc ran his shooting gallery.

The table at the gallery was littered with a tangled mess of discarded heroin envelopes, miniature ziplock coke packets, and crack vials. Doc was asking what we had purchased, telling us (without even waiting for an answer) the brand names of what was good that night—Rambo, 007, SunShine, Latin Power, O.J., Mandela—what was "open," and where the cops were patrolling. We added our bit of information to the street-savvy pool of knowledge to be imparted to the next customer: "Knockout's open on 117th but is crazy hot, and SunShine in Jefferson Park just closed." I was somewhat disappointed that everything of significance from our last two rain-drenched hours striving to buy heroin could be summed up in such a matter-of-fact sentence.

As my eyes continued to adjust to the flickering candlelight, I tried to discern what—or who—the two bundled shapes were on the far side of the room. My reconnoitering was interrupted by a loud knock on the plywood plank door. Two new clients, Slim and his friend Flex, walked through the hole in the wall, stamping their feet and shaking off melting snowflakes with the satisfied expressions of eager customers entering a welcoming place of business. Apparently, the rain had turned into snow flurries. Slim sat down next to me and, to my surprise, immediately engaged me in a relaxed, affable conversation about how the pitcher on the SunShine line had run out of heroin just when it was his turn to buy.

It took me a few seconds to realize that I had earned Slim's friendly familiarity by waiting at his side along the chain-link fence in the Jefferson Park playground. I was almost embarrassed not to have recognized him right away. His had been one of the more aggressive rasping voices that had complained threateningly each time someone at the front of the line had purchased more than a couple of packets or taken too long to count his money. Slim had been left stranded without his "cure" and had been forced to go three blocks farther downtown to purchase DOA, a less reputable brand. On the DOA line, he had met Flex, who was now sitting next to him, his brow knit in earnest concentration while he dumped his precious powder into the same kitchen spoon ("house cooker") that Mikey had just finished using.

Meanwhile, Doc was asking Mikey if he needed a "tie" for his arm. I had not watched what Mikey had done beforehand. I kicked myself for my lapse in concentration; I had meant to document potential vectors for infectious diseases from the micropractices of preparing injections in a shooting gallery. Ethnographic methods are important for improving public health messages and programs that do not address the everyday pragmatic realities of street-based injectors (Bourgois 2002; Bourgois and Bruneau 2000; Bourgois et al. 2006; Ciccarone 2003). On the run from law enforcement, addicts often find themselves injecting in filthy sites with no running water. They frequently clean out their bloodied syringes in the same containers from which they draw their water. They often share their cookers (usually bottle caps, old spoons, or the bottoms of crushed beer cans) in which heroin is dissolved, as well as their "cottons"—cigarette filters or pinches of real cotton swabs for trapping undissolved particles. At busy shooting galleries, clients sometimes inject water pink from the blood residues of the previous half dozen injectors (Bourgois and Bruneau 2000; Koester, Booth, and Wiebel 1990). We know that needle sharing can transmit HIV, but it is not clear whether the sharing of other types of drug paraphernalia can also spread the virus. However, hepatitis C and abscesses, which are more highly infectious than HIV, are very likely spread through these "indirect sharing" practices (Bourgois, Prince, and Moss 2004; Ciccarone et al. 2001; Ciccarone and Bourgois 2003; Koester et al. 2003).

In my irritation, I was only vaguely aware that Doc's offer to hold Mikey's tie was impatiently refused. Mikey unrolled his shirtsleeve to expose a scrawny white forearm with a long line of red prick marks. It took him less than twenty seconds to shoot up. He flexed his fist a few times to make his veins pop out and then hit a vein far up toward his wrist artery, just beyond where the last red pockmark had been left from his injection the morning before. Once the needle was a few millimeters below the skin he pulled back on the stopper with his thumb to make sure blood flooded the syringe's chamber. This is called "registering" and indicates that the needle tip is squarely inside the vein and has not pierced right through or rolled off the casing of the vein into the surrounding tissue. Registering is a crucial part of shooting up because if an injector carelessly injects the heroin into the muscle or fatty tissue surrounding the vein, it will balloon up into a painful bruise. More important, the expectant addict will miss the initial euphoric rush that comes when a successful hit of heroin is released directly inside a racing blood vessel and pulses within seconds up the arm, through the heart, and into the brain for a bull's-eye of sedated warmth and relaxation.

Slim and Flex heated their heroin and loaded the house needle with the same swift, efficient hand motions that Mikey had used—as well as the same dirty water, the same dirty cooker spoon, and the same crumpled cigarette filter cotton. Mikey was already heading out the door with a barely audible "I'll see you later," followed by further spasms from his hollow, racking cough. Perhaps he was concerned that Doc might demand another two dollars from him should he overstay his welcome, perhaps he was irritated by my repeated injunctions to have his lungs checked out at the local hospital for pneumonia, or perhaps he was just being commonsensical about the real dangers of hanging out for longer than strictly necessary in an East Harlem shooting gallery well past midnight on a stormy winter night—especially when you are white. More to the point, he had already hustled—several times!—the only easy victim in this space. It was time to move on and scrounge up enough money for his next fix before his body once again started aching for heroin sometime around sunrise.

Doc, either to express companionship and solidarity with me or to create a moral hierarchy in which he might seem more worthy of trust, converted my concern over Mikey's pneumonia-like cough into a forum where Mikey was berated for not taking care of himself. For a moment everyone injecting around the table sounded like wise, elderly matrons eager to impart their words of wisdom to an errant child wearing inadequate clothing on a cold day. Slim clucked something about how important it is to wear a warm hat, and he actually pulled a large red, yellow, and green wool Rastafarian cap out of his pocket and covered his overgrown afro. We were all clearly happy with ourselves to be able to share our righteous concern over the behavior of a wayward dopefiend.

In the wake of this newfound respectability, Doc stood up and began, somewhat precipitously, to clean off the table. Throughout the tidying process, in an effective attempt to welcome, reassure, and further evaluate me, Doc kept up a steady, happy chatter about "the decent place" that he tried to run, how he was "not gonna let things get dirty," how he "ran a classy joint," and so on. Indeed, within minutes, most traces of the past several hours of injecting had been wiped up. The table looked spotlessly clean and orderly. Pushing his offended housekeeper scenario to the limit, Doc reproached Flex, who was nodding heavily from the effects of his injection, for having carelessly left fresh litter scattered around him. In the same breath of righteousness, Doc picked up the open house hypodermic needle that Flex had also dropped on the table in front of him, carefully capped it, and laid it strategically in the center of the table, ready for the next customer. Doc did not bother rinsing the syringe to kill any trapped HIV; he simply shrugged when I suggested that maybe it should be cleaned.

Slim had not "hit" yet. He was carefully adding some powder cocaine into his spoon of already heated and dissolved heroin solution. Slim was preparing a "speedball," the contradictory combination of stimulant and depressant that is highly appreciated by street addict connoisseurs. Speedballs became the rage among even the most down-and-out dopefiends when the Colombian cartels, in response to the 1980s "War on Drugs" and its crackdown on bulky and less profitable marijuana shipments (Bourgois 2003b: 350n77) began flooding the U.S. market with low-volume, high-value, inexpensive cocaine. Once Slim had finally loaded his works, I expected him to take off his jacket and roll up his sleeve, or at worst take off his shoes or roll up his jeans and search for a clean vein below the knees. Instead, Slim arched back his neck and called over to one of the dark forms huddled, under a mound of covers and plastic bags, on the old mattress against the far wall.

Pops, a true veteran heroin addict who was considerably older and even frailer than Doc, jumped eagerly to his feet. Perhaps he was anticipating a "taste"—that is, a drug tip—for the service he was about to render, or maybe he was just trying to be helpful. Nobody likes to be taken for granted, but in this instance there was a worse fate to be had—Pops might be thrown out of the gallery if he did not prove himself useful. Pops vigorously massaged Slim's jugular while holding the loaded syringe high above his head, well out of harm's way. The wavering silhouette thrown by the candlelight reminded me of the Statue of Liberty, although the hypodermic needle full of heroin, coke, and perhaps HIV, hepatitis C, and abscess bacteria from the traces of a previous customer's blood was substituting for the torch of freedom.

I tried to ignore this spectacle—and almost succeeded—acting as if it were totally normal for a shriveled old man to jab a syringe into a middle-aged man's neck. I was unable, however, to prevent myself from noticing how carefully Pops pulled back the hypodermic's plunger to make sure blood from the neck's vein spurted into the syringe before injecting its contents. His head cocked tensely to the side, Slim let out a steady stream of directions and feedback. Somehow he remained motionless throughout the operation: "That's right; keep steady; you're in. Steady now; that's right; slowly; that's right. Go ahead! Come on! YEAH!"

Slim dropped back into his chair to allow the competing waves of cocaine and heroin to flush through his synapses. Moments later, he burst into urgent conversation as the initial coke rush from his speedball overwhelmed the heroin in the mixture. I forgot to notice if Slim paid Pops or gave him a taste.

In the meantime, Flex had become sufficiently roused from his nodding to pursue the same speedball high as Slim had, except that Flex "chased it" by "stemming," that is, smoking crack in a four-inch-long cylindrical glass pipe, or "stem," with crumpled wire mesh stuffed down one end. Crack is merely an alloy of cocaine and baking soda. Its psychoactive ingredient is the same as that of powder cocaine, except that unlike cocaine, crack releases the psychoactive agent efficiently when it is burned, resulting in a faster euphoric rush than injection or sniffing because the capillaries in the lungs pass the drug almost instantaneously into the brain's synapses.

Pops had dragged himself back out of the range of the candlelight to collapse onto a filthy mattress in the self-effacing manner of a hired helper. Desperate to trap as much of his body heat as possible and to deflect the occasional raindrops falling from the charred rafters high above us, he swathed himself in an amorphous pile of ragged blankets that he then wrapped with ripped sheets of plastic. When Pops realized that I was looking directly at him, he shyly nodded his head and propped himself up on his elbows. He gave me a faint smile, only to break eye contact moments later to withdraw once again, exhausted and shivering, into his ragged patchwork of covers.

After finishing my bottle of malt liquor, I stood up and stretched so as to obtain a clearer look into the back recesses of the room, where a second bundled shape had begun emitting, at unpredictable intervals, deep guttural moans of delight. This explicitly happy, relaxed form turned out to be an elderly woman. Her eyes lidded three-quarters shut as if to appreciate more fully the internal peace of her heroin nod, she also had a glass crack stem balanced delicately between her fingers as if it were an imported cigarette. With the phlegmy rasp that is the trademark of superannuated dopefiends, her almost obscene groans of pleasure seemed to burst forth involuntarily, from deep inside her blankets. Everyone seemed to think her choruses of bizarrely protoerotic bliss were completely normal. It was as if she were the shooting gallery's speedball conductor—she effectively paced and punctuated the rise and fall of the various combinations of coke, crack, and heroin tides that were washing through the synapses of the patrons, some of whom were "conversating" in an animated way while others nodded deeply.

Every now and then the old woman would fumble with her crack pipe, light it up, and temporarily snap to a wide-awake consciousness. On these occasions, she contributed enthusiastic affirmations to whatever was being said in the nearest conversation audible to her. For example, she interrupted one of Doc's reveries over "the good place" he ran with "Yes, that's a fact. And ain't it something! We been gettin' straight every day now for almost a year. I know it's hard to believe but it's the truth. Keepin' warm and staying straight every day—mmm-hmmm." Slim and Flex, meanwhile, were rallying their energies around Flex's crack stem, which they were now earnestly passing back and forth—almost grabbing it from each other—reminding me of preteen buddies huddled around a forbidden cigarette in a school yard. Somehow ferreting out additional stashes of crack from the recesses of their pockets, sleeves, and hems, they repeatedly lit up tiny chunks of the precious stuff. Each inhalation precipitated a burst of happy conversation. The advantage of the speedball high for crack smokers is that the heroin they inject, or sniff, provides an underlying stabilizing foundation for their coke-induced exaltation. This prevents them from losing control to the hyperparanoid fantasies that massive, concentrated ingestion of cocaine often brings on—the sense that "coke bugs" are swarming over their skin, for example, or a panic that inspires them to sprint away from imaginary police officers or attack possible assailants.

Only Doc and I clung to any vague pretense of sobriety, but Doc soon changed that by drawing water into his syringe from the filthy water jug under the table and then dissolving in the house cooker the jumble of heroin shavings-cum-cocaine he had scraped from the sides of the empty packets cleaned off the table earlier. He also added the used cottons from the night's previous injections into the mix to eke out any residue (and viruses and bacteria) trapped in their fibers. He then dropped his jeans, shuffled over closer to the fire, squatted in the flickering light, and shot himself up in one of the veins below his knee. The coke part of his makeshift speedball was the first part of his high to hit him. All of a sudden he was standing above me at full height, gesturing excitedly. Oblivious to whatever it was that he was telling me, I focused all my attention on the open needle that was clutched in his right hand as he began to pace the small space between me, the table, and the fire. To my dismay he began punctuating his more emphatic remarks by jabbing the needle at me.

Doc's cocaine-inspired diatribe proved to be contagious; it galvanized the group back into a single, "conversating," coke-rushing unit. Following the unpredictable ebbs and flows of the group's contradictory chemical tides, the room's speedball roller coaster dissolved a few minutes later into yet another ebb of heroin-induced relaxation. Eventually, Doc, too, became calmer. He sank into the front bucket seat of a long-gone car that he had dragged from the back of the shooting gallery closer to the fire.

Only moments later, however, he was shivering and announced aggressively that someone needed to break up a large hunk of nailed plywood boards that lay near the entrance to feed the fire. Flex, presumably still flush from the crack he had just finished smoking with Slim, jumped to his feet, seized the plywood boards, and began whacking at them with an oversized club of gnarled iron gas piping. His positioning of the plywood on an unstable marble step created the acoustics of an oversized drum. Soon the entire building was echoing with each bang. Our hands over our ears, we shouted at him to stop, but this merely encouraged him to swing faster and harder, sweat flying off of his contorted face. He started to look angry and I happened to be the person sitting closest to him, directly in the path of his metal club. Was he about to bug out into cocaine paranoia and hallucinate me into an evil white enemy undercover cop?

Slim rose from his cot, cursing Flex for potentially attracting the attention of the police with this outrageous racket. Others in the gallery, quickly oscillating from their heroin highs to cocaine-induced anxiety, began shouting obscenities at Flex, but no one dared stop him physically because his iron pipe was swinging faster and faster. Slim's mention of the police flooded me with a new worry: that I could be trapped for three days in an overcrowded New York City "bullpen," waiting to be arraigned by a Narcotics Circuit judge overwhelmed with cases due to the recent Tactical Narcotics Team crackdown. I flashed on the prison rape stories I had been tape-recording in the crack house where I normally spent my evenings. U.S. drug policies, along with the growing concentrations of unemployed populations in the inner cities, have turned prisons and jails throughout the country into chaotic race-segregated cesspools. The United States has the highest per capita incarceration rate of any industrialized nation in the world, and African Americans are approximately seven times more likely than whites to be in prison, primarily due to ethnic disparities in drug arrests since the escalation of the War on Drugs in the 1980s. This is exacerbated, of course, by the dramatic statistical rise in poverty rates during these same decades. Sociologist Loïc Wacquant (2002, 2006) identifies the explosion in the size of the incarcerated African American population as the government's new way of managing race and class relations since the time of the War on Poverty and the civil rights movement. As factories move out of big cities and overseas in search of lower labor costs, ever larger proportions of the population in the United States have been pushed into generating income through crime and the underground economy (Duster 1987; Wilson 1996).

The planks finally gave in, and Flex surveyed us proudly, panting and wiping his brow. I was surprised to find that everyone was instantly happy with him again. Both Slim and Doc praised him for his hard work, and Doc busily stacked the shredded wood into a neat pile by the fire. I realized that I—rather than my coke-pumped friends—had been the paranoid one during this incident. I had misjudged the aggressive street tone of their shouts and curses. In fact, I was embarrassed at myself for my lapse in street-smart sensitivity. Despite having lived in East Harlem for almost four years at this point, and spending most of my nights among dealers and addicts on the street (Bourgois 2003b), I was still confused by the nuances of emphasis that distinguish genuinely volatile rage from normally stylized emphatic discourse.

In the ensuing calm, I began to appreciate my role as Doc's guest of honor. Treated to candy, popcorn, potato chips, and even a second quart of malt liquor that Doc sent Slim out to buy for me, I realized that these tasty snacks paralleled the gallery's speedball pleasure principle of maximizing sensory input through contradictory unhealthy chemicals. The unhealthy substances in which I was indulging, however, were packaged legally by billion-dollar multinational corporations allowed by the government to pack huge quantities of sugars, salts, and nonmetabolized fats into our increasingly obese and diabetic bodies.

Settling into the preferential fireside seat Doc had given me, I remembered my initial "research aim": to place these most broken-down of heroin addicts in the historical and structural context of mainstream America (Bourgois 2004). I steered the conversation away from their constant references to the logistical particulars of their narcotized lifestyles and toward the topic of the larger array of power constraints ripping apart their lives and destroying their communities. I wanted to explore their relationship to a society that has managed to turn them into the actual agents devastating themselves and everyone around them while simultaneously suggesting they were "getting over" on the system in a lifelong sprint after narcotic euphoria. So I encouraged them to discuss their parents' experiences of migration from the rural South, the "chump change" jobs they had held in their youth, and, of course, their experience of racism as African Americans. Doc's mother, I soon learned, had been forced to flee her sharecropping community in "Carolina" when her uncle was lynched "for lookin' at a white woman the wrong way."

But Doc most definitely did not consider himself to be a structural victim of a racist society. He was not interested in confirming a college professor's political economic analysis of how the unemployed children of rural immigrants displaced by the closing of factories were victimized. He did not subscribe to dreams of hopeful struggle and liberation. His oppression was fully internalized. Like most poorly educated people in the United States, Doc took full responsibility for his poverty, illiteracy, and homelessness and failed to see the structural economic and political policy forces that dole out a disproportionate share of suffering, unemployment, poverty, and poor health to African Americans, Latinos, and Native Americans.

It was 4:30 in the morning and my legs were shivering uncontrollably from the cold. I bid everyone goodbye and hurried home through the blizzard outside. Warm in my bed ten minutes later, like most employed and housed people in the United States, I tried not to think about how physically painful it is to be a homeless addict in the middle of winter.

Conclusion: Confronting Inner-City Apartheid

The breakdown of both public-sector services and private market forces in the U.S. inner city is overwhelming. Miles and miles of abandoned buildings and rubble- and garbage-strewn vacant lots along with the millions of drug-shattered lives all across the urban United States are testimony to a profound political and economic dysfunction in how resources are distributed to the socially vulnerable. Except for the massive investment in the counterproductive and ineffectual War on Drugs, the government has failed to intervene on behalf of desperately poor inner-city residents. The private sector has also failed to help anyone but the real estate tycoons who come in to gentrify and exacerbate the problems of poverty and segregation by pricing the poor out of their former neighborhoods of refuge (Dávila 2004). In fact, the East Harlem neighborhood in which this shooting gallery was located is now in the advanced throes of a violent gentrification, expelling the poor Puerto Rican and African American population that used to call these streets home. The disproportionate ethnicity- and class-specific statistics on life expectancy, disease burden, infant mortality, homicide, suicide, childhood hunger, addiction, family income, and homelessness also clearly point to a profoundly racist political economy in the United States that punishes the poor by subjecting them to far more than their share of social suffering. The United States has the highest levels of income inequality and arguably the worst overall quality-of-life indices of any wealthy industrialized nation in the world.

U.S. common sense blames poverty on character flaws and lack of moral fiber. Individual responsibility reigns supreme; public responsibility for protecting the citizenry's human right to access basic social services—shelter, income, employment, health care (including drug treatment)—is not on the U.S. political agenda (Farmer 2003). Within the inner city itself, the glaring objective horrors enveloping the community—inadequate jobs, decrepit housing, racism, inferior public infrastructure—are understood and often acted upon with self-destructive self-blame. Doc, for example, may be the primary agent for the spread of HIV in his community. We can righteously criticize his individual irresponsibility, or we can constructively address the larger political policies that limit public health outreach and direct the police to arrest aging addicts for needle possession.

As an anthropologist I consider participant-observation ethnography to be a useful methodological tool for violating class and ethnic apartheid and documenting extreme social suffering. Immersing oneself full-time in such disorienting settings as the underground worlds of crack dealers and heroin injectors, however, is a frightening and personally draining experience that can lead to analytic confusion. On an immediate descriptive level, given the tremendous ideological polarization around poverty in the United States, a raw presentation of ethnographic data without a critical theoretical analysis risks fueling the racist stereotypes and blame-the-victim convictions that dominate U.S. popular culture. Power and historically structured forces that impose social inequality are hard to see unless one actively trains a discerning eye on those forces. In a vacuum, descriptions of interpersonal violence and drug abuse make individuals appear pathological. The application of cultural relativism, geared toward understanding the logics for actions without imposing moral judgments, is a useful first step. For example, public violence can be understood as a judicious investment in "human capital" given limited alternatives. Dealers, addicts, and just plain wannabes need to engage in visible displays of aggression periodically if they are to maintain credibility on the street. Should they fail, they will be mugged, ripped off, and ridiculed (Bourgois 2001).

The underground economy and the social relations thriving therein are best understood as an oppositional reaction to social and material marginalization. This oppositional resistance to oppression, however, is rooted in drug dealing/using and leads to the further destruction of the community. The physical violence imploding U.S. inner cities is largely self-contained: "black on black" and "brown on brown." It is interpreted by most people—including most inner-city residents themselves—as proof that homeless drug addicts and street-level dealers deserve their fate. The brutality of racist white police officers that periodically surfaces in the press pales before the everyday sense of fear and distrust that most inner-city residents feel when they suddenly hear footsteps running behind them on the street at night. People begin blaming themselves and the individuals around them rather than recognizing the political and economic forces driving a social system that destroys record numbers of its citizens.

Memoirs from the Nazi Holocaust have taught us that under conditions of extreme oppression, victims can become perpetrators (Bourgois 2005; Levi 1988). Discussions of jail experiences that I have tape-recorded echo these findings. The interpersonal violence of fellow inmates, rather than the brutality of guards or the humiliation of institutional rules, becomes the primary subject of conversation. Victims often lash out at those around them, becoming ruthless administrators and agents of violence and terror (Bourgois 2001). Inmates throughout history and around the world sometimes become the enforcers and executors of the most barbaric dimensions of their own torture. This is one of the most fundamental premises of the experience of politically structured suffering, leading to what Bourdieu calls "the misrecognition" of the larger structural fault lines of power that turns people into monsters (see his theory of "symbolic violence" in Bourdieu 2000).

We need a pragmatic understanding of the material forces driving addiction on the street (Bourgois 2003a). The multibillion-dollar illicit drug industry—the only equal-opportunity employer thriving in U.S. inner cities since at least the 1980s—offers a powerful material base for so-called youth street culture. It would be naive and atheoretical to think that the dramatic economic vigor of the international drug trade could be neutral ideologically or culturally. The playground where Mikey bought his heroin is located two blocks away from the neighborhood's magnet high school, and on most days throughout the 1980s and 1990s, money and drugs flowed there in fistfuls. Why should we be surprised that East Harlem posted one of the highest high school dropout rates in the country during those years? The War on Drugs has only exacerbated the problem. Government statistics confirm that heroin was cheaper and of higher quality on U.S. inner-city streets during the mid-2000s than ever before; in the mid-2010s it continues to drop in price and increase in purity. The drug economy has been outcompeting the legal, entry-level economy for the hearts and minds of too many inner-city youth for too many decades because they cannot find decent legal jobs and they are trapped in some of the most expensive cities in the world.

Heroin and crack dealers believe with a vengeance in the American Dream. They hope to go from rags to riches through private entrepreneurship (Bourgois 2003b). Most will be crushed in their endeavor as they fall prey to violence, drug addiction, and/or paralyzing depression. Most of the crack dealers and heroin addicts whom I have befriended over the past two decades worked at legal jobs in their childhoods. In fact, many dropped out of school in order to make money to obtain the childhood "necessities"—candy, potato chips, sneakers, basketballs, baseball cards—that most preteens in the United States are able to buy with their allowance money.

The material alternative to entry-level employment that the drug industry offers could explain all by itself the powerful appeal of street culture. In the case of youth street culture in the United States, however, racism conflates with an economically generated appeal to create an even more dynamic and persuasive alternative to white middle-class suburban culture. The inner-city resident who does not faithfully imitate white middle-class society's modes of interaction at the workplace will be fired—or, worse yet, ridiculed into submission. Selling drugs on the street offers a real economic alternative to low-wage service jobs in which the cultural identities of inner-city youth are a source of humiliation rather than an asset.

The extraordinary vitality of cultural expression on the poorest, most violent streets in the United States wells forth in opposition to this conjugation of racism and marginalized employment. The appeal of the oppositional style even crosses class, ethnic, and national boundaries, as the hugely successful gangsta rap/hip-hop music industry proved in the 2000s. Ironically, however, on the street, where this alternative cultural framework is rooted in the drugs economy and its logic for violence, the outcome destroys individuals and communities. Worse yet, this destructive dynamic leads to blaming the victim, thereby cementing in place a status quo of gross socioeconomic inequality.

EXERCISE

Are the drug users described in this chapter responsible for their own situation in life? Discuss ways in which this might be said to be true and ways in which it is not. See if the class can arrive at a consensus regarding the question.

REFERENCES

Bourdieu, Pierre. 2000. *Pascalian Meditations*. Stanford, CA: Stanford University Press.

Bourgois, Philippe. 2001. "The Power of Violence in War and Peace: Post–Cold War Lessons from El Salvador." *Ethnography* 2 (1): 5–37.

———. 2002. "Anthropology and Epidemiology on Drugs: The Challenges of Cross-Methodological and Theoretical Dialogue." *International Journal of Drug Policy* 13 (4): 259–69.

———. 2003a. "Crack and the Political Economy of Social Suffering." *Addiction Research & Theory* 11 (1): 31–37.

———. 2003b. *In Search of Respect: Selling Crack in El Barrio*. Cambridge: Cambridge University Press.

———. 2004. "U.S. Inner-City Apartheid and the War on Drugs: Crack among Homeless Heroin Addicts." In Arachu Castro and Merrill Singer, eds., *Unhealthy Health Policy: A Critical Anthropological Examination*, 303–14. Walnut Creek, CA: AltaMira Press.

———. 2005. "Missing the Holocaust: My Father's Account of Auschwitz from August 1943 to June 1944." *Anthropological Quarterly* 78 (1): 89–123.

Bourgois, Philippe, and Julie Bruneau. 2000. "Needle Exchange, HIV Infection, and the Politics of Science: Confronting Canada's Cocaine Injection Epidemic with Participant Observation." *Medical Anthropology* 18 (4): 325–50.

Bourgois, Philippe, and Eloise Dunlap. 1993. "Exorcising Sex-for-Crack: An Ethnographic Perspective from Harlem." In Mitchell S. Ratner, ed., *Crack Pipe as Pimp: An Ethnographic Investigation of Sex-for-Crack Exchanges*, 97–132. New York: Lexington Books.

Bourgois, Philippe, Alexis Martinez, Alex Kral, Brian R. Edlin, Jeff Schonberg, and Dan Ciccarone. 2006. "Reinterpreting Ethnic Patterns among White and African American Men Who Inject Heroin: A Social Science of Medicine Approach." *PLoS Medicine* 3 (10): e452.

Bourgois, Philippe, Bridget Prince, and Andrew Moss. 2004. "Everyday Violence and the Gender of Hepatitis C among Homeless Drug-Injecting Youth in San Francisco." *Human Organization* 63 (3): 253–64.

Bourgois, Philippe, and Jeff Schonberg. 2009. *Righteous Dopefiend*. Berkeley: University of California Press.

Ciccarone, Dan. 2003. "With Both Eyes Open: Notes on a Disciplinary Dialogue between Ethnographic and Epidemiological Research among Injection Drug Users." *International Journal of Drug Policy* 14 (1): 115–18.

Ciccarone, Dan, Josh Bamberger, Alex Kral, Brian Edlin, Chris Hobart, A. Moon, E. L. Murphy, Philippe Bourgois, Hobart W. Harris, and D. M. Young. 2001. "Soft Tissue Infections among Injection Drug Users—San Francisco, California, 1996–2000." *Morbidity & Mortality Weekly Report* 50 (19): 381–84.

Ciccarone, Dan, and Philippe Bourgois. 2003. "Explaining the Geographic Variation of HIV among Injection Drug Users in the United States." *Substance Use & Misuse* 38 (14): 2049–63.

Dávila, Arlene. 2004. *Barrio Dreams: Puerto Ricans, Latinos, and the Neoliberal City*. Berkeley: University of California Press.

Duster, Troy. 1987. "Crime, Youth Unemployment, and the Black Urban Underclass." *Crime & Delinquency* 33 (2): 300–315.

Farmer, Paul. 2003. *Pathologies of Power: Health, Human Rights, and the New War on the Poor*. Berkeley: University of California Press.

Gans, Herbert. 1996. *The War against the Poor: The Underclass and Anti-poverty Policy*. New York: Basic Books.

Koester, Stephen, Robert Booth, and Wayne Wiebel. 1990. "The Risk of HIV Transmission from Sharing Water, Drug-Mixing Containers and Cotton Filters among Intravenous Drug Users." *International Journal of Drug Policy* 1 (6): 28–30.

Koester, Stephen, Robert Heimer, Anna E. Barón, Jason Glanz, and Wei Teng. 2003. "Re: 'Risk of Hepatitis C Virus among Young Adult Injection Drug Users Who Share Injection Equipment.'" *American Journal of Epidemiology* 157 (4): 376.

Levi, Primo. 1988. *The Drowned and the Saved*. Raymond Rosenthal, trans. New York: Summit Books.

Wacquant, Loïc. 2002. "From Slavery to Mass Incarceration: Rethinking the 'Race Question' in the US." *New Left Review*, January/February, 41–60.

———. 2006. *Prisons of Poverty*. Minneapolis: University of Minnesota Press.

Wilson, William Julius. 1996. *When Work Disappears: The World of the New Urban Poor*. New York: Alfred A. Knopf.

RITUAL AND RELIGION

14

A Pilgrimage to the Past: Civil War Reenactors at Gettysburg

Matthew H. Amster

It was nine o'clock on a hot Friday morning in early July 2005 when I pulled my car into the parking lot at the Gettysburg National Military Park to meet a group of Civil War reenactors. When I had first contacted the group, back in April of that year, I had explained that I was an anthropologist doing research on reenactors and that I was interested in joining them on their visit to Gettysburg that summer. The group's leader invited me for the Fourth of July weekend, when there would be a Living History demonstration, and allowed me, along with one of my students, to wear his loaner uniforms, generally reserved for potential new recruits. As the reenactors assembled into their regiments, my student and I made a quick change out of our shorts, T-shirts, and sandals into our new clothes for the weekend: heavy wool pants and coats and misshapen leather boots, accessorized with leather sacks and an array of Civil War–era military gear, including bedrolls. We were also handed heavy replica Springfield rifles, and before we had time to absorb what was happening we were nineteenth-century infantrymen lined up for some basic training and drills. Soon we were heading out in military formation, our normal lives transformed.

It was then that I had my first flicker of a surreal moment. For just an instant—with a haze rising around us from the gravel under our feet, the group moving along the trail in unison, the sound of our gear clanging, and a sea of blue uniforms with rifles pointed skyward—I momentarily grasped just a tiny bit of what it might have felt like to be one of these men in the 1860s, marching in the hot sun with a heavy rifle under someone else's orders. Even though I'd been doing this only for a very short time, something visceral occurred that gave me a taste of what makes reenacting appealing. I began to think about the difficult life of the infantrymen who wore these hot wool uniforms, carried all this gear, and walked in these uncomfortable shoes, not just for "fun" on a weekend but for

Reflecting on America, 2nd edition, edited by Clare L. Boulanger, 167–179 © 2016 Taylor & Francis. All rights reserved.

Figure 14.1   The author (left) and anthropology student Mike Leader at a Living History encampment, Gettysburg National Military Park, July 2005

months or years, experiencing homesickness, hardships, disease, and death. As time went on and I got to know reenactors better, I learned how such uncanny moments—described as "period rush," "going into the bubble," "time travel," or "Civil War moments"—are a significant part of what keeps them coming back year after year.

Who Are Civil War Reenactors?

When I moved to Gettysburg to teach anthropology, one of the first bits of advice I was given was to leave town in the summer. People warned me that nearly two million visitors descend each year, most in the summer months, transforming the otherwise relatively tranquil town into a bustling historical fantasy. In Gettysburg one often encounters people walking the streets in period dress, including women leading bands of tourists on "ghost tours" and Civil War reenactors who stroll the streets dressed as if it were still 1863. At first glance, the hobby seems quaint and, at times, fanatical, particularly the element within the reenacting community that talks about lost souls roaming the battlefield, engages in ghost hunting, recounts sightings of such paranormal phenomena as floating "orbs" of light, and tape-records the night air to hear the dead soldiers speak. While such beliefs and practices are common, at the heart of the hobby is a sincere love of history and a desire to breathe life and relevance into this history through reenacting.

American Civil War reenacting groups are found in such unlikely places as England, as well as other European countries, and Canada (Hunt 2004), though most come from places close to where the war was fought. There are no reliable statistics on how many people have participated in the hobby, but estimates range from 15,000 to more than twice that number (Cushman 1999: 52). According to Tony Horwitz, whose book *Confederates in the Attic* was published in 1999, when the hobby may have been at its peak of popularity, there are "over 40,000 reenactors nationwide," and "one survey named reenacting the fastest growing hobby in America" (126). A number of reenactors with whom I spoke claimed that the hobby has diminished in recent years, particularly since 9/11; they speculated that it may not be as appealing to reenact combat during times of actual war. Others theorized that the popularity of reenacting can be linked to the influence of media, with Ken Burns's documentary series *The Civil War* and such feature films as *Gettysburg, Gods and Generals*, and *Glory* having fueled interest in the hobby in the 1990s. Whatever the reasons for its popularity, reenacting has grown considerably from its early days in the 1960s, around the time of the Civil War centennial, when the current form of the hobby is said to have begun.

Reenacting is a mainly male activity (although at the more mainstream events whole families can participate), and most reenactments are "blindingly white affairs" (Horwitz 1999: 137), despite the existence of some black reenacting groups, including an all-black Union regiment that regularly marches through Gettysburg on the anniversary of Lincoln's Gettysburg Address and on Remembrance Day, when thousands of reenactors parade through the town. Usually, however, reenactors are white males, although their socioeconomic backgrounds can vary. It is often pointed out that one can find people from very diverse lifestyles and careers reenacting side by side. As one reenactor said to Horwitz (1999: 134) during an event: "See that general over there? He's probably pumping gas at Exxon during the week."

Most reenactors concentrate on doing specific "impressions," typically of either northern "Union" or "Federal" soldiers, commonly referred to as "Yanks" or "Yankees," or of southern "Confederate" soldiers, also referred to as "Rebs" or "Johnny Rebs." While some reenactors are willing to portray either side in the conflict—in reenactor parlance known as "galvanizing," or switching sides—most tend to have strong affinity with a particular side. One reason some do not galvanize is simply the expense, since even an entry-level outfit, like the standard infantry kit complete with replica Springfield rifle, costs more than a thousand dollars. Civilian attire is also an option for reenactors, and people specialize in a range of period impressions, portraying, for example, sutlers (private merchants and craft specialists who provision soldiers), medical practitioners, and missionaries.

Authenticity is a big issue for reenactors, and there is a broad spectrum in terms of individual levels of commitment. At one extreme are the most devoted and serious reenactors, referred to as "hard-core" or "campaigners," who go to great lengths to be authentic. At the other end of the spectrum are more family-oriented "mainstream" or "garrison"-type hobbyists for whom authenticity is less critical. When spending time with reenactors, one often hears the expression "farb," or the adjective form "farby" (and various derivatives, such as "farb fest"), in relation to anything that is inauthentic or modern. The term is commonly said to derive from the phrase "far be it from authentic," though there are other suspected etymologies (Thompson 2004: 291). References to farbs and farby items are rampant in reenactor discourse, and it is a common insult among reenactors to call someone a farb. A farby item can be virtually anything that would not be considered period—whether this is the presence of a cooler, a vehicle, a filtered cigarette, or simply an attitude or demeanor. Among hard-core reenactors, even items out of sight, such as undergarments, may be criticized as farby.

Most reenactors come to Gettysburg as part of local regiments attending one of the various events held there, the largest being a three-day battle reenactment that takes place each year, usually around the anniversary of the actual battle, July 1–3. This annual reenactment, held on private land, is a for-profit commercial venture that draws tens of thousands of paying spectators and thousands of reenactors, each of whom also pays a small registration fee to participate and camp on-site. During particularly significant years, such as the 150th anniversary of the battle in 2013, the event tends to draw even larger numbers. In addition to the private reenactment held away from the Gettysburg National Military Park, a large regular gathering of reenactors takes place in Gettysburg each year in November to commemorate the anniversary of Lincoln's Gettysburg Address. Also, a steady trickle of reenactor groups visit Gettysburg throughout the year to offer Living History demonstrations in cooperation with the National Military Park.

For Civil War enthusiasts—reenactors and nonreenactors alike—Gettysburg is a place of great emotional significance, as the battle that took place there is considered a turning point in the Civil War. For many, visiting Gettysburg and Civil War battlefields is equivalent to a pilgrimage experience. Gatewood and Cameron (2004: 213), who conducted research on tourists visiting the park, found religious elements in the experiences of many battlefield tourists, noting that those who initially come with a casual interest are increasingly drawn to the emotional power of the landscape as "impressions of the site become more complex and more layered with repeated visits." It was precisely the pilgrimage aspects of battlefield tourism and reenacting that drew me to this research, as I had previously examined the phenomenon of religious pilgrimage elsewhere (Amster 2003).

The main purpose of this chapter is to give voice to reenactor stories and viewpoints in order to shed light on what motivates people to participate in this hobby. I conducted research from 2004 to 2006, mainly over the summer months. My methodology included participant observation and interviews with dozens of reenactors. Most of the interviews took place immediately before or after reenactments, when I would spend time in reenactor camps. I conducted interviews with individuals from a broad cross section of the reenactor community—men and women, young and old, experienced and inexperienced, and, most important, Union and Confederate. (Unfortunately, I did not have the opportunity to interview any African American reenactors, who tend not to take part in summertime activities at Gettysburg because African American regiments did not fight at Gettysburg.) Each year, I attended both the annual commercial reenactments and a range of Living History demonstrations in the park, including the one in which I myself participated as a Union infantryman. By joining a reenactor group and "going native," I got my most vivid glimpse of "the life" —as some reenactors call it—and the unforgettable chance to "feel the itch of the wool."

"Civil War Moments"

When one asks Civil War reenactors why they reenact, invariably a number of "official"-sounding answers are offered: to educate the public, to commemorate and honor those who died, for love of country, and to better understand details of history. While all of these are, to a certain extent, true, there seems to be an unspoken agreement among reenactors that in interacting with the "public" a certain facade must be maintained to shield their motives. It does not take much probing, however, to learn that there are a host of other reasons people choose to reenact, most prominent among them being that it is fun.

So *why* is reenacting fun? Reenactors often stress an intense camaraderie that accompanies involvement in the hobby: the good friends they make and the people they meet; the pleasure of telling stories around the campfire at night, singing Civil War songs and drinking; and the deep bonding with others who share their interest in history. During my own participation in firing demonstrations, I could not help but notice how much the men enjoyed simply using their weapons. For such demonstrations, as well as in battle reenactments, actual gunpowder is loaded in the rifles, though no bullets are used. At one point, after a particularly intense round went off and the smoke cleared, the man next to me, sporting a wide grin, commented blissfully to himself, "Love the sound. Love the feel." As Jim, a naval reserve officer in his mid-forties, put it:

> It's the ultimate guy hobby. You've got camping, firearms, and the occasional beer, you know, weekends out with nature. It all makes sense. You have guys giving you all those fancy, you know, honor-my-great-granny-type stuff and some of them might believe it, but most of them are just here because it's a good time. You hang out with your friends, you do something that's somewhat interesting, and you learn a little bit, maybe you help someone learn a little bit, and you have a good time doing it.

Jim, who resides in the Philadelphia area, has a passion for both military history and firearms, and he readily admits that these interests are what motivate him to reenact. Having done Civil War reenacting for more than a decade, Jim is also now among a growing group who have become involved in reenacting other wars. World War I, for example, has recently increased in popularity as a subject of reenactment (Thompson 2004).

As I questioned Jim further about his particular motivations, he talked about how the hobby allows him to think concretely about the challenges of facing combat, something he has never actually experienced and does not want to experience. He said he often asks himself: "Could I have done what they did? Could I have spent time in the field the way they did? How would I have reacted in the same circumstances?" Jim was quick to point out that one can never really know how a soldier might have felt during a Civil War battle, but at least by doing some of the things reenactors do, one gets closer to the experience. "Whether it's eating hardtack or nasty salt pork or sleeping in the cold, marching in the rain," he said, "you know *they did it*."

Over and over, I heard similar comments about the deep experiential value of reenacting and the unique pleasure it brings. Wayne, a fifty-two-year-old Union reenactor from the Baltimore area, described his special moments in the heat of battle:

> You get into certain reenactments or certain times and it's only milliseconds, it might last a few seconds. You're in a long line of battle, the breeze is a'blowing, the flags are a'fluttering, the smoke's coming up, they're yelling commands, and for those small seconds you are almost transported back in time and [you] say, "I'm living this." It gives you a time capsule, a time machine, to come back in time and experience something, even if it's for a little part of time. You almost put yourself back in that time period. Of course, you're not having the bullets go past your ear, you're not having blood splattered on you, you're not having bombs exploding in the air, but it's just small periods—you can blot out everything and you're there, you're actually there. So that's what pulls me. I enjoy it, I enjoy it immensely.

Bruce, age fifty-one, from the Lancaster, Pennsylvania, area, expressed similar reasons he was drawn to reenacting. He also cited family connections that drew him to the battle of Gettysburg specifically, including a great-uncle killed by friendly fire and another relative who drowned while on guard duty. As a deeply committed Christian, Bruce saw no conflict between his love of reenacting and his religious beliefs; indeed, the two merged in his work—teaching history at a Christian school. He had been reenacting for five years and traced his love of the Civil War back to his childhood, when he began collecting Civil War artifacts at five years old. For Bruce, reenacting is a kind of "men's club" for people who like history. "I get personal satisfaction because it is fun. I like to camp, I love the camaraderie. I think the relationships that we build with our fellow reenactors come the closest to understanding what a soldier's heart is." He also brings students to Gettysburg and pointed out that this is an effective way to teach history. "A person standing out there in a hot uniform, with a smoking pole, is gonna grab somebody's attention, and hopefully they are going to learn from us what they don't learn from their teachers at school."

For many people I interviewed, their interest in reenacting was linked to personal experiences in the military, memories of combat; for others, it fulfilled their fantasies about military life. As a teenager from Central New Jersey commented, through reenacting "you go into the military without paying the consequences of being in the military." For some veterans, reenacting can provide a kind of alternative to combat and perhaps even have a therapeutic effect. Keith, a professor at a major research university, became a reenactor because it helped him process some of his memories from the Vietnam War and offered him a place where he could proudly wear an American military uniform without feelings of shame. Many of his academic colleagues could not relate to his military past or his interest in reenacting, but he had much in common with friends in the reenacting community. Simply carrying a rifle and marching in formation evoked powerful bodily memories that allowed him to think about his relationship to the military and his own, otherwise muted, patriotic feelings.

Jerry, a Virginia resident in his late forties, first became involved in reenacting in his teens and then later joined the army for two years, a career choice he attributed to his prior involvement in reenactment. But Jerry far preferred Civil

War reenacting to being in the actual military. He had been reenacting for twenty-five years and estimated that he had been to more than three hundred reenactments and experienced roughly seven hundred battles; he was considering stopping because the hobby was beginning to bore him. For Jerry, the camaraderie around the campfire at night was by far the best part of reenacting, although what kept him coming back most of all was his sense of commitment to the group he founded and the men who depended on his leadership. For him, having "Civil War moments" (or "time bubbles," as he called them) was no longer important, and such experiences were fewer and farther between.

"Civil War moments" can be both individual and shared. One group of men told me about a collective moment when they were simultaneously affected by what sounded eerily like actual bullets whizzing by their ears. After the fact, they speculated that the sound was caused by an echo off a nearby barn. One of the men called this a "Civil Wargasm," bringing up jokes about "multiple Civil Wargasms," a term that Horwitz (1999) uses in *Confederates in the Attic* to describe a whirlwind tour of Civil War sites. Another man told me that his first Civil War moment occurred before he became a reenactor, while he was a spectator watching a battle; the experience led him to become involved in the hobby.

Cushman (1999) lists commemoration, instruction, and entertainment as the three main reasons people reenact, adding the kind of special moments on which I focus here as a fourth reason. As he describes it, "Reenactors also reenact in order to lose track of time, to fool themselves, to experience a mystical moment when the seemingly impermeable boundary between the present and the past suddenly dissolves" (62). A common characteristic of these moments is that they are marked psychologically by a temporary loss of orientation, one that mimics what reportedly happened to soldiers in battle at Gettysburg:

> One of the most prevalent themes among soldiers who did record their thoughts in diaries and letters around that time is confusion. Men were stupefied by the experience of battle—the deafening noise, the whirlwind of pain and death, the numbness of shock and horror—and had no idea what had just happened. Even the more sober and clearheaded would only have seen and remembered what occurred within a few feet of them, as that is as far as their vision and consciousness allowed them to record. (Desjardin 2003: 14)

It is thus the small and often chaotic details of battle, rather than the broader tactical view, that make reenacting seem realistic. As I sat down with Jason, a fifty-year-old Confederate soldier from Indiana, he had just come back from a long, hot reenactment, and it was clear he was overwhelmed with emotion. He described the event in which he had just participated as incredibly "real," in part because of the frenzy. "We pushed the Yanks back, and they pushed us back, and then we pushed them back and it was just so totally real." Slumped over on the rough ground, wiping the sweat from his brow, he spoke of his feelings, particularly toward his fellow soldiers:

> Going up that hill elbow-to-elbow with your guys, it's just being full of worry for them and, you know, everything that goes through a soldier's mind. You think about home in a heartbeat, and you think about your buddy next to you, and you think about getting the job done for your officers. And then at the same time you gotta

think, "Am I gonna make it?" You know, I don't know if I'm gonna make it. And then you make it! And the jubilation is just incredible. We weren't in somebody else's footsteps but we re-created somebody else's hard fight today. We didn't feel the bullets enter, but we felt the rest of the pain they felt, we felt the rest of the fear they felt, the anxiety, you know, "Am I going to be OK today?" By that I mean, am I going to do right by my fellows today? You know, what it really all boils down to is you're fighting for the guy next to you, you're not fighting for the officers, you're not fighting for the president whether he's in the White House, or in Mobile, or in Richmond; you're fighting for the guy next to you. And you know at the end of the season—there's no doubt in your mind at the end of a season—that if you had to kill somebody to protect your buddy, you would, for real . . . not just powder.

Referring to the same battle, a group of Confederates from Delaware told me, "It was so real it was incredible. It had us all torn apart."

For many Confederate reenactors, their involvement in the hobby is often linked to their political views. As one told me, "The war is still on, the war is still on." He then launched into a scathing critique of contemporary American politics and asserted that "the issues haven't changed . . . it's the same song, just a different choir." As Horwitz (1999: 386) points out, for many people from the South, "remembrance of the War had become a talisman against modernity, an emotional lever for their reactionary politics." Similarly, Strauss (2003), who conducted participant-observation research among Confederate reenactors, points out that while one will not normally hear overtly racist comments, Confederate reenactors "had more in common with their Neo-Confederate counterparts than they were willing to admit" (160), including views that he describes as "symbolically manifesting discomfort with the eroding state of white hegemony in the United States" (159). Strauss also found that Confederate reenactors were often "adamant in their refusal to galvanize" (155), which I also found to be true of many Confederate reenactors, including those of southern heritage who live in northern states. When I asked a group of Confederates from New York State if they ever portrayed Union soldiers, they told me in all seriousness that it was sacrilegious, in their view, to don a Union uniform, citing their "rebel blood" and adding, "Nothing but Dixie. Won't catch me in a blue suit."

Union reenactors, for their part, tend to portray Confederates as fanatical and point out that Confederates take reenacting "too seriously," citing the cliché that for some the war has never ended. While there is some truth in these observations, I noted far more similarities than differences between Union and Confederate reenactors. I would argue that playing up the differences is part of the performance and fun of reenacting. Confederate reenactors often told me that Union reenactors were more disciplined in terms of their military formations and procedures, which the Confederates said reflected actual differences, though this is historically questionable. Confederate reenactors also claimed that Union camp life was "cold." In both Union and Confederate camps at the commercial reenactment, however, there was a surprisingly strong family orientation, and the differences between these enemies were more subtle than most reenactors were willing to admit. Nonetheless, some even refused to set foot in the other camp, though a family-friendly atmosphere prevailed in both camps. For Jason, who was divorced, reenacting provided him the opportunity to spend time with his fourteen-year-old son, Dylan, in his second year of reenacting. Jason talked about the values he hoped to instill in his son at these events. "You know, fourteen is where you lose a kid. He's not gonna get lost," he said, nodding toward Dylan. "Not while he's out here doing this with us. It consumes your focus."

Despite the carnival-like mood and commercialized aspects of Gettysburg reenactments, many people claimed to have experienced profoundly special moments, even with blaring loudspeakers and the presence of spectators in the grandstands. After a major battle, a group of teenage reenactors from central New Jersey described how the crowds completely disappeared as a group of them shot off a volley and three men across from them suddenly went down (known as "taking a hit"). "I felt it right there for at least five seconds," one said, pointing out that this was enough to make the whole weekend worthwhile. Others with whom I spoke said they preferred smaller events, especially those without spectators, where things "can get a little more intense." Describing an event at a remote Living History farm in upstate New York, a reenactor noted how "you can time warp a little bit better, or time travel a little bit better, because there's really nothing around you other than what is there in the camp."

Many female reenactors also described experiences of period rush. Carol from San Antonio, in her late thirties, had just come back from the thick of battle, where she had been serving for the first time as an "ice angel," bringing ice chips to soldiers. She was glowing with excitement: "It was overwhelming, I almost cried 'cause you just almost feel it. You feel like you're actually out there trying to fight for your ground." Julie, an experienced reenactor in her late thirties who traveled to Gettysburg each year with her husband and two children, described her relationship to reenacting as an "addiction" that allows you to "leave the twenty-first century behind." She herself portrays a Union soldier. "It's so funny," she told me, "I can't wait to get out into 90-degree weather in wool and shoot at each other, and smell the gunpowder, and campfires." Similarly, her seventeen-year-old daughter, Megan, said, "When I went out the first time, I came back and I went 'Mom, I'm never putting on a dress again.' I had black powder all over my face, but it was absolutely wonderful. I was sweaty, I was sticky, but it was fun." Another woman in her twenties, who had just gone into battle as a Confederate soldier, told me: "It's such an adrenaline rush while you're out there. You forget everything in the world and you're just marching to the beat of the drum, climbing over fences and walls. It's fun. I love it."

Ultimately, part of the allure of such Civil War moments is their rarity. As one reenactor told me, "I've done this event so many times ... man, I'm all out of magic moments." Another reenactor, in response to my question about whether he had experienced anything "special" or "magical" in a battle that particular day, said:

> No, I didn't go through the bubble, I'm afraid. That truly is a rare thing. You can't psych yourself up for it, you can't put yourself in the mood, it's just something that happens. You know when it's real when you suddenly catch yourself, and you jerk back to reality and say, "What, am I going psychotic or something?" You can't pretend to do it and make it happen. It's 'cause it really is that true experience, as though, in your mind anyway, that you are really there for that split second. It's a beautiful moment.

As powerful as such experiences are, they always remain partial. And, as Cushman (1999: 56) points out, "No matter how completely they identify with their roles, contemporary Civil War reenactors do not come away from reenactments with post-traumatic stress disorder caused by their reenacting." While many take the hobby very seriously, I never got the impression that any of the reenactors with whom I spoke *really* believed they were capable of time traveling or that they became other people, although it was clear that they enjoyed the illusion of being in such moments, the ultimate payoff for the hard work of living as soldiers of the era did. As Bruce, the history teacher, said, "While we're not facing the bullets and the shrapnel and guts flying all over the place, there are some things that I believe are very similar, like the friendships, the experiences, the heat, the smell." Finally, as a sixty-year-old Union officer told me, "We only do an impression. We don't live like it really was. I wouldn't want that anyway. I don't want diarrhea, I don't want lice, I don't want fleas. And, of course, there weren't too many soldiers pushing sixty years old running around there either, unless they were generals on a horse."

Authenticity and Experience

As a discipline, cultural anthropology places great emphasis on the value of participant-observation fieldwork as a key methodology through which anthropologists gain access to other people's perspectives. In a sense, reenactors also use and gain from this methodology, although, since "informants" from the Civil War are long dead, reenactors can only participate and observe through re-creating the experience. While my own immersion in reenactor culture was brief, I emerged with a better grasp of what motivates reenactors to pursue this hobby and with an appreciation of the sincerity, passion, and fun involved.

I also began to see reenacting as having characteristics similar to many found in cultures around the world, particularly in its religious and ritual aspects. Throughout history, human beings have performed rituals to express and reaffirm key values of their cultures, and reenactors, too, can be seen in this mold, carrying out their activities to maintain links to history, forebears, and place. Whenever people hold auspicious rituals—whether of a world religion or a remote indigenous culture—there is often an implicit understanding that in repeating acts believed to have been passed down for generations, one gets closer to something essential or primordial. In re-creating the past through acts of remembrance, reenactors may have more in common with ritual practitioners who call up ancestors and divine spirits, Sunday churchgoers, and New Age pagans than they do with other hobbyists, such as those who are passionate about sports, coins, stamps, or the perfect lawn.

In a very real sense, then, what reenactors do when they gather for a weekend and put on their uniforms is not simply have fun, make good friends, and escape the modern world—they also reaffirm links to their heritage as Americans. This experience is heightened, as I have described above, within the seemingly authentic circumstances and performances that result in intense and powerful bursts of emotion that are part of what keep people coming back. When such bursts occur, reenactors are like religious pilgrims traveling to a sacred site, as both groups seek to connect to something beyond their everyday circumstances. As such, reenacting has a quasi-religious (and perhaps civil religious) element. Of course, as with any religious ritual or cultural practice, aspects of reenacting change over time, and authenticity is always illusory (Amster 1999). This brings me to the topic of the Gettysburg National Military Park and its efforts to restore the landscape of the original battlefield.

In recent years, the park administration at Gettysburg has committed to a major project of battlefield restoration—referred to as "rehabilitation"—with the aim of returning the landscape to its 1863 condition. Virtually every reenactor I spoke with applauded the park for its vision, which includes the ongoing removal of approximately seven hundred acres of "nonhistoric" trees and the restoration of fence lines and other features of the viewscape that can affect how tourists experience the battlefield. All of this is a reenactor's dream, as it allows him to experience more accurately the actual locations of battles as the soldiers might have seen them and improves tactical understanding of military events. As Bruce pointed out, the removal of trees helps reenactors learn about the battles in a multisensory way: "You're seeing it, you're feeling it, you're smelling it. You know, it's one of those things—the more senses you bring into learning, the better you're gonna learn it. So I don't have any problem with what they're doing right now." Another reenactor described how the recent removal of a large stand of trees from the lower end of Little Round Top allowed him to get "a whole new perspective" on specific events. "When you see that opened up like that," he said, "then you can understand, then you get a better picture of why and how things transpired in there." His only complaint about the project was that, "unfortunately, it is going to take ten years to get it complete."

Figure 14.2   Trees being removed near Little Round Top, Gettysburg National Military Park, January 2005 (photo by author)

Another project undertaken by the park is the removal from the battlefield of nonperiod architecture, such as the former Visitor Center and Cyclorama building, the latter constructed at great expense and with much fanfare in the 1960s and located near the heart of the battlefield. The park administration demolished these buildings, in part, because they were located on "sacred" ground and interfered with visitors' ability to see the battlefield as it was at the time of the Civil War.

These attempts to provide a more "authentic" tourist experience, which have increasingly drawn on input from reenactor groups, represent a new approach to heritage and memory. As Jim Weeks (2003: 187) points out, this trend has "pulled away from the family-friendly Gettysburg of the earlier era to create an authentic experience for enthusiasts." Gettysburg, he observes, is now starting to resemble "a kind of giant hobby set for middle-class white America" (198). Critiquing this mind-set, Weeks cites an example of a newspaper report by a black male who visited Gettysburg and had the uncomfortable experience of coming across a Confederate reenactor, pointing out one of the more obvious pitfalls that can accompany the obsessive pursuit of authenticity. One of my colleagues recently asked me, "What happens if Asian Americans want to get involved in reenacting? Would they be accepted?" These are good questions. There were, in fact, some Asian Americans who fought in the battle of Gettysburg, but it is telling that I have not yet seen an Asian American reenactor, or any black reenactors aside from those who belong to all-black reenacting groups. Thus, in seeking to create accurate impressions, reenacting and battlefield "rehabilitation" both run the risk of promoting forms of exclusion, not just by implicitly limiting the participants in a reenactment but also by neglecting the possibility of other forms of commemoration, such as might be reflected in nonperiod architecture or allowing nonhistoric trees to stand as a different type of tribute on the battlefield.

Coming full circle, then, I return to my first day of reenacting and the events immediately following my own brief Civil War moment, described in the opening passages. As our group left the dusty path and crossed a modern road, we immediately encountered a group of tourists who stopped to take our picture. By then, I was fully back to present-day reality. Then, as we marched past General Meade's Union headquarters on one side and the Cyclorama building (still standing at the time) on the other, one of the men in my line, chatting idly, glanced over at the building and said, "It will be nice to get that off the battlefield." It was clear that his desire to see a more authentic battlefield landscape was entirely heartfelt, even though I find such views extreme, having some sympathy for the architectural preservationists who see this building as a valuable piece of history as well. In any case, being there in formation on the battlefield with reenactors gave me a better perspective on what was taking place from the viewpoints of both the reenactors and the park administration, now converging on the idea of the battlefield as "sacred ground" that is best commemorated through accurate historical representation. Having been freshly jarred out of my own brief time bubble by "farby" elements—the road, cars, tourists, the modernist building—in that moment I could more fully appreciate the ever-present challenges such pilgrims to the past face in their attempts to achieve authenticity.

Questions for Discussion

Why do reenactors feel so strongly about authenticity? How does this relate to their personal feelings about the reenacting experience? In what ways do the recent efforts to rehabilitate the battlefields in the Gettysburg National Military Park resemble the aims of reenactors?

References

Amster, Matthew H. 1999. "'Tradition,' Ethnicity, and Change: Kelabit Practices of Name Changing." *Sarawak Museum Journal* 54 (75): 183–200.

———. 2003. "New Sacred Lands: The Making of a Christian Prayer Mountain in Highland Borneo." In Ronald A. Lukens-Bull, ed., *Sacred Places and Modern Landscapes: Sacred Geography and Social-Religious Transformations in South and Southeast Asia*, 131–60. Tempe: Program for Southeast Asian Studies, Arizona State University.

Cushman, Steven. 1999. *Bloody Promenade: Reflections on a Civil War Battle*. Charlottesville: University Press of Virginia.

Desjardin, Thomas A. 2003. *These Honored Dead: How the Story of Gettysburg Shaped American History*. Cambridge, MA: Da Capo Press.

Gatewood, John B., and Catherine M. Cameron. 2004. "Battlefield Pilgrims at Gettysburg National Military Park." *Ethnology* 43 (3): 193–216.

Horwitz, Tony. 1999. *Confederates in the Attic: Dispatches from the Unfinished Civil War*. New York: Vintage Books.

Hunt, Stephen J. 2004. "Acting the Part: 'Living History' as a Serious Leisure Pursuit." *Leisure Studies* 23 (4): 387–403.

Strauss, Mitchell D. 2003. "Identity Construction among Confederate Civil War Reenactors: A Study of Dress, Stage Props, and Discourse." *Clothing and Textiles Research Journal* 21: 149–61.

Thompson, Jenny. 2004. *War Games: Inside the World of Twentieth-Century War Reenactors*. Washington, DC: Smithsonian Books.

Weeks, Jim. 2003. *Gettysburg: Memory, Market, and an American Shrine*. Princeton, NJ: Princeton University Press.

15

Memories of Burning Man

S. Megan Heller

On Friday, March 20, 2015, my family and I drove east toward Joshua Tree National Park on our way to BEquinox, a gathering of the Los Angeles Burning Man community. My husband and brother sat in the front seats of my black Toyota Prius; I sat sandwiched in the back between our two young children (the eldest already a Burning Man veteran) in their protective car seats. Our tents, costumes, a borrowed easy-up shade structure, food, water, and additional camping gear were piled four feet high on the roof rack. As we slowly climbed higher into the California desert, the Joshua trees grew taller and their branches multiplied. Their small palm fronds reached up into the sky as if in ecstasy.

Every summer in Nevada, an enormous effigy of a man, arms similarly outstretched toward the sky, is constructed from wood and burned amid tens of thousands of revelers. They make the annual pilgrimage to the remote, barren Black Rock Desert, enduring relentless sun, wind, and dust, to participate in the Burning Man ritual. Many participants feel that the opportunity to act and express oneself freely is exceedingly rare in the United States, and so they consider the temporary circular desert city created for the weeklong event to be a sacred setting for transformation. They return year after year to cocreate Black Rock City, a place where they play together and become radically transformed by its unforgiving ecology and experimental social context.

Those who are moved by their experiences at Burning Man can become active participants in regional Burning Man communities like the one I have been studying in Los Angeles. My research into the Burning Man movement takes me to smaller, local events throughout the year. Our destination that day was a private campground near Joshua Tree National Park, where BEquinox was already under way. It was the third gathering of the Los Angeles Burning Man community at that location. March is on the opposite pole of the year from the Nevada Burning Man event, hence the name of the event is the Burning Man Equinox, shortened to BEquinox. Rather than wait half a year to return "home" to Black Rock City, organizers of this event worked to bring the Burning Man experience to Southern California, creating a time and place for "BE"-ing in their chosen community. The capital letters suggest a transcendental or existential way of being at the event that requires one to confront such issues as personhood, mortality, sacredness, and relationships with others.

The four-day event would culminate in the communal burning of a wooden sculpture, or effigy, on Saturday night. Members of the Los Angeles Burning Man community were motivated to gather in this (more accessible) California desert to remember and attempt to re-create the ecstatic feelings of togetherness they had experienced at Burning Man. In the social sciences, such feelings have been called "communitas" (Turner 1982) and "collective effervescence" (Durkheim 1995). At various times, I too had experienced these deep feelings of belonging in the context of Burning Man, especially during its rituals and while volunteering. Like all participants who attend the event repeatedly, I had come to consider myself a member of the community. Such insider status would not have been possible if I had chosen a more typical anthropological field site within a community based on birth and kinship.

As we approached the BEquinox event, familiar feelings of anticipation, anxiety, and ambivalence surfaced, as they do when I drive through Nevada on my annual pilgrimage to Black Rock City. Safe inside my vehicle, I feared the intensity of the desert outside. Memories of the approach to Black Rock City percolated in my brain. I recalled how, after the twelve-hour journey (which I often spread out over two days), the city shows itself first as hazy black dots against a stark landscape; if I arrive after dark it appears as a concentration of bright lights in the distance against a black night. I recalled how there are no trees or bushes in the Black Rock Desert and how it feels to step out onto that lifeless, flat, alkaline lakebed that extends for miles, ringed by majestic pastel-colored mountains. In Joshua Tree, the flora and the mountains differed, yet the familiar colors of a desert connected me to my desert "home" in Nevada.

I reminded myself that if I could endure a week in the deadly Black Rock Desert, this one would feel like an oasis. Then it dawned on me that I also felt trepidation about the people I would meet—whom I would treat as friends, although we might be strangers. As I approached the BEquinox event, I wondered if a little regional gathering of "burners" at an ordinary campground could possibly produce the same feelings as the enormous spectacle I had become accustomed to witnessing in Black Rock City amid thousands of participants. I wondered if I would know anyone at this spin-off event and if I would feel any kinship with those I met.

As we drove along the perimeter of the campground, I pointed out where the effigy stood. A large wooden sculpture had been erected where I had witnessed *Seraphim* burn two years before. Thus far the city of Los Angeles has not allowed any such burns to take place within city limits. (In November 2015, the city refused to provide permits even for Decompression, an event without a burn.) Luckily, there was this campground not too far away that agreed to host these burns. This year's effigy was a twenty-foot hypercube. Six dimensions of cubes (frames with no sides) receded to the center, and a large sphere was suspended in the middle. The straight lines of the cubes and the curved edges of the sphere were strong and rigid, and yet movement seemed possible, as if at any moment the effigy might begin to pulsate, like a rib cage or the sides of an audio speaker. Paul Hudson, I learned, designed this sculpture and named it *Earthstar*. A crew of volunteers transported and built it, working together to create something that the community would sacrifice a short time later.

Burning Man has a playful, secular culture involving many ritual practices. Rituals often involve artists creating spaces for participants to write inscriptions and assemble altars, which are subsequently burned in a communal rite. As anthropologist Lee Gilmore (2005, 2010) has documented, participants in Burning Man like the fact that these rituals offer opportunities for spirituality without the dogma of an organized religion.

In addition to the celebratory ritual of burning the Man, participants regularly build and burn sculptures of an even more sacred type, referred to as Temples. The meanings ascribed to the temples most often relate to death, loss, and other personal struggles. Rachel Bowditch (2007) documented the origin of the Temples by interviewing San Francisco Bay Area artist David Best, who built the *Temple of the Mind* in 2000 and dedicated it to a friend who had died in a car crash. Best built many structures out of recycled wood from a puzzle factory, creating a large shelter of ornate latticework on which people were invited to write and leave objects. Some people have had intense emotional reactions during the Temple burns, as I did in 2001, shortly after my father died of cancer.

Best attempted to create a more uplifting cathartic experience the next year when he named his creation *Temple of Joy*, but because of the terrorist attack on the World Trade Center the previous September, participants continued to use the structure primarily as a site for mourning (Bowditch 2007). Other artists have followed in Best's footsteps, creating a series of Temples built lovingly by large groups of volunteers referred to collectively as the Temple Crew. Each year the Temple Crew burns its monument in a solemn rite at the conclusion of the event on Sunday, the night after the Man burns. Throughout the week preceding this burn, participants write inscriptions about personal experiences and leave photographs or other meaningful objects at the temple. In this way, altars publicly address losses due to suicide, estrangement from family members, sexual abuse, lost loves, and illness, as well as describe positive events such as coming out of the closet and falling in love.

Anthropologist Sarah Pike (2005) found that at Temple sites, participants can mourn openly and work through taboo topics that are not addressed in traditional religious contexts. Altars, inscriptions, and rituals display a cultural bricolage of symbols and practices from the world's major religions as well as Native American, pagan, and animist traditions. Participants marshal various ritual practices and direct them toward personal ends.

The cultural practices of Burning Man also include rites of passage, which mark transitions from one state to another. One example is passing through the Greeters Station, the threshold of the event, as one transitions into the role of "participant." A participant is expected to play and interact with others as part of the community, to learn the rules and customs, to volunteer, and not to be a passive "spectator" who just consumes the culture without contributing something to it. At the entrance to the campground, men and women in eccentric attire directed our car forward along the dirt road and then to a stop. As we opened the windows on the driver's side, hot, dry desert air rushed into our air-conditioned vehicle.

A shirtless man greeted us warmly and explained that after handing over our tickets we would be welcomed properly at the Greeters Station up ahead.

The event organizers had sold only one thousand tickets for BEquinox, responding to community members who wanted to keep this regional burn small and intimate. I handed three of these tickets, which cost me a total of $330, to the man at the window, along with three signed "hold harmless" agreements and three driver's licenses. He congratulated me for being so organized. He checked to be sure the names on the tickets and agreements matched the licenses and then passed the licenses back to us, along with three wristbands. There would be no coming and going; once inside, we were expected to make the place our home for the duration of the event.

Volunteers working the gate buzzed around the cars and gathered under a shade structure next to the road. A kind-eyed woman approached my window, gestured to the kids next to me, and asked if they were my children. I replied, "Yes," and she handed me a clipboard with hold harmless agreements to fill out on each child. I tried to concentrate on the paperwork and complete it quickly, but the friendly chatter of the volunteers distracted me. The forms specified that I was to give the name of an emergency contact who was not at the event. I scribbled my mother's information and tried not to imagine what type of emergency would require them to contact her in Sacramento.

Then another woman approached us from beyond the shade structure. She hollered toward our car, asking if we were with Kidsville. My husband responded briskly, "Maybe." She hesitated slightly in her approach, and I responded in a friendlier tone, "Do you know if they have any room for us there?" indicating our wish to join the camp. She smiled and warmly invited us to camp with her and the other families, going on to explain how to get there and recognize it, and some of the activities they had planned. I thanked her and she retreated contentedly. My husband inched the car forward and eventually pulled to the side of the road to let other cars pass us. Finally, I finished the children's paperwork and the gate volunteer took the clipboard from me. She put wristbands on each of the children and two additional ones on my wrist, explaining that they had numbers on them corresponding to the children's so I could be reunited with them by Black Rock Rangers should we became separated. Finally, we were allowed to proceed down the road.

As we approached the Greeters Station, I recognized the lane dividers, white cloth triangles blowing in the wind. The familiar shape of those used to demarcate the fourteen Greeters Stations at the entrance to Black Rock City stirred up feelings of nostalgia in me. As there were only two lanes to be divided at BEquinox, the decorations may not have been necessary, but they clearly signaled that we had arrived. Greeters smiled at us and waved us over into the right-hand lane, where a topless woman greeted me through the window with a warm "Welcome home!"

Although the greeting was familiar, I initially found it peculiar in this context. I was accustomed to the notion that Black Rock City had become my home. Startled, I thought, was Joshua Tree my home as well? Yet it was appealing to believe I could have a similar feeling of attachment to this place, developing deeper roots closer to my actual place of residence. Passing through the threshold, or *limen*, I was already contemplating my habitual way of BEing and my relationships to others. I felt myself opening up to unanticipated possibilities.

The greeters are masterful at orienting new arrivals quickly to the Burning Man social context.

They handed us a printed copy of the "BEquinox Survival Guide," which included information about the event. They also handed us a map of the campground with information about the art installations, as well as stickers with the BEquinox logo, making sure that my daughter got one of her own. "Where can I buy a soda?" my husband asked one of the greeters. Typically no vending is allowed at Burning Man events (coffee drinks and ice for coolers at Black Rock City are exceptions). The community operates on a "gift economy" basis in which gifts are given freely, without expectation of reciprocal gifts. The greeter paused as if to respond in earnest, then smiled knowingly at my husband's joke and went on to tell us about a party happening on Saturday night at Awesome Town camp, at which there would be a twenty-dollar cover charge. "Don't worry," he assured us, saying that the five of us were definitely on the guest list. Through this banter about transactions that were not going to take place, the two men established their social capital, leaving monetary exchange and typical hierarchies behind.

Gift giving is a social practice that binds individuals in the Burning Man community and distinguishes its events from market-oriented gatherings. Anthropologist Marshall Sahlins (1972) uses the term "generalized reciprocity" to describe gift giving that is altruistic or done with only a vague expectation of return. According to psychological anthropologist Alan Fiske (1993), social relationships operate according to four basic models: "communal sharing," "equality matching," "market pricing," and "authority ranking." At Burning Man events one can see clearly how communal sharing is highly valued and promoted through altruistic gift giving, in stark contrast to the market pricing and authority ranking that predominate in most U.S. cities and the equality matching of barter economies. Robert Kozinets and John Sherry (2005), who have written extensively about the gift economy at Burning Man, describe how relationships at the event are ideally based on the principles of sharing with and caring for one another. Even bartering and other quid pro quo practices are frowned on, viewed as antithetical to the goal of breaking down barriers between people who are trying to form a community.

As we drove away from the Greeters Station and into the campground, my husband continued joking about the gift economy by talking about all the hand-blown glassware we had brought to sell at BEquinox. I laughed at the memory of other festivals and events we have attended at which small-scale entrepreneurship proliferates. Although I appreciated the novelty of handmade crafts and the convenience of purchasing food, I felt disconnected from others in the role of consumer. I was relieved to arrive into the comfort and safety of a gift economy, where I would not be sold anything by anyone, I would not be expected to give tips or donations, and I could leave my wallet in my car all weekend. Whatever people at this event had brought with them—games, food, drinks, art, transportation, toys, music, shade, special effects, fire—they had brought it to share freely with others.

One of the main activities at a Burning Man event is wandering—one wanders into and through other people's camps, discovering what they have to offer, and one also wanders out into the open spaces to interact with larger-scale art projects. As my husband and brother set up our desert abode, I took the children to explore Kidsville and beyond. Our immediate neighbors at BEquinox had a little shade, so I walked over and introduced myself, hoping they would ask us to join them in the shade, which they did. We played with their baby for about thirty minutes on a blanket spread out in front of their tents. They gave my daughter a juice box and shared their sunblock with all of us. I was grateful to be out of the sun for a bit. As I chatted with our campsite neighbors, I learned that they lived quite close to us in the "default world," as the world outside Burning Man is labeled. People I meet in Black Rock City come from all over the world; we can stay in contact by e-mail or phone or wait and see if we ever run into each other again. But people I met at this regional event were often my actual neighbors, and I realized how much easier it could be to develop ties with them in the default world.

After a while we thanked the family and moved on. I put my son in his stroller and we wandered into the center of Kidsville, where the organizers had erected a large yellow shade structure. I met a few of the parents in charge, but because there were no activities happening there yet to pique my daughter's interest, they directed us to the big tree by the lake where someone was doing activities for kids.

We wandered slowly to the lake—really a pond in terms of size. Some kids were gathered under a tree behind two little white walls forming half of a playhouse. They were busy with some type of hands-on activity that I could not see. A group of adults sat nearby in what appeared to be a smoking area made of adobe. A few coffee cans were available for their cigarette butts, and there were several benches shaded by palm fronds. Rather than approach either group directly, I found a seat between them and made myself comfortable rocking the baby's stroller. I suggested to my daughter that she join in the kids' activity at the playhouse. She was shy, she explained, frowning and hunching her shoulders. "They might be doing face painting," I said, something I knew she would enjoy. Immediately she perked up and marched over to investigate.

I was also feeling shy, but pretended not to be. As I rocked the baby, I eavesdropped intently, listening to the smokers' conversation and waiting for my chance to join in. A man with an accent talked loudly about the probability of intelligent life on other planets. He went on to describe the accelerating speed of technological advancement on this planet and the possibility of our inventing an even higher form of intelligence. He described a future in which information would become the most valuable commodity and objects, including food items, could be synthesized easily. Some of what he described sounded scary to me, but the tone of the conversation was of optimistic imaginings, as if such a reality were imminent and ought to be embraced.

When the group dispersed, the man engaged me in a conversation. I learned that he was born in Russia. Earlier in my life I had studied Russian language and culture, and I had visited Russia as part of a performing arts group. We talked about Mikhail Gorbachev and the radical changes brought about through his policies of glasnost, or openness, which inadvertently led to the dismantling of the Soviet Union. Eventually our conversation came around to the man's experiences at Burning Man. He described a campmate who was radically transformed by the event. He characterized the campmate as a typical "frat boy" who surprised everyone by coming out as a homosexual. Members of the Burning Man community often use "frat boy" to refer to a distasteful version of mainstream masculinity, symbolized by a man who joined a fraternity in college. This sort of man is viewed as obnoxious and the opposite of the social misfits, artists, and hardworking volunteers who are attracted to Burning Man and its countercultural norms.

After coming out, the "frat boy" underwent a dramatic transformation. He became freer to wear what he wanted and love whom he wanted. Stories of transformation are common at Burning Man events. This one was remarkable because the change was so unexpected and profound. Because the "frat boy" was so much more relaxed, his face looked like that of a different person. I thanked my conversation partner for sharing this story with me.

I rejoined my daughter, whose fingernails had been painted while I was chatting. She insisted on applying pink nail polish to my toenails. Afterward, we started walking together toward the effigy, *Earthstar*, pushing the baby's stroller in front of us. Immediately, however, we encountered an interactive art project. It was a large purple-and-blue board with teardrop-shaped pieces of paper pinned to it. My daughter, recognizing this as an invitation to participate, asked to write on one of the teardrops herself. A sign near the board instructed participants to share a story of grief on one of the pieces of paper. I read the sign aloud to her and explained what "grief" means, and then I helped her write her story with the pens provided. This is what she had me write: "Grandpa—Why did you die before I was born? I wanted to meet you. Love, Sophia." Then she took the pen from me and drew several smaller teardrops on the paper.

I was quite moved by her unprompted memorial to my dead father. I remembered grieving when he was ill, lamenting how he would never know my children. Actual tears welled in my eyes as I pinned my daughter's story to the board. My father's ashes dwell in a box in our living room; this conspicuous location was inspired by my time in Japan with a Japanese host family who kept an ancestral shrine in the main living area. Death is so rarely discussed openly in American culture. At BEquinox, I appreciated my child's ability to understand her own loss and to use the ritual practices of Burning Man to express her emotions and speak to her ancestor.

We continued our journey toward *Earthstar*, walking away from the lake into the open space where the effigy stood apart from any structures or shrubs that might catch fire. The wooden square appeared to grow in size as we approached. We found pens there as well, and we each picked one up. My daughter doodled along the base of the sculpture; I selected a surface about three feet off the ground and drew a picture of my husband's colon, part of which had been removed two months earlier. Next to my drawing I wrote, "Bye Bye Sigmoid!" It felt good to acknowledge the grueling period of illness and recovery my family had just endured. My drawing was a playful attempt to move past this unexpected event.

Laughing inwardly at my private joke, I felt a cathartic release of some of the anxiety I had experienced on account of this diseased organ. I looked forward to witnessing the burning of *Earthstar* and the incineration of this symbolic source of my recent distress. I had been at BEquinox for only two hours, and already I felt a shift in my subjectivity. I felt more relaxed, content to wander and encounter people and things with an open mind. I also felt an opening up to the possibility of being a healthier and happier family in the future.

The following morning I returned to the lake and ran into one of my research informants, whom I will call Mick. As was his habit, Mick introduced me to his female companion as "my anthropologist," which sounded like "my therapist" the way he said it. The introduction made me blush, because I would have preferred to keep our anthropologist–informant relationship a secret so as to protect his anonymity. Mick had called me recently to say that his life had improved greatly since 2009, when I had been interviewing him. He wanted me to know he was no longer the sad man he was then. He thanked me for listening to him, giving me some of the credit for his transformative experience. He told me about the woman he was dating, his self-help course, and the new performance art he had taken up—clowning. He was training to perform as a clown for children in hospitals, a radical departure from his current job selling alarm systems. He sounded like a more hopeful man, excited about the new direction in his life.

In 2009 I used several different research methods to answer the question "What happens to people who report having transformative experiences at Burning Man?" I relied primarily on a style of interviewing, based on psychoanalysis, in which the informant is interviewed multiple times and leads the conversation. This allowed me to collect rich ethnographic information about a small number of informants, focusing on what they, not I, considered salient about the events they experienced. Over the course of a year, I established intimate, trusting relationships with sixteen participants, all California residents, who spoke to me in great detail about their lives and their experiences at Burning Man. I audio-recorded our monthly conversations. I also video-recorded each person for one hour at the event in Nevada and had the person fill out a questionnaire. As I analyzed the data, I compared my observations with the self-reports of my informants. I sought to understand my informants' unique developmental pathways and the psychological and cultural processes that produced their reported experiences.

When I conducted these interviews I often learned that an informant was suffering in some way. Mick had been going through a particularly difficult period in his life. He was fighting a custody battle for his daughter, whose mother was addicted to methamphetamine and had left Mick to move in with her drug dealer. Mick was trying to prove to the court that he was the more reliable parent, but he was nursing a broken heart and a broken ego. He consumed alcohol, food, and video games in abundance; however, these various forms of play did not fill the void left by his ex-girlfriend. She continued to be a source of drama and disappointment. In the privacy of our interviews, he expressed a yearning to find a romantic partner who would love him and stay with him.

Throughout my research I often encountered Mick at various Burning Man community events in the Los Angeles region. In public, Mick seemed like a jolly man. He had a big belly and he looked quite dashing in a bowler hat. He seemed to have fun drinking and dancing, participating as a judge at a cook-off, and helping to build effigies for burning. When I met him, Mick clearly separated his Burning Man life from his family life. He did not want anything to jeopardize his case that he was the fitter parent. So even when he was going to daytime, family-friendly Burning Man events, he usually left his daughter with her grandmother.

After Mick was eventually awarded custody of his daughter, he embarked on the process of integrating his two lives. In 2013 he brought his mother and daughter to the first BEquinox and rented an RV for them. He had become lead builder of the Los Angeles regional community's effigy, *Seraphim*. He had worked hard to build it, prepare it for transport to Nevada, and assemble it for the burn there, and then he built it a second time to be burned in Los Angeles. The structure was a wooden pergola, twenty feet by twenty feet, with angels of four different ethnicities adorning its four corners. In the center was a twenty-five-foot-tall vortex, shaped like an ice cream cone, which was designed to hold a secret steel angel, the "Human Spirit," to be revealed when the structure burned.

Fifty or so volunteers built the first *Seraphim* in seven months and erected it at Burning Man in 2012 as part of a huge ring around the Man formed by thirty-three CORE (Circle of Regional Effigies) Project effigies. They were burned on the Thursday night of the event. Afterward, Mick was asked to build a second *Seraphim* in time for Decompression, a regional event that took place in a state park in downtown Los Angeles in October. He and seven other volunteers built the second effigy in just five weeks. Just before Decompression, however, the Los Angeles Fire Department revoked the event's burn permit. So after simply displaying the sculpture, Mick and his team put it in storage while they figured out where it could be burned. In March 2013 the first BEquinox was organized at this private campground, the only place that would allow the stigmatized, fire-loving community to gather for its ritual.

"I am a Temple builder," Mick told me with pride as we stood beside the second *Seraphim* in 2013, preparing to watch it burn. In 2012 Mick had assumed a great deal of responsibility as the lead builder on the project. He put a lot of work into managing volunteers and dealing with the drama that so often occurs in such collaborative projects. Fortunately, it appeared that he was a skillful leader. He worked well with people, trained them if necessary, and tried to make the job seem easy. He was able to make executive decisions and give orders while keeping everyone feeling heard and happy. But in his absence, all the members of the team that was supposed to assemble the structure at the beginning of Burning Man had quit. When he arrived two days before the event, he had to finish assembling the project by himself.

Mick called the process of working on the project a "crucible," a container into which all these different personalities were poured. In the end, either their relationships would hold together or they would break apart, he explained. Despite what had happened, Mick suspected that his team might reunite when he put the call out for volunteers to build the next effigy. When I asked him why they would come back after things fell apart in the desert, he said that the people volunteering on the project were outcasts and misfits who had become friends. The project gave them "something to do on a Saturday instead of sit around and watch TV." The sculpture was just temporary, a memory, he said, but the relationships that formed around it were lasting.

At gatherings such as BEquinox, participants "play" the culture of Burning Man into existence using their imaginations as well as their hands. Burning Man is an intentional community, a reaction to feelings of dislocation and alienation that participants attribute to commoditized experiences in the default world. The culture of Burning Man is meant to be a radical departure from that world and an invitation to participate in the creation of alternative possibilities. Those who become absorbed in the countercultural world of Burning Man may become radicalized in the same way some people become radicalized by religious experiences or political movements. At Burning Man some people find a place in something larger than themselves—a family, a culture, a social network, a historical happening, a purpose. They may become more hopeful about the future and less fearful of change. They may adopt a new cultural identity and a new set of principles by which to live (at least some of the time).

Burning Man founder Larry Harvey wrote the official Ten Principles of Burning Man in 2004 as a model of what had emerged in the desert and a model for guiding the culture as it spreads to regional communities throughout the world:

The Ten Principles of Burning Man

Radical Inclusion
Anyone may be a part of Burning Man. We welcome and respect the stranger. No prerequisites exist for participation in our community.

Gifting
Burning Man is devoted to acts of gift giving. The value of a gift is unconditional. Gifting does not contemplate a return or an exchange for something of equal value.

Decommodification
In order to preserve the spirit of gifting, our community seeks to create social environments that are unmediated by commercial sponsorships, transactions, or advertising. We stand ready to protect our culture from such exploitation. We resist the substitution of consumption for participatory experience.

Radical Self-Reliance
Burning Man encourages the individual to discover, exercise and rely on his or her inner resources.

Radical Self-Expression
Radical self-expression arises from the unique gifts of the individual. No one other than the individual or a collaborating group can determine its content. It is offered as a gift to others. In this spirit, the giver should respect the rights and liberties of the recipient.

Communal Effort
Our community values creative cooperation and collaboration. We strive to produce, promote and protect social networks, public spaces, works of art, and methods of communication that support such interaction.

Civic Responsibility
We value civil society. Community members who organize events should assume responsibility for public welfare and endeavor to communicate civic responsibilities to participants. They must also assume responsibility for conducting events in accordance with local, state and federal laws.

Leaving No Trace
Our community respects the environment. We are committed to leaving no physical trace of our activities wherever we gather. We clean up after ourselves and endeavor, whenever possible, to leave such places in a better state than when we found them.

Participation
Our community is committed to a radically participatory ethic. We believe that transformative change, whether in the individual or in society, can occur only through the medium of deeply personal participation. We achieve being through doing. Everyone is invited to work. Everyone is invited to play. We make the world real through actions that open the heart.

Immediacy
Immediate experience is, in many ways, the most important touchstone of value in our culture. We seek to overcome barriers that stand between us and a recognition of our inner selves, the reality of those around us, participation in society, and contact with a natural world exceeding human powers. No idea can substitute for this experience.

A set of principles does not constitute a religion, but it might form the charter for a culture. The Burning Man culture is a reaction to the social relations that have arisen within a capitalist economic system. The principles are an attempt to create a more perfect community within the extant system without undermining the fact that people must make a living in it.

One could view this emerging culture as a novel ideological synthesis between capitalism and communism—a way of having the best of both. The Ten Principles of Burning Man champion communal means of viewing the self and one's labor as part of a collective while upholding the liberties that Americans have come to cherish. In the Burning Man community a person can enjoy the decadence of a capitalist city and the intimacy of a small commune without the constant drama of having to live with friends every day.

There is, however, an undercurrent of anarchy pervading the Burning Man community. It is a crass anarchy that distrusts authority, burns things, and wears punk styles of clothing. It is also a more philosophical type of anarchy that boasts of the possibility of a stateless society constituted out of voluntary associations and agreements maintained without the use of force.

The Los Angeles regional Burning Man community embraces the ten principles and suggests an eleventh: gratitude. The community includes this bonus principle in such publications as the pamphlet I received at the entrance to BEquinox. As the culture of Burning Man spreads, the traditions, customs, principles, and rituals become increasingly real, and yet there remains room for innovation. Burning Man events are centered on a strong foundation of past practice, but there is also a degree of flexibility, perhaps because of the emphasis on the transformative potential of playing.

I thought about gratitude the morning after *Earthstar* burned, when my family returned to the smoldering site where it had stood. We milled about the edge of the flattened sculpture and watched the volunteers tending to the scarred earth, using rakes and magnets to separate the coals from the metal. My inscription and my daughter's doodles were obliterated, but our sentiments lingered. I felt gratitude for our lives and for the rituals that helped me find and express that feeling.

Questions for Discussion

What ways of playing are available to you in adulthood? In what ways are these activities meaningful to you? Do they help you express emotion, form social bonds? What do you learn from playing with others?

References

Bowditch, Rachel. 2007. "Temple of Tears: Revitalizing and Inventing Ritual in the Burning Man Community in Black Rock Desert, Nevada." *Journal of Religion and Theatre* 6 (2).

Durkheim, Émile. 1995. *The Elementary Forms of Religious Life.* Karen E. Fields, trans. New York: Free Press.

Fiske, Alan Page. 1993. *Structures of Social Life: The Four Elementary Forms of Human Relations—Communal Sharing, Authority Ranking, Equality Matching, Market Pricing.* New York: Free Press.

Gilmore, Lee. 2005. "Fires of the Heart: Ritual, Pilgrimage, and Transformation at Burning Man." In Lee Gilmore and Mark Van Proyen, eds., *AfterBurn: Reflections on Burning Man*, 43–62. Albuquerque: University of New Mexico Press.

———. 2010. *Theater in a Crowded Fire: Ritual and Spirituality at Burning Man*. Berkeley: University of California Press.

Harvey, Larry. 2004. "The 10 Principles of Burning Man." Burning Man Project, Philosophical Center. burningman.org/culture/philosophical-center/10-principles (accessed October 26, 2015).

Kozinets, Robert V., and John F. Sherry Jr. 2005. "Welcome to the Black Rock Café." In Lee Gilmore and Mark Van Proyen, eds., *AfterBurn: Reflections on Burning Man*, 87–106. Albuquerque: University of New Mexico Press.

Pike, Sarah M. 2005. "No Novenas for the Dead: Ritual Action and Communal Memory at the *Temple of Tears*." In Lee Gilmore and Mark Van Proyen, eds., *AfterBurn: Reflections on Burning Man*, 195–214. Albuquerque: University of New Mexico Press.

Sahlins, Marshall. 1972. *Stone Age Economics*. New York: Aldine de Gruyter.

Turner, Victor. 1982. *From Ritual to Theatre: The Human Seriousness of Play*. New York: Performing Arts Journal Publications.

16

WHEN WORLDS COLLUDE: GROUNDHOG PHIL AND THE SUPER BOWL MEET ON CANDLEMAS

Robert Myers

This is a short story about three annual events that happened on the same day for the first time on Sunday, February 2, 2014. The story is one of evolving mythologies, shifting importance, adaptive functions, and overlapping connections in modern U.S. society. These events illustrate the decline in formal religion and the rise of secular entertainments in a media-saturated world. The coincidence of the events offers a simple model of a sacred/secular old/new dichotomy mediated by a pragmatic mythology of imported lore linking animals and weather. In these events we see the persistence of prophetic belief in the midst of material, high-tech society, as well as the embeddedness of chance in a world keen on knowing the future. Connecting threads of winter celebrations and weather forecasts—along with European pagan, Christian religious, and commercial secular prophecies used to manage the unknown—bears out the anthropological tradition of making the strange familiar and the familiar strange.

CANDLEMAS

Set on February 2 by the Catholic Church centuries ago to compete with European pagan fire festivals and beliefs, Candlemas is one of the feast days on the wheel of the year, falling midway between the winter solstice and the spring equinox (Fitzgerald 1991). Candlemas marks both the cultural end of winter and the turn toward spring and, as a pivotal time, is associated with profound beliefs and rituals. For centuries it was an important midwinter event on the liturgical calendar, the final feast day optimistically heralding spring and divine salvation. Today, only the most devout Catholics, Anglicans, and Episcopalians are familiar with

Reflecting on America, 2nd edition, edited by Clare L. Boulanger, 193–203 © 2016 Taylor & Francis. All rights reserved.

Candlemas. (By word-processing standards, the event is obscure: Microsoft Word neither recognizes the term *Candlemas* as a proper noun nor offers it as a correction.)

Known variously as the Feast of the Presentation of the Lord at the Temple, the Meeting of the Lord, the Encounter (in the Eastern Church), and the Feast of the Purification of the Blessed Virgin Mary, Candlemas is recorded in Luke 2:22–40 as the day when Joseph and Mary went to the temple forty days after the birth of Jesus to present the newborn formally, as required by Jewish law, and to complete Mary's purification after birthing a male (had Mary had a girl, the ritual would have taken place eighty days after the baby's birth). This ritual required the sacrifice of a pair of "turtledoves or young pigeons" (or a lamb for those who could afford one) and a small redemption payment of five shekels (Leviticus 12:8; Exodus 13:12–15). The culmination of the presentation of Jesus was Mary and Joseph's encounter with Anna the Prophetess and Simeon (i.e., Saint Simeon the Righteous), the "just and devout" man of Jerusalem who had been told he would not die until he had seen the son of God born of a virgin. Together, Simeon and Anna revealed to Mary and Joseph their forecast of all-time highs and lows: Mary's infant was the Messiah, the son of God, who would save the world through the sacrifice of his own life ("Simeon" n.d.; Stanton 2014).

By the sixth century, the Western Church was celebrating the feast day with processions in which celebrants held lighted candles blessed by the priests (CatholicCulture.org n.d.). This accounts for the name Candlemas, or Candle Mass, but there is more to candles than illumination. In *The Golden Bough*, Sir James Frazer ([1922] 1996: 36–37, 162) notes the magical qualities associated with candles in European folklore. Celebrants take Candlemas candles home, where they serve as talismans providing sacred protection from all sorts of disasters, including extreme weather. In Hungary, according to Dorothy Spicer in *The Book of Festivals* (cited in Fitzgerald 1991), February 2 is called Blessing of the Candle of the Happy Woman (Gyertyazsenteio Boidog Asszony). In Poland, it is called Mother of God Who Saves Us from Thunder (Swieto Matki Boskiej Gromnicznej) or Mother of God of the Blessed Thunder Candle. Traditionally, Poles brought home candles blessed by priests and used them "to protect a dying person from Satan or as an aid in the ritual 'cleansing' of a new mother. . . . The candle's most important function, however, as suggested by its name, was to protect a house from lightning and thunder; nineteenth-century prayer books contained special prayers used during thunderstorms" (Silverman 2000: 48).

In France, the popular day was a time to light candles and to make and enjoy crepes. The day was associated with the saying "If the candle be fair and clear, we'll leave winter behind. If the sky be neither clear nor fair, we'll have more wine than water" (Delors 2009).

Chambers' Book of Days, published in 1869, catalogs numerous British customs relating to February 2, among them the practice of removing all holly and Christmas decorations on the eve before February 2 to prevent misfortune (Hillman and Clerici 2004). The book also includes one of four poems written by Robert Herrick (1591–1674) on the occasion of Candlemas:

> Down with the rosemary and bays,
> Down with the mistletoe;
> Instead of holly now upraise
> The greener box for show.

The holly hitherto did sway,
Let box now domineer,
Until the dancing Easter day
Or Easter's eve appear.

The youthful box, which now hath grace
Your houses to renew,
Grown old, surrender must his place
Unto the crisped yew.

When yew is out, then birch comes in,
And many flowers beside,
Both of a fresh and fragrant kin',
To honour Whitsuntide.

Green rushes then, and sweetest bents,
With cooler oaken boughs,
Come in for comely ornaments,
To re-adorn the house.

Thus times do shift; each thing in turn does hold;
New things succeed, as former things grow old.

Several British weather proverbs link midwinter's Candlemas beliefs; for example, "If Candlemas be fair and bright / Come, winter, have another flight / If Candlemas brings clouds and rain / Go winter, and come not again." An old Scottish couplet goes: "If Candlemas Day is bright and clear / There'll be twa winters in the year." From Germany, there is this: "For as the sun shines on Candlemas Day / So far will the snow swirl until the May" (Dunwoody 1883: 101–2; Yoder 2003: 52). In our modern world, however, Candlemas is virtually unknown except in the town prominently associated with a midwinter ritual of small-mammal prophecy.

GROUNDHOG DAY

Punxsutawney, Pennsylvania, the self-proclaimed "Weather Capital of the World," rises to national prominence every February 2 as home to Punxsutawney Phil, the most famous animal weather prophet in the nation. Groundhog Day has been celebrated in Pennsylvania at least since 1841, and continuously since 1886. Annual ritual treks to Gobbler's Knob, the sacred ground where Phil's prophecy is revealed, have been taking place since 1887. The Bill Murray film *Groundhog Day*, directed by Harold Ramis, catapulted the event to national prominence in 1993, but even before that Phil was famous far beyond his burrow. He has visited or been visited by the governors of various states, he met President Reagan in the White House in 1986, and he was on *The Oprah Winfrey Show* in 1995. His prophecy has been shown live on the Jumbotron in New York City's Times Square and broadcast live by The Weather Channel (TWC) for years. Whether or not Phil sees his shadow on February 2, his augury is carried by most electronic and print media outlets. The result is said to determine whether spring will come soon or only after six more weeks of winter.

Beliefs in the ability of a badger to predict spring were brought to the United States by German immigrants during the eighteenth century ("Groundhog Day" n.d.), and in the absence of badgers, the beliefs were transferred to the plentiful groundhogs. Groundhogs (*Marmota monax*), variously called woodchucks, whistle pigs, land beavers, and ground squirrels, resemble neither hogs, pigs, beavers, nor squirrels. They are members of that small group of animals that fully hibernate, going into a deep coma "where the body temperature drops to a few degrees above freezing, the heart barely beats, the blood scarcely flows, and breathing nearly stops" (Punxsutawney Groundhog Club n.d.b). Thus they experience near death but are reborn, in the case of Phil, to foresee the arrival of spring. Phil has eternal life; he receives special care throughout the year and is given a secret magical elixir "groundhog punch" each summer at the Groundhog Picnic to prolong his life another seven years. The 2014 event was said to be the 128th in his career. Although there are other groundhog weather predictors, Phil is "the only true weather forecasting groundhog. The others are just impostors" (Punxsutawney Groundhog Club n.d.a).

On Groundhog Day, Phil is surrounded by twelve disciples called the Inner Circle of the Punxsutawney Groundhog Club, attired formally in black top hats, black ties, and topcoats. Members of the all-male group have special roles and titles: Rainmaker, Iceman, His Protector, Thunder Conductor, Big Chill, Sky Painter, Coal Front, Stump Warden, Fair Weatherman, Shingle Shaker, Big Windmaker, and His Scribe. Membership in the Inner Circle is for life, or until a member gets tired of all the work required. In public Phil is addressed by his formal title, "Seer of Seers, Prognosticator of Prognosticators, Weather Predictor Extraordinaire, National Treasure, and Most Photographed Pennsylvanian." The considerable efforts of the Inner Circle result in a mock-serious event of dramatic proportions. The president of the Inner Circle asserts that the group's role is "to promote the town and have fun," a function that belies the huge amount of work and considerable scale of philanthropy by its members (Punxsutawney Groundhog Club n.d.c)

On February 2, 2014, between 20,000 to 30,000 people gathered at Gobbler's Knob and stood for hours before dawn in muddy, rainy, nearly freezing weather waiting patiently for Phil's prophecy. At dawn, the climax of the event, Phil was pulled from his artificial burrow on the grand stage where all the members of his Inner Circle and other dignitaries had gathered. Phil revealed his prophecy in groundhogese to the president of the Inner Circle, who translated it into English. Then Phil was held high and presented to the cheering multitudes. His presentation bore a striking resemblance to the depiction of the prophet Simeon's presentation of the Christ Child in the painting *Presentation of Jesus in the Temple* (*La présentation de Jésus au Temple*) by French painter James Tissot (see "Presentation of Jesus" n.d.).

Phil remained calm and focused throughout the event, as one would expect of an archetypal prophet. He was undistracted from his mission despite being surrounded by the pressures of prophecy, thousands of cameras and cell phones, and loud cheers from his followers. He carefully selected his prophecy, which had been written out in two forms by handlers. His words, which rank Phil as the poet laureate of woodchucks, read in part:

A Super Bowl winner I will not predict,
But my weather forecast, you cannot contradict.

Why, that's not a football lying beside me
It's my shadow you see
So, six more weeks of winter it shall be! (quoted in Rice 2014)

Officially, according to the true believers of his fan club, Phil has prophe-sied correctly 100 percent of the time (Punxsutawney Groundhog Club n.d.a). Others, however, have been more critical of his abilities. He may have seen his shadow 100 out of 116 times, but he has been accurate only 39 percent of the time (Daniel 2013; Stormfax Weather Almanac 2015). The National Climatic Data Center found that he did poorly during the period 1988–2014 (Edwards 2015; National Oceanic and Atmospheric Administration [NOAA] n.d.). Evaluating temperatures for the six weeks after February 2 for 250 cities over thirty years, the graphics department of the *Washington Post* found that "while Phil was tech-nically right more times than not in some cities (it's bound to happen in some areas because temperatures across the country do not rise and fall uniformly), the average temperatures between shadow and non-shadow years were slight at best" (Elliott and Tan 2015).

The 2014 Groundhog Day weekend events were covered live by a popular team of Weather Channel broadcast stars: Jim Cantore, the public face of TWC and 2013 inductee into the Punxsutawney Weather Discovery Center Meteorologist Hall of Fame, and Jen Carfagno, who graduated from nearby Penn State's mete-orology program. Throughout Saturday, Cantore and Carfagno interacted with residents and tourists on Main Street as they broadcast local events, reported local weather, and linked viewers to the upcoming Big Game. Carfagno gave the key-note address at a banquet held by the Punxsutawney Groundhog Club the night before. There, at Punxsutawney High School ("Home of the Chucks"), some five hundred attendees from numerous states and at least three other countries sang patriotic songs, offered prayers, and enjoyed a sumptuous feast featuring large groundhog-shaped cookies for dessert. (One colleague noted the commun-ion wafer–like symbolism of the cookies.) After Phil's prophecy on Sunday, the major event of the long professional football season, dubbed the "Weatherbowl," quickly supplanted Groundhog Day celebrations.

Super Bowl XLVIII

Since 1967, the National Football League has held the Super Bowl annually to determine the champion professional football team. Super Bowl games have usu-ally taken place in January, but in recent years the football season has edged into February. Super Bowl Sunday has become an informal national holiday, inspiring countless Super Bowl viewing parties, where interest in the game's halftime show and the expensive commercials shown during the game rival interest in the game itself.

Americans love statistics, cloaking nearly every event, especially those that take place in the areas of sports and weather, in mantles of numbers. "Numbers are America's tranquilizers," one Italian journalist has concluded, explaining that Americans use numbers as an element of control (Severgnini 2014). In the case of 2014's Super Bowl XLVIII, enough statistics were published to make one comatose (except where noted, the facts below were gathered from "Super Bowl XLVIII" n.d.; "Super Bowl XLVIII Halftime Show" n.d.):

- The game was said to match the top defensive team against the top offensive team, with the status of each supported by volumes of statistics.
- A total of 82,529 fans attended the game at MetLife Stadium in East Rutherford, New Jersey.
- Television viewers totaled 111.5 million; this was the largest audience in U.S. television history until Super Bowl 2015.
- The halftime show, featuring Bruno Mars and the Red Hot Chili Peppers, had even more viewers, estimated at 115.3 million. Bruno Mars, who had just won a Grammy Award for Best Pop Vocal Album the week before, was the first Super Bowl halftime performer under thirty years old and the first with (some) Puerto Rican ancestry ("Bruno Mars" n.d.).
- The halftime performance generated 2.2 million tweets.
- The league ordered 84,000 "warm-welcome kits" to be placed on the stadium seats in anticipation of freezing weather (Baker 2014).
- The price for a thirty-second commercial to air during the game was $4 million.
- The total financial impact of this single game was estimated in the double-digit billions.
- Competitive prophecies, usually called "bets" or "wagers," on the game made throughout the United States and abroad generated many collective kings' ransoms.

The modern prophets known as sportswriters, economists, bookies, and weather forecasters had a field day with the Super Bowl. Sportswriters predicted which teams would make it to the Super Bowl as soon as the season began (e.g., "2014 Predictions" 2014). Wagers placed on the game in Las Vegas set records. Every aspect of the event generated bets, from the coin toss to who would be the MVP to point spreads to the length of the national anthem (previously between 1 minute and 34 seconds and 2 minutes and 25 seconds [SB Nation 2014]; in 2015 the anthem ran 1 minute and 53 seconds [SuperBowlBets.com 2015]). Many wagers were made simply on the basis of the emotional appeal of favored regional teams. Overall, bets on the game amounted to an estimated $12 billion, more than the gross domestic products of many nations and more than the annual revenues of such Fortune 500 companies as Visa, Marriott, Heinz, and Hershey (Chase 2014).

In addition to competitive prophecies about outcomes, Super Bowl superstitions abound among obsessed fans. Ritual control over events has always held an attraction, especially with respect to high-profile, high-tech sports. As reported on a CNN blog: "According to a poll released in January [2014] by the Public Religion Research Institute, about half of all Americans believe that some element of the supernatural plays a role in sporting events." Believers "put on certain underwear, danced in little circles, gave their TVs a pep talk." Compared with fans of other sports, football fans are "more likely to pray for their teams, perform pregame rituals or believe their teams are cursed" (Burke 2014).

Above all, uncertainties of weather predominated in predictions for Super Bowl XLVIII. This was the first Super Bowl played outdoors (i.e., in a stadium with no dome or other roof) in a cold-weather city. Speculation about the weather on game day began as soon as the date and location were announced in August 2011 and formed the subject of comments by the NFL's commissioner, Roger Goodell, on September 27, 2011. The *Farmers' Almanac* prophesied "stormy weather . . . with copious wind, rain, and snow" at least eighteen months before the game (Weatherbee 2013).

As the date of the game approached, articles about the possibility of inclement weather on February 2 proliferated. *Weatherbowl* replaced *Super Bowl* in the terminology of weather people and weather companies, self-servingly promoted by The Weather Channel, which committed two hundred personnel to on-site game-day coverage. (The worse the weather, the more viewers for TWC; few watch when the weather is good.)

Close to game time, the *New York Times* reported that "questions about the weather for the first outdoor cold-climate Super Bowl have upstaged even the point spread" (Anderson 2014). Another *New York Times* article quoted meteorologist Bernie Rayno: "This will be the most talked-about Super Bowl weather. It's going to be a very busy week for meteorologists across the country." Rayno noted, "It's not rocket science: You have cold air, you have increased chance of snow" (quoted in Belson 2014a). Commissioner Goodell "poked fun at the worrywarts, with fake snowflakes falling from the ceiling during his annual state of the league address" two weeks before the game. The *Times* quoted Goodell: "'Of course, we cannot control the weather,' he said. 'I told you we were going to embrace the weather; here we go'" (Belson 2014b). Goodell "all but dared the weather gods to make it snow on Super Bowl Sunday" (Belson 2014a).

Despite the availability of data collected by thousands of private weather stations, NASA weather satellites, an impressive collection of National Weather Service (NWS) radar stations, weather balloons, and buoys, analyzed by several hundred weather and climate specialists, accurate weather prediction more than seven to ten days into the future remains problematic. Today's best weather prophecies are only marginally accurate more than four to five days ahead of time.

Complex mathematical algorithms ground vast amounts of weather data in atmospheric science. NWS supercomputers named Tide and Gyre analyze more than 1.7 billion observations per day, "whizzing through 213 trillion calculations per second," (NOAA 2008, 2013), to yield scientific predictions. This is as close as we can come to knowing the future. However, it places us squarely in the interpretive realm of weather forecasting described by Bruno Latour in *Science in Action* (1987) and *We Have Never Been Modern* (1993); supported by Gary Alan Fine's *Authors of the Storm* (2007), a detailed ethnography about the "culture of prediction" in an NWS forecast office near Chicago; and succinctly distilled by anthropologist James Peacock (2001: 88) in the line "Fact, as well as theory, is interpretation." Ninety years ago British meteorologist Sir Napier Shaw (1926: 123), who applied sophisticated mathematical methods, noted rather harshly, "Every theory of the course of events in nature is necessarily based on some process of simplification of the phenomena and is to some extent therefore a fairy tale" (cited in Stewart 1947).

All predictions for weather on the day of the 2014 Super Bowl passed through human interpretations with barely a nod to the "science" of weather prediction.

Table 16.1 Candlemas, Groundhog Day, and Super Bowl Compared

Event	Candlemas	Groundhog Day	Super Bowl
Type	Sacred, religious	Secular, local → national	Secular, national
Important for	Roman Catholic and Anglican Churches	Community, nation	Nation (informal holiday)
Origin, basis	Christianity	U.S. community folklore adapted from European folklore	U.S. professional sports competition
Began	40 days after birth of Jesus, ca. 4 B.C.	February 2, 1887	January 15, 1967
Timing of ceremony	February 2, midwinter	February 2, midwinter	Variable, early February
Supernatural qualities	Virgin birth	Near-death hibernation and revival; annual elixir of life	Magical rituals by fans and players
Presentation of	Infant Jesus	Groundhog Punxsutawney Phil	Winner's team trophy and MVP trophy
Prophecy	Savior of mankind	Arrival of spring	Best pro football team
Prophets	Simeon, Anna	Mammal invested with prophetic powers: "Seer of Seers"	Sportswriters, bookies, statisticians, weather forecasters when outside
Prophetic time	Eternity	Annual	Annual
Dominant gender during ceremony	Mary the Mother must be purified; the prophet Simeon presents infant Jesus; Anna's role minor	All-male Inner Circle presents Phil	Male players and sports executives
Communicated by	Bible (Luke 2:22–40), disciples, liturgical calendar; religious art over centuries	Community, news media; television; The Weather Channel; popular movie Groundhog Day	National news media, television, social media
Role of weather	Weather peripheral; blessed candles protect against storms, thunder, and lightning	Weather central; presence or absence of shadow determines arrival of spring	Weather important in outdoor cold-weather location
Prophetic accuracy	100% accuracy for believers	100% accuracy for believers; weather experts say percentage is much lower	Game outcome unpredictable; in 2014, game-time weather equally unpredictable

Two weeks before the game, the *New York Times* reported that "the long-range fore-cast from John Gresiak, senior meteorologist at AccuWeather.com, called for 'partly cloudy skies with a 30 percent chance of a snow shower, with a high of 36 for the day, so the probable game-time temperature would be 32'" (Anderson 2014).

As late as January 25, one blogger using a Global Forecast System weather model speculated that a nor'easter would hit New York City during the Saturday and Sunday of the big weekend. This was soon shifted to an event coming on the Tuesday after Super Bowl Sunday, but the game-day temperature was predicted to be 23 degrees, with an inch of snow (Lion of the Blogosphere 2014). Eliot Abrams of AccuWeather more cautiously commented that predictions for the game-day temperature fluctuated between the teens and the 50s (Belson 2014b).

Ground truth (as a meteorologist might say) met prophecy on February 2. TWC managing editor and on-camera star Sam Champion said, "There's something romantic about being out there in the cold and the snow," but by game time his view was that something dramatic had happened. "It's almost like this beautiful oasis in the middle of all we've been seeing," he said. "It's almost like the seas are parting just in time for the game" (quoted in Baker 2014). The weather at game time in New Jersey turned out to be partly cloudy and 53 degrees, 10 to 15 degrees above normal and only 9 degrees below the record high of 62 set in 1973 (Associated Press 2014). On February 2, it was warmer in New Jersey than in Anchorage, Alaska, and in both Denver and Seattle, home cities for the teams.

CONCLUSION

Midwinter provides a pivotal moment for important events. The annual cycle turns—spring is close enough to think about, to hope for, to predict or prophesy, yet the vagaries of winter linger and threaten. The unusual coincidence, collision, collusion of Candlemas, Groundhog Day, and the Super Bowl in 2014 highlighted important prophetic moments for groups separated by time and rationale, with diverse origins, audiences, timing, and purposes, yet each grappling with an unknown future. We go to great lengths to know the future, but, despite our best efforts, it retains an elusive air of mystery.

QUESTION FOR DISCUSSION

Compared with people in many other parts of the world, Americans seem especially concerned with weather. Why do you think this is so?

REFERENCES

Anderson, Dave. 2014. "New York Area Weather Has a History with the Super Bowl." *New York Times*, January 25. www.nytimes.com/2014/01/26/sports/football/new-york-area-weather-has-a-history-with-the-super-bowl.html (accessed November 12, 2014).

Associated Press. 2014. "Super Bowl XLVIII Played in Abnormally Warm Weather." The Weather Channel, February 3. www.weather.com/sports-recreation/superbowl/news/photos-super-bowl-xlviii-played-abnormally-warm-weather-20140202 (accessed November 28, 2014).

Baker, Geoff. 2014. "Brrr. How Will Fans Weather First Cold-Weather Super Bowl?" *Seattle Times*, January 30/31. seattletimes.com/html/seahawks/2022797732_superweather31xml.html (accessed November 27, 2014).

Belson, Ken. 2014a. "Do Not Adjust Your Set: Super Bowl Snow May Be Real." *New York Times*, January 24. www.nytimes.com/2014/01/25/sports/football/wild-card-at-super-bowl-snow. html?action=click&contentCollection=Pro%20Football&module=RelatedCoverage&region= Marginalia&pgtype=article (accessed November 12, 2014).

———. 2014b. "Not Quite 75 and Sunny, but a Mild Day Dispels the Worries about the Weather." *New York Times*, February 2. www.nytimes.com/2014/02/03/sports/football/not-quite-75-and-sunny-but-a-mild-day-dispels-the-weather-worries.html?_r=0 (accessed November 12, 2014).

"Bruno Mars." n.d. Wikipedia. en.wikipedia.org/wiki/Bruno_Mars (accessed November 22, 2014).

Burke, Daniel. 2014. "For Some Fans, Super Bowl Has Supernatural Twists." CNN, Belief blog, January 31. religion.blogs.cnn.com/2014/01/31/for-some-fans-super-bowl-has-supernatural-twist (accessed November 22, 2014).

CatholicCulture.org. n.d. "Ordinary Time: February 2nd." www.catholicculture.org/culture/ liturgicalyear/calendar/day.cfm?date=2014-02-02 (accessed October 27, 2015).

Chase, Chris. 2014. "Seattle's Super Bowl Win Made Gambling History." *USA Today*, For the Win blog, February 4. ftw.usatoday.com/2014/02/seattle-seahawks-super-bowl-prop-bets-odds (accessed November 12, 2014).

Daniel, Matt. 2013. "Groundhog Day 2013: How Accurate Is Punxsutawney Phil?" EarthSky, February 2. earthsky.org/earth/groundhog-day-2013-how-accurate-is-punxsutawney-phil (accessed October 26, 2015).

Delors, Catherine. 2009. "La Chandeleur, Candlemas." Versailles and More, February 2. blog. catherinedelors.com/la-chandeleur-candlemas (accessed December 12, 2014).

Dunwoody, H. H. C. 1883. *Weather Proverbs*. Washington, DC: Government Printing Office.

Edwards, Phil. 2015. "Punxsutawney Phil: Incompetent—or Evil?" Vox, February 2. www.vox. com/2015/2/2/7963267/punxsutawney-phil-accuracy-evil (accessed February 4, 2015).

Elliott, Kennedy, and Shelly Tan. 2015. "30 Years of Groundhog Forecasts, Mapped." *Washington Post*, Wonkblog, January 31. www.washingtonpost.com/blogs/wonkblog/wp/2015/01/31/40-years-of-groundhog-forecasts-mapped (accessed February 14, 2015).

Fine, Gary Alan. 2007. *Authors of the Storm: Meteorologists and the Culture of Prediction*. Chicago: University of Chicago Press.

Fitzgerald, Waverly. 1991. "Celebrating Candlemas." School of the Seasons. www.schoolofthe-seasons.com/candlemas.html (accessed November 21, 2014).

Frazer, James. (1922) 1996. *The Golden Bough*. Abridged ed. New York: Penguin.

"Groundhog Day." n.d. Wikipedia. en.wikipedia.org/wiki/Groundhog_Day (accessed October 26, 2015).

Hillman, Michael, and Michele Clerici, eds. 2004. "February 2nd." *Hillman's Hyperlinked and Searchable Chambers' Book of Days*. www.thebookofdays.com/months/feb/2.htm (accessed December 12, 2014).

Latour, Bruno. 1987. *Science in Action*. Cambridge, MA: Harvard University Press.

———. 1993. *We Have Never Been Modern*. Cambridge, MA: Harvard University Press.

Lion of the Blogosphere. 2014. "Superbowl Nor'easter Update 1/24/2014 18Z." January 25/26. lionoftheblogosphere.wordpress.com/2014/01/24/superbowl-noreaster-update-1242014-utc (accessed November 20, 2014).

National Oceanic and Atmospheric Administration. 2008. "NOAA Names Kyger to Manage Nation's Climate and Weather Supercomputer." February 12. www.noaanews.noaa.gov/sto-ries2008/20080212_kyger.html (accessed May 15, 2014).

———. 2013. "NOAA's National Weather Service More than Doubles Computing Capacity." July 29. www.noaanews.noaa.gov/stories2013/2013029_supercomputers.html (accessed May 5, 2014).

———. n.d. "Groundhog Day." National Climatic Data Center. www.ncdc.noaa.gov/customer-support/education-resources/groundhog-day (accessed February 14, 2015).

Peacock, James. 2001. *The Anthropological Lens: Harsh Light, Soft Focus*. 2nd ed. New York: Oxford University Press.

"Presentation of Jesus at the Temple." n.d. Wikipedia. en.wikipedia.org/wiki/Presentation_of_Jesus_at_the_Temple (accessed November 12, 2014).

Punxsutawney Groundhog Club. n.d.a. "Groundhog Day: About Groundhog Day." www.groundhog.org/about/about-groundhog-day (accessed February 4, 2014).

Punxsutawney Groundhog Club. n.d.b. "Groundhog Day: Fun Facts." www.groundhog.org/about/fun-facts-faq (accessed February 4, 2014).

Punxsutawney Groundhog Club. n.d.c. "Groundhog Day: Inner Circle." www.groundhog.org/about/inner-circle (accessed February 4, 2014).

Rice, Doyle. 2014. "More Winter! Groundhog Punxsutawney Phil Sees Shadow." *USA Today*, February 2. www.usatoday.com/story/weather/2014/02/02/groundhog-day-punxsutawney-phil/5101379 (accessed February 4, 2014).

SB Nation. 2014. "Super Bowl Odds and Prop Bets 2014." www.sbnation.com/super-bowl-odds-prop-bets (accessed November 22, 2014).

Severgnini, Beppe. 2014. "How to Explain Americans." *New York Times*, June 14. www.nytimes.com/2014/06/12/opinion/severgnini-how-to-explain-americans.html?emc=eta1&_r=0 (accessed November 12, 2014).

Shaw, Napier. 1926. *Manual of Meteorology*, vol. 1. *Meteorology in History*. Cambridge: Cambridge University Press.

Silverman, Deborah Anders. 2000. *Polish-American Folklore*. Urbana: University of Illinois Press.

"Simeon." n.d. Wikipedia. en.wikipedia.org/wiki/Simeon_(Gospel_of_Luke) (accessed November 12, 2014).

Stanton, David. 2014. "Sermon Given at Matins on Candlemas." Westminster Abbey, February 2. www.westminster-abbey.org/worship/sermons/2014/february/sermon-given-at-matins-on-candlemas-2014 (accessed October 27, 2015).

Stewart, George R. 1947. *Storm*. New York: Modern Library.

Stormfax Weather Almanac. 2015. "Groundhog Day." www.stormfax.com/ghogday.htm (accessed February 15, 2015).

SuperBowlBets.com. 2015. "2015 Super Bowl bets." www.superbowlbets.com (accessed October 26, 2015).

"Super Bowl XLVIII." n.d. Wikipedia. en.wikipedia.org/wiki/Super_Bowl_XLVIII (accessed November 22, 2014).

"Super Bowl XLVIII Halftime Show." n.d. Wikipedia. en.wikipedia.org/wiki/Super_Bowl_XLVIII_halftime_show (accessed November 22, 2014).

"2014 Predictions for Super Bowl, MVP and More." 2014. *USA Today*, September 3. www.usatoday.com/story/sports/nfl/2014/09/03/preseason-predictions-super-bowl-xlix-mvp-awards/14973901 (accessed November 29, 2014).

Weatherbee, Caleb. 2013. "The 'Days of Shivery' Are Back! Read Our 2014 Forecast." *Farmers' Almanac*, August 25. farmersalmanac.com/weather/2013/08/25/2014-us-winter-forecast (accessed November 12, 2014).

Yoder, Don. 2003. *Groundhog Day*. Mechanicsburg, PA: Stackpole Books.

17

METAKINESIS: HOW GOD BECOMES INTIMATE IN CONTEMPORARY AMERICAN CHRISTIANITY

Tanya M. Luhrmann

Within the past fifty years, middle-class Americans have begun to worship their God(s) in a manner markedly different from before. Mainstream churches have seen their congregations dwindle; evangelical, New Age, and other more demanding faiths have seen their membership explode. And what the new congregants seem to want from these religiosities—and from evangelical Christianity in particular—is intense spiritual experience. We in the academy have focused on evangelical Christianity's claim that the Bible is literally true. That claim is undeniably important (Crapanzano 2001), but at least equally important is that today's religious practice puts intense spiritual experience—above all, trance—at the heart of the relationship with God. The most interesting anthropological phenomenon in American evangelical Christianity is precisely that it is not words alone that convert; instead, congregants—even in ordinary middle-class suburbs—learn to have out-of-the-ordinary experiences and to use them to develop a remarkably intimate, personal God. This God is not without majesty, but He has also become a pal.

How does God become real to people? A widely read book, Susan Harding's *The Book of Jerry Falwell* (2000), argues that in evangelical Christianity, what makes God come alive to people is the mastery of God's word. Harding's book seeks to understand the compelling power and appeal of Falwell's brand of evangelical fundamentalism. The book is specifically cast as an account of conversion, and from the beginning Harding presumes an identity between the culture and practice of Christianity on the one hand and its language on the other. Harding describes her book as an attempt "to show how Bible-based language persuades and produces effects" (xii). She dismisses the "considerable literature, both popular and academic, on how various ritual practices and psychological techniques trigger

Reprinted with permission, from Luhrmann, Tanya M. 2004. *American Anthropologist* 106 (3): 518–28. © American Anthropological Association. Republished in *Reflecting on America*, 2nd edition, edited by Clare L. Boulanger, 205–222 (© 2016 Taylor & Francis). All rights reserved.

experiences that result in conversion" (35). Those experiences may "pave the way for radical shifts in belief and commitment" (35), but they are not necessary. The appropriate question, Harding says, is this: "How does the supernatural order become real, known, experienced, and absolutely irrefutable?" (36). Her answer is that it can do so through language alone.

Among conservative Protestants and especially fundamentalists, Harding argues, it is the Word, the Gospel of Jesus Christ, that converts the unbeliever. The conditioning and techniques examined by many social scientists do not "cause" conversion to Christ; all they do, according to Harding, is "prepare a person's heart" (36) to accept the Gospel. Harding's first chapter's title and its concluding sentence state the basic argument: "Speaking is believing." "Generative belief, belief that indisputably transfigures you and your reality, belief that becomes you, comes only through speech" (60).

Yet the patterns of new American religious practices suggest that rituals and psychological techniques are not ancillary to contemporary spirituality but central to it. Congregants seem to want to experience the Gospel in intensely bodily ways that make the message of the Gospel come alive for them in a way it had not previously. Since the late 1960s evangelical and fundamentalist Christianity has exploded as a cultural phenomenon, as has the New Age in all its many forms (like modern witchcraft and modern Santeria). In 1996, 39 percent of Americans described themselves as "born again" or "evangelical" (Gallup and Lindsay 1999: 68). Even Judaism, whose traditional and Reform rabbis look askance at intense spirituality because it distracts the faithful from their religious obligations, has seen an increased interest in an immediate spiritual experience of divinity, from the growth of such institutions as the Kabbalah Centre in Los Angeles, teaching kabbalah as a practice accessible to all (a heretical idea in the past), to Chabad and Hasidic shuls promoting an experience-centered religiosity (e.g., Kamenetz 1997). There are many explanations for this shift and many anxieties about its political and social implications (see, e.g., Fogel 2000), but its behavioral implications are clear: these religions greatly value intense religious experience. They encourage participants to experience the divine vividly, immediately, and through unusual moments of altered consciousness (Wuthnow 1988).

Harding (2000) is certainly accurate when she reports that evangelical Christians often say that they are converted by the Word alone. But conversion is a complex process, and above all else a learning process. Converts do not make the transition from nonbeliever to believer simply by speaking—by acquiring new concepts and words. They must come to believe emotionally that those new concepts and words are true. And this, as Saba Mahmood (2001: 844) points out in an Islamic context, is a matter of "skills and aptitudes acquired through training, practice and apprenticeship." As many anthropologists have noted, those skills are often bodily and the training often emotional (Boddy 1989; Csordas 1994; Desjarlais 1992; Lambek 1981; Mitchell 1997; Whitehead 1987; see also the rich discussion in Rambo 1993). What is striking about American religion since the 1960s is that bodily phenomena are now often seen as the chief means of forging a relationship with a personal and personable God.

When we take an ethnographic look at what these converts actually learn in the process of becoming evangelical Christians, we see that their new cognitive/ linguistic knowledge is embedded within other kinds of learning that not only make that knowledge real but also make this God as gritty as earth and as soothing as a summer breeze. Converts do indeed acquire what Harding (2000: 19) calls a "shared elementary language" of faith (see also Keane 1997). There are words and phrases to describe their new life in Christ (their "lexicon"), themes that structure the logic of their new understanding (their "syntax"), and a common plotline that describes the way they decided to join this way of life (their "conversion narrative"). This knowledge is important; it is necessary for conversion. But it is not sufficient.

For converts to these intensely experiential American evangelical Christianities, God becomes a buddy, a confidant, the ideal boyfriend. It is not mere words that make Him so but rather learned techniques of identifying the presence of God through the body's responses—particularly in the absorbed state we call trance—and learned techniques that frame that responsiveness into the experience of intimate relationship. This is not to say that every convert has these intense experiences of absorption, but the religion models the practices that produce these experiences as central to the experience of God.

We can describe this process as *metakinesis*, a term used in dance criticism to depict the way emotional experience is carried within the body so that the dancer, using his or her own style, conveys the emotion to the observer (Martin 1983: 23–25). Today's new believers learn to identify bodily and emotional states as signs of God's presence in their lives, identifications that imply learning processes quite different from those entailed by linguistic and cognitive knowledge. Then the believers put these bodily experiences to use through new relational practices that are in turn another kind of learning process.

These three different kinds of learning—cognitive/linguistic, metakinetic, and relational—are psychologically distinct. Linguistic/cognitive knowledge tends to be the domain of cognitive science, emotional and altered states tend to be studied by developmentalists and those interested in psychopathology, and relationship practices tend to be studied by attachment theorists, often with a psychoanalytic bent. Together, they enable converts to do something quite remarkable: to construct, out of everyday psychological experience, the profound sense that they have a real relationship with a being that cannot be seen, heard, or touched. Through practice evangelicals can perceive a God who is in some fundamental sense more tangible than the God of our fathers. We have yet to come to terms with this enormous social fact.

THE ETHNOGRAPHY

Horizon Christian Fellowship in Southern California employs the no-frills, ordinary-folks approach characteristic of the "new paradigm" Christian churches (Miller 1997). Like other such churches, Horizon has a rock band on Sunday morning; the pastors have an informal, anti-intellectual style; many congregants meet in small Bible fellowships during the week; and the church's large worship meetings are held in a gym. Such churches call themselves "Bible-based," by which they mean that the written Bible is literally true and the only decisive authority. They are also entrepreneurial, well organized, and extremely effective. Horizon is an offshoot of perhaps the prototypical new paradigm church, Calvary Chapel, which began to grow in the mid-1960s by reaching out to the countercultural Jesus movement on Southern California beaches; it now has more than twenty-five thousand members and nearly a thousand "seeded" churches around the country. These days Horizon serves about five thousand mostly white congregants at its main church campus. It has seven associated churches in San Diego and claims eighty offshoots around the world. Horizon runs a preschool, an elementary school, a junior high, a high school, a school of evangelism with a master's program in divinity and pastoral studies, outreach evangelism in the United States and abroad, youth programs, summer camps, and constant concerts, "getaways" and social events. The specific and much-reiterated goal of this busy institution is to lead each worshipper to have a vividly personal relationship with Jesus (see also Ammerman 1987).

The great majority of Americans (96 percent) say that they believe in God—or, at least, in a power "higher than themselves"—when asked in a Gallup survey. The percentage has remained more or less constant for fifty years (Gallup and Lindsay 1999: 24–25). At the same time, those who have come to Horizon have usually developed a faith quite different from that in which they were raised (Miller 1997). Most congregants say that they believed "intellectually" in Christ in their childhoods and that as adults they discovered a "new" life in Christ. How does a congregant learn to turn an amorphous, often intellectual belief in God into the rich personal experience modeled in such religious sites?

Seen from another angle, this ethnographic puzzle is the central practical issue for a church like Horizon. The established Horizon congregation is acutely aware of newcomers; after all, the point of an evangelizing institution is to convert. Yet learning to be a true Christian is understood as a lifelong goal. As so many tracts say, faith is a journey in which the believer aims always to grow in the knowledge and love of God. While sermons talk of accepting Jesus as a one-time commitment (come, today, to the altar to be saved), they speak in the same breath of a long-term process of "dying to self" so that gradually and with difficulty one learns to put God's desires above one's own. Being "saved" is both a singular event that an individual celebrates like a birthday and an ongoing process.

As a result, there is no sharp distinction between newcomers and longtimers. At Horizon, newcomers learn about the faith in two institutional settings. The first of these is the service. There are as many as five services throughout the weekend, each often packing the gym. They are usually led by different pastors and are sometimes structured differently, but they all focus on an hour-long sermon based on a particular biblical text. The services have the anonymity of all large groups. During the week, however, congregants often attend more intimate fellowship gatherings in other congregants' homes, where they participate in the small-group worship Robert Wuthnow (1994) finds to be so characteristic of contemporary American religion. Despite variation among these gatherings, all home fellowship meetings involve personal testimony about Jesus and biblical teaching.

Print and audiovisual materials are also important vehicles for learning about the faith. Horizon's well-appointed church bookstore sells an impressive array of Christian goods. Many of its items are obviously intended as learning tools—more than a hundred guides to prayer and Bible study are available, with prominent displays for what are seen as basic manuals. The sermon, or message, delivered at each service is audio-recorded and sold at the store for a nominal fee so that congregants can listen to it again in their cars. The store also offers a wide selection of Christian novels, videos, and music. The music section has a chart that helps congregants identify what Christian music they will like based on their favorite kinds of mainstream music. The music for sale ranges from folk to disco, its difference from the mainstream only in its lyrics. The wider commercial success of these products is stunning.

From 1997 to 2000 I carried out fieldwork with a colleague, Richard Madsen, to try to understand how adults create personal relationships that feel to them authentic and mutually reciprocal with an intentional being who does not exhibit any of the normal signs of existence. In addition to Horizon we studied three other "new religion" sites, but in this chapter I will draw primarily on the Horizon research to describe the three kinds of learning that took place: cognitive/linguistic, metakinetic, and relational. The cognitive/linguistic learning actually contains its own analytic triad of learning forms—the lexical, the syntactic, and the specific conversion narrative.

Cognitive/Linguistic Knowledge

Lexicon

At Horizon, not all of the knowledge presented in the written materials is taken equally seriously by congregants, at least to judge by the content of their conversation. Few congregants spoke in their interviews about "the Rapture" and "the end times," concepts that are central to the best-selling Left Behind novel series (e.g., LaHaye and Jenkins 1995), volumes of which are planted front and center in the bookstore and which many congregants seemed to have read. But certain phrases did reverberate through the manuals, the church services, other books, and the transcripts of our interviews. As newcomers became full-fledged members of the community, these phrases became part of their speech patterns.

The most important phrase was "to walk with God." This phrase describes the daily experience of living one's life as an evangelical Christian. According to the manuals, "to *walk* with God" refers both to developing a relationship with God and to managing the everyday challenges to one's faith: temptation, frustration, disappointment. This, for example, is how one congregant used the term when she described her goal for a women's Bible study group started with students in Horizon's School of Evangelism, where she works: "It's really just interacting with them so that they can get to a different level of their walk with God" (all quotations from congregants are taken from a series of taped interviews conducted in May 2000). "To walk with God" describes the way God is incorporated into one's life; people accept that there are different degrees of that incorporation, more being better. "Walking with God" suggests a daily, folksy presence. As another congregant said, "To me, well, now that I am walking with the Lord I know that, like, I feel that God talks to me all day long. . . . I just think God's with me all the time."

Another common phrase in the lexicon is the "Word of God." This phrase refers overtly to the written Bible, but it connotes the relationship congregants believe God has with each individual Christian. One man said, "I went [to church] for several weeks in a row and I heard the Bible and it was addressing me and speaking to me personally. . . . I was realizing that it is a love story, and it's written to me." This is an amazing claim: that the written Bible, a text that is the same for all who read it (issues of translation aside), is at the same time written uniquely and with love for each of us individually. "The Bible says," he continued, "that the word of God is actually written on the tablets of your heart."

Syntax

By *syntax*, I mean an underlying logic that knits together different phrases; syntax organizes the narratives around meaningful phrases like "my walk with God." Syntax is like the grammar of this sort of religious commitment. The sermons at Horizon, along with the books and videos sold by the church, model the kind of people Christians are, what they struggle with and to what end. New congregants are not so much learning a specific, concrete story as they are learning ways to tell a range of stories.

Albert Lord (1960) famously distinguished "formula" and "theme" as building blocks for the great stories told by singers of tales, the Homeric bards among them. Such singers, he argued (with Milman Parry), did not memorize and precisely reproduce the thousands of lines of text found in the great epics. Instead, they composed anew each time in what Parry and Lord called the "oral-formulaic" tradition. They became familiar with large and small plots that could be elided or elaborated as the occasion demanded, and they learned to use common phrases associated with the tale. "Rosy-fingered dawn" is a formula, a phrase often evoked to describe the Iliadic morning; the tragedy of Achilles and the deception of the Trojan horse are themes. Similarly, Horizon congregants become familiar with formulaic phrases like "walking with God," and part of what it means to be a Christian is to apply those phrases in describing your daily life. Another part of being a good Christian is to learn the themes—the syntactic knowledge—that organize the way that life is understood and experienced.

Horizon's syntactic themes are well represented in its sermons, or messages. Here is one such sermon, captured in my notes from a service one morning in May 2000.

> Someone, somewhere, has to start a revolution. The people of this government, they've been to Harvard and Yale, they just passed a law saying that pornography can be shown on television at any time, because it's protected by the freedom of speech. But that's not what free speech is about; we all know that free speech is about having the freedom to criticize the government, not to allow rubbish on television. . . .
>
> Remember, that we are the children of God. You ladies [and here the room got very silent], you are the daughters of God. . . . Lift your head out of the gutter. You are noble. . . . [When] you realize this, and you say to God, I'm here in a place full of body odor and bodies, a fleshly material place, and can You please help me, He will help you. Even when you want to pray so badly and you can't really get it out, it's okay because there's a spirit inside of you helping it to come out. And if you are praying and being with Jesus, the devil won't distract you. He'll say, she's got the helmet of righteousness on. She can't be reached. And he'll move on. Because his time is short. Short. And your time is infinite. So don't numb your feeling, don't dull yourself with alcohol and drugs. Feel good. Reach out. Start living. Smell every flower. Live like that, live with God. Be alive. He loves you. (field notes, May 28, 2000)

In a sermon like this, the pastor is teaching a way of thinking about how to live in the world as a Christian: what it is to be a person (you need to be responsible;

you are noble, a child of a mighty Lord), what the world is like (full of rubbish, full of people who have been to Harvard and Yale but can't see what's morally obvious, a place of bodies and odors), who God is (He's responsible, He's pure, He loves you), and why a Christian person needs God (to keep you pure, to give you armor for protection from the devil, to help you be fully alive). Interwoven with these more general spiritual themes are some remarkably concrete politics. It is also worth noting that a good Christian might "want to pray so badly and ... can't really get it out." These Christians expect that prayer does not come easily and naturally. It is a skill that must be learned, as a relationship to God must also be learned. That is part of the logic of the faith.

Conversion Narrative

While congregants learn specific phrases to depict their new religiosity and thematic plots to describe God's human world, each also learns a specific personal narrative to depict his or her own entry into committed evangelical Christianity. This narrative form stands out from the other kinds of narratives, like the sermon above. It is both more personal and more stereotyped. This combination of the very personal and the stereotyped is hardly unique to evangelical Christians. Anthropologist Jon Christopher Crocker (1985: 206) describes the recruitment of Bororo shamans as exhibiting a similar combination of cultural expectations (everyone knows that the shaman-to-be must see a stump or anthill or stone move suddenly in the forest; catch a small wild game animal, such as a wild turkey; dream of attempted seduction; and so forth) and intensely personal experience: "Their details and sequences are standardized almost to the point of collective representations, known by most adult non-shamans. Yet the shamans I knew best spoke of them with vivid sincerity, adding variations and personal reactions at once idiosyncratic and consistent with the general pattern" (see also Crapanzano 2001: 102ff.).

In these accounts, congregants said that they knew God, or knew about God, in an abstract way as children, then they had a wild ride through drugs, sex, alcohol, and depravity; they hit bottom and realized that their lives were empty, unsatisfying, and unfulfilled. They accepted Christ (often as a result of coming to a Bible-believing church on a whim) and were filled with love, acceptance, and forgiveness. A male congregant, who worked in construction for Horizon, told us that he grew up in a house without religion, although he knew that "there was someone I was accountable to, and that was God." By the time he was thirteen, he had already experimented and realized that "it all amounted to emptiness." The sense of emptiness, he said, "really hit when I was thirty-eight." He had tried drugs, what he called "Buddhism," existentialism, one romance after another, but never, apparently, a Christian church. "Because of drugs, [I] lost everything. I lost my business, lost my place, lost my hope. Absolutely rock bottom." Homeless, he moved in with friends, and someone invited him to Horizon. When he went, he said, "I just knew it. Without a doubt." Eight of the ten people we interviewed gave us some version of this story of self-destruction, despair, and redemption.

Should we trust these stories? If accurate, they are an alarming glimpse into American (or at least Californian) life. It is possible that some congregants at Horizon learn, like Augustine, to stretch their little sins until they become an abyss of wickedness. It is also possible that a church like Horizon offers the structure to enable an addict to abandon his addiction, just as the fast-growing Pentecostal churches offer women a tool with which to detach their men from drink (e.g., Brusco 1995). In any event, the message of the narrative is clear: I was lost, so deeply lost, so lost that no one could love me—and then God did, and I was found.

METAKINESIS

In the religious context I use *metakinesis* to refer to mind–body states that are subjectively and idiosyncratically experienced even as they are known to the group as the way God's real presence in daily life is revealed. The process of learning to have these experiences cannot be neatly disentangled from the process of learning the words to describe them. A congregant must use language to describe, and thus to recognize, the moment of entering the state, yet congregants do not use the appropriate phrases the way they use phrases like "my walk with God." In identifying metakinetic states, congregants identify—and thus psychologically organize—bodily phenomena that seem new and distinctive to them, which they come to interpret in ways congruent with the group's understanding of God. They seem to be engaging a variety of bodily processes that are integrated in new ways and synthesized into a new sense of their bodies and the world. Some of these processes could be called dissociative in that they involve states in which attention is narrowed and manipulated to produce noticeable shifts in conscious awareness; individuals may feel that they are floating or not in control of their bodies. Others involve hallucination-like events in which people see or hear things that observers do not. In addition, specific and dramatic mood elevations lead to extended periods of time during which individuals are self-consciously and noticeably happier. As a result of these phenomena, congregants literally perceive the world differently and attribute that difference to the presence of God.

Horizon and the Calvary Chapel movement more generally do not place doctrinal or ritual emphasis on what Christians often call the "gifts of the Holy Spirit" (see Robbins 2004). No one speaks in tongues in public ritual, and spiritual authority is understood to rest in the Bible, not in private experience. Yet the singular point of the services, sermons, Bible study groups, and prayer manuals is that one should build a personal relationship to God through prayer. *Prayer* is a commonplace word, tinged with the mystery of the sacred but ordinary in a way that words like *meditation, visualization,* and *trance* are not. Still, the act of prayer demands that we focus our attention inward and resist distractions.

Most of us remember the prayer at services we attended as children. I would bow my head and my mind would wander to my dress's scratchy collar and what I would do that afternoon. In mainstream Christian and Jewish services, that is what prayer often is: a dutiful, closed-eyed silence while the leader intones, followed by a period of quiet during which it is all too easy to remember items you need to add to the shopping list. Horizon sets out to change those habits by modeling a relationship to God as the point of life—and, incidentally, of going to church—and modeling prayer as the practice on which that relationship is built. And with this emphasis, prayer becomes the conduit of anomalous psychological experience it was for the nineteenth-century reformers, the medieval ecstatics, and the early pastoralists who sought to be still and hear the voice of God.

The taught structure of this prayer is deceptively dull: prayer is about talking with God. But the taught practice asks the congregant to turn inward with great emotional attention. In the service, in the early period of worship before the pastor speaks, people start singing songs to God—songs *to* God, not *about* God. People shut their eyes, hold out their hands, and sway back and forth, singing of how much they love Him and yearn for Him. Some have tears on their cheeks. Then the music fades, and congregants remain standing, eyes shut, deeply absorbed in their thoughts. Sometimes the bandleader prays out loud, softly describing "how much we seek to glorify You in our hearts." Prayer, says a popular manual, is a yearning for God (Burnham 2002). That private, absorbed yearning is visible on the faces of those who pray.

There are perhaps a hundred prayer manuals and books about prayer at the Horizon bookstore. These books, the sermons, and home fellowships insistently and repeatedly assert that none of us prays as seriously as we can or should; all urge us to pray more intensely. Despite Horizon's literal interpretation of the Bible and overt hostility toward charismatic phenomena, in fact the practical theology invites congregants to assume that truth is found inwardly and not through external experts. God is to be found in personal experience, as He speaks to you directly in your prayers and through His text. Pastors hasten to say that anything He says to you in private must be confirmed through His Word, but in fact the Bible is learned not as a text to be memorized but as a personal document, written uniquely for each believer.

I see this emphasis on prayer as having two effects. First, it encourages people to attend to the stream of their own consciousness like eager fishermen, scanning for the bubbles and whorls that suggest a lurking catch. Perhaps, because memory is adaptive and perception obliging, people begin to note natural discontinuities and actually interpret them as discontinuous rather than smoothing them over with the presumption of a simple integrated self. Second, the emphasis on prayer demands that people engage in practices that help them go into trance.

Trance is an ominous-sounding word, but I mean something relatively straightforward by it: that one can become intensely absorbed in inner sensory stimuli and lose some peripheral awareness (Spiegel and Spiegel 1978). Trance is the consequence of shifting our awareness from the external to the inward. When we daydream, play, or read, we do this naturally to some extent, but trance at the religious level is often a learned ability. The degree of mental concentration Horizon encourages in its praying congregants responds to practice (Luhrmann 1989). There are no known bodily markers of a trance state, but as the absorption grows deeper, people become more difficult to distract, and their sense of time and agency begins to change. They live within their imaginations more, whether that be simple mindfulness or elaborate fantasy, and they feel that the experience happens to them, that they are bystanders to their own awareness, more themselves than ever before, or perhaps absent—but invariably different. In addition, trance practice appears to encourage the wide variety of anomalous phenomena (hallucinations, altered states, mystical awareness, and so forth) often called "spiritual" (Luhrmann 1989; Roche and McConkey 1990; Tellegen 1981; Tellegen and Atkinson 1974).

Whether because they pay new attention to their awareness or because these new practices alter their conscious experience, all the congregants interviewed spontaneously associated the process of "getting to know Jesus"—which one does through prayer and reading the Bible—with occasional experiences that involved heightened emotions and unusual sensory and perceptual phenomena, which they identified, labeled, and discussed.

One of the less dramatic of these metakinetic states was "falling in love with Jesus." People said that you could spot newly committed Christians because they got "this goopy look" on their faces when you asked them if they loved Jesus. They repeatedly spoke of Christ as their lover or their greatest love and described this love in physical terms. Even the men did so, although for them He was more buddy than boyfriend. When I asked John (a construction worker) whether the phrase "falling in love with Jesus" made sense to him, he said, "Absolutely . . . the closer you get the more of his love you feel and it is undeniable. You become flooded. You become absolutely radiant." Is that different from falling in love with a woman? "He will never disappoint me. He will never let me down. He'll tell me the absolute truth and He will never push me. He will never force me to do anything. He will always encourage. Granted, he's perfect."

"Falling in love with Jesus" is an emotional state, not the general way of being in the world as "walking with God" denotes. People spoke about this experience as if it were indeed the intense love of early adolescence, with the confidence that the beloved truly is perfect and that his perfection is a kind of miraculous confirmation of one's self. One was not necessarily in prayer when one felt it, but it emerged through the process of establishing a relationship through prayer. One woman compared her connection with God "to a relationship with the man of my dreams." Another spoke for an hour about her love of God and ended our interview by talking about people who might tell her that God is selfish to want her exclusive love. "And you know what? They're right. They are right. He wants to be loved." Falling in love with the Lord was a giggly, euphoric experience. Because of this, it could also be seen as merely the first step on the road to true Christianity. A pastor spoke scoffingly to us about people who had fallen in love with Christ but didn't realize that there were rules and responsibilities to being Christian. He went on to compare the experience of being a true Christian to being married: sure, you fell giddily in love and there was all the romance, but you had to get past that and do the dishes and pay for the car.

Then there was "peace"—the "peace of God that passeth understanding." Like "falling in love with Jesus," peace had a bodily quality and was treated as an emotional state or a mood. People often spoke of this peace as something God gave to them. They felt sad for those who did not feel it and often used the word in the context of turning responsibility for some decision they needed to make over to God. "Falling in love" was the first phase of a peaceful relationship with God, what one evangelical writer describes as the "first love" years (Curtis and Eldredge 1997: 30). A person "new in Christ" may experience "peace" immediately, but peace is also associated with mature Christian faith. Peace results from the engagement of the yearning, sometimes anguished spirit; the true prayer may begin in pain, but it ends in peace. Peace is the sense of being spiritually heard and emotionally satisfied, of being calmed through the act of relating to God. While the concept and its evocation are shared by all Christian traditions, at Horizon the word was likely to be used to evoke the shape of a feeling rather than a political goal. One man said, "I almost stopped [on his way down to the altar during an alter call] but I felt peace, so I went forward."

In addition to these emotional phenomena, nearly half of the congregants also reported a variety of what a psychologist would call unusual sensory events—phenomena of thought, not mood. These are not everyday events for these Christians. They are not, however, as rare as one might think even in the wider population. Many people (in the United States, roughly one in ten; see Bentall 2000) hear an apparently hallucinated external voice at least once in their lives, and for most of them this is not a symptom of illness. Horizon congregants do seem to experience hallucination-like events: individuals were very clear about the difference between hearing God's voice "inside" and "outside" their heads. One congregant, making that distinction, remarked, "There are rare times when I hear a definite voice, but ... it's hard to explain. Like just a small tiny push or something, like a thought in your mind." It is possible that the trancelike practice of prayer may evoke such sensory events—that would be in accord with what we know scientifically about the relationship between concentration practices and anomalous experience (e.g., Cardena, Lynn, and Krippner 2000; Luhrmann 1989). Whether prayer induces such phenomena or not, individuals do become differently aware of themselves through prayer. To some extent, we impose coherence on our conscious experience retrospectively (Gergen 1991; Kunzendorf and Wallace 2000). These congregants learn to identify and highlight these moments of discontinuity and come to understand them as signs of God's presence in their lives.

Sometimes the term *Holy Spirit* is used to indicate such moments, although that term is also used more broadly. But even moments too trivial to be glorified as the Holy Spirit are reported and associated with God nonetheless. A man who served as one of the many associate pastors called them "these quirky things that happen that there is no scriptural support for. Every person I talk to," he continued, "has some oddball supernatural experience that sounds crazy, unless you're a Christian." The story that prompted his comment was this:

I'm pretty much a new believer at this point and I'm driving and I hear the evangelist say on the tape, "Dennis, slow down. You are going too fast." It certainly wasn't something on the tape; it was something I heard. So, I slowed down and immediately a cop passed me and pulled over another guy who was also speeding, in front of me. I thought, God is really doing something here.

Congregants also reported tactile sensations, as this woman did when I asked her how she sensed God:

One time I was praying for this woman who had dated this guy who was into this Satan worship and she felt like there were demons in her. We were praying for her and stuff and I felt like there was a hand on my head. . . . And sometimes I just feel when I'm driving along, sometimes I can feel it on my body and sometimes it's just more inside. He is just such a comfort to me, and it's just so great.

Again, what a psychologist would call sensory hallucinations are not everyday events for these Christians, but they are clearly significant, common in many evangelical accounts of prayer and divine connection (e.g., Burnham 2002; Curtis and Eldredge 1997) and meaningful enough for nearly half of our interviewees to bring up in a comparatively short formal interview.

Other moments are more complex. Many congregants described answering the "altar call" as an emotionally overpowering experience accompanied by a conscious loss of bodily control. Congregants remembered that God took over their bodies (this can be described as submission to God's will) and carried or pushed them up to the altar. One said that "it was like someone had lifted me up out of my seat and I pretty much ran down there. I was walking real fast down there. It was like it wasn't me; it was kind of like he was pushing me up there. It was kind of cool. And I was just crying . . . I was weeping. I was crying so much. I was so happy." These memories recall moments that are both bodily and profoundly emotional, that stand out sharply from everyday experience and are identifiable by physical sensations. For those who experience them, these moments mark God's spiritual reality in their lives.

RELATIONAL PRACTICE

At Horizon, the goal of worship is to develop a relationship with God. Developing that relationship is explicitly presented as the process of getting to know a person who is distinct, external, and opaque, and whom you need to get to know in the ordinary way. "Acquaint thyself with God," says a classic evangelical guide. "God is a Person and He can be known in increasing degrees of intimate acquaintance" (Tozer 1961: 116). This is a striking characterization, the more so at Horizon because the intimacy is modeled so concretely. God is not only first principle, an awesome, distant judge, and a mighty force, nor is He only *spouse*, a formal term. He is also *boyfriend* (for women), *buddy* (for men), and *close friend* and *pal* (for both). Several congregants began their explanations of the process of developing a relationship with God by asking me whether I had a boyfriend. Congregants described God and Jesus as people you need to meet personally, as if you were out for coffee and had to figure out what the person across the table from you really meant. As one congregant said, "It's just like any relationship. If I had a best friend and we never hung out, where would our friendship be?" Another remarked: "The closer you get to a human being, the better you can get to know them. It's the same with Jesus, the more time I spend reading the Bible, the more time I spend praying, the closer I get to Him and the better I get to know Him."

As that congregant's comments suggest, the two practices thought to create that relationship are Bible reading and prayer. They are taught as two sides of a personal conversation: the worshipper speaks to God through prayer and receives His answer through His Word. But the printed text of the Bible is the same for all, of course. A congregant's relationship with God is supposed to be unique, private, and personal; he or she is meant to understand that this common text is a "love story . . . written to me," as the congregant put it. What seems to enable congregants to experience this personalization of a common text is their ability to identify their own bodily reactions as indicating God's responsiveness when they read the Bible and pray.

At Horizon reading the Bible is modeled as an interactive process, a way to know God better and to learn what He has to say specifically to you in this love letter that He has written. God is understood to be communicating when, as one congregant put it, "a verse just jumps out at me," or when one is overcome by a powerful bodily feeling—peace, or intense joy, or the sense of relaxation one might feel in the wake of a burden being lifted. Another congregant told this story:

> All of a sudden I was in the book of Isaiah. . . . I felt that the Spirit was leading me. . . . I started reading about what the chosen fast was, which was to break the bonds of wickedness. And something about it made me think about my family members and how I wanted to pray for my family members. Like that was the answer for me. I really felt that God brought me to that Scripture and that this is where I need to be. . . . It was just such an amazing thing. It was like two o'clock in the morning, and I remember reading it wide awake, and as soon as I read that it was a relief, and then I felt really sleepy. It was comforting. And so that's an example of how I think God speaks to me through the Word.

She knows that God "speaks" to her because she feels different when she reads a particular line of Scripture: that Scripture then becomes what He "says" specifically to her.

Metakinetic states—when God gives you peace, speaks to you outside your head, carries you down to the altar—give a kind of reality to God because they create the experience of social exchange between opaque individuals, between individuals who cannot read each other's minds and must exchange goods or words in order to become real to each other, in order to know each other's intentions. Adam, then a college undergraduate, told a story about how he did not understand what a pastor was talking about when he spoke of being filled with the Holy Spirit. Then Adam went on a trip to Acapulco with his friends and got high.

> And this night I was laying on the bed over to the side and all these guys were talking and stuff and I was quiet. I hadn't said a word in like over an hour because I was communing with Him again, and He was telling me all these things. . . . Usually when I'm high I'm kind of tingling and stuff, but this time I felt a wave going through me, through all my body. . . . I felt like I was floating. I was like, *dude*. . . . Overwhelmingly I knew that it was Him and He said, this is Me, filling you up. For the first time it was like I was being filled with the Holy Spirit and I knew what that meant because I was filled with it and I was floating.

He was, of course, high. But at that time, he was often high. He experienced this high as different, as identifiable through bodily sensations, and as proof of God's spiritual presence in his life.

Congregants seem to use more dramatic experiences as models for their experience of everyday interactions. Later in the conversation, Adam went on to describe the way he experienced prayer on a daily basis: "When we worship we sing songs and I just close my eyes and it's like I'm talking to Him again and communing with Him. *It's the same experience I had in . . . Acapulco*. It's like me and Him talking. He knows me, He knows my name, and we just talk back and forth. . . . It's so cool" (emphasis added). It was not, of course, the same experience: Adam felt the body wave only once. But he uses that dramatic initial experience as his mnemonic marker for his ongoing experience of his relationship with God.

Dramatic experiences like hallucinations do not, in fact, seem to be nearly as central to the process of building that ongoing relationship as the metakinetic states, like "peace" and emotional responses, that congregants come to interpret as God's participation in a daily personal dialogue with them. One learns to know God by having a relationship with Him through His text, and part of that involves just getting to know the kind of "person" He is. Texts and sermons constantly discuss particular biblical passages and ask how God is reacting. "How is God feeling at this point?" one book asks in describing the Eden story (Curtis and Eldredge 1997: 79). Congregants read biblical passages over and over, noting their thoughts about particular verses or what others have said about them. Bibles are accreted with the personal history of reading; the typical congregant's Bible is stuffed with notes and Post-its, its pages marked up in different colors; papers from past meetings stick out from the unbound sides. But a significant part of developing that relationship with God is learning to feel God actually interacting, and that demands that worshippers pay attention to their own bodily states as they read, as memories of previous readings wash over them, and as they think about the associations of particular verses for their lives. A guide for Bible study begins with this how-to advice: "This Bible study has been created to help you search the Scriptures and draw closer to God as you seek to understand, experience, and reflect His grace. . . . Before you begin each chapter, pray for attentiveness to how God is speaking to you through His Word and for sensitivity to His prompting" (Heald 1998: v).

Adam described his ongoing relationship with God:

> I wake up in the morning and I thank Him for nothing bad happening throughout the night because you never know what can happen. I thank him for letting me sleep well and I ask that he blesses my day, that it will go okay, and I'm not hurt, and whatever He wants me to learn that day I'll learn. When I talk to Him, He's always listening. He doesn't talk to me verbally like, "Adam, this is God." It's more like a feeling I get inside of me that I know He is listening. Or when I go to bed at night . . . I'll read some scripture. Like now I'm studying Acts. . . . I'll pray that he opens my heart so that I can kind of be transported back into that time so it makes sense to me. . . . By reading the Bible, that's His Word. That's where He talks to you.

Adam knows from "more of a feeling I get" that God is listening. He is used to that feeling. From his personal history, he has many memories of prayers where he spoke to God and felt familiar emotions that made him confident God was listening and answering. Through these Adam attains a comforting familiarity with who God is in the relationship and who he, Adam, is in that relationship. And Adam experiences that relationship as special and good.

This is a God who cares about your haircut, counsels you on dates, and sits at your side in church. One congregant talked about the fact that God speaks to her through His Word on the page, but He also interacts in a more personal manner, when He "puts a thought" into her mind. Then she talks to Him the way she talks to anyone—just more intimately. "Sometimes I feel a real closeness to Jesus. . . . I just talk to Jesus through the day." As another congregant said, "You start to know the fulfillment and comforting feeling that God gives you. Sometimes, sitting in church, I have this overwhelming feeling that God is speaking to me and sitting right there with me. . . . It's just so much peace." A congregant I'll call Alexis said that at first it was a great struggle for her to pray, but prayer eventually became easy. I could see from the way she prays that she has learned to interpret God's presence through her own bodily experience. She did not, she said, ask the Lord whether she should paint her toenails, but then she seemed to hesitate, as if she wondered whether she should. She experienced Him as a person deeply involved in her everyday life. That, she knew, was amazing. "It's a very humbling experience, because you're talking to the Creator, and you're an ant. . . . You know, He created the human race so that He could have fellowship and He could have a relationship with us. It's almost like—I wonder whether he's lonely, or was lonely. . . . It just kind of blows my mind."

Conclusion

Why now? What is it about American life today that has led people to search out psychologically anomalous experiences and to use them metakinetically to build their own relationships with God? Two tentative explanations present themselves.

The first is the rise of television and modern media. The literary scholar Mark Hansen (2000) points out that the radical technological innovations of our time have fundamentally altered the conditions of our perception. Technology, he argues, changes the very way we experience with our bodies. Television, the virtual reality of the internet, and the all-encompassing world of music we can create around us seem clearly to be techniques that enhance the experience of absorption, the experience of being caught up in fantasy and distracted from an outer world. We play music to create the shell in which we work or to soothe ourselves from a daily grind. We put on headphones on buses and subways specifically to create a different subjective reality from the frazzled one that sways around us. We park our children in front of videos in the hope that they will be transported into their own little universes so that we can cook or clean around them undisturbed. A classic book on trance says that "the trance experience is often best explained . . . as being very much like being absorbed in a good novel: one loses awareness of noises and distractions in the immediate environment and, when the novel is finished, requires a moment of reorientation to the surrounding world" (Spiegel and Spiegel 1978: 23). Today, television and movies, with their gripping images and mood-setting music, are likelier to provide this degree of absorption.

The second explanation is what one might call the attenuation of American relationships. This is a controversial issue, but a great deal of sociological data suggest that the American experience of relationship has become thinner and weaker. Robert Putnam's (2000) massive analysis of the decline of civic engagement in the United States argues powerfully that Americans have become increasingly disconnected from friends, family, and neighbors through both formal and informal structures. Union membership has declined since the 1950s. Membership in parent–teacher associations has plummeted. Fewer people vote in presidential elections (except in the South). And data collected since 1975 show that people have friends to dinner less often (and go out with friends no more often): "The practice of entertaining friends has not simply moved outside the house, but seems to be vanishing entirely" (Putnam 2000: 100). Time diary studies suggest that informal socializing has declined markedly. Between 1976 and 1997, the practice of taking family vacations (with children between eight and seventeen years old) nose-dived, as did "just sitting and talking" together as a family (Putnam 2000: 101). Even the "family dinner" is noticeably in decline.

Putnam uses these data to argue that social capital is on the wane in the United States. The data also suggest, however, that Americas might feel more lonely. They are certainly more isolated. More Americans live alone now than ever before: 25 percent compared to 8 percent in 1940, and none in our so-called ancestral environment (Wright 1995). It is possible that this increased isolation contributes to a putative increase in mood disorders (Wright 1995), as isolation is a leading risk factor for depression. Isolation certainly increases morbidity and mortality (Cacioppo and Hawkley 2003).

What may be happening is that Horizon congregants and others like them are using an ease with trancelike phenomena, supported by our strange new absorbing media, to build an intensely intimate relationship with God that protects them against the isolation of modern social life. After all, the most striking consequence of these new religious practices is the deeply felt conviction that God is always there on a personal level, always listening, always responsive. In the evangelical setting, congregants learn to use their own bodies to create a sense of the reality of someone external to them. That learning process is complex and subtle: it involves developing a cognitive model of the relationship, experiencing a metakinetic responsiveness that can be interpreted as the presence of another being, and participating repeatedly in instances of apparent dialogue. The experience of faith for these Christians is a process through which the loneliest of conscious creatures come to experience themselves as existing in a world awash with love. It is an astonishing achievement. In the end, the question Harding asked in 2000—How does the supernatural become real, known, experienced, and absolutely irrefutable?—is the most profound question we ask of faith.

Questions for Discussion

How is the experience of evangelical Christians, as described in this chapter, similar to other spiritual experiences, both within and outside Christianity, with which you are familiar? How is it different? In each instance, what encourages religious adherents to become totally committed to the reality of their beliefs?

References

Ammerman, Nancy. 1987. *Bible Believers*. New Brunswick, NJ: Rutgers University Press.
Bentall, Richard. 2000. "Hallucinatory Experiences." In Etzel Cardena, Steven Lynn, and Stanley Krippner, eds., *Varieties of Anomalous Experience*, 85–120. Washington, DC: American Psychological Association.
Boddy, Janet. 1989. *Wombs and Alien Spirits*. Madison: University of Wisconsin Press.
Brusco, Elizabeth. 1995. *The Reformation of Machismo: Evangelical Conversion and Gender in Colombia*. Austin: University of Texas Press.
Burnham, Sophy. 2002. *The Path of Prayer*. New York: Viking Compass.
Cacioppo, John, and Louise Hawkley. 2003. "Social Isolation and Health, with an Emphasis on Underlying Mechanisms." *Perspectives in Biology and Medicine* 46 (suppl. 3): 39–52.

Cardena, Etzel, Steven Lynn, and Stanley Krippner, eds. 2000. *Varieties of Anomalous Experience*. Washington, DC: American Psychological Association.

Crapanzano, Vincent. 2001. *Serving the Word*. New York: New Press.

Crocker, Jon Christopher. 1985. *Vital Souls: Bororo Cosmology, Natural Symbolism, and Shamanism*. Tucson: University of Arizona Press.

Csordas, Thomas J. 1994. *The Sacred Self: A Cultural Phenomenology of Charismatic Healing*. Berkeley: University of California Press.

Curtis, Brent, and John Eldredge. 1997. *The Sacred Romance: Drawing Closer to the Heart of God*. Nashville: Thomas Nelson.

Desjarlais, Robert R. 1992. *Body and Emotion: The Aesthetics of Illness and Healing in the Nepal Himalayas*. Philadelphia: University of Pennsylvania Press.

Fogel, Robert. 2000. *The Fourth Great Awakening and the Future of Egalitarianism*. Chicago: University of Chicago Press.

Gallup, George, Jr., and D. Michael Lindsay. 1999. *Surveying the Religious Landscape: Trends in U.S. Beliefs*. Harrisburg, PA: Morehouse.

Gergen, Kenneth J. 1991. *The Saturated Self: Dilemmas of Identity in Contemporary Life*. New York: Basic Books.

Hansen, Mark. 2000. *Embodying Technesis: Technology beyond Writing*. Ann Arbor: University of Michigan Press.

Harding, Susan Friend. 2000. *The Book of Jerry Falwell: Fundamentalist Language and Politics*. Princeton, NJ: Princeton University Press.

Heald, Cynthia. 1998. *Becoming a Woman of Grace*. Nashville: Thomas Nelson.

Kamenetz, Rodger. 1997. "Unorthodox Jews Rummage through the Orthodox Tradition." *New York Times Magazine*, December 7, 84–86.

Keane, Webb. 1997. "Religious Language." *Annual Reviews in Anthropology* 26: 47–71.

Kunzendorf, Robert G., and Benjamin Wallace, eds. 2000. *Individual Differences in Conscious Experience*. Philadelphia: John Benjamins.

Lambek, Michael. 1981. *Human Spirits: A Cultural Account of Trance in Mayotte*. Cambridge: University of Cambridge Press.

LaHaye, Tim, and Jerry Jenkins. 1995. *Left Behind: A Novel of the Earth's Last Days*. Wheaton, IL: Tyndale House.

Lord, Albert B. 1960. *The Singer of Tales*. Cambridge, MA: Harvard University Press.

Luhrmann, Tanya Marie. 1989. *Persuasions of the Witch's Craft: Ritual Magic in Contemporary England*. Cambridge, MA: Harvard University Press.

Mahmood, Saba. 2001. "Rehearsed Spontaneity and the Conventionality of Ritual: Disciplines of Salal." *American Ethnologist* 28 (4): 827–53.

Martin, John. 1983. "Dance as a Means of Communication." In Roger Copeland and Marshall Cohen, eds., *What Is Dance? Readings in Theory and Criticism*, 22–27. New York: Oxford University Press.

Miller, Donald E. 1997. *Reinventing American Protestantism: Christianity in the New Millennium*. Berkeley: University of California Press.

Mitchell, Jon P. 1997. "A Moment with Christ: The Importance of Feelings in the Analysis of Belief." *Journal of the Royal Anthropological Institute*, n.s., 3 (1): 79–94.

Putnam, Robert D. 2000. *Bowling Alone: The Collapse and Revival of American Community*. New York: Simon & Schuster.

Rambo, Lewis R. 1993. *Understanding Religious Conversion*. New Haven, CT: Yale University Press.

Robbins, Joel. 2004. "Globalization of Pentecostal and Charismatic Christianity." *Annual Review of Christianity* 33: 117–43.

Roche, Suzanne, and Kevin McConkey. 1990. "Absorption: Nature, Assessment and Correlates." *Journal of Personality and Social Psychology* 59: 91–101.

Spiegel, David, and Herbert Spiegel. 1978. *Trance and Treatment: Clinical Uses of Hypnosis*. New York: Basic Books.

Tellegen, Auke. 1981. "Practicing the Two Disciplines for Relation and Enlightenment: Comment on 'Role of the Feedback Signal in Electromyography Biofeedback—The Relevance of Attention.'" *Journal of Experimental Psychology: General* 100: 217–26.

Tellegen, Auke, and G. Atkinson. 1974. "Openness to Absorbing and Self-Altering Experiences ('absorption'): A Trait Related to Hypnotic Susceptibility." *Journal of Abnormal Psychology* 83: 268–77.

Tozer, A. W. 1961. *The Knowledge of the Holy: The Attributes of God, Their Meaning in the Christian Life*. New York: Harper & Row.

Whitehead, Harriet. 1987. *Renunciation and Reformulation: A Study of Conversion in an American Sect*. Ithaca, NY: Cornell University Press.

Wright, Robert. 1995. "The Evolution of Despair." *Time*, August 28, 50–57.

Wuthnow, Robert. 1988. *The Restructuring of American Religion: Society and Faith since World War II*. Princeton, NJ: Princeton University Press.

———. 1994. *Sharing the Journey: Support Groups and America's New Quest for Community*. New York: Free Press.

IDEOLOGY

18

LITTLE BOYS WRIT BIG: GENDER, ECONOMY, AND *THE BIG BANG THEORY*

Clare L. Boulanger

Ultimately, this will be an essay about the television program *The Big Bang Theory*, but not quite yet. In emulation of one of the show's lead characters, Sheldon Cooper, who seizes every opportunity to expound on the nature of the universe, I will open with an extended exposition that seems like a digression. If you bear with me, I hope you will see that it is not.

THE UTILITY OF NEOTENY IN BIOCULTURAL EVOLUTION

Neoteny is recurrent in human evolution. By *evolution*, I mean, as Darwin ([1859] 2006) did, "descent with modification," not the Lamarckian quest for perfection (see Packard 1901) that continues to dominate popular thought. Evolution is not any sort of a quest; it is merely what results when certain variants within species fail to thrive in particular environments. These variants are winnowed out, or at least whittled down, while other variants live to adulthood and reproduce, thus sending their genetic material into the next generation. There it may enjoy continued success, or it may be winnowed out in the next environmental shift.

Neoteny—that is, the retention of immature characteristics—seems to have figured in a number of the biological and cultural changes that have taken place among humans and their ancestors over time, though it has generally been a means to an end and not the end in itself. Human beings and fetal chimpanzees have traits in common; take, for example, open skull sutures. In the chimp the skull sutures knit before birth, but human skull sutures do not knit until well after birth so that the infant's huge head can squeeze through

Reflecting on America, 2nd edition, edited by Clare L. Boulanger, 225–235 © 2016 Taylor & Francis. All rights reserved.

the birth canal. Clearly, when our ancestors started to become human in terms of brain size, infants whose skull sutures remained open were likelier to survive (see Gould 1977, 1980).

Fetal and infant chimps have other traits we see in human beings but not in adult chimps, like thin body hair and flat facial profiles. I hasten to add that human beings are *not* infantile chimpanzees—millions of years have passed since the separation of the human and chimp ancestral lines—but if infants had the above characteristics in the ancient population that gave rise to both humans and chimps, then these characteristics would be raw material for further evolutionary developments.

Biological neoteny is not difficult to effect—it requires no radical genetic restructuring. It is "simply" (and doubtless the reader understands that nothing in genetics is actually simple) that at least some of the genetic actions that bring about maturity do not take place. In any population there is variation regarding the rate of maturity—some individuals mature quickly, others more slowly—so those that mature slowly may constitute the vanguard for a neotenous turn in a species's evolutionary path. This would seem to be the path down which humans traveled.

Neoteny is the centerpiece of most forms of domestication. This was strikingly demonstrated by a fox-taming experiment begun in the 1950s by the Russian geneticist Dmitry Belyaev (Trut 1999). The foxes selected to breed were those that retained, at least for a little while longer than others, the trusting disposition of infancy. Hence over the generations the foxes became more docile, but a startling suite of physiological changes accompanied this change in behavior. Traits generally seen only in young foxes—floppy ears, piebald coats, and tails that curled over the back—became commonplace in the experimental fox population. The researchers concluded that the genes whose action led to a properly vicious mature fox also triggered several other aspects of adulthood, and if a fox did not mature in its behavior, it would also not mature in its ear shape, coat color, and tail position. If all of this is sounding eerily familiar, think of your floppy-eared, spotted, curly-tailed dog presenting its vulnerable belly to you for scratching. It is just as you always suspected—your dog, for all of its life, is just an overgrown puppy.

But dogs are not immature in key ways. An adult dog is capable of mating and reproducing even if it has floppy ears and a juvenile temperament. In other words, neoteny may transform the appearance and/or the behavior of a species, but so long as such changes do not prevent organisms from breeding and rearing offspring successfully, the definition of maturity also changes. Dogs mature, but not like their forebears did.

Maturation is a biological process, but in humans it is also a cultural one. When our ancestors became cultural beings, they infused their life experience with meanings far more elaborate than mere survival required. The cultural definition of maturity was not just a matter of an individual reaching an age when he or she could reproduce; in fact, the process of becoming mature could include any number of milestones. Maturity, in terms of when it occurred and how it occurred, varied from society to society, and it also varied within societies, in the sense that maturity for boys was often defined differently from maturity for girls. This is a point to which I will return, but first I need to say something about the concept of economy.

All societies have economies—systems of production, distribution, and consumption of goods and services. The cultural meanings of production, distribution, and consumption are mutually involved with cultural definitions of maturity and gender. The ability to produce in sufficient quantities to sustain a household, whether production be assessed in slaughtered game, gathered vegetables, farm crops, or wages, is the measure of an adult, as opposed to a child, in many societies. Both men and women can take at least a quiet pride in their productive activities, but the value of production is boosted by the extent to which products are involved in distribution activities. It is distribution that stands out from the ethnographic record as a means not only of attaining adult status but also of enhancing that status at the expense of others. Men, more often than women, compete for status in this way, by, for instance, throwing lavish feasts in the manner of the New Guinean "big man" (e.g., Strathern 1975) or, in the United States, buying a round of drinks at a bar. In society after society, men are grandiose givers, converting material wealth into a growing circle of dependents.

In contrast, consumption is regularly seen, across the ethnographic record, as unmanly. Although everyone must consume, in many cultures this act is hidden or at least downplayed. The ultimate consumers are children, but women and those gay men who are thought to "receive" rather than "give" in the act of sex are frequently consigned to the same degraded gender category of Not Men (Kulick 1997). If a man fails at giving or, even worse, is repeatedly reduced to receiving, he is mocked as something less than a man. Further, other men are motivated to place him and/or keep him in this "lower" position so as to bolster their own masculinity.

The tripartite mission that David Gilmore (1990) identifies as a near-universal model for manhood proper is all about giving. The ideal man (1) protects his loved ones (that is, he is willing to give his life), (2) provisions his household (giving the food and necessities he produces or procures), and (3) fathers many children (giving even of his biological essence). The rites of passage meant to transform boys into men are often rigorous if not outright perilous, but this sort of ordeal is believed to be necessary in order to prepare men for the dangers they will have to face when they take up the tripartite mission in full. Despite these extreme demands on boys, it is recognized in many societies that rites of passage may not work; manhood in its ideal form is, as the Meskwaki (formerly known as Fox Indians) put it, "the Big Impossible" (Gearing 1970, cited in Gilmore 1990: 15). Even so, a boy who flinches during circumcision or runs away from a fight can be dogged by these experiences for the rest of his life, and in his now-questionable adulthood he may forever pursue, with a fervor fueled by a desperate attempt to prove himself, the benchmark of which he has fallen short.

Today's Americans may not see manhood in the picture painted above; they may also fail to understand what is so shameful about consumption. Consumption in our own economy is something to be flaunted, not kept behind closed doors. Children and women certainly consume, but so do men. If a man owns a flashy car, the biggest of big-screen TVs, the smartest of smartphones, and the latest in sports equipment, his masculinity, at least in American terms, is not in question; indeed, it is on display.

Consumption may have come to prominence in the United States because Americans have deployed their power and wealth to break up the production process and scatter its pieces all over the globe. An American man makes little if anything for himself, but this does not compromise his status as a man. His shirt may have been manufactured in Cambodia using cloth and buttons from China, but he hardly feels beholden to a poor seamstress halfway around the world on this account. She shares her meager amount of control over production with a host of similarly disempowered laborers; she has no power at all over distribution, since that process, as well, has been hacked into specialized tasks taken up by container packers, truckers, marketers, and so on; and our American consumer has purchased his clothing with money, a depersonalizing medium that he believes, with reason, releases him from the burden of social debt. Once he pays for his shirt, the contract between buyer and seller is closed, only to be reopened at the will of the consumer (if he has the money) and not that of the producer or distributor. Because production and distribution have been socially diminished in this way, Americans often entertain the magical notion that goods simply appear on store shelves. My American students have marveled at the fact that for foragers and horticulturalists, subsistence seems so hard-won when, as I've heard many times, "all we have to do is go to the supermarket."

Thus in recent times consumption has become the mainstay of the American economy, so much so that when President George W. Bush declared a "war on terror" in the wake of the 9/11 attacks, he assured consumers that they need not exercise fiscal discipline in response. On the contrary, this would be a war supported by continued shopping, as opposed to the belt-tightening that wartime conditions generally demand. Basing an economy on consumption is risky, however, in that a constant flow of new and alluring products must be generated. In American society, there is perhaps no one better placed to innovate in the area of cutting-edge product development than the young, reasonably affluent male, adept in the use of gadgets and possessed of more leisure time than many men around the world enjoy, insofar as he is able to defer the tripartite mission of masculinity. Modern captains of industry—Bill Gates (Microsoft), Steve Jobs (Apple), Sergey Brin and Larry Page (Google), and Mark Zuckerberg (Facebook)—began as whiz kids for whom work was a good deal more like play. The Eternal Boy, who can turn consumption back into production, is a vital player in today's economy (Boulanger 2005).

I suspect that among readers there are two objections brewing at this point. Of course American women can be and have been innovators, too. But the innovative girl-woman has not been enshrined in cultural icons—there is no Girl Genius to complement the Boy Genius, no sayings about women comparable to "Men are little boys writ big" or "The only difference between men and boys is the price of their toys." Immaturity in a woman may be thought by some to be sexually attractive, by others to enhance her powers of persuasion, but it is seldom viewed positively even if it produces a positive result, and it is certainly not seen as a source of inventiveness. Boyishness in men, on the other hand, is regarded with a sneaking admiration. Americans say "Boys will be boys" with exasperation but also with endearment. We do not generally say "Girls will be girls," but even if we were to do so, it would hardly have the same sense.

It is also the case that an American man is as capable as any other man in the world of taking up Gilmore's tripartite mission, although in the United States nowadays the ability to father numerous children is valued primarily in those impoverished socioeconomic spaces where men cannot manage to protect or provision kin. Men committed to Gilmore's mission used to be considered "good husband material" and likely still are by a number of potential partners. Compared to the Eternal Boy, however, "good husband material" might appear to be somewhat stodgy. The Eternal Boy generally does not lack for partners, either—prospective lovers may be attracted to his delight in play, his extraordinary creativity, his moments of childlike need for his mate. Taken together with the fact that in today's economy these very traits could land the Boy a decent job or even his own company, we can expect his kind will continue to be favored not only by economic but also by sexual selection.

That said, even the Eternal Boy, not to mention his mate, may be plagued by the uneasy feeling that in this historical moment, when maturity in men would seem to be undergoing yet another neotenous adjustment, we have not quite succeeded in consigning prior forms of masculinity to the past—culture, unlike biology, keeps a record of change many of us are capable of reading. The protector/provisioner/procreator remains with us in the iconic form of the Real Man, and the Eternal Boy may dream that someday he will *truly* mature along these lines. But the dream is a troubled one, because in the present day the Real Man is, paradoxically, becoming more and more unreal.

And now, at long last, we have arrived at the apartment door of Eternal Boys Sheldon Cooper and Leonard Hofstadter.

MEN AT PLAY: THE *BIG BANG* CAST OF CHARACTERS

Before we enter, however, I have to mention that most of what I recount below about the popular, long-running television series *The Big Bang Theory* pertains to the first six seasons. Television shows are works in progress, and plotlines that were unthinkable during the earliest years of a program's run are often explored as audience interest wanes in the tried and true. I will provide some updating in the conclusion of this article, but in the meantime, avid fans will have to bear with what they will recognize as outdated material.

Sheldon and Leonard—I should perhaps introduce them more formally as Drs. Cooper and Hofstadter—are the central characters of *The Big Bang Theory*. They share an apartment, and both are employed as researchers at the California Institute of Technology (Caltech). While Leonard's work is experiment based, Sheldon, as a theoretical physicist, truly lives the life of the mind, and he seizes every opportunity to lord this over his roommate. Both men, however, see themselves as having an intellectual edge over their friend and colleague Howard Wolowitz, who holds a mere master's degree in engineering. Of the three, however, only Howard produces anything of practical value, although his inventions are often, to say the least, unglamorous, and occasionally comically flawed—his malfunctioning waste-disposal system, designed for installation on the International Space Station, comes to mind. Nonetheless, Howard's long-term work on space-related instruments eventually wins him a stay on the station.

There is a fourth member of this core group of boy-men—Dr. Rajesh Koothrappali, an astrophysicist who also works at Caltech. This character bears the burden of representing multiple forms of diversity; that is, in addition to "child," Raj embodies other figures that are Not Men (again see Kulick 1997) in the American scheme of gender. He is not only an Indian national with a noticeable accent, but

immigration > feminizing

he is also the most feminine member of the group, the combination reminiscent of Linke's (1997) work on how immigration is often represented as a feminizing force. It is continually stressed, however, that Raj is not gay, despite his exceedingly close relationship with Howard, his extensive knowledge of women's fashion and "chick flicks," and his penchant, generally ascribed to his foreignness, for making offhand remarks that throw his sexuality into question.

As an aside here, I feel compelled to point out that no major character in the series is gay. There are also no African Americans or Latinos in the regular cast. Thus a straight white middle-class male fan of *The Big Bang Theory* can generally expect easy laughs, uncomplicated by what for him may be uneasy topics.

Sheldon, Leonard, Howard, and Raj are all boy-men, but they are childish in different ways. A viewer with a background in psychology might ascribe Sheldon's bizarre behavior to a high-functioning form of autism, but this possibility is never mentioned, likely because a frank presentation of disability might compromise the lighthearted atmosphere. We know only that Sheldon was "tested" when he was young and proved "not crazy," a diagnosis that is both comic and devoid of scientific authority. Sheldon is brilliant (though not infallible) when it comes to physics, but he has no "emotional intelligence" and needs his friends to inform him when, for instance, they are being sarcastic. For Sheldon, everything must be rule governed—he draws up a roommate agreement for Leonard and a relationship agreement for his girlfriend. Each night of the week is assigned its own meal (e.g., Pizza Night) and its own activity (e.g., Halo Night), and if these routines are disturbed, Sheldon becomes more so. Sheldon's insistence on absolute predictability contrasts with the chaos of his Texas childhood, during which his God-fearing mother would frequently fight with her drunken lout of a husband. Neither parent understood such a gifted, neurotic son, but Sheldon's mother knew her duty as a Christian woman and reared him as strictly, though also as lovingly, as his idiosyncrasies allowed.

In contrast to Sheldon's mother, Leonard's mother is cold and cruel. An eminent psychologist, she treated Leonard's birth and upbringing like an extended laboratory experiment, one that could not help but yield disappointing results. Leonard is thus the rejected child, constantly craving the parental approval he will never receive. It makes sense that Leonard and Sheldon are close, as Leonard is accustomed to poor treatment at the hands of people who have no empathy for others. It also makes sense that Leonard is attracted to women who dominate him. While Leonard is in many respects the most mature among his friends, he continually undercuts this status through unmanly self-doubt.

Howard, on the other hand, is brimming with self-confidence when we first meet him, though this is rooted in a vast capacity for self-delusion. Until he gets married—a development that doesn't take place until the fifth season— Howard lives with his mother, a passive-aggressive, perennially constipated avatar of Jewish matriarchy. In keeping with a long tradition of invisible characters on American television, Howard's mother is never actually seen, but she is heard, as she and her son snipe at each other constantly. Despite this endless shouting match, Howard is utterly dependent on his mother while he lives at her house, and she clearly babies him, making his favorite foods and even cutting his meat. Howard's mother always refers to his colleagues and even his lovers as his school playmates, and Howard has to remind her, testily, that he is a grown man despite the fact that everything about his living situation belies this. Before he begins to date his wife-to-be, Howard's involvements with women are largely of the fantasy kind, but he never gives up hope that a real woman might someday find him as charming as he considers himself to be.

During the show's early seasons, Raj is the only one of the four boy-men whose parents are still happily married, and he videochats with them regularly. Even so, Raj is a rebellious child, though he is rebelling not so much against his parents as against Mother India. Raj describes his homeland in the same terms an ethnocentric American might choose—dirty, smelly, overcrowded, awash in superstition. On those occasions when Indian food is the takeout of choice, Raj is unenthusiastic. Were Raj to return to India, he knows the pressure from his parents to marry and have children, exerted to some degree even across the ocean, would become unbearable. But it is adulthood he is avoiding, not attachment. Raj has engaged in a smattering of short-lived trysts, but he craves a steady female presence in his life. His quest is complicated, however, by the fact that when we first meet him he is selectively mute, unable to converse with young women unless he has been drinking alcohol.

Sheldon and his cohort may be boyish as men, but they were not boyish as actual boys, in that their intelligence set them apart from others. Sheldon, Leonard, and Howard all suffered childhoods of bullying at the hands of their peers, with the classic repertoire of physical insults—noogies, wedgies, swirlies, and the garden-variety beating—supplemented by verbal abuse. It is not disclosed whether Raj endured similar treatment in India, but his family was clearly concerned with his fondness for dressing up and playing make-believe long after a normal child might have abandoned such pastimes. As a teenager, Sheldon had no interest in romance, but the other three men entered a new phase of humiliation in adolescence as their attempts to find love were rebuffed. Despite their desire to mature in at least this respect, Leonard, Howard, and Raj were thus routinely returned to the status of Not Men by the actions of other men and even of women. Howard revisits this aspect of his teen years during his stay on the International Space Station, where his fellow astronauts belittle him and subject him to a number of pranks.

There is some revenge to be had, however, in that all four men make enough money to spend it lavishly on consumption. Their incomes are converted into toys of many types—video games, action figures, faux weaponry, character costumes. While the boy-men appreciate both science fiction and fantasy, they maintain a purist boundary between the two and become incensed when, for instance, *Star Trek* is confused with *Star Wars*. A significant portion of their spending goes toward building their reading, video, and toy collections involving comic-book superheroes. Most superheroes are not only male; they are the epitome of manhood, pursuing the "protect" mandate of the masculine tripartite mission to the exclusion of all else. In line with the idea that manhood, even in our own society, is "the Big Impossible," superheroes are the quintessential Real Men who embody the unattainable. Sheldon, tall but slight, Leonard and Howard, short of stature, and the effeminate Raj are further from the superhero ideal than most men. Their obsession with superheroes may stem from a need to compensate for what they so profoundly lack.

In 1978, Nancy Chodorow wrote that it is imperative for men to participate fully in the child-rearing process, because in the literal absence of a father, or in the "absence" that is created by emotional distance, a boy can only fantasize about what being a man is like, and his fantasies are abstract and outsized. But Chodorow recognized that a boy who has never truly known what it is to be a man can hardly model manhood for his son. Sheldon and his friends piece together an image of Real Manhood from the most preposterous tales of our age. They do not have to live up to this image—they are reasonably successful as boy-men, and any disadvantages that accrue from their immaturity can be surmounted through steady salaries and the growing cultural acceptance of a neotenous version of masculinity. Nonetheless, they evince a sort of wistfulness as classic manhood recedes further into the realm of fantasy.

BABES IN TOYLAND

Penny = just penny (no last name)

At first the only woman (aside from Howard's mother) who intrudes on this boy-man idyll is Penny. Coming off a relationship that has gone sour, Penny moves into the apartment across the hall from Sheldon and Leonard. Leonard is instantly smitten, though initially Penny does not consider him boyfriend material. She is pretty and vivacious, and while she has moved to L.A. to pursue a career in acting, she is working as a waitress at the Cheesecake Factory until her "big break" comes through. That "waitress" is only a way station on a proper career path is indicated by the fact that we have yet to learn Penny's surname. The surnames of the boy-men, all professionals despite their immaturity, are known to us from the earliest episodes of the program, but as of this writing Penny remains, simply, Penny.

In most societies—ours is no exception—the definition of maturity for women (often, tellingly, referred to as "girls") is less stringent than that for men. If manhood in our society is undergoing a neotenous adjustment, womanhood already includes a certain degree of neoteny that men are meant to counteract—the child-like helplessness of women, so many a fairy tale goes, is what inspires men to protect, provision, and procreate in line with the tripartite mission. Such myths impugn the competence of American women, many of whom, singly or in couples, sustain their households more than adequately, yet even these women may dream of a Prince Charming in moments of difficulty. Penny is a capable woman in a number of ways, but she has only a high school education, is profligate with what little she earns, and carried on with teenage-type promiscuity and alcohol abuse into her twenties. Leonard, with whom Penny develops an on-again, off-again relationship, would dearly love to be her Prince Charming, but she is resistant. In men, commitment-shyness is thought to be yet another indicator of immaturity, but there is more to Penny's reluctance to marry or even speak the words "I love you" to Leonard. Just as Penny does not want to settle for the Cheesecake Factory as her permanent place of employment, she is afraid to settle down with Leonard. In each instance, Penny is plagued by the nagging sense that she can do better.

Bernadette, destined to be Howard's wife, is also working at the Cheesecake Factory when Penny arranges for the future couple to meet. Unlike Penny, Bernadette is far more assured that her stint as a waitress will be only temporary, since she is simultaneously earning her PhD in microbiology. Hence we soon learn *her* surname—Rostenkowski—which is additionally significant in that it identifies her as the shiksa goddess who is, for Howard, forbidden fruit. However, Howard is accustomed to violating the rules of Judaism—for one thing, his diet is defiantly nonkosher—so Bernadette's Catholicism does not pose much of an obstacle to their relationship.

Bernadette is childlike in that she is very short and sounds like a cartoon mouse—in fact, her voice is noticeably higher now than it was when her character first appeared. She can, however, drop her voice into a far lower register when she is angry, making it clear that one reason her relationship with Howard has worked out so well is that she will become, over the course of her life with him, more and more like his mother.

The third woman who has insinuated herself into the world of the boy-men is Amy Farrah Fowler, whose surname we know immediately, not only because she is a professional woman with a PhD in neurobiology but also because she regularly introduces herself using her full name. At first Amy appears to be the female version of Sheldon—erudite and averse to all forms of physical intimacy—and the two agree to date only to please their respective mothers, who yearn for signs of normalcy from their children. Over time, however, Amy's libido is awakened, and she plots to transform a resistant Sheldon into the ideal mate.

While Amy's primary love object is heterosexual, she has powerful feelings toward Penny. Bernadette and Amy constitute Penny's entourage, and Penny has come to enjoy their adulation as her own social circle seemingly has narrowed. Like the boy-men, Bernadette and Amy were bullied as teens, and for them Penny is the popular girl whose friendship they could never have hoped to win in high school. Hence Amy's longing for Penny is not depicted as a bisexual struggle in which Amy is drawn to a man and a woman simultaneously, but rather as the girl-crush she was denied in her teen years. Just as Raj is not gay, Amy is not a lesbian. She is merely a woman whose sex drive is thwarted no matter where she directs it.

The three women form an unlikely cohort of their own, but it is not the mirror image of the men's cohort. Occasionally the women get caught up in the men's obsession with video games or superheroes; the women also indulge, every once in a while, their more stereotypically feminine desire to be princesses. This desire is much stronger on the part of Bernadette and Amy than of Penny, who has known something of the life of a princess, having once been elected to the Corn Queen's court in her small Nebraska hometown. These rare flights of fancy on the part of the women generally do not endure, however—they know to put their toys away at the end of the day. *Smart women = homosexual*

CONCLUSION

> America is neither dream nor reality. It is a hyperreality. It is a hyperreality because it is a utopia which has behaved from the very beginning as though it were already achieved. Everything here is real and pragmatic, and yet it is all the stuff of dreams, too. It may be that the truth of America can only be seen by a European, since he alone will discover here the perfect simulacrum.
>
> [EPI ATT] —Jean Baudrillard, *America*

As previously mentioned, neoteny, in biological terms, is a relatively straightforward evolutionary path to take, insofar as the genetic material for immaturity is already in place and all that needs to be done is to disable those genes or genetic processes that bring about adulthood. However, just because this path is available does not mean that a species will follow it. There should be some benefit associated with delaying or even reworking maturity that outweighs the obvious costs. An operational biological maturity—that is, one that leads to successful reproduction—is generally too valuable a stage of life to suffer alteration.

Maturity as culturally understood is no less valuable, for the same reason, but it is even more easily transformed in line with new circumstances. In the United States, neoteny has frequently been drawn upon to construct not only the American Man but also the country, which is regularly represented as youthful, especially in comparison to what former U.S. defense secretary Donald Rumsfeld once sneeringly referred to as "Old Europe." The Cowboy, that classic symbol of Manifest Destiny, has considerable license, in his youth, to shirk adult responsibilities. He is happiest riding off into the sunset, away from the encroaching urbanism for which his pioneering activities have cleared the way. But as Stephen Crane (1898) wrote in an iconic short story, eventually "the bride comes to Yellow Sky," bringing lace curtains and Sunday school and all the other trappings (multiple interpretations intended) of civilization, and the Cowboy realizes he must sheath his guns and submit to domestication even as he occasionally glances westward with nostalgic yearning.

Now that the West has been won, and an agrarian economy has given way to postindustrialism, the brawn of the Cowboy has likewise given way to the inventive brain of the Eternal Boy. Compared to the Cowboy, the Eternal Boy faces down far more fearsome enemies—ogres, dark lords, aliens—but all on a computer screen, and all as a rehearsal for real tests of strength he may never undergo. It would seem as though he experiences life through simulacra, save that these simulacra have *become* life, just as his Eternal Boyishness has become an acceptable version—indeed, an economically necessary version—of manhood in today's America.

Even so, for the sake of society beyond economy, the issues of reproduction and child rearing cannot be cast aside, unless technology someday spares us those "chores." *The Big Bang Theory*, almost despite itself, has been chronicling a slow march, with the boy-men gradually constructing a fully operational masculinity from the neotenous bits and pieces available. As I write, the show's eighth season has concluded with a cliffhanger episode whose implications have yet to be revealed, so I will not discuss them here. I can say that over the seventh and eighth seasons Sheldon's relationship with Amy deepened, and he has admitted that engaging in "coitus" (a word that is habitually mispronounced on the show) at some point is not beyond the pale. Leonard and Penny are finally engaged, although, significantly, Penny accepted Leonard's proposal when her self-esteem was at its lowest; it has recovered given her career shift into pharmaceutical sales, but her success at this job has added stress to the couple's relationship. Since the death of Howard's mother (a plot twist sadly necessitated by the death of the actor who provided the voice-over), Howard and Bernadette have become home owners; Raj, who can now talk to women, had a girlfriend throughout season eight. Despite these developments, manhood remains elusive in its definition and its actualization both on *The Big Bang Theory* and in real American life. The frontier is now a matter of what gender, adulthood, and economy will be in the future.

When the pre-Aztec Toltec empire collapsed, its existence was preserved by the Aztecs, who transformed its heroes into gods and its capital city, Tula, into the home of the fantastical feathered serpent Quetzalcoatl. This example—and there are many others across the ethnographic and historical records—shows us that what human beings destroy they may also convert to myth, often depicting how the Glorious Victim must be sacrificed so that society can "move forward." Comic-book superheroes, with their preternatural physiques, embody the manhood of the past distorted through the lens of modernity. As "action" figures, especially when they are given life (of a sort) on a movie screen, they may on occasion be inspiring to boy-men who are struggling to fashion adulthood in these times, but they are also plastic statues, immobilized and powerless in "mint-in-box" packaging, that Sheldon, Leonard, Howard, and Raj greedily, almost desperately, consume.

EXERCISE

Analyze another long-running American TV program for what it can tell us about gender (and/or race, class, and sexuality) in the United States.

REFERENCES

Baudrillard, Jean. 1988. *America*. Chris Turner, trans. London: Verso.

Boulanger, Clare L. 2005. "*American Pie*: Good to Eat, Good to Think?" *Anthro-at-Large: The Bulletin of the Federation of Small Anthropology Programs* 12 (1): 2–6.

Chodorow, Nancy. 1978. *The Reproduction of Mothering: Psychoanalysis and the Sociology of Gender*. Berkeley: University of California Press.

Crane, Stephen. 1898. "The Bride Comes to Yellow Sky." *McClure's Magazine*, February, 377–84.

Darwin, Charles. (1859) 2006. *On the Origin of Species by Means of Natural Selection*. Mineola, NY: Dover.

Gearing, Frederick O. 1970. *The Face of the Fox*. Chicago: Aldine.

Gilmore, David D. 1990. *Manhood in the Making: Cultural Concepts of Masculinity*. New Haven, CT: Yale University Press.

Gould, Stephen Jay. 1977. *Ever since Darwin: Reflections in Natural History*. New York: W. W. Norton.

———. 1980. *The Panda's Thumb: More Reflections in Natural History*. New York: W. W. Norton.

Kulick, Don. 1997. "The Gender of Brazilian Transgendered Prostitutes." *American Anthropologist* 99 (3): 574–85.

Linke, Uli. 1997. "Gendered Difference, Violent Imagination: Blood, Race, Nation, History." *American Anthropologist* 99 (2): 559–73.

Packard, Alpheus S. 1901. *Lamarck: The Founder of Evolution*. London: Longmans, Green.

Strathern, Andrew. 1975. *The Rope of Moka: Big-Men and Ceremonial Exchange in Mount Hagen, New Guinea*. Cambridge: Cambridge University Press.

Trut, Lyudmila N. 1999. "Early Canid Domestication: The Farm-Fox Experiment." *American Scientist* 87 (2): 160–69.

19

WARMAKING AS THE AMERICAN WAY OF LIFE

Catherine Lutz

Sometimes a people's problems are as visible as rivers discolored and foaming with pollutants or as homeless women and men living in lean-tos under highway bridges. Other troubles are more deeply hidden and so likely to persist without solutions or even names. So it is with America's permanent and massive mobilization for war. Long before 9/11, nearly every aspect of the American way of life began to depend on, entwine with, or suffer from a massive investment in arms and armies. The evolution from a nation that enshrined its suspicion of the militarist states of eighteenth-century Europe in its Constitution to a nation in which war readiness is a way of life was mainly a twentieth-century phenomenon, one that emerged most strongly during and following World War II. It has entailed corresponding disinvestment in other ways of life, unintended social and cultural consequences, and blowback from overseas.

How large has this investment been? Looking back in time and across the world today, no military has come close to rivaling the global scale of the U.S. military's reach and the lethality of its weapons. Not the Roman, not the British, not the Ottoman, not the Soviet, and not the Chinese militaries. As of 2013, the military budget of the United States was larger than those of the seven nations with the next-largest military budgets combined (Stockholm International Peace Research Institute [SIPRI] 2015).[1] The U.S. Department of Defense has millions of employees, thousands of bases established in every state and each corner of the globe, recruiters trawling for young people in every school and mall

Author's Note: I would like to thank Anna Christensen and Austin Miller for their invaluable assistance with the research for this chapter.

in America and its territories, and people writing reams each day on nuances of strategic thought, planning interventions for virtually every nation on Earth, and creating new weapons. For decades, U.S. civilian and military planners have dreamed of and executed a plan to establish an unconquerable empire of bases overseas and a national industrial and educational policy centered on the production of advanced weaponry.

Many Americans will immediately ask, what is wrong with that? Isn't the scale of our military made necessary by a dangerous world and made easily possible by our affluence? Isn't it a force for good both domestically and abroad? I argue that the evidence is that the massive and long-term mobilization for war in the United States has misshapen cultural values; increased various forms of inequality, most importantly those of race, class, gender, and sexuality; served as a massively antidemocratic force by accelerating the corporatization of government and legitimating secrecy and violation of the rule of law; and exported violence, toxins, and authoritarianism. Since 2001, for example, more than 350,000 people, most of them civilians, have died in the post-9/11 wars the United States has initiated (Costs of War Project 2015). Each year, PCBs and greenhouse gases from military and military-industrial operations have poured into the world's air and water supplies, and scientific talent has been massively detoured from the task of producing medical cures or teaching. And while affluence may be both cause and effect of the large U.S. military, many thinkers from across the political spectrum note that the decline of American power is ongoing and the result of overinvestment in military matters.

This chapter does three things: it describes the scale and uses of the U.S. military; outlines its broad social, economic, and political impact, especially within the United States; and then asks what beliefs and social processes contribute to Americans' inability to see the gargantuan U.S. military as a massive and enduring problem.

THE SCALE AND USES OF THE U.S. MILITARY

The United States has the largest budget for the production of violence of any government, anywhere, ever. The wealth involved is staggering, with national security spending in 2015 estimated to be more than $1 trillion (Center for Defense Information 2014). When the official Department of Defense budget is released each year, the figure is far smaller than that, but the true number is much larger because it includes separate congressional allocations for the wars in Iraq and Afghanistan, military spending buried in other areas of the federal budget such as the Department of Energy and Department of State, interest payments on the debt for past and current wars, and Department of Veterans Affairs spending.

Despite the size of this figure, it represents only a fraction of the actual drain of military spending on the nation, as Stiglitz and Bilmes (2008) demonstrated in their study of the eventual total costs of the Iraq War. They put the price tag for that war alone at $3 trillion. Their total is so much higher than the official budget figures because they include macroeconomic effects, such as the higher oil prices that the war prompted, and more local costs, such as lifetime disability payments to veterans wounded in the war, the economic costs of withdrawal of the civilian labor of the National Guard and Reserve, the costs in lost economic productivity of those who died (the notorious "value of statistical life," or VSL), and the health care costs for the tens of thousands of soldiers with such serious injuries as brain damage, blindness, burns, nerve damage, facial deformation, and mental breakdown.[2] The long Cold War was even pricier: the nuclear arsenal the United States built during those years is estimated to have cost $5.5 trillion, and the likely cost of cleaning up U.S. nuclear weapons facilities will come close to matching that of making the weapons in the first place (Schwartz 1998).

The U.S. military is far and away the country's largest employer, leaving Walmart, the Postal Service, and General Motors in the dust. It has more than 3 million workers, 2.5 million of them soldiers and 700,000 civilians. Approximately 1.4 million soldiers are permanent employees and the rest, in the Reserves and National Guard, are temp workers of a sort, called up only when needed. The Pentagon pays the wages of millions more Americans through weapons and other contracts, with the overall result that the military's direct and indirect employees constitute about 5 percent of the U.S. workforce. Other militaries have claimed larger percentages of their nations' workers; the relatively modest size of the U.S. direct military workforce has to do with the preference for more capital-intensive rather than labor-intensive advanced weaponry.

Since the early twentieth century, American military dollars have gone to hire industrial, scientific, and technical workers who design and produce weapons. The funding stream is so massive that fully one-quarter of the scientists and technicians in the United States now work on military contracts (Korb 1986–87: 41). To generate the needed workforce, the military has had an intimate and shaping relationship with U.S. universities, providing 41 percent of all federal funds for engineering research and 45 percent of all federally funded support to graduate students in computer science. From 1993 to 2015, fifteen universities, particularly the University of Alaska, received funds from the U.S. Air Force and U.S. Navy to work on the High-Frequency Active Auroral Research Program (HAARP), a project investigating how upper-atmosphere processes could be controlled in order to enhance the military's ability to control enemy communications and conduct surveillance. In 2013, Penn State received $187 million in Department of Defense research contracts (Wright 2014). As a result of their deep dependence on the Pentagon, the University of California system and other universities now actively lobby Congress for increases in military spending. While the assumption is that this research is "basic" rather than applied and devolves to the good of society as a whole, Pentagon spending on research is oriented toward the needs of warmaking rather than toward prioritizing knowledge needed to solve pressing social problems. Because the Department of Defense spends such a significant amount of money on research, it influences the direction of scholarly research more generally and directs young people who apprentice on professors' military contracts into military work.

Increasingly, the Department of Defense also subcontracts out work formerly done only by men and women in uniform. At least three dozen private military companies are currently working for the Pentagon. Between 1994 and 2002, the Pentagon entered into more than three thousand contracts with such firms, valued at over $300 billion (Singer 2003). The rise of these "private warriors" is both the outcome of privatization efforts during the 1990s that restructured the military along neoliberal lines and the result of lobbying by military corporations for ever-larger chunks of the budget. Employees of these companies, including KBR (formerly Kellogg Brown & Root), Vinnell, DynCorp, and Academi (once Blackwater USA), play roles that once belonged to people in uniform, taking on jobs such as base construction and logistics, the training of foreign soldiers, and the provision of security details for bases and officials (such as the forty DynCorp gunmen who once guarded the president of Afghanistan). The Defense Department counted 45,349 contract employees in Afghanistan in 2014 (Deputy Assistant Secretary of Defense 2014). These workers, some poorly compensated migrants from the global South, others better-paid U.S. citizens, bring great profit for the corporations that sell their services to the Pentagon. Massive contract fraud has been uncovered in this additional war-for-profit set of operations since the war in Iraq began (O'Brien 2006).

The U.S. arsenal consists of a baroque array of weapons and other technologies. At the pinnacle are six thousand active deployed nuclear warheads.[3] The arsenal includes highly sophisticated and expensive missiles of a bewildering variety, including AIM-120 AMRAAM missiles, which cost $386,000 apiece, and the newest fighter aircraft, the F-22 Raptor, which "possesses a sophisticated sensor suite allowing the pilot to track, identify, shoot and kill air-to-air threats before being detected" (U.S. Air Force 2015). Other especially controversial components of the arsenal are cluster bombs, which rain many small bomblets across an area as large as three football fields. They are "triple threats" in the sense that they can explode in the air, on impact, or when unexploded bomblets on the ground are disturbed, even years later. While the United States has appeared to be adhering to most provisions of the international ban on chemical and biological weapons, the Pentagon admitted using white phosphorus in Iraq and continues research on other such banned weapons and maintains the capacity to reintroduce them to the arsenal. The United States is also one of only a handful of countries that have refused to sign the Ottawa Treaty, the international agreement banning land mines and other weapons of mass destruction that have killed or maimed millions.

The elements of the U.S. arsenal are produced by some of the nation's largest and most profitable corporations, including Lockheed Martin, Boeing, Northrop Grumman, Honeywell International, and United Technologies. Their profit margins have consistently topped the list of American companies. With their research and development costs and infrastructure costs subsidized and other business risks socialized, they have had almost double the return on equity compared with other manufacturing corporations (Marullo 1994). Their products are expensive: the Hughes Missile Systems Company of Tucson, for example, makes the Tomahawk Cruise Missile, a 3,200-pound submarine-launched missile that can carry conventional or nuclear warheads. Hughes has produced 4,170 of these missiles, at a cost to the Department of Defense of $1.4 million each.

The Pentagon's investment in weapons research and promotion of the interests of weapons makers together make the United States the world's largest arms producer and dealer. In 2012, U.S. companies accounted for 58 percent of total arms sales and nearly a third of all international arms transfers (SIPRI 2014). Other countries can order U.S. weapons direct from the factory, or they can buy them on government credit. U.S. exports of major weapons increased by 23 percent between 2005 and 2009 and again between 2010 and 2014 (Wezeman and Wezeman 2015: 2). U.S. arms sales agreements from 1999 to 2006 totaled $124 billion, and the numbers increased radically after September 11, 2001, with arms sales to the top twenty-five recipient countries increasing fourfold in the five years after that date in comparison with the previous five.

It matters far too little to the sellers whether those who buy weapons ultimately use them on their own people or in eventual combat against the United States or U.S. interests. When the United Nations held a vote in 2006 on starting to negotiate a treaty regulating international conventional arms transfers, the United States was the only country that voted against it. Despite some domestic attempts to enforce codes of conduct for arms dealing, abuses are widespread. Turkey, for example, has received extensive military arms and other forms of aid from the United States that it has used to fight a long-term war against its own Kurdish minority. More than 30,000 have died in that war, and between 650,000 and 2 million Kurds were made refugees in the 1980s. Common as well is what is known as blowback, the most infamous recent example being Osama bin Laden himself, trained by the CIA in the proxy war the United States fought against the Soviet Union in Afghanistan (Scheuer 2004: 30).

The U.S. military also stands out in world historical context for its imperial structuring and reach—that is, the fact that it is the world's first and only truly global empire (while the British could claim to be so in the first half of the twentieth century, they did not have military presence in and surveillance of nearly as many places). There are currently 250,000 U.S. troops overseas, stationed at 686 official bases. They are housed in facilities worth nearly $140 billion and on the 493,000 acres the U.S. military owns or rents (U.S. Department of Defense 2014b). Many more secret or unacknowledged facilities should be added to this list. There the military stores extensive amounts of weaponry, including nuclear bombs and missiles, the presence of which in any particular country the U.S. government refuses to acknowledge (Lutz 2008).

The U.S. military also engages in extensive training of other militaries through the International Military Education and Training (IMET) and Foreign Military Financing programs. This puts American soldiers, sailors, airmen, and marines in an estimated 130 (out of the world's 192) countries. As is the case with arms deals, human rights concerns and the laws of warfare have often taken a backseat to strategic and opportunistic thinking. While claiming to professionalize other militaries, U.S. trainers sometimes teach assassination and torture techniques. Exposure of the official nature of these practices occurred in 1996 when School of the Americas torture manuals were released to the public (U.S. General Accounting Office 1996). Systematic patterns of training proxy militaries to "do the dirty work" are well documented, most recently in Colombia, where the United States supports security forces that have massacred civilians suspected of supporting guerrillas (Selsky 2001). The goal of the IMET program, as well, is to create in foreign militaries a sense of shared identity of interests with and obligation to the United States. Finally, the exposure of the American "extraordinary rendition" program, which has accelerated during the war on terror, shows how cooperation with other militaries has often been in service to outsourcing responsibility for human rights abuses committed in the name of the United States (Mayer 2005).

THE DOMESTIC SOCIAL IMPACT OF THE U.S. MILITARY: THE WAGES OF WAR

The more than $20 trillion of federal spending on military equipment, personnel, and operations over the period since 1945 has been the United States' largest public works and public employment effort since at least 1947, and as such, that spending has had profound effects. These include (1) increasing levels of class and race inequality, given how the Pentagon budget redistributes wealth around the country; (2) increasing gender inequality through the hypercitizenship that soldiering, long and still an overwhelmingly male occupation, culturally bestows and through the support it gives to a militarized, violent version of masculinity; (3) severe erosion in the quality of democratic processes; (4) massive environmental damage from military production and operations; and (5) cultural changes that include the rise of values such as ethnocentrism and belligerence.

How does spending on the military affect levels of race and class equality? To judge by the advertising and the numbers of people of color who join the military, the effect must be very positive: blacks made up 18 percent of the enlisted armed forces in 2012 but only 13 percent of civilians of comparable age (U.S. Department of Defense 2012: 74). The military advertises itself as an equal opportunity employer and has numerous antibias programs, at least since it was forced to desegregate in 1947 and particularly since it has had to rely on volunteers since 1973. Many poor and African American and Latino youth do achieve individual advancement through their choice of military work.

The overall statistics, however, are much more mixed and demonstrate how wrong it is to use individual stories to tell institutional ones. "Returns to service" is a commonly used economic measure of whether social mobility results from soldiering. These returns vary by historical cohort, military occupational specialty, gender, and other factors, with the experiences of World War II and Korean War–era veterans being generally positive. Veterans of the Vietnam War era and later, however, tend to earn less than demographically comparable nonveterans of all racial groups. Further, the earnings gap between young veterans and nonveterans is greater for whites than for African Americans—in other words, black youth do less poorly than white youth—but the unemployment rate for black and minority vets as a whole remains higher than that for white veterans (Barley 1994; Bryant and Wilhite 1990; Congressional Budget Office 1989; Crane and Wise 1987; U.S. Congress, Office of Technology Assessment 1992). Training in a select group of military jobs, including especially electronics and equipment repair, does bring positive returns to service. However, these are fields in which minorities have been underrepresented due to bias. In addition, civilian training programs in the same fields give people even higher rates of return in terms of their longer-term wages. These facts have had a hard time swimming against the widespread belief that military service provides discipline and life skills that improve an individual's employment prospects or will eventually bring higher wages.

Moreover, the impact of enlistment on college attendance of African Americans has been a subject of great controversy, with some college admissions officers arguing that the military diverts many young black men from college who would otherwise go. In fact, African American recruits have often and increasingly come from a wealthier segment of the black population than white recruits in relation to the white population. The strong presence of JROTC and recruiters in majority-black high schools, coupled with students' exposure to military advertising, has meant that the military often wins out in competition with colleges for black youth.

More important even than these effects of military recruitment are the effects of the military's procurement budget, which is much larger than that for personnel. Tax money that goes into weapons contracts is money that disproportionately benefits male middle- and upper-class whites who dominate the management of the corporations that get Pentagon contracts. These are also the people who are disproportionately the technical, engineering, and scientific workers dominant in today's high-tech weapons industries.

Nonetheless, a job in the peacetime military has been a much better choice than a job at Walmart for the short term. Many people with families choose military work in order to have health care for their children. In wartime the trade-offs change radically, however, and political opposition to the current war and the danger of grave bodily harm caused black enlistment rates to plummet from 24 percent of new recruits in 2000 to 14 percent in 2005 as the Iraq War began to take many casualties.

How does having a military of the sort operated by the United States affect gender equality? Women currently make up less than 15 percent of the U.S. armed forces, having been recruited primarily in response to a shortage of male recruits (U.S. Department of Defense 2013: 16). As a group, women receive negative returns to service—that is, they earn less after being in the military than do their nonveteran female peers (Markusen and Yudken 1992: 163–65). Moreover, in the thirty U.S. labor markets with a large military presence, women in the civilian sector are more likely to be unemployed and to earn less than comparable men.

Much harder to measure but even more devastating is the amount of sexual assault and harassment within an institution that still defines masculinity for many Americans. By the military's own estimate, 26,000 troops were victims of unwanted sexual contact in 2012 (Vanden Brook 2014). At the military academies, 48 percent of women and 10 percent of men indicated perceiving some form of sexual harassment in academic year 2013–14 (U.S. Department of Defense 2014a: 7). In addition, the prohibition of abortion in military hospitals can result in particularly difficult situations for deployed women. Even harder to assess but fundamentally important is the shaping of American masculinity by the notion that to be a man is to be ready to fight to defend a nation construed as a nation of women and children. One of the intangible returns to service that brings young men to the recruiting office is the promise that they will be seen and rewarded as "super-citizens" and "real men." The higher rate of domestic violence in military families compared with civilian families is one index of the problems engendered by the violent notion of masculinity associated with military work.

A third impact of maintaining a large military in the United States over the past seventy years has been the erosion of the democratic process. The military has provided the opportunity for the expansion of government secrecy and the notion of exemption from the law on the grounds of national security. The Pentagon classified budget, or "black budget," was $30 billion in 2007, up about 50 percent since 9/11, and the intelligence agencies receive billions more without oversight. The problem of militarization undermining democracy was visible to President Dwight D. Eisenhower in the late 1950s. In his last public speech as president, in January 1961, Eisenhower famously identified the new "conjunction of an immense military establishment and a large arms industry . . . [whose] total influence—economic, political, even spiritual—is felt in every city, every Statehouse, every office of the Federal government," entailing "potential for the disastrous rise of misplaced power." The cumulative result of the subsequent years of military and military-industrial influence has been that huge sections of the federal budget no longer conform to Article I of the U.S. Constitution, which requires that the uses of all Treasury moneys be publicly decided upon and publicly published and accounted for. Long gone as well is enforcement of the article's requirement that wars be declared by Congress, not the executive. It is also assumed that the president can order the use of nuclear weapons without Congress's approval, given the assumption that there would not be time for the president to consult with congressional leaders were the United States to come under nuclear attack.

At the local level, democracy has also suffered in the hundreds of military base communities where the governments negotiate on steeply uneven playing fields with base commanders over such things as the behavior of troops in civilian areas. The tax bases of these communities are also deeply impoverished, given the fact that the bases are federal property and so tax exempt, but the towns retain the financial burden of providing public services to both large base populations and civilian populations.

Fourth, the military has been a major unacknowledged contributor to environmental decline in the United States and globally through the processes of manufacturing weapons; the damage done during training, maneuvers, and operations; and the disposal of old and used weapons. Like civilian industry, military operations have environmental costs in water and air pollution and the heavy use of fossil fuels, which contributes to global warming and resource depletion. Unlike in the civilian sector, however, national security justifications, secrecy, and legal exemptions have allowed military-related toxins to flow freely into local water and air. Military operations have astounding rates of use of fossil fuels and so contribute even more than other government operations to global warming. The military consumes 2 to 5 percent of the total electricity used annually in the United States and more aluminum, copper, nickel, and platinum than many countries' total demand for these materials. Tens of thousands of military vehicles, in constant use, guzzle gasoline; a single F-16 fighter aircraft consumes 900 gallons of fuel per hour; a carrier battle group consumes 10,000 barrels of oil a day when under way, as numerous groups are each day around the world. In the 1980s, the U.S. military consumed an average of 37 million barrels of oil annually, enough to run all the urban mass transit systems across the United States for fourteen years. And it has released fully one-third of the global total of ozone-depleting CFC-113 into the atmosphere (the rest of the world's militaries are responsible for another third; see Singer and Keating 1999). Many of the thousands of current and former defense sites around the country have been declared unfit for other human use but continue to cause illness in those exposed to their effects in underground water supplies and air.[4] Environmental cleanup at the Hanford Site—which made plutonium until 1989—had cost taxpayers $30 billion as of 2009 (Oregon Department of Energy 2009: 1), with another $113 billion estimated by 2090 (Cary 2014).

Finally, the building of a large and imperial military has created fundamental cultural changes in the United States beyond those related to the social changes just mentioned. As Kathy Ferguson has noted, the military has been able to win monumental struggles over the meaning of "America" (Ferguson and Turnbull 1998). Making incursions into every facet of American life and identity, it has helped define true manhood and true womanhood and has suggested that certain values that are championed in the military—discipline, loyalty, courage, and respect for authority among them—are ultimately American values and superior to other kinds. Less explicitly, warmaking has promoted belligerence and ethnocentrism as quintessential American values. Ironically, the frequency of war and the nation's origin in wars of aggression against Native Americans have had a compensatory response in the development of the idea of the United States as a "peace-loving nation." As Tom Engelhardt notes in *The End of Victory Culture* (1995), Americans see themselves as simply and only responding to mortal threats rather than as pursuing interests through violence. The favored American war story is one in which the United States has fought only defensive wars, responding to attacks from duplicitous and racialized others. The unpopularity of the preemptive Iraq War hinged on its violation of that story, although the Bush administration initially attempted to claim that the United States was in imminent danger of attack by Iraq with weapons of mass destruction.

The scale and depth of cultural militarization of the United States is indexed by the simultaneous growth and blurring of the boundary between the "civilian" and the "soldier." While the all-volunteer force that replaced the draft in 1973 has meant that the military has increasingly been demographically and politically different from the rest of the U.S. population—more Republican, more working-class, and more often from a second- or third- generation military family—the appearance that there is a growing gap between civilian and military worlds is deceptive. On the one hand, this is true—fewer individuals and families in the United States have intimate experience with military life compared with thirty or sixty years ago. More important, however, the militarization of everyday life has grown significantly in this same period, meaning that civilians are much more likely to have positive views about the military, to have paid significant parts of their federal and even local taxes to support the military, and to consume media products and political discourse that could have or might as well have emerged from within the public-relations arms of military institutions. The idea of civilian control of the military, central to the democratic design of the nation, is made increasingly meaningless when, as C. Wright Mills (1956) observed at the beginning of the Cold War's militarizing momentum in the 1950s, a military definition of the situation reigns in all corners of society.

AMERICA'S MENTAL ARMOR: BELIEFS AND PRACTICES THAT SUPPORT MILITARIZATION

When historians look back in one hundred years at the United States of today, how will they judge the fact that warmaking by the most powerful military ever assembled was at the venerated core of this country? Will they see it, as I think they should, as an unforgivable violence foisted on the world and the nation itself? Will they categorize the United States of today with the militarizing Japan, Germany, and Soviet Union of the 1930s and 1940s or the Argentina and Guatemala of the 1970s and 1980s? One indication that they might lies in the evaluations of many of the world's people today, who tell interviewers that they distrust the United States, see its policies as having made the world less safe from terrorism, and increasingly see it as having a negative influence on the world.[5]

But such comparisons to other militarist states are seen as over the top at best in the contemporary United States. Why is that so? How can a nation's view of itself be so far from the facts as seen by most of the rest of the world, and how can the nation be so hostile toward confrontation with those facts? A number of conditions make this disjuncture possible, and their effect, at best, is to restrict public debate in the United States to a narrow range of options about when, where, and how to deploy the military and how to size it properly for the job. At worst, they silence discussion altogether.

The military and its vast size and noxious uses have been deeply and pervasively normalized. Cordoned off by secrecy and political belligerence, the military has been designed to operate outside many aspects of the law that govern everyday life and Teflon-coated by cultural veneration. While I will return to the first two factors later, the respect accorded the military needs first mention.

No institution in the United States is more revered than the military, and no institution's financial and moral support is thought more unquestionable in the halls of Congress, over the media airwaves, and at the backyard barbecue. We know this from polls that show even religious institutions garner less respect, and the other institutions of our common governance are in the basement of popular affections. This situation has made it simply impossible for Americans to criticize the military as an institution or to argue that less military might mean more security. Reverence for the military is a relatively recent phenomenon (officers of a certain rank have always merited high status, but the vast bulk of the institution and the uses to which it has been put have not), but it has now reached the point that the one tenet that unites Americans across the widest range of the political spectrum is the idea of "supporting," or endorsing the sacrifice and needs of, U.S. soldiers (or at least the enlistees—and therein lies a tale of class submerged, with popular films feeling free to poke at the puffy chests of generals and the occasional lower-ranked officer-sadist, but treating enlistees as victims, survivors, or heroes). The veneration is also seen in widespread mimicry, as when John Kerry began his acceptance speech at the Democratic National Convention in 2004 with a military salute and the announcement that he was "reporting for duty!" and when George Bush made his 2003 aircraft carrier appearance costumed in a military flight suit.

This is not to say that everyone is perfectly content with the military. Many Americans on the right complain that it does not get enough money, that it softens its standards for women recruits, that it allows itself to be drawn into the orbit of UN peacekeeping missions, and that its activities bleed into domestic uses. More left-leaning citizens argue that the military has been tasked with inappropriate jobs, such as the invasion of Iraq, that its budget needs "trimming," and that corruption sometimes erupts within its procurement process.

Behind these differences, there is seemingly thorough agreement that the United States needs a large military, that it should and can use that military to do good in the world, and that the one it has is selfless and honorable. In this consensus, soldiering expresses a love for the community greater than any other form of work and deserves commemoration at sporting events, school graduations, and multiple national holidays. In the terms of this consensus, the military is inevitable, even good, because war is part of human nature and violence has the power to get things done. These hegemonic cultural ideas matter deeply; they squash debate about the military and legitimate the system as it is.

How can this consensus have emerged when the core of the military's business is killing? (And if this bald statement grates, it may be because, as Elaine Scarry notes in *The Body in Pain* [1985], war's central bloody bodily fact is often conflated with war's ostensible purposes. It may also be because the Pentagon has been working to rename many of its coercive operations as humanitarian or nation-building efforts.) How can the consensus hold when profits and self-interest are central to when and where the military is deployed and how it spends its budget, and when the effects of military action are so broad and devastating for those on both ends of the rifle? To understand this consensus is to understand the legitimation of war and empire, and to begin to understand how warmaking has become the American way of life, as much as the malls and television shows and highways and families at play that are the nation's more visible face and self-image.

When I teach courses on war, I find my students deeply attached to a number of ideas about war and about the U.S. military that solidify the military's hold on the U.S. budget, foreign policy, and cultural terrain. These ideas represent widespread American beliefs that serve as key supports for people's faith in the naturalness and necessity of the military as it exists. These cultural ideas matter deeply, as they prop up the system and substitute for other, more helpful ways of thinking about violence and the state. A number of sociological factors also play into the normalization and veneration of the military, including the advertising used to raise a volunteer army and the cumulative effect of the nation's 25 million veterans, many well organized to act politically on questions of military budget and policy, but here I focus on the cultural narratives that have emerged in response to these and other factors.

They include, first, the notion that the military is an essential and necessary institution because war is deeply coded in human nature, biologically conceived, and therefore inevitable. Humans are territorial, greedy, and aggressive by nature, and war runs on such human instincts and motives. This is despite the fact that social science, including military science, has repeatedly demonstrated that this is not the case: by rough estimate, a mere fraction of 1 percent of humans throughout history have gone into battle, and when they do, they require extensive, extreme resocialization to kill.

Almost as central to American belief and certainly as ill conceived is the idea that violence is an economical and effective way to get things done—the belief that, as Cohn and Ruddick (2004) put it, violence "works." In comparison, other ways of creating social change take much more time, money, and patience, and they have uncertain outcomes. This belief in the efficacy of violence flies in the face of the evidence, too, and even of some U.S. military doctrine emphasizing the importance of restraint in the use of violence. We know that, particularly in the second half of the twentieth century, political will and collaborative nonviolent direct action have often achieved goals that violence has failed to achieve and that violence has often accomplished no more than to bring others into resentful and temporary compliance. Jonathan Schell (2003: 186) identifies the fall of the Soviet Union as "the most sweeping demonstration so far of the power of 'politics' without violence." He quotes Václav Havel's belief that by operating within the confines of a violent system, "individuals confirm the system, fulfill the system, make the system, *are* the system" (196). In addition to his discussion of Solidarity, Schell addresses the success of what he calls "nonviolence from the top down" (211), particularly Gorbachev's policies of perestroika and glasnost.

A caveat: The dominance of pragmatism in American worldviews has meant that winning has become the measure of many things. When the U.S. military is thought to be winning a fight, Americans support that war. When things stop working, the public calls on the military to withdraw. This is not exactly a moral vacuum, but it is a morality with a difference: if something works, the reasoning goes, it must be right. The nation's power, by definition, makes its people and their military and warmaking right.

Another of the tenets that supports the normalization of a gigantic military in the United States is the idea that war and soldiering have brought benefits to the nation and to individuals. Military service is thought to produce unity, discipline, and patriotism, and military research into new technologies of war is widely believed to have generated spin-offs both concrete, such as sophisticated computing and advances in emergency medicine, and economic, such as the prevention of recession and the creation of jobs. Wars, it is believed, are "good for the economy"—again, against the evidence. Military spending creates far fewer jobs than do equivalent amounts of spending for education or health care (Anderson 1982). And economists have demonstrated the long-term harm of war-generated deficit spending and the diversion of research and development into other domains; for example, Markusen and Yudken (1992) highlight the deterioration of the U.S. auto, steel, and consumer electronics industries as research and development resources were diverted to the military, as well as the decline in investment in public infrastructure such as sewers and mass transit (which fell 21 percent from 1965 to 1977 as military spending skyrocketed).

The role of imperialism in U.S. militarization has remained largely invisible because of the belief that the military's extensive activities overseas are not only defensive of the United States and its "national interests" but also altruistic—that is, the United States is said to "gift" other nations with military security, providing the world's police force, free of charge or self-interest. Americans commonly believe that the United States has military bases around the world in order to defend the countries they are in and ultimately to defend democracy—also against the evidence. U.S. bases and military aid were plentiful in the Philippines of Ferdinand Marcos and in South Korea under its several dictatorships and are newly proliferating in autocratic states in Central Asia and the Middle East. Moreover, rather than gifting, the United States has been able to extract significant financial, training, and strategic benefits from this basing. The Japanese, for example, will be paying $10 billion (and by one official estimate the eventual total will be more on the order of $26 billion) to relocate a U.S. Marine Corps base now on Okinawa to Guam.

Another thing that makes it so hard for Americans to see militarization and its effects is the hygienic distance they are able to keep from the bloody core of war. Unlike uncivilized nations, Americans continue to believe, their nation does not revel in violence and death; rather, the U.S. military kills reluctantly and surgically, avoiding civilian deaths. This would certainly appear to be the case when the nightly news and mainstream internet sites are so free of blood and splattered brain matter, with broken bodies displayed at a tasteful distance, if at all. There was public dismay when it became clear that many U.S. soldiers were collecting, displaying, and reveling in gruesome images of war, including horrors and tortures they themselves had produced. The home-front response was quickly managed, with the official message being that these were states of exception the soldiers were in, or that the actions were those of sick, outlier soldiers.

Finally, the normalization of American militarization has been accomplished through the science of public relations, which strategists recognize as the central fact, strategy, and technique of modern war. Military leaders are deeply committed to the idea that winning a war or winning the battle for funding war preparation requires tactical moves on political and home-front terrain. This means winning hearts and minds through advertising and PR spin of everything military, from what service members do each day to motives for joining to specific operations around the world. While most of the advertising, showing proud parents and self-assured, generous-spirited young people in uniform, is directed at convincing the American public to join the military or to support their children in doing so, it has the additional and very important effect of shaping how Americans who have never been in the military see it.

CONCLUSION

How will this—the American militarized way of life—all end, or will it end? Despite all the problems just identified and despite the lack of support for the war in Iraq, the militarized status quo seems to have a firm grip on national hearts and budgets. A small elite's agenda and offspring dominate Congress, an elite that benefits from a large, interventionist military, directly through the military-industrial complex and indirectly through the unequal global terms of trade that militarization has helped enforce. The United States also has large middle and working classes that believe they benefit from military spending, and some may even receive paychecks that seem to prove it. They may find the rule of the rich somewhat suspicious, but they have been unwilling to risk the level of comfort they have achieved, even if it is a house of cards built on indebtedness.

Like the empires of the past and their vast militaries, however, the U.S. empire and the military that supports it cannot go on forever. Overinvestment in military power has often been a symptom of empires whose other forms of power, economic and political, are already in decline. Moreover, military spending and intensified military interventionism only accelerate the descent as those military endeavors—arms sales perhaps to the side—entail underinvestment in other, more economically generative, activities.

Signs of trouble are on the horizon. The U.S. military is having trouble recruiting youth: when a *Wall Street Journal* columnist suggests offering citizenship to foreign mercenaries willing to fight in place of U.S. youth who will not go, it is clear that the business as usual of the past many decades may be nearing an end. Recently some of the strongest critiques of militarism have been coming from conservatives and libertarians; traditionally interested in limiting the state, they seem ready to make common cause with progressives on this issue. Widespread counterrecruitment sentiments and efforts, antiwar political candidates, and appeals to the "Golden Age" ideal of an America where freedom and democracy were much more robust are all cultural signs that there is hope for change. If these critiques were to expand to consider some of the above-explored mental armor that supports militarism, the system itself might contract more rapidly.

The primary pushes for change, however, are going to be transnational and systemic. The collapse of world support for the idea of a United States that dominates the world militarily and economically has already begun, as indicated by polls and the withdrawal of all but Britain and a handful of surrogate states from serious joint military action with the United States. More important, the financial architecture on which the U.S. military and state operate is shaky indeed, with unprecedented levels of personal and national debt and dollar hegemony under threat. Should oil no longer be traded in dollars, should China or other nations call in the massive amount of wealth they have in U.S. Treasury bonds, or should debt-ridden or unemployed U.S. taxpayers fail to pay the bills, there could simply be much less money with which to buy arms and soldiers. In such a context, ethical claims and convictions—secular and religious—against violence and imperial hubris might finally be heard.

Questions for Discussion

How do you think your own life has been shaped by war or preparation for war? How might your future be affected if the United States were to have a much smaller, less interventionist military?

Notes

1. These data are for 2014.
2. This estimate does not include the costs for a long list of other items, including health care for veterans absorbed by families or private insurance, the economic costs that come with oil price volatility, and the costs of tighter monetary policy as a result of the inflationary pressures that war produces.
3. According to the Federation of American Scientists (fas.org), along with these six thousand ready-to-launch weapons, the United States has another four thousand readily deployable warheads.
4. Examples include areas in and around naval bases in Groton, Connecticut; Vieques, Puerto Rico; and Otis Air Force Base on Cape Cod. For decades, the U.S. Navy dumped sulfuric acid, torpedo fuel, waste oil, and incinerator ash in Groton. On Vieques, used as a military bombing range, there are high rates of cancer in surrounding neighborhoods, and fishermen have brought suit against the navy for water pollution (Apuzzo 2005; Dorfman 2004).
5. The Pew Global Attitudes Project (www.pewglobal.org) conducted a seventeen-country survey in 2005, and in January 2006 the BBC World Service completed a poll of the public in thirty-five countries concerning the U.S. invasion of Iraq (World Public Opinion 2006).

References

Anderson, Marion. 1982. *The Price of the Pentagon.* Lansing, MI: Employment Research Associates.

Apuzzo, Matt. 2005. "Base Closings Leave Behind Large Swaths of Pollution." Associated Press, Environmental News Network, May 31. www.enn.com/top_stories/article/1666 (accessed October 27, 2015).

Barley, Stephen R. 1994. *Will Military Reductions Create Shortages of Trained Personnel and Harm the Career Prospects of American Youth?* EQW Working Paper WP26. Philadelphia: National Center on Education Quality of the Workforce.

Bryant, Richard, and Al Wilhite. 1990. "Military Experience and Training Effects on Civilian Wages." *Applied Economics* 22 (1): 69–81.

Cary, Annette. 2014. "New Hanford Cleanup Price Tag Is $113.6B." *Tri-City Herald*, February 19. www.tri-cityherald.com/news/local/hanford/article32167617.html (accessed October 27, 2015).

Center for Defense Information. 2014. "Total U.S. National Security Spending, 2014–2015." March 13. www.pogo.org/our-work/straus-military-reform-project/defense-budget/2014/total-us-national-security-spending.html (accessed October 27, 2015).

Cohn, Carol, and Sally Ruddick. 2004. "A Feminist Ethical Perspective on Weapons of Mass Destruction." In Sohail H. Hashmi and Steven P. Lee, eds., *Weapons of Mass Destruction: Religious and Secular Perspectives*, 405–35. Cambridge: Cambridge University Press.

Congressional Budget Office. 1989. *Social Representation in the United States Military*. Washington, DC: U.S. Congress.

Costs of War Project. 2015. "Human Costs of War: Direct War Death in Afghanistan, Iraq, and Pakistan, October 2001–April 2015." Watson Institute for International Studies, Brown University. watson.brown.edu/costsofwar (accessed October 28, 2015).

Crane, Jon R., and David A. Wise. 1987. "Military Service and Civilian Earning of Youths." In David A. Wise, ed., *Public Sector Payrolls*, 119–46. Chicago: University of Chicago Press.

Deputy Assistant Secretary of Defense. 2014. "Contractor Support of U.S. Operations in the USCENTCOM Area of Responsibility." October. www.acq.osd.mil/log/PS/reports/CENTCOM%20Census%20Reports/5A_October_2014_Final.pdf (accessed October 28, 2015).

Dorfman, Bridget. 2004. "Permission to Pollute: The United States Military, Environmental Damage, and Citizens' Constitutional Claims." *Journal of Constitutional Law* 6 (3): 613–14.

Engelhardt, Tom. 1995. *The End of Victory Culture: Cold War America and the Disillusioning of a Generation*. Amherst: University of Massachusetts Press.

Ferguson, Kathy E., and Phyllis Turnbull. 1998. *Oh, Say, Can You See: The Semiotics of the Military in Hawai'i*. Minneapolis: University of Minnesota Press.

Korb, Lawrence. 1986–87. "The Defense Budget." In Joseph Kruzel, ed., *American Defense Annual*. Lexington, MA: Lexington Books.

Lutz, Catherine. 2008. *The Bases of Empire: The Global Struggle against US Military Posts*. London: Pluto Press.

Markusen, Ann, and Joel Yudken. 1992. *Dismantling the Cold War Economy*. New York: Basic Books.

Marullo, Sam. 1994. *Ending the Cold War at Home: From Militarism to a More Peaceful World Order*. New York: Lexington Books.

Mayer, Jane. 2005. "Outsourcing Torture." *New Yorker*, February 14.

Mills, C. Wright. 1956. *The Power Elite*. New York: Oxford University Press.

O'Brien, Tim L. 2006. "All's Not Quiet on the Military Supply Front." *New York Times*, January 22.

Oregon Department of Energy. 2009. *Hanford Cleanup: The First 20 Years*. Salem: Oregon Department of Energy. www.oregon.gov/energy/NUCSAF/docs/HanfordFirst20years.pdf (accessed October 28, 2015).

Scarry, Elaine. 1985. *The Body in Pain: The Making and Unmaking of the World*. New York: Oxford University Press.

Schell, Jonathan. 2003. *The Unconquerable World: Power, Nonviolence, and the Will of the People*. New York: Metropolitan Books.

Scheuer, Michael. 2004. *Imperial Hubris: Why the West Is Losing the War on Terror*. Washington, DC: Potomac Books.

Schwartz, Stephen I., ed. 1998. *Atomic Audit: The Costs and Consequences of U.S. Nuclear Weapons since 1940*. Washington, DC: Brookings Institution Press.

Selsky, Andrew. 2001. "U.S. Green Berets Train Colombians." Associated Press, May 5.

Singer, J. David, and Jeffrey Keating. 1999. "Military Preparedness, Weapon Systems and the Biosphere: A Preliminary Impact Statement." *New Political Science* 21 (3): 325–43.

Singer, P. W. 2003. *Corporate Warriors: The Rise of the Privatized Military Industry*. Ithaca, NY: Cornell University Press.

Stiglitz, Joseph E., and Linda Bilmes. 2008. *The Three Trillion Dollar War: The True Cost of the Iraq Conflict*. New York: W. W. Norton.

Stockholm International Peace Research Institute. 2014. "Sales by Largest Arms Companies Fell Again in 2012 but Russian Firms' Sales Increased Sharply." Press release, January 31. www.sipri.org/media/pressreleases/2014/top100_january2014 (accessed October 27, 2015).

———. 2015. SIPRI Military Expenditure Database. April. www.sipri.org/research/armaments/milex/milex_database (accessed October 27, 2015).

U.S. Air Force. 2015. "Fact Sheets: F-22 Raptor." September 23. www.af.mil/AboutUs/FactSheets/Display/tabid/224/Article/104506/f-22-raptor.aspx (accessed October 27, 2015).

U.S. Congress, Office of Technology Assessment. 1992. *After the Cold War: Living with Lower Defense Spending*. OTA-ITE-524. Washington, DC: Government Printing Office.

U.S. Department of Defense. 2012. *2012 Demographics: Profile of the Military Community*. Washington, DC: Office of the Deputy Assistant Secretary of Defense. download.militaryonesource.mil/12038/MOS/Reports/2012-Demographics-Report.pdf (accessed October 27, 2015).

———. 2013. *2013 Demographics: Profile of the Military Community*. Washington, DC: Office of the Deputy Assistant Secretary of Defense. download.militaryonesource.mil/12038/MOS/Reports/2013-Demographics-Report.pdf (accessed October 27, 2015).

———. 2014a. *Annual Report on Sexual Harassment and Violence at the Military Service Academies: Academic Program Year 2013–2014*. Executive summary. Washington, DC: Department of Defense. sapr.mil/public/docs/reports/MSA/APY_13-14_MSA_Report_Executive_Summary.pdf (accessed October 27, 2015).

———. 2014b. *Base Structure Report—Fiscal Year 2014 Baseline: A Summary of the Real Property Inventory*. Washington, DC: Department of Defense. www.acq.osd.mil/ie/download/bsr/Base%20Structure%20Report%20FY14.pdf (accessed October 27, 2015).

U.S. General Accounting Office. 1996. *School of the Americas: U.S. Military Training for Latin American Countries*. Washington, DC: GAO.

Vanden Brook, Tom. 2014. "Sexual Assault in the Military by the Numbers." *USA Today*, May 2. www.usatoday.com/story/nation/2014/05/02/military-sexual-assault/8630871 (accessed October 28, 2015).

Wezeman, Pieter D., and Siemon T. Wezeman. 2015. "Trends in International Arms Transfers, 2014." SIPRI Fact Sheet, March 2015. books.sipri.org/files/FS/SIPRIFS1503.pdf (accessed October 28, 2015).

World Public Opinion. 2006. "World Public Says Iraq War Has Increased Global Terrorist Threat." February 28. www.worldpublicopinion.org/pipa/articles/international_security_bt/172.php?nid=&id=&pnt=172 (accessed November 10, 2015).

Wright, Austin. 2014. "Universities Chase Big Defense Dollars." American Defense International, August 13. www.americandefense.net/2014/08/13/universities-chase-big-defense-dollars (accessed October 28, 2015).

20

AMERICAN CULTURAL DENIAL: THE CATs' COMPASS

E. L. Cerroni-Long

And Keep Your Powder Dry, subtitled *An Anthropologist Looks at America*, is a book written by one of the most influential anthropologists of her times as part of an attempt "to develop a series of systematic understandings of the great contemporary cultures so that the special values of each may be orchestrated in a world built new" (Mead [1942] 1965: viii). That such an objective now sounds not only unrealistic but also quaintly obsolete clearly indicates how far American cultural anthropology has moved away from its foundational disciplinary commitment to the scientific study of culture. Also, any basic review of the social science literature on Americans (e.g., Wilkinson 1992) clearly reveals the striking scarcity of anthropological contributions. I believe that these two facts are connected, in the sense that the disciplinary path taken by American anthropologists since the mid-1970s has been at least partially defined by their inability—or unwillingness—to apply the theoretical and research approaches of their discipline to "complex" societies, and especially to their own. I also believe that this phenomenon has been at least partially catalyzed by cultural reasons, to the extent that denying the existence of American culture is a very culture-specific American tendency.

THE CULTURAL CONTEXT OF AMERICAN ANTHROPOLOGY

Franz Boas is considered the father of modern cultural anthropology precisely because he zeroed in on the species-specific adaptive aspect of culture and saw cultures, in the plural, as the product of this process. This was a breakthrough conceptual development because it provided a more useful lens than the one offered by the concept of society for studying and understanding human behavior. The Boasian concept of culture called attention to the interaction between a population and its environment on the one hand and its history on the other, and it emphasized how all aspects of behavior both emerge from and affect the adaptive social processes underlying such interactions. Boas was a German Jew who immigrated to the United States, and while he was very successful in establishing cultural anthropology as an academic discipline in this country, he also saw many of his students and disciples moving steadily away from his own theoretical position and embracing, instead, psychological models of culture.

This, in my view, was a consequence of the Americanization of cultural anthropology, and it was triggered by the profound interest Americans have in the "mental premises" of human behavior. Psychology is such an extraordinarily successful and influential discipline in the United States because it encompasses the modern version of the theological preoccupations that characterized the religious dissidents who so crucially contributed to the ideological foundations of American culture. The great attention Americans give to exploring the boundaries of the self and the constant tension perceived to exist between the individual and the community, the need for affiliation and autonomy, and the corrupting drives of the body and the redeeming influence of morality all emerged from an intellectual tradition that made the data collected by cultural anthropologists the "mirror for humanity" through which such preoccupations could be more effectively expressed and social amelioration attempted.

And then, in the last quarter of the twentieth century, postmodernism could easily be grafted onto such an ideological tradition. While postmodernism—as the epistemological translation of the zeitgeist catalyzed by consumer capitalism (Jameson 1991)—has affected the entire Western (and Westernized) intellectual world, its impact on anthropology has been particularly acute in the United States (Cerroni-Long 1999). My contention is that postmodernist notions fit certain characteristics of American culture particularly well, and this is what has made them particularly influential.

Postmodernism's emphasis on narcissistic self-reference and interpretive autonomy, its implicit denial of structural constraints (even the constraint of facts versus the freedom of fiction), and its alluring play on the potential for personal self-invention and reinvention were bound to resonate very strongly with American competitive individualism. In the postmodern world, as the British prime minister Margaret Thatcher famously stated, "societies do not exist, only individuals do." Translated into disciplinary terms, this means that culture, as a behavioral framework, is denied, and the *jouissance* of individual choice is celebrated and documented. Thus, a 2003 print advertisement for the Center for the Ethnography of Everyday Life at the University of Michigan was headed by a banner proclaiming: "Everyday? Yes. Ordinary? No." It continued by declaring: "Before the abstractions of social science, there are people's stories, the emotional worlds of disappointment and uncertainty, and the brave coping of everyday life" (*Anthropology News*, October 2003, 59). One can almost hear the crescendo of Hollywood music introducing a movie on "the American Dream"!

This is as should be expected. Academic practices are as affected by culture as any other form of human expression, and that is why there are national, culture-specific schools of anthropology (see Barth et al. 2005). Indeed, it would be foolish to expect that because anthropology focuses on the study of culture, it is somehow exempt from the influence of culture. But because of their training, anthropologists should be particularly sensitive to the cultural embeddedness of their theory-building and research approaches. Cultural reflexivity and cross-cultural analysis should be the tools brought to bear on the cultural specificity of their perspectives. As Mary Douglas (1995: 93) points out, "The pressing agenda for anthropologists [is] not how to escape from our own cultural bias, but how to generate theoretical questions from a systematic comparison of different cultural biases." There seem to be two prerequisites for this. First, we have to model culture in a way that permits us to truly operationalize ethnographic research. Second, we have to engage in cross-cultural, comparative analyses in a more effective and dedicated way than has been done in the last fifty years.

Unfortunately, the application of the comparative method in anthropology still suffers from association with social evolutionism. Indeed, in a chapter titled "The Comparative Method and Its Application," Robert Carneiro (2003: 250–61) highlights such correlation and argues that the method came under specific attack by Boas and the Boasians. Certainly, wariness about the pitfalls of social evolutionism has contributed to marginalizing comparativism in anthropology and has obscured the fact that such a method can be used very effectively (as, for example, it continues to be used in area studies) outside the evolutionist paradigm.

Methodological resistance to comparativism and current theoretical contestation of the culture concept both have led to little ethnology being done in the American context over the last twenty years. As one of the grand old men of anthropology has noted: "To compare and contrast cultures, the task of ethnology, we must have dependable pictures of other cultures" (Werner 2003: 7). Such comparable units of analysis have become increasingly unavailable as ethnographic research has abandoned its holocultural focus, and even fragmentary analyses of American culture remain especially scarce. What anthropologists have typically contributed, instead, are either social assessment studies (e.g., Baker 2003; Forman 1994; Naylor 1998; Spindler and Spindler 1990; Tannen 1998) or ethnographic thumbnail sketches (e.g., Moffatt 1989; Perin 1988). On the other hand, ethnographic-type research and writing are now used by sociologists, psychologists, other assorted social scientists, and even journalists and travel writers. Consequently, some valuable recent attempts at anthropological analyses of American culture (e.g., Carroll 1988; Hall and Hall 1990) have been given very little attention, dismissed as "trivially anecdotal" and theoretically irrelevant (Greer 1989).

This is unfortunate, because a holistic understanding of American culture could also provide a useful framework for analyzing ethnicity and, especially, the thorny issue of continuing interracial conflict in American life. I discovered this backward, having come to the United States to study ethnicity and realizing that both ethnic and subcultural groups can be studied only with reference to the characteristics of the culture in which they emerge. Thus, a robust theory of culture can also provide a unique handle on how to distinguish a culture from an ethnic group, and each of them from a subculture.

BEHAVIOR IS THE KEY

I was first exposed to ethnicity in Hawaii. By that time I had spent almost a decade studying the culture of Japan, a country that happens to be just as ethnically homogeneous as my native Italy, where I was raised and trained as an Asian studies scholar. What particularly struck me in Hawaii was the behavior of the Japanese Americans, which seemed to differ in consistent and interesting ways from that of both mainstream Americans and the Japanese. This discovery triggered my interest in becoming an anthropologist as well as my formulation of a theory of culture that would provide a useful framework for the study of both subcultural and ethnic variation (see Cerroni-Long 1993a).

In line with the theoretical founders of cultural anthropology, I came to believe that "we *are* our culture" (Mead [1942] 1965: 21), but I also distanced myself from the typically American attempts at searching for the mental causes of culture. Certainly, culture must affect cognitive and emotional processes (and that is why it influences intellectual endeavors, such as anthropological research), but culture neither emerges nor gets transmitted, and certainly cannot be studied, on the basis of some mental blueprint, be it "modal personality," "values orientation," or "collective unconscious." Rather, I became convinced, culture is an open system of behavioral constraints, constituted by environmental, historical, and social factors, shaping the behavior of people born and raised in a particular society. A society, in turn, can be defined as an enduring human group, recognized as distinct from all others and in which all the functions necessary for the continuation of communal life are performed by in-members. In line with this, an ethnic group is any community viewing itself as culturally distinct from others to which it is fundamentally related at the sociopolitical level. In other words, at a minimum, ethnicity differs from culture to the extent that an ethnic group has no political sovereignty, and a sovereign political structure is an extremely important component of the system of behavioral constraints constituting a culture (Cerroni-Long 2001). Consequently, in broad general terms, many cultures coincide with nation-states (as, indeed, in the case of "the culture of Japan"), and many ethnic groups (such as the Maori or the Basques) could be defined as "nations without states" (Cerroni-Long 2001).

A culture, then, is not a "thing," but nonetheless it profoundly affects and characterizes human behavior—more than factors such as age, sex, personality, socioeconomic status, and ideology—simply because of the pervasiveness of the behavioral constraints it encompasses. In a similar way, a disease is not a thing either, but it may mold behavior, frame lifestyle choices, define one's sense and presentation of self, and affect everyday activities. As diseases can be studied only through patients' symptoms, cultures can be detected only through observation and documentation of the behavior of their "carriers"—that is, people whose behavior is recognizably different from the behavior of members of different cultures. Without human carriers, human diseases would not exist, so it must be understood that one's culture enables behavior just as it constrains it. As in a traffic jam, which both is caused by and affects the behavior of drivers caught in it, each individual shapes the culture just as he or she is shaped by it.

However, being born and raised in a particular culture leads to a form of blindness; we consider our own behavior "natural" and take it so completely for granted that we are not consciously aware of its cultural specificity. That is why, typically, anthropologists study—at least in the early phases of their training—cultures different from their own. Engaging in "native anthropology" is fraught with difficulties, especially since it removes the comparative frame of reference through which we easily identify the characteristics of foreign behavior (Cerroni-Long 1995). But cultural analysis is important and necessary precisely because cultures differ. "As soon as there is contact with another culture (and this has always been the case), there is potential for conflict" (Carroll 1988: 3). I would add that intercultural encounters can also lead to interest, excitement, and pleasure (the international tourist industry and the travel-writing literature are built on this). Documenting cultural differences proves that there are many ways to be human, which deepens our understanding of human behavior, and can provide tremendous examples of different approaches to social organization and of the culture-wide consequences of particular institutional choices, be they polygamy, theocracy, or economic reciprocity.

The most dangerous type of reaction to intercultural encounters, however, comes from the unwillingness to recognize the legitimacy of cultural differences, leading to the ethnocentric denial of the common humanity of the culturally "others" and to the concoction of all sorts of ideological justifications—such as supposed "racial" inferiority and "innate" evil tendencies—for their exploitation or victimization. Unfortunately, ethnocentrism is a tendency found in most cultures, and when combined with military power, it can lead to the most aberrant phenomena, ranging from slavery to colonialism. The blindness leading to ethnocentrism, however, has nothing to do with cultural denial. Confronted with specific questions about the characteristics of their culture, most people will recognize their cultural membership, correlating it perhaps to attachment to particular customs or to the recognition of a specific cultural heritage with which they identify. In fact, a strong sense of cultural identity—and superiority—is often behind strong ethnocentrism. Not so with Americans. Even those who claim to "love their country" and to be "proud to be American" will generally discount that a distinctive American culture exists (Cerroni-Long 2004; Naylor 1998: 42–45).

I suspect that this has partly to do with the extreme competitive individualism that seems to be such a deep-rooted social norm in American culture, but I also think that it may be connected with the confused, conflicted ways ethnicity is seen in the American context.

ETHNOGENESIS AND THE CATs

When I started studying ethnicity in the United States in the late 1970s, I encountered an interesting phenomenon. Whenever I mentioned my research interests to "the natives" in informal social situations, the most common reaction I got was mild embarrassment. People would smile uncomfortably and often tried to change the topic of conversation. Intrigued, I started pressing on with clarification questions, and it emerged that people thought I was planning to study either "racial" groups or majority–minority relations—topics they felt constituted a negative aspect of American society, certainly not appropriate for inspection by a foreigner. And when I argued that, in a country like the United States, everybody had an ethnic background, they would stare at me in sincere amazement and shake their heads, smiling sadly, as if I had made a rather poor joke.

So, on top of denying that an American culture exists, mainstream Americans tend to deny their ethnic roots. The fact is that most mainstream Americans feel, as Margaret Mead ([1942] 1965: 31) acutely pointed out, that "however many generations we may boast of in this country, however real our lack of ties in the old world may be, we are all third-generation, our European ancestry tucked away and half forgotten, the recent steps in our wanderings over America immortalized and over-emphasized." In spite of the ever-increasing relevance of ethnic identity for American minority groups, and in spite of the demographic changes brought about by the mounting growth of immigration into the United States since the mid-1960s, mainstream Americans still identify much more readily on the basis of coming from the same town, living in the same neighborhood, having gone to the same school, working for the same company, or even liking the same rock band than on the basis of sharing common ethnic roots.

Partly, of course, this has to do precisely with the negative connotation ethnicity has acquired in the United States because of the nation's colonial and immigrant history. Ethnicity (often mislabeled as "race") has traditionally defined the colonized and enslaved, the "fresh off the boat," the social outsiders. Ethnicity is what must be erased in the process of becoming an American—a process that typically takes place over three generations. Thus, American culture gets defined in terms of absence; it is what remains after all traces of ethnicity are erased. No wonder so many Americans deny ethnicity's reality!

Furthermore, the "melting pot" ideology, together with a long record of intergroup marriage, has convinced members of the American mainstream that their ethnic roots simply cannot be traced. Thus, the closest they can come to a cultural definition is to think of themselves as WASP—or white, Anglo-Saxon, and Protestant—a term highlighting their preoccupation with "racial," historical, and religious categories (Robertiello and Hoguet 1987).

These are also typically abstract categories. Because they do not recognize that culture is expressed through behavior, Americans are often sincerely puzzled by the ease with which they are identified as Americans when traveling abroad. Also, because they are not able to identify the ethnic origins of their patterns of behavior, they are unable to trace their roots. And the critique of "culturalist essentialism" mounted by so many American anthropologists (e.g., Goode 2001) both feeds and fits into these views. As a consequence, I have come to see what I do in some of my classes as "teaching ethnicity" rather than teaching about ethnicity (Cerroni-Long 1993b).

When I introduce my students to the concept of ethnogenesis—the process by which a new set of "people" emerges from particular historical circumstances favoring either intense cultural intermixing or subcultural isolation—they initially take notes dutifully but with little interest. But when I go on to illustrate this process by describing the emergence of American culture from the amalgamation of three distinct European populations—of Celtic, Anglo, and Teutonic backgrounds—which through intermarriage and other forms of close contact merged their cultural characteristics into a new system of behavioral constraints, they sit up and pay real attention. For many of them this analysis is a revelation of enormous proportions. For the first time in their lives they feel that they have a recognizable, documented, legitimate ethnic heritage. As I describe the American cultural patterns that can be traced back to Irish, English, or Germanic ancestry, they seem to delight in relating their own behavior to its ethnic roots. And they seem to think that being designated by the acronym CAT—for Celtic, Anglo, Teutonic—is so much cooler than being a WASP! Also, it gives members of the mainstream a way out of being defined simply as American and, implicitly, as part of the socially dominant and culturally hegemonic group in the United States—a characterization they seem to abhor.

The enthusiasm for these discoveries, however, and for the new perspective from which behavior can be analyzed and identity defined is often short-lived. In the class in which I teach about American culture and intracultural diversity, the final assignment requires each student to engage in reflexive cultural analysis by writing a paper titled "What is it like to be _____?" in which the blank should be filled in with the name of the national, ethnic, or subcultural group with which the student identifies. This comes at the end of a semester dedicated to the analysis of American culture—as expressed in the behavioral patterns of the mainstream population—and of the major ethnic and subcultural groups found within it. We do a lot of documentary readings, we see illustrative films, and we have lengthy analytical discussions. Also, students are given detailed guidelines on what aspects of their own behavior they should reflect on, describe, and analyze in order to answer the assignment question. But to no avail. While members of minority groups generally breeze through the assignment and turn in very well-documented descriptions of their ethnic-specific patterns of behavior, the great majority of students who are members of the mainstream answer "What is it like to be an American?" in the most abstract, mentalistic way.

Having conducted this exercise once or twice a year for more than twenty years and in several universities, I have accumulated an imposing array of papers documenting in no uncertain terms the ways students perceive what it is like to be an American. "Americanness," they all agree, resides in a set of mental attitudes, acquired early on from parents and role models, that serve as guidelines for daily behavior. Indeed, even those students who reject the premises of the assignment and, against my specific request, fill in the blank of the paper title with their own names—proclaiming their unique individuality and denying any form of sociocultural membership—even these "paladins of exceptionalism" submit papers strikingly similar to those written by their more docile cultural brethren. In their remarkable uniformity, all of these papers show not only how Americans conceive of what motivates their behavior—the set of mental guidelines they claim to follow in their daily lives—but also, and to me more interestingly, provide a set of *words* that seem to operate as the master tropes of the American experience. I have come to call this set of terms "the CATs' compass," and I believe that it provides some important insights into American culture.

THE CATS' COMPASS

Cognitive scientists have been giving increasing attention to the "metaphors we live by" (Lakoff and Johnson 1980) in order to document the experiential basis of human thought (Johnson 1990). Such an approach strongly supports cultural relativism, since it highlights the embeddedness of thought in experience—which is inescapably culture-specific—and the concomitant interpretation of experience through metaphorical elaborations that are, again inescapably, derived from "cultural knowledge." The case of proverbs is the clearest illustration of the "directive force" of behavioral prescriptions that have the ring of timeless universality precisely because they express culture-specific themes (White 1987). Psychological anthropologists have long attempted to relate cultural specificity to differences in "worldviews" or in "cultural themes," but these approaches have "typically failed to specify the range of domains in which a given theme, alleged to be central to a culture, applies" (Quinn and Holland 1987: 35). The theory of culture I adopt in my research bypasses such preoccupations, which derive from a search for the prime causes of culture, and aims instead at describing culturally characteristic patterns of behavior, relating them to some of the specific factors that may have influenced their emergence but also placing them in the systemic context that has stabilized and perpetuates them. Still, native views on what guides behavior, whether or not empirically confirmed through participant observation, reveal a lot about culture-specific ideals. I would argue that the recurrent words used in expressing these ideals may provide even better insights into the building blocks of cultural themes.

In the case of my students' papers, there are seven words that recur with striking regularity: *challenge, control, comfort, competition, community, change, and choice*. Because they all begin with the letter *c*, I have labeled them the "7Cs" of American culture. Also, I have arranged these terms around a seven-point star—representing a compass (Figure 20.1)—and have tried to superimpose them on the "social factors wheel" (Figure 20.2) for the system model of culture I have adopted. In the process, I discovered that *each* of these seven ideas could be seen as central to one of the social factors listed. For example, "competition" is certainly at the core of the American economic structure, but it could be argued that it also shapes American social and political structures, and it is a core norm, value, and belief. Similarly, Americans definitely value "choice"—which they often define as "freedom"—but they also believe in it and use it as a social norm, incorporating it into their social, economic, and political structure. In other words, these seven words and the concepts they represent pervade American culture at all levels and seem to constitute the metaphorical filters through which people give meaning to their behavior and in the process reinforce it.

Do these concepts determine behavior? I do not think so. Behavior is shaped by culture-specific systemic constraints, which certainly include mental constructs such as norms and values but also very material ones such as climatic conditions and availability of natural resources (see Figure 20.2). Nevertheless, psychological anthropologists argue that cultural knowledge "is typically acquired to the accompaniment of intermittent advice and occasional correction rather than explicit, detailed instructions; but it is learned from others, in large part from their *talk*" (D'Andrade 1981, cited in Quinn and Holland 1987: 22; emphasis added). If "cultural knowledge" is defined as the webs of signification giving

The CATs' compass

Figure 20.1   The CATs' Compass

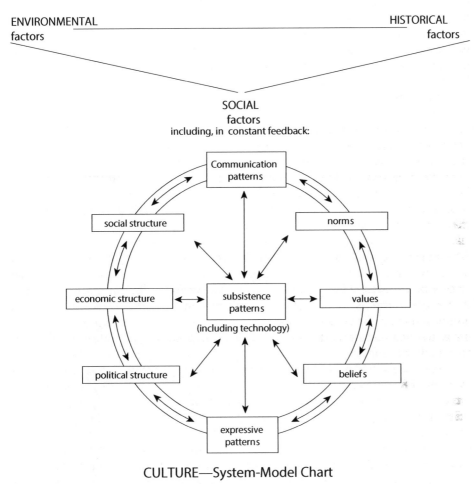

CULTURE
System-Model Chart

ENVIRONMENTAL
factors

HISTORICAL
factors

SOCIAL
factors
including, in constant feedback:

Communication
patterns

social structure

norms

economic structure

subsistence
patterns
(including technology)

values

political structure

beliefs

expressive
patterns

CULTURE—System-Model Chart

Figure 20.2   Culture System Model

Source: Adapted from E. L. Cerroni-Long, *Diversity Matters* (Trieste, Italy: COER Press, 2001), 22.

meaning to behavior, then I would agree that any holistic ethnography should attempt to dissect it and analyze it. From its foundations, cultural anthropology aimed at balancing etic and emic perspectives, and the natives' point of view is certainly helpful for understanding representational, if not operational, knowledge. In attempting to sort out the three levels of behavioral analyses available to researchers—what people do, what people think they do, and what people say they do—anthropologists like me tend to be most interested in documenting the first level, but in sorting out the cultural "package," we need to acknowledge and take into account the way the natives interpret their behavior or describe what they consider their behavioral guidelines, as my American students inevitably do in their papers. More usefully, the actual words being employed recurrently in the process of describing a perception of behavioral guidelines may reveal the often unrecognized linguistic signification structure being applied in giving order to experience.

In a way, then, the "7Cs" of American culture could be seen as the canons for American expressive style, the idée fixe array filtering the American experience and giving it shape. There is nothing mystical or amenable to psychoanalytic treatment in this. Expressive style is certainly not "national character," but it may serve as a useful framework for discussing cultural characteristics from a behavioral perspective. Style accommodates a rich repertoire of behavioral patterns, encompassing communication, inclinations, and identification. Above all, describing a culture through the expressive style of its members takes into account the core research methodology of cultural anthropology, which continues to be focused on the observation of, and interaction with, individuals and small groups in natural settings.

In her discussion of "cultural misunderstandings" between the French and the Americans, Raymonde Carroll (1988) attempts just such a description, but in spite of facilitating its understanding by presenting it through the lenses of cross-cultural comparison, the way she organizes the ethnography—around topics such as "home," "friendship," and "the telephone"—seems so haphazard as to partly justify her critics' theoretical discomfort. Hall and Hall (1990) do somewhat better, systematically addressing American use of time and space, educational and work attitudes, communication style, and psychological framework, but their theory of culture as shaped by the way information is organized, transmitted, and perceived leads to descriptions that constantly shift from expressive style to institutional structures, often mixing representational and operational aspects of cultural knowledge.

Organizing the description of American expressive style along the lines of traditional holistic ethnographies—that is, the topics listed in the "social factors wheel" in Figure 20.2—leads on the one hand to the difficulty of relating behavior to its institutionalized expressions and on the other to the pitfall of belaboring the trivial and the trite (Holmes and Holmes 2002). By the time Alexis de Tocqueville published the two volumes of *Democracy in America* in 1835 and 1840, the view of Americans as "isolated by self-reliance" was already well established (Wilkinson 1992: 11); what is interesting from an anthropological point of view is to look at how individualism gets expressed in American behavior and to trace the impact of the self-reliance social norm at the level of the cultural system as a whole.

Unfortunately, current trends in cultural anthropology have taken us increasingly away from any attempt at holistic descriptions of American culture. The rare exceptions come from anthropologists so steeped in psychological theories of culture that the ethnographic material they present seems incidental, being chiefly geared toward supporting a particular view of the human mind (e.g., Nuckolls 1998; Stein 2004). What remain are anthologies collecting the reflections of various social scientists on different aspects of American culture (e.g., DeVita and Armstrong 2002; Jorgensen and Truzzi 1974; Plotnicov 1990; Spradley and Rynkiewich 1975).

The collection edited by Spradley and Rynkiewich (1975) takes its title from the lead article, "Body Ritual among the Nacirema," a piece by Horace Miner, originally published in 1956, that has become a bit of a classic in the literature on American culture. In this short article, the author describes bodily preoccupations as being central to the culture of a group he calls the Nacirema, whose rituals he describes using full-fledged anthropological jargon. The reader eventually realizes that *Nacirema* is *American* spelled backward, and amusement is derived both from the unusual perspective the article gives on common American patterns of behavior and from the gentle irony the author bestows on the anthropological approach itself. Rereading this piece half a century after its publication, however, also highlights how unexplored the Nacirema have unfortunately remained. In spite of its strong economic and political influence on the rest of the world, American culture is still not well understood, least of all by its own members, who deny its reality and are puzzled by foreign recognition of its characteristics, and even more so by the real distaste these trigger across many national boundaries. International relations are, first and foremost, intercultural relations, and cultural reflexivity—the ability to recognize the cultural matrix of our behavior rather than considering it the universal norm—seems a crucial first step on the path toward peaceful coexistence. The characteristics of the CATs' compass offer an introductory glimpse into the culture of a people that is still awaiting a comprehensive ethnography.

EXERCISE

Gather information on your ethnic background by looking into documents on your family history and/or interviewing older relatives. Be prepared to discuss the results of this research in class. Is this ethnic background still somehow in evidence in your family? Were you or any of your relatives treated differently from others because of this background? How is this background related to "being American"?

REFERENCES

Baker, Lee D., ed. 2003. *Life in America: Identity and Everyday Experience*. Oxford: Blackwell.

Barth, Fredrik, Andre Gingrich, Robert Parkin, and Sydel Silverman. 2005. *One Discipline, Four Ways: British, German, French, and American Anthropology*. Chicago: University of Chicago Press.

Carneiro, Robert L. 2003. *Evolutionism in Cultural Anthropology: A Critical History*. Boulder, CO: Westview Press.

Carroll, Raymonde. 1988. *Cultural Misunderstandings: The French–American Experience*. Chicago: University of Chicago Press.

Cerroni-Long, E. L. 1993a. "Life and Cultures: The Test of Real Participant Observation." In Philip R. DeVita and James D. Armstrong, eds., *Distant Mirrors: America as a Foreign Culture*, 148–61. Belmont, CA: Wadsworth.

———. 1993b. "Teaching Ethnicity in the USA: An Anthropological Model." *Journal of Ethno-Development* 2 (1): 106–11.

———. 1995. *Insider Anthropology*. Arlington, VA: American Anthropological Association/NAPA.

———. 1999. "Anthropology at Century's End." In E. L. Cerroni-Long, ed., *Anthropological Theory in North America*, 1–18. Westport, CT: Bergin & Garvey.

———. 2001. *Diversity Matters*. Trieste, Italy: COER Press.

———. 2004. "Comparing US." *FOSAP Newsletter* 11 (2): 2–4.

D'Andrade, Roy Goodwin. 1981. "The Cultural Part of Cognition." *Cognitive Science* 5 (3): 179–95.

DeVita, Philip R., and James D. Armstrong, eds. 2002. *Distant Mirrors: America as a Foreign Culture*. 3rd ed. Belmont, CA: Wadsworth.

Douglas, Mary. 1995. "The Cloud God and the Shadow Self." *Social Anthropology* 3 (2): 83–94.

Forman, Shepard, ed. 1994. *Diagnosing America: Anthropology and Public Engagement*. Ann Arbor: University of Michigan Press.

Goode, Judith. 2001. "Against Culturalist Essentialism." In Ida Susser and Thomas C. Patterson, eds., *Cultural Diversity in the United States: A Critical Reader*, 434–56. Oxford: Blackwell.

Greer, Herb. 1989. "Not So Very Alike." *Times Literary Supplement*, July 13, 372.

Hall, Edward T., and Mildred Reed Hall. 1990. *Understanding Cultural Differences*. Yarmouth, ME: Intercultural Press.

Holmes, Lowell D., and Ellen Rhoads Holmes. 2002. "The American Cultural Configuration." In Philip R. DeVita and James D. Armstrong, eds., *Distant Mirrors: America as a Foreign Culture*, 3rd ed., 4–26. Belmont, CA: Wadsworth.

Jameson, Fredric. 1991. *Postmodernism, or, The Cultural Logic of Late Capitalism*. Durham, NC: Duke University Press.

Johnson, Mark. 1990. *The Body in the Mind: The Bodily Basis of Meaning, Imagination, and Reason*. Chicago: University of Chicago Press.

Jorgensen, Joseph G., and Marcello Truzzi, comps. 1974. *Anthropology and American Life*. Englewood Cliffs, NJ: Prentice-Hall.

Lakoff, George, and Mark Johnson. 1980. *Metaphors We Live By*. Chicago: University of Chicago Press.

Mead, Margaret. (1942) 1965. *And Keep Your Powder Dry: An Anthropologist Looks at America*. New York: William Morrow.

Moffatt, Michael. 1989. *Coming of Age in New Jersey: College and American Culture*. Brunswick, NJ: Rutgers University Press.

Naylor, Larry L. 1998. *American Culture: Myth and Reality of a Culture of Diversity*. Westport, CT: Bergin & Garvey.

Nuckolls, Charles W. 1998. *Culture: A Problem That Cannot Be Solved*. Madison: University of Wisconsin Press.

Perin, Constance. 1988. *Belonging in America: Reading between the Lines*. Madison: University of Wisconsin Press.

Plotnicov, Leonard, ed. 1990. *American Culture: Essays on the Familiar and Unfamiliar*. Pittsburgh: University of Pittsburgh Press.

Quinn, Naomi, and Dorothy Holland. 1987. "Culture and Cognition." In Dorothy Holland and Naomi Quinn, eds., *Cultural Models in Language and Thought*, 3–40. Cambridge: Cambridge University Press.

Robertiello, Richard C., and Diana Hoguet. 1987. *The WASP Mystique*. New York: Donald I. Fine.

Spindler, George, and Louise Spindler. 1990. *The American Cultural Dialogue and Its Transmission*. London: Falmer Press.

Spradley, James P., and Michael A. Rynkiewich, eds. 1975. *The Nacirema: Readings on American Culture*. Boston: Little, Brown.

Stein, Howard F. 2004. *Beneath the Crust of Culture: Psychoanalytic Anthropology and the Cultural Unconscious in American Life*. Amsterdam: Rodopi.

Tannen, Deborah. 1998. *The Argument Culture: Moving from Debate to Dialogue*. New York: Ballantine Books.

Werner, Oswald. 2003. "Ethnographers, Language Skills and Translation." *Anthropology News*, March, 7.

White, Geoffrey M. 1987. "Proverbs and Cultural Models: An American Psychology of Problem Solving." In Dorothy Holland and Naomi Quinn, eds., *Cultural Models in Language and Thought*, 151–72. Cambridge: Cambridge University Press.

Wilkinson, Rupert, ed. 1992. *American Social Character: Modern Interpretations from the '40s to the Present*. New York: HarperCollins.

21

LIVING UP TO OUR WORDS

Paul Durrenberger

This chapter is adapted from remarks Professor Durrenberger made at the 2014 meeting of the Society for Applied Anthropology (SfAA) when he received the Society's Malinowski Award. The speech was dedicated to Robert O'Brien, an anthropologist whose activism in the areas of environmental protection, workers' rights, and LGBT issues distinguished his tragically brief career.

Thanks for the introduction and thank you all for honoring me with this award. I thank Kendall Thu and Barbara Dilly for putting me up for this and filling out all the paperwork it required. I'd also like to thank all of the people who wrote letters of support. And I want to thank my wife, partner, and collaborator, Suzan Erem, for all that she has been and is to me now.

I dedicate my talk today to the memory of Robert O'Brien, who died in Philadelphia on June 1, 2012, at the age of forty-four. He epitomized the values and outlook I advocate here and helped to lead the struggle for equality and dignity.

I won't make a case for applied anthropology. We applied anthropologists have already done that with our work:

- On city streets and battlefields, and in hospitals, we have saved lives.

- In the World Bank and U.S. Agency for International Development we have given voice to untold numbers of otherwise voiceless people.

- We have put fishing peoples into fisheries management and users into IT products from copy machines to computer programs.

Reprinted with permission, from Durrenberger, Paul. 2014. *Human Organization* 73 (4): 299–304. © Society for Applied Anthropology. Republished in *Reflecting on America*, 2nd edition, edited by Clare L. Boulanger, 265–274 (© 2016 Taylor & Francis).

- Archaeologists have preserved the memory of labor struggles and documented the conditions of enslaved Africans that would otherwise have escaped the notice of history.
- We are in the ecovillages, farmers' markets, and alternative agriculture movements.
- In the Occupy Movement we have helped to organize the 99 percent.

That's a wide swath through contemporary government, corporations, and development organizations, working with and against these institutions. Nobody needs to make a case for applied anthropologists. We are here.

Further, though applied anthropology is focused on practical results, it is hardly atheoretical. Walter Goldschmidt (2001) argues that in fact applied anthropology is a testing ground for theory. Through working *with* people as opposed to *on* them, we have learned that:

- The tragedy of the commons has become a comedy of economists (McCay and Acheson 1987).
- Malinowski's ([1922] 1984) critique of methodological individualism and Economic Man has been validated time and again (Durrenberger 2009).
- Privatization is not a viable solution to resource management problems (Acheson 2000; Carrier 2015; Durrenberger and Palsson 2015).
- Whenever you hear "all things being equal," you have a good reason to stop listening.
- Objective ethnography cannot be dismissed as simply "the objectivist narrative," one story among many, . . .
- nor is it the exclusive domain of disengaged observers (Singer 1995).

These discoveries reiterate the wisdom of Malinowski's classic ethnography:

- Assume nothing.
- Listen to the people you want to understand.
- Don't substitute your understandings for theirs.
- Honor your observations.

Who else but anthropologists can scrap all prior assumptions about human nature and examine living social orders firsthand for answers?

Thomas Weaver's (2002) compilation of Malinowski Award Addresses suggests common themes through four decades—concern for

- inequality,
- policy and influencing policy makers,
- empirical and accurate reportage, and·
- public service.

I rephrase these as

- be empirical,
- work for change,
- serve the people.

And that's what I want to talk about tonight.

Unlike many of you, I've been institutionalized for most of my life. I've recently finished fifteen years at Penn State, Pennsylvania's land-grant college, created to serve the people but hijacked to become another branch of Monsanto U—that is, a research and development arm of agribusiness. Before that, I spent twenty-five years at the University of Iowa, that state's liberal arts university whose chief role is to serve the pharmaceutical industry.

Anthropology is rooted in the academy. So let's pause to understand the role of universities in our economic and ideological systems.

The American working class has two segments. One does the work. The other manages the workers. The ruling class grants the managerial part of the working class privileges in return for its service, such as suburban houses or urban lofts, cars, and the chance to get kids into the managerial class via university educations (Ehrenreich 1990).

The role of universities is to make this system seem reasonable, natural, and inevitable, and to reassure the students of what they've heard since they were born—that their inherent merit entitles them to privileges—but that they have to prove it by what we, the soft-handed, are pleased to call "hard work." Graduation certifies that we have convinced reasonable people to take absurd systems seriously and function in them without going too crazy too often.

Sound familiar?

So that's what I've devoted *my* life to. In fact, a course I developed on business anthropology was explicitly designed to help students get jobs within the system.

A young woman named Erin Holland graduated from Penn State with a degree in anthropology. She was working with a marketing firm in Pittsburgh, and her employers wanted to hire more anthropology graduates. I went to Pittsburgh to visit her and talk with her bosses, who agreed to let Erin work with me on the business anthropology course.

I wanted to check with the people who hire anthropologists to see what skills they needed, so in 2007 I went to the Ethnographic Praxis in Industry Conference (EPIC) to ask them.

They told me PhDs were too set in their ways. They wanted people who could think like anthropologists. And they wanted people who could

- work on schedule,
- work in teams, and
- make themselves intelligible to their bosses.

These skills are well beyond the reach of many PhDs.

So Erin and I developed a syllabus to teach these skills. Undergraduates would have to learn how to think like anthropologists in other courses; this one was just for technique. Further, these techniques could help the students get work right out of college. They wouldn't need to go to graduate school.

At another EPIC I heard anthropologists who worked at Xerox (Watts-Perotti et al. 2009) discuss the future of paper in business. Their ethnographic observations convinced them paper was useful only for patching between computer applications that didn't interface very well. Yet. They reminded us of the Kodak Corporation's discovery of digital photography and its ten-year plan to deal with it. And that five years later, Kodak was out of business.

That was five years ago. By now technology has just about wiped out the need for paper. I couldn't get that out of my mind as I returned to my teaching at Penn State. I was already well along in a course on global processes and local systems. At the meeting of that class after I returned, I told the students to scrap all their assignments. They were all for a paper this or paper that, and paper was no longer in the future.

But, I admitted, I was at a loss as to what else to do. So their first assignment was to let me know what they would like to do instead. On paper, of course. They told me: animations, videos, a teach-in, dramatic presentations, art.

A grad student, Nuno Ribeiro, worked with others who called themselves the Anthro 450 Collective to bring together all of these elements into one coherent evening event held in a large auditorium.

The evening's emcee assured the unsuspecting spectators that the uniformed security guards were there to ensure their safety. The leader of this group happened to be a prison guard during his working hours, so his demeanor added a note of verisimilitude.

At that time, Victoria's Secret's campaign for its Pink line at universities was very much in the news. Some students who were also members of United Students Against Sweatshops (USAS) learned that Pink goods were produced in sweatshops.

The evening began with a Victoria's Secret fashion show. When students posing as workers rose from the audience to announce where the merchandise had been produced, the "security guards" forcibly removed them.

Another USAS group went to Pittsburgh to video the protests against the G-20 meeting. It was the same scene we see enacted around the planet—the mass of police in riot gear and gas masks with their batons . . . the running crowd . . . the tear gas. I had asked my students to avoid getting hurt or busted because we needed their video for our class, after all.

USAS follows in the tradition of other great student protest movements, like the civil rights movement, the anti–Vietnam War movement, the South Africa divestiture movement, and the environmental movement. The goal of USAS is to ensure that merchandise that bears a university's licensed logos is not made in sweatshops. The activism of the students in USAS did more than just spice up our class project. When a USAS member was arrested at Penn State and assessed an outrageous fine by the university, I organized a faculty response with a letter to President Spanier and collected money from my colleagues to pay the fine.

That's when I confronted Penn State's culture of fear.

There's a lot of fear in academia. Undergrads are afraid of exams; grad students are afraid of crossing professors, losing funding and sponsorship; junior faculty are afraid of not getting tenure. By the time people are tenured, fear has become a habit.

One faculty member whose son had been arrested refused to sign the letter because he was coming up for tenure. A very senior colleague told me at great length that while he sympathized, he could do nothing because one line of his funding came directly from the president's office. That's what the ruling class is counting on. A fearful faculty cannot teach boldness.

When USAS organized a sit-in at the president's office, I participated. When the USAS students organized an action in front of Old Main, I led my class out to join them. And when they got a meeting with the president, Suzan and I did role-play training to help ensure they wouldn't be shooting blanks when they faced a dismissive and arrogant administration.

That worked. An otherwise shy USAS representative refused to allow President Spanier to talk over him. When it became obvious that the administration lawyers were evading the issues, the USAS representatives caucused and then walked out. That was a great victory and left the administration stunned. Students don't act that way!

What did we accomplish? I expect Penn State merchandise is still made in sweatshops, but our efforts produced a handful of dedicated, savvy, and smart organizers who are now working with unions and other activist organizations in Pennsylvania and other parts of the world. All without PhDs.

Be empirical, work for change, serve the people.

I gave no tests. Taking tests is *not* a useful skill. It only ratifies a fallacious ideology of meritocratic individualism. I organized class meetings as student-led discussions of student-submitted questions about assigned readings. The questions and discussion let me know which students had done the reading.

At the end of the semester I asked students to write a brief essay on what they'd learned. One of the most poignant was written by a young woman who said that she'd learned the most important lesson of her university education in one of my classes: "There but for the grace of God go I."

In other words, she's just like everyone else: vulnerable, weak, helpless, exposed. Anything that happens to anyone else could happen to me—to her—to you.

Taking that seriously motivates solidarity—people joining together to defend the weakest among them because they know that an injury to one is an injury to all. This is what we learn from Nuer and Bedouin with their segmentary systems (Evans-Pritchard 1940, 1949) and what we learn from the longshoremen who load and unload ships at our ports every day.

Early in 2000 when the International Longshore and Warehouse Union in California heard about the troubles of their brother longshoremen in South Carolina, the members immediately started to organize support. The dockers did this even though they belonged to a different union. Even though their international union told them not to. Even though the national labor confederation, the AFL-CIO, refused to back them.

When dockers in Europe, Latin America, and Asia ignored their national unions and joined the South Carolina local, there was a real prospect of shutting down global trade networks. The dockers knew the loss of the longshoremen's local in Charleston would be a loss to all longshoremen.

Suzan and I spent three and a half years working on a book about that story, *On the Global Waterfront*. The union purchased a thousand copies to give to all its members and sparked what one observer called a cultural revolution on the waterfront. Longshoremen were sitting in their pickup trucks on their breaks reading the book, with each page making them think about solidarity and their role in it. The same thing happened in California and in Australia. Spanish dockers had the book translated into Spanish.

Sometimes it helps to recognize and record people's actions. It lets people know they are not invisible. It prepares them for the next battle. The books we write *can* make a difference.

Supporting those who are most threatened, those at the bottom, serves the interests of all workers. How does that pertain to anthropologists?

Are we not also workers? Like the hotel workers who have served us at our conferences? For one brief moment anthropologists showed sufficient courage to join the struggle and show solidarity with our fellow workers.

The 1999 meeting of the American Anthropological Association (AAA) was in a Chicago hotel close to the Congress Hotel and not far from a large homeless shelter. Suzan and I were taking a big plastic bag full of leftover food from the meeting to the homeless shelter when we passed a picket line at the Congress Hotel. The workers there had been out on strike for a long time. The conjunction of the surplus high-end food on my shoulder, the homeless shelter, and the picket line caused me to wonder aloud what a bunch of anthropologists could do about anything. Aside from sit in a hotel and talk about the problem. We are, after all, academics.

Suzan, who learned about organizing in the labor movement, pointed out that our meetings themselves are a resource and that we could have some clout if we agreed to meet only in facilities whose workers were represented by unions.

As president of the Central States Anthropological Society, I drafted a proposal to the Executive Board of the AAA, but that didn't go anywhere. Then I drafted a motion and took it to the Section Assembly for a vote. "But that would cost more," some protested. I provided data to refute that claim, and the motion carried with a huge majority. The AAA Executive Board adopted the motion and it became policy.

Then came 2004. The AAA contracted to meet in the San Francisco Hilton. But the hotel had locked out its workers and refused to negotiate with the representatives of their union. Perhaps the dispute would be resolved before our meeting. But time wore on, and nothing happened.

Finally, AAA staff and leadership canceled the San Francisco venue. Other organizations joined us, and before long the San Francisco Hilton was negotiating with its workers and soon they were back to work with a new contract.

What the AAA did worked. It accomplished something. That was solidarity. We anthropologists led the way for other scholarly organizations. But only because the policy was in place.

Why should we professors support the unions of the other segment of the working class? Look at the data from the Economic Policy Institute's yearly *State of Working America*. Having a union raises workers' wages, closes the gender and race gaps, and increases the chances workers will have health and pension benefits. A union contract provides a shield against arbitrary and capricious bosses. Work for change. Serve the people. It's something we can do.

Did it cost more? That's like the argument that a higher minimum wage decreases the number of jobs. If you're empirical, you'll learn that that has never happened. Ever. And it's the same for hotel costs. Union hotels don't cost more. The wages of workers don't determine the prices of products. (If *adjunct* wages determined university tuition rates, there wouldn't be half as much student debt in this country as there is today.)

However, there *were* costs. The AAA had to pay a stiff penalty for breaking the contract. The AAA meeting was disrupted. Some members couldn't give their papers; some could not get to their job interviews; some lost the price of their air tickets. But how can we weigh the cost of not getting a job interview, not giving a paper, not meeting friends, against the benefit of helping hotel workers in their struggle for representation? The logic of solidarity means that when you need that kind of help, you can trust that someone will be there to help you. There but for the grace of God go you.

Those in the managerial part of the working class are supposed to have the logic of solidarity educated out of them. For years they learned: the market determines everything equitably. You get what you deserve. *You* don't need any help.

I don't know how it would have played out for the Charleston longshoremen if the dockers in California or Spain had asked the cost of their actions. Or if they'd been afraid to act. But that would have made all the shipping companies very happy because it would have been their signal that they wouldn't need to put up with longshoremen's unions anymore. Anywhere. The ruling class likes that kind of message.

For a brief moment, the AAA made a difference to working people. During the same period I was on the Society for Applied Anthropology Board of Directors, and the members would not even entertain the idea of such a policy of solidarity with unions. Thus the society violated a union boycott and met in Baltimore in 2012, and right now we are meeting in Albuquerque, a city whose hotel workers are not represented by unions.

But I was talking about universities. So let's get back to that.

The focal point for corporate universities, as for corporations, is the bottom line. The main task of faculty is to bring in enough outside money to convert departments from cost centers to profit centers. The administration gets half of any research money a faculty member receives. This money is used to pay for utilities, maintenance, and the expenses of a huge bureaucracy, especially administrative salaries, which are typically three times those of any faculty members.

Because teaching returns only a part of tuition money, it is a largely unrecompensed use of faculty time. So administrators hatched a plan of hiring qualified but low-paid people to teach. Then they elevated researchers to higher levels of prestige and sometimes salary. So the pattern shifted from having a largely tenured faculty involved in teaching to having a small core of tenured researchers who don't teach and a large, low-paid, and rotating group of adjunct teaching staff.

That's where many of our younger colleagues are today, and that's why so many of them are talking about unions. In one of her articles on the Baltimore debacle in the *SfAA News*, Betsy Taylor (2012: 28) says:

> The labor problems of the "working poor" in hotels and hospitality industries are converging with the labor problems of the "working poor" in academe and professions. It is inaccurate to argue that we should accept bad wages and work conditions for hotel workers to create cheap meetings for underpaid anthropologists. The same forces *push down all wages*.

There but for the grace of God go us all.

One of the courses that adjuncts often teach is the introductory anthropology course that every university offers every semester. Across this country and others a lot of students take that course. That means a huge market for a universal book that has lots of pretty pictures and makes a lot of money for the publishing house and doesn't make any administrators or students uncomfortable. So came the age of bland bad intro books that cost 130 bucks a pop.

To me, that's a class issue. I was discussing this with Dean Birkenkamp of Paradigm Publishers when I said in frustration, "What this country needs is a good ten-buck intro book." He said, "You write it and I'll publish it." So Suzan and I put our heads together and wrote *Anthropology Unbound: A Field Guide to the 21st Century* (2007).

We start with the assumption that every person on the planet deserves one share of the planet. No more; no less. We acknowledge that the world is not a fair place and explain why that is, but we also suggest that the people who read the book bend their efforts toward *making* the world a fair place.

I've taught the book. It's tough to teach. It makes you truthful. But then again, as anthropologists, isn't that our *job*?

So I've given you a few good reasons for those of you still at universities to think of deinstitutionalizing yourselves. And maybe figuring a way to join with others in the same boat and organize for common benefit. You can't rely on the organizations you now have. That's for sure.

And these days a PhD is an impediment, not an asset. At a university you will barely get paid to use what you know about anthropology. What does it get you if the best you can look forward to is a low-paying, marginalized adjunct position? You will simply prop up the corporate university that churns out PhDs who will only become adjuncts or teaching and research assistants.

Corporate universities have followed the rest of industry in substituting capital for labor. From the advent of the first recording devices, forward-looking administrators have anticipated the day they could mechanize lectures. Nowadays the internet removes even the necessity for classrooms with the advent of massive open online courses, or MOOCs.

But no one is immune. Machines can replace anyone. Political scientist Benjamin Ginsberg (2013), of Johns Hopkins, is a step ahead with his plan for massive open online administrations—MOOAs. Administrators everywhere face the same problems, so they standardize solutions with best practices. With MOOA, one administrator can resolve the problems of all with a few keystrokes. The only downside, Ginsberg points out, is unemployment among university administrators. But thankfully they're qualified for work in the growing industries of retail sales, hospitality, and food services. Then they might see the wisdom of union representation.

But let's get real. With no resident students, classes, or administrators, vast areas of dormitories, classrooms, and administrative offices will be vacant, and mostly they're climate controlled. A bottom-line solution is to convert this space to concentrated animal feeding operations, or CAFOs, fattening hogs, chickens, and turkeys—perhaps in conjunction with the now Chinese-owned corporation Smithfield Foods—to finally achieve the dream of the university as a profit center.

Work for change? I know something about CAFOs, because I've studied them.

Kendall Thu and I offered the first warnings to the people of Iowa in the mid-1990s. The Iowa swine industry kept saying, "We'll do for Iowa what we did for North Carolina," so we went to North Carolina and found that none of the consequences was good for the environment, local economies, rural residents, the wider economy, or most farmers. We returned to Iowa and said, "Hey, you don't *want* what the swine industry did for them."

In the mid-1990s, as an academic, I naively thought the best thing we could do was to get good scientific information into the hands of state decision makers. Kendall organized a series of workshops, convened scientists, and edited a two-volume series on the consequences of industrial swine production. He found funds to print the volumes and send them to every legislator in the state.

But the process of industrial swine production continued apace. For the citizens' groups organizing against it, we put together a less technical book, *Pigs, Profits, and Rural Communities* (Thu and Durrenberger 1998). And the juggernaut rolled on.

Why? We wrote a paper about that too (Durrenberger and Thu 1997). The biggest contributor to the Republican governor's campaign was the state's largest industrial swine producer. The governor had a line item in his budget for the dean of agriculture at Iowa State to prove scientifically how beneficial industrial swine production was. So the industry bought a governor, the governor bought Iowa State, and Iowa State proved it was all good. Just like we'd seen in North Carolina.

No amount of information can influence that process. It's a political process, and Kendall was correct to see that the only meaningful way to engage it was via political action. An elegant analysis didn't mean squat. My academic naïveté prevented me from seeing political realities.

How can anthropologists, their heads in the clouds of academe, enter the political process? Well, we have to be willing to *get* political. Weaver's collection of twentieth-century Malinowski Award talks is full of calls from Malinowski for anthropologists to organize to have some effect on public policy. It has never happened.

As chair of AAA's Public Policy Committee, Kendall tried to organize a policy think tank that would be like the Brookings Institution, providing reporters with the scientific take on environmental issues, agricultural questions, immigration, the nature of marriage and family, and other policy matters. Imagine if anthropologists could speak with the authority of the Brookings Institution or the Cato Institute or the Heritage Foundation. Imagine anthropologists instead of economists as the go-to people for reporters. That was the idea.

AAA allocated money to start such an institute. With that backing, Kendall brought it to SfAA and suggested a joint venture. How would that look? The board wanted details. Kendall came back the next year with a plan. I was on the SfAA Board of Directors and heard my colleagues articulate reason after reason not to participate in such a venture. It might be "too political"—as though every other speaker on this podium before me hadn't enjoined us to be political.

The politics of industrial agriculture might be too big an objective for a couple of academic anthropologists to take on. But the politics of SfAA and the AAA? Surely all of us together can manage that.

I tell you now: Do what all of the Malinowski speakers before me have urged. Be *better*, be *stronger*, be *braver* than the anthropologists and leaders who came before you.

So I've said some things that we're not supposed to say. I've said there is a class system in America that includes

- a ruling class,
- a working class, and
- lots of anthropology classes.

I've suggested that our organizations don't live up to our ideals. All of this has probably made some folks uncomfortable. I hope so, because that might just be sufficient to motivate some change.

I'm truly honored to receive this award, and I've enjoyed speaking to you tonight. But now it's up to *you* to do the hard part—live up to the legacy all of the Malinowski speakers have left you.

QUESTION FOR DISCUSSION

What is wrong with the idea that merit entitles you to privileges?

REFERENCES

Acheson, James M. 2000. "Clearcutting Maine: Implications for the Theory of Common Property Resources." *Human Ecology* 28 (2): 145–69.

Carrier, James G. 2015. "Retrospect." In E. Paul Durrenberger and Gisli Palsson, eds., *Gambling Debt: Iceland's Rise and Fall in the Global Economy*. Boulder: University Press of Colorado.

Durrenberger, E. Paul. 2009. "The Last Wall to Fall: The Anthropology of Collective Action in the Global System." *Journal of Anthropological Research* 65 (1): 9–26.

Durrenberger, E. Paul, and Suzan Erem. 2007. *Anthropology Unbound: A Field Guide to the 21st Century*. Boulder, CO: Paradigm.

Durrenberger, E. Paul, and Gisli Palsson, eds. 2015. *Gambling Debt: Iceland's Rise and Fall in the Global Economy*. Boulder: University Press of Colorado.

Durrenberger, E. Paul, and Kendall M. Thu. 1997. "Signals, Systems, and Environment in Industrial Food Production." *Journal of Political Ecology* 4: 27–39.

Ehrenreich, Barbara. 1990. *Fear of Falling: The Inner Life of the Middle Class*. New York: Harper.

Evans-Pritchard, E. E. 1940. *The Nuer: A Description of the Modes of Livelihood and Political Institutions of a Nilotic People*. Oxford: Clarendon Press.

———. 1949. *The Sanusi of Cyrenaica*. London: Oxford University Press.

Ginsberg, Benjamin. 2013. "Forget MOOCs—Let's Use MOOA." Minding the Campus, June 13. www.mindingthecampus.org/2013/06/forget_moocslets_use_mooa (accessed October 28, 2015).

Goldschmidt, Walter. 2001. "Notes toward a Theory of Applied Anthropology." *Human Organization* 60 (4): 423–29.

Malinowski, Bronislaw. (1922) 1984. *Argonauts of the Western Pacific*. Long Grove, IL: Waveland Press.

McCay, Bonnie, and James M. Acheson. 1987. *The Question of the Commons: The Culture and Ecology of Communal Resources*. Tucson: University of Arizona Press.

Singer, Merrill. 1995. "Beyond the Ivory Tower: Critical Praxis in Medical Anthropology." *Medical Anthropology Quarterly* 9 (1): 80–106.

Taylor, Betsy. 2012. "Best Practices in Ethical Planning of Professional Meetings." *SfAA News* 23 (4): 26–28.

Thu, Kendall M., and E. Paul Durrenberger, eds. 1998. *Pigs, Profits, and Rural Communities*. Albany: State University of New York Press.

Watts-Perotti, Jennifer, Mary Ann Sprague, Patricia Wall, and Catherine McCorkindale. 2009. "Pushing New Frontiers: Examining the Future of Paper and Electronic Documents." *Ethnographic Praxis in Industry Conference Proceedings*, August, 1: 197–208.

Weaver, Thomas, ed. 2002. *The Dynamics of Applied Anthropology in the Twentieth Century: The Malinowski Award Papers*. Oklahoma City: Society for Applied Anthropology.

About the Contributors

Matthew H. Amster teaches cultural anthropology at Gettysburg College. He has published numerous articles on sociocultural change among the Kelabit of Sarawak, Malaysia, exploring such diverse topics as religious pilgrimage and conversion, gossip and social networks, and the implications of cross-border movement along the international frontier. Most recently, he has begun a new research project in Denmark, looking at Viking reenactment and Norse-inspired religious movements.

Clare L. Boulanger is professor emeritus at Colorado Mesa University. Her ethnographic work has spanned the urban jungles of Borneo and the exotic land known as New England. In addition to editing this anthology (and its previous edition, published by Allyn & Bacon in 2008), she has written *A Sleeping Tiger: Ethnicity, Class, and New Dayak Dreams in Urban Sarawak* (University Press of America, 2009) and the textbook *Biocultural Evolution: The Anthropology of Human Prehistory* (Waveland, 2013). Regarding her chapter on *The Big Bang Theory*: she has always felt that television has far more ethnographic value than is generally granted; besides, she greatly enjoys watching it.

Philippe Bourgois is professor of anthropology and director of the Center for Social Medicine at the Semel Institute for Neuropsychiatry, Department of Psychiatry, University of California, Los Angeles. He is the author or editor of several books on U.S. inner-city poverty, including the award-winning *In Search of Respect: Selling Crack in El Barrio* (Cambridge, 1995), *Righteous Dopefiend* (coauthored with Jeff Schonberg; California, 2009), *Ethnicity at Work: Divided Labor on a Central American Banana Plantation* (Johns Hopkins, 1989), *Violence in War and Peace* (coedited with Nancy Scheper-Hughes; Blackwell, 2004), and *Violence at the Urban Margins* (coedited with Javier Auyero and Nancy Scheper-Hughes; Oxford, 2015). He is currently coauthoring a book focusing on the carceral and psychiatric diagnosis–mediated management of inner-city poverty in the United States.

E. L. Cerroni-Long developed an interest in Asia during her early childhood in Italy. After earning a doctorate in Oriental studies at the University of Venice, she continued her academic training at the University of Kyoto, where her actual experience with a "foreignness" she had previously understood only from books was sufficiently unsettling to inspire her to study anthropology in the United States, a country whose ethnic makeup intrigues her. She specializes in cross-cultural research and is the editor of *Anthropological Theory in North America* (Bergin & Garvey, 1999). Currently she teaches at Eastern Michigan University in Ypsilanti.

Lara Descartes received her PhD in anthropology from the University of Michigan in 2002. After working with Dr. Conrad Kottak at the Alfred P. Sloan Foundation's Center for the Ethnography of Everyday Life, she became a faculty member in the Department of Human

Development and Family Studies at the University of Connecticut. She is currently professor of family studies at Brescia University College in Ontario. She has published on the topics of LGBT health and aging, qualitative research, informal support, work and family, and media and family. Her current work is with sexual-minority single parents.

Micaela di Leonardo, who received her PhD from the University of California at Berkeley in 1981, is professor of anthropology and performance studies at Northwestern University. She is a cultural anthropologist with broad interests in social and economic inequalities arising from differences in class, race, gender, and sexuality, as well as the representations and misrepresentations of those inequalities. Her primary geographic focus is American urban life, but she also works in and teaches on global political economy. She is the author of *The Varieties of Ethnic Experience* (Cornell, 1984) and *Exotics at Home* (Chicago, 1998) and editor of *Gender at the Crossroads of Knowledge* (California, 1991), *The Gender/Sexuality Reader* (coedited with Roger N. Lancaster; Routledge, 1997), and *New Landscapes of Inequality* (coedited with Jane L. Collins and Brett Williams; School for Advanced Research, 2008). Currently she is working on two books: an analysis of race and American media through the optic of an ignored but extraordinarily popular black radio show, *The Tom Joyner Morning Show*; and an ethnography of political economy and public culture in New Haven, Connecticut.

Paul Durrenberger taught at the University of Iowa for twenty-five years and at Penn State for fifteen years. He has done fieldwork in highland and lowland Thailand, Iceland, Alabama, Mississippi, Iowa, Chicago, and Pennsylvania. He and his wife and collaborator, Suzan Erem, wrote the introductory text *Anthropology Unbound: A Field Guide to the 21st Century*, now in its third edition. In addition to books, academic articles, and informal works, he has written radio commentaries. His informal essays have been collected and published as *American Fieldnotes*; he has also written a memoir, *At the Foot of the Mountain: A Journey through Existentialism, Anthropology and Life*. He now lives in rural Iowa with Suzan (visit the website at dracohill.org).

Ilana Gershon is associate professor in the Department of Anthropology at Indiana University. She is interested in how new media affect highly charged social tasks, such as breaking up and hiring, in the United States. She has written about how people use new media to end romantic relationships in her book *The Breakup 2.0: Disconnecting over New Media* (2010). She has also published a book comparing Samoan migrant experiences in the United States and New Zealand, titled *No Family Is an Island: Cultural Expertise among Samoans in Diaspora* (2012). She has a new edited volume, *A World of Work: Imagined Manuals for Real Jobs* (2015), a collection of imagined job manuals for real jobs around the world, written for people who want to know how to be, for example, a professional wrestler in Mexico or a professional magician in Paris. Her current research addresses how new media affect hiring in the postrecession U.S. workplace.

Paul Grebinger is emeritus professor of anthropology in the College of Liberal Arts at Rochester Institute of Technology. He completed his undergraduate degree at Columbia University when Marvin Harris was chair, and Harris's theory of cultural materialism permeated the intellectual ether of the Department of Anthropology. On completing his PhD at the University of Arizona in 1971, Grebinger specialized in prehistoric archaeology of the American Southwest. By the 1980s, however, he had refocused his interests on historical American material culture and technological change. He is currently conducting research into the role of horticultural industries in transforming the nineteenth-century American landscape.

Beth Hartman is a PhD candidate in cultural anthropology at Northwestern University. She is also a musician, a dancer, and a certified Feldenkrais practitioner. She has been researching contemporary striptease-related practices—exotic dance, neo-burlesque, and fitness/leisure pole dancing—in the midwestern United States since 2011. She published an article on the methodological challenges of conducting ethnographic research on stripping in the *International Journal of Communication* (2013). Her chapter in this volume is her first published work on neo-burlesque.

Sarah Hautzinger is professor of anthropology at Colorado College, and her work emphasizes the institutional processes related to interpersonal, state, and transnational levels of conflict and violence. Her book *Violence in the City of Women: Police and Batterers in Bahia, Brazil* (California, 2007) explores the creation of all-women police stations in a newly democratizing Brazil. With Jean Scandlyn, she wrote *Beyond Post-Traumatic Stress Disorder: Homefront Struggles with the Wars on Terror* (Left Coast, 2014), based on five years of collaborative fieldwork with students and community partners. She has also published on tourist economies, research methods, feminist naming quandaries, and community-based teaching and learning.

S. Megan Heller is a lecturer at the University of California, Los Angeles, where she received her PhD in anthropology. She also studied demography at the University of California at Berkeley and established the Black Rock City Census Lab, an interdisciplinary team that conducts mixed-methods research on the population that attends the annual Burning Man event in Nevada. Earlier in her life she lived and studied in Japan and Nepal, and she also visited Russia as part of a performing arts group. Today, her research is devoted to the study of adult play and transformative experiences.

Brandi Janssen is clinical assistant professor of occupational and environmental health at the University of Iowa and director of Iowa's Center for Agricultural Safety and Health. As an anthropologist, she applies ethnographic research and participatory techniques in addressing the health and safety concerns of farmers in Iowa.

Autumn Kelly was the research assistant for the project reported in Chapter 7. At the time of the research, she was an undergraduate at the University of Michigan, Ann Arbor, majoring in anthropology.

Ann Kingsolver is professor of anthropology at the University of Kentucky. She has conducted ethnographic research on the United States for thirty years, listening to how people make sense of global capitalist ideology and practices in relation to identities and livelihoods. Her books include *NAFTA Stories: Fears and Hopes in Mexico and the United States* (Lynne Rienner, 2001) and *Tobacco Town Futures: Global Encounters in Rural Kentucky* (Waveland, 2011) as well as the edited volumes *More than Class: Studying Power in U.S. Workplaces* (SUNY Press, 1998) and *The Gender of Globalization: Women Navigating Cultural and Economic Marginalities* (with Nandini Gunewardena; School for Advanced Research, 2007).

278 Reflecting on America

Conrad P. Kottak earned his PhD from Columbia University, following which he conducted extensive research in Brazil and Madagascar. He has published numerous works on these societies as well as several popular textbooks, including *Window on Humanity: A Concise Introduction to Anthropology*; *Anthropology: The Exploration of Human Diversity*; and *Cultural Anthropology*. He is currently professor emeritus of anthropology at the University of Michigan, where he has been teaching since 1968. Among the honors he has received are an excellence in teaching award from the College of Literature, Sciences, and the Arts of the University of Michigan in 1992 and the American Anthropological Association's AAA/Mayfield Award for Excellence in the Undergraduate Teaching of Anthropology in 1999. He was elected to the membership of the National Academy of Sciences in 2008.

Tanya M. Luhrmann holds a position in the Anthropology Department at Stanford University. Previously, she served as director of the Clinical Ethnography Project for the Committee on Human Development at the University of Chicago. Focusing on the question of how people know what is real, she has carried out research among modern-day witches in Britain (*Persuasions of the Witch's Craft*; Harvard, 1989), the postcolonial elite of India (*The Good Parsi*; Harvard, 1996), and American psychiatrists who come from different "cultural" backgrounds within the profession (*Of Two Minds*; Knopf, 2000). The members of each of these groups come to believe something that may not in fact be recognized as "real" by others, and it is the development of conviction—an anthropological process producing a psychological result—that she has illuminated through her work.

Catherine Lutz is Thomas J. Watson, Jr., Family Professor of Anthropology and International Studies at Brown University. Her books include *Homefront, Unnatural Emotions, Reading National Geographic* (with Jane Collins), *Carjacked* (with Anne Lutz Fernandez), and *Breaking Ranks* (with Matthew Gutmann). She has written and spoken widely in a variety of media, consulted with civil society organizations, served as president of the American Ethnological Society, and been the recipient of a Guggenheim Fellowship. She is currently codirector of the Costs of War project (watson.brown.edu/costsofwar).

Robert Myers is professor of anthropology and public health at Alfred University in Alfred, New York, where he has taught for twenty-eight years. He received his BA in German from Davidson College, his MA and PhD in cultural anthropology from the University of North Carolina at Chapel Hill, and his MPH in international health from the Harvard School of Public Health. He has studied in Europe, conducted fieldwork in the Caribbean, and spent two years at the University of Benin in Nigeria on a Fulbright Fellowship. These experiences lend perspective to his primary interest: the cultural relationships between people in the United States and their weather, as these relationships are shaped by pervasive weather information and evolving social media in the era of climate change.

Richard H. Robbins, University Distinguished Teaching Professor at the State University of New York at Plattsburgh, received the 2005 American Anthropological Association/McGraw-Hill Award for Excellence in the Undergraduate Teaching of Anthropology. He has produced such teaching-oriented volumes as the popular textbook *Cultural Anthropology: A Problem-Based Approach* (seventh edition, Cengage, 2016) and *Global Problems and the Culture of Capitalism* (sixth edition, Pearson, 2014). His most recent work is *Debt as Power* (with Tim Di Muzio;

Manchester, 2016). In his teaching, he has taken full advantage of new pedagogical tools, creating and maintaining websites associated with his books.

Jean Scandlyn has always sought to apply anthropological perspectives to the study of U.S. society and culture. She began her career as a registered nurse, working in hospitals and as a visiting nurse and running women's reproductive health clinics. Wanting to better understand how people make decisions about their health, she turned to medical anthropology. Since receiving her doctorate in anthropology, she has taught courses on a variety of topics, including gender, global health, medical anthropology, qualitative research methods, and social science theory. Her research focuses on adolescence and young adults in the contemporary United States. She is coauthor, with Sarah Hautzinger, of *Beyond Post-Traumatic Stress Disorder: Homefront Struggles with the Wars on Terror* (Left Coast, 2015).

Richard Wilk is Distinguished Professor of Anthropology at Indiana University, where he runs the new Food Research Center and a PhD program in food anthropology. He has also taught at the University of California (Berkeley and Santa Cruz), New Mexico State University, and University College London, and has held visiting professorships at Gothenburg University, the University of Marseilles, and the University of London. Early in his career he worked as an applied anthropologist with UNICEF, USAID, Cultural Survival, and a variety of other development organizations. Today his research is devoted to understanding the relationship between climate change and consumer culture, and to the even more formidable problem of the everyday food consumption of students at Indiana University.